John Valdimir Price is lecturer in English Literature at the University [.d.]burgh. He is author of *The Ironic Hume* (1965), *David Hume* (1968), and *Tobias Smollett: The Expedition of Humphry Clinker* (1973); and he has edited, with E. C. Mossner, David Hume's *A Letter from a Gentleman* (1967).

A. Wayne Colver is Professor of Philosophy at California State University, Fresno.

THE NATURAL HISTORY
OF RELIGION

DIALOGUES CONCERNING
NATURAL RELIGION

To render it still more ~~unsatisfactory~~ unsatisfactory, said Philo, there occurs to me another Hypothesis, which must acquire an Air of Probability from the Method of Reasoning so much insisted on by Cleanthes. That like Effects arise from like Causes: This Principle he supposes that Foundation of all Religion. But there is another Principle of the same kind, no less certain, and derived from the same source, viz. That where several known Circumstances are observed to be similar, the unknown will also be found similar. Thus, if we see the Limbs of a human Body, we conclude, that it is also attended with a human Head, tho the first from us. Thus, if we see, thro a Chink in a Wall, a small part of the Sun, we conclude, that were the Wall ~~removed~~ removed, we should view the whole Body.

In short, this Method of Reasoning is so obvious & so familiar, that no Scruple can ever be made with regard to its Solidity.

The Natural History of Religion

BY DAVID HUME

Edited by A. Wayne Colver

AND

Dialogues concerning Natural Religion

BY DAVID HUME

Edited by John Valdimir Price

OXFORD
AT THE CLARENDON PRESS
1976

Oxford University Press, Walton Street, Oxford OX2 6DP

OXFORD LONDON GLASGOW NEW YORK
TORONTO MELBOURNE WELLINGTON CAPE TOWN
IBADAN NAIROBI DAR ES SALAAM LUSAKA ADDIS ABABA
KUALA LUMPUR SINGAPORE JAKARTA HONG KONG TOKYO
DELHI BOMBAY CALCUTTA MADRAS KARACHI

ISBN 0 19 824379 0

Printed in Great Britain
at the University Press, Oxford
by Vivian Ridler
Printer to the University

PREFACE

THIS will not be the first occasion upon which two of Hume's
major contributions to philosophical religion have appeared in
the same volume, but it is the first time since their initial publication that either has been edited comprehensively. For this
edition of *The Natural History of Religion* and the *Dialogues concerning Natural Religion*, we have attempted to present Hume's texts
in their most authoritative versions. Though each of us has
been responsible for editing only one text, we have scrutinized
and checked the other's work. We have tried to resolve every
question about editorial procedure and presentation solely in terms
of whether or not Hume's best interests were being met. We have
assumed that the primary interest of the reader is (or ought to be)
in what Hume said and not in what we or others might make of it.
In consequence, we have limited ourselves to the dull duties of
editors. Believing firmly that study of Hume's text, its revisions,
changes, and sources, is both intellectually rewarding and intrin-
sically valuable, we have sought to give the modern reader as much
aid in knowing exactly what Hume wrote, and in understanding
contexts, as we can.

Thus, the approach in these texts is bibliographical and textual,
not philosophical or critical. A text is not necessarily the place for
commentary, explanation, or evaluation, and while we have certain
ideas about the interpretation of these texts, we have tried to keep
them from intruding on the editorial presentation. In this respect,
both texts, and more noticeably that of the *Dialogues*, differ from
former editions in that critical commentary on the arguments is
excluded.

Though *The Natural History of Religion* and the *Dialogues* were
published some twenty-two years apart, Hume was working on
both in the 1750s, a fact that could be inferred from the occasional
similarities in phrasing. It was not felt that the integrity of Hume's
Four Dissertations was violated by extracting and publishing *The
Natural History of Religion* in the same volume as the *Dialogues*. If

anything, publication of the two in the same volume creates a coherence of topic that probably would have seemed attractive to Hume. In reading the two works together, we have both been impressed (as, doubtless, other readers have been before us) with the diversity and flexibility of Hume's mind. The learning and scholarship displayed in *The Natural History of Religion* complement the philosophical inquiry and creative scepticism of the *Dialogues* in surprising and informative ways. Having read more treatises and essays than we care to remember on religion, natural and revealed, of the eighteenth century and earlier, we can readily appreciate the versatility of an author who can adapt an apparently intransigent topic to such literary forms as the dialogue and the historical survey.

These two editions, then, represent not so much a collaboration as a consolidation. Hume turned his literary and philosophical abilities to religious subjects on other occasions, most notably in the *Enquiry concerning Human Understanding*, but the *Natural History of Religion* and the *Dialogues* represent his most searching and self-contained pronouncements upon the central issues of religion. In presenting to the modern reader authoritative editions of these two works, we aim at neither conversion nor apostasy, just textual verisimilitude.

A. W. C.
J. V. P.

CONTENTS

Frontispiece

> The frontispiece shows part of p. 45 of Hume's manuscript of the *Dialogues* (cf. p. 195 in this volume). It is reproduced by permission of The Royal Society of Edinburgh.

ABBREVIATIONS

The following abbreviations are observed in both works:

Letters	*The Letters of David Hume*, ed. J. Y. T. Greig, Oxford: The Clarendon Press, 1932.
New Letters	*New Letters of David Hume*, ed. Raymond Klibansky and Ernest C. Mossner. Oxford: The Clarendon Press, 1954.
R.S.E.	Hume's manuscripts in the possession of The Royal Society of Edinburgh, by volume and folio number.
Treatise	*A Treatise of Human Nature*, ed. Ernest C. Mossner. London: Penguin, 1969.

Page references to *The Natural History of Religion* are to the edition by Wayne Colver in this volume.

The Natural History of Religion

BY

DAVID HUME

The text of the first edition of 1757
edited, with textual and explanatory notes
by
A. WAYNE COLVER

TO
JIM AND FLORENCE

ACKNOWLEDGEMENTS

PERHAPS the most congenial duty that is incurred by any editor is the acknowledgement of his indebtedness to friends and colleagues. Since I have operated for the past two years on the amiable assumption that everyone was as interested as I in providing Hume with appropriate scholarly clothes, I have been wholly without shame in calling on other people for help. But before I could do much calling, the text had to be established, and had it not been for my secretary, Aurora Avakian, who typed the text of the first edition with patience, good humour, and remarkable accuracy, this project never would have been begun. Gene Bluestein and Roger D. Chittick, both of the English Department, have each saved me many a tedious hour by instantly clarifying an obscurity or identifying a reference. Russell Leavenworth, also of the English Department, read the entire typescript in its nearly final form and made several helpful suggestions. My former colleague, Richard Toscan, now at the University of Southern California, verified two references that a library thief made it impossible for me to check, and his wife, Joyce, saved me time and anguish by doing invaluable bibliographical work in the libraries of Southern California. Robert Harlan and Engel Sluiter, both of the University of California, rendered similar assistance from Berkeley. Stephen Benko, from the Department of History, assisted me in construing three Latin passages; he should not, however, be held accountable for my departures from his sober, literal, accuracy. He also rendered invaluable assistance by checking the accuracy of the Loeb translations against the texts Hume uses. Paul F. Kinzel, of the French Department, appreciably reduced my labours by checking two of the French references. Wallace Nethery, director of the Hoose Library of Philosophy, made it possible for me to secure a photocopy of the 1767 edition of the *Essays and Treatises*, thus making a collation of all editions possible. Ronald J. Mahoney, head of Special Collections, placed his bibliographical knowledge generously and enthusiastically at my disposal and has called my attention to many an arcane reference that would otherwise have escaped me. Philip Gaskell, Librarian of Trinity College, Cambridge, and William B. Todd, of the University of Texas, have both generously given me bibliographical information and assistance. The readers and editorial consultants of the Clarendon Press have made more contributions to this text than can conveniently be listed. It has been a great pleasure to work with them.

Two persons, however, must be singled out for special mention. My long-time friend and colleague, Earl Lyon, has subjected every line of this edition to exacting scrutiny. His keen critical awareness and his impatience with loose thinking, and its invariable reflection in even looser writing, have rendered this edition very much less imperfect than it would otherwise have been. Finally, there is my wife, Ginny, who not only indulged my curious behaviour while I was absorbed in this project, but also carefully read the typescript, made innumerable suggestions for its improvement, and discovered and eliminated over two dozen textual errors that had survived nine readings. Without her support and encouragement nothing would have been possible.

CONTENTS

NOTE ON THE TEXT

THE original manuscript of the *Natural History of Religion* has not survived and the bound proof sheets used by Green and Grose in the preparation of their edition of 1875 have vanished from the shelves of the National Library of Scotland. In consequence, the earliest text of the *Natural History* is that contained in the first edition of the *Four Dissertations*. In this edition two leaves (C12 and D1) have been cancelled in all copies known to me. Fortunately, the changes Hume made on them were recorded by Green and Grose. The modifications are minor, but how they came to be made at all is a story of some interest.[1]

The *Natural History* was most likely written between 1749 and 1751; during this period Hume was also engaged in writing his *Dialogues Concerning Natural Religion*. It is impossible to determine which he began first. We may reasonably assume that they were conceived at the same time. Certainly they exhibit like sentiments, and the effect of each is, in its own way, devastating to the cause of natural religion. As it turned out, Hume completed and published the *Natural History* in 1757, while the *Dialogues*, revised in manuscript in 1761 and again in 1776, just before his death, was not published until 1779.

The earliest allusion to the *Natural History* occurs some years after its completion in a letter from Hume to Andrew Millar (12 June 1755):

There are four short Dissertations, which I have kept some Years by me, in order to polish them as much as possible. One of them is that which Allan Ramsay mentioned to you. [This is the *Natural History of Religion*.] Another of the Passions; a third of Tragedy; a fourth, some Considerations previous to Geometry & Natural Philosophy.[2]

---

[1] In the account that follows I rely heavily on the long and detailed article by E. C. Mossner, 'Hume's *Four Dissertations*: an Essay in Biography and Bibliography', *Modern Philology*, xlviii (1950), 37–57. The reader who wishes a fuller account than I provide, but one that is less detailed than that given in the above article, is directed to chapter 24 of Mossner's *Life of David Hume* (Austin, Tex. 1954).

[2] *Letters*, i. 223.

These dissertations, running, according to Hume's estimate, to about a quarter of the length of his *Enquiry Concerning the Principles of Morals*, were offered to Millar for fifty guineas; Millar accepted the bargain and directed his printer to set the essays in type. However, before the fourth dissertation on Geometry had been set, Hume was persuaded by Lord Stanhope, one of the most distinguished mathematicians of his day, that it was defective and he directed Millar to withdraw it. To take its place, as Greig surmises, Hume dashed off two essays, 'Of Suicide' and 'Of the Immortality of the Soul', in which he argues that the reasons advanced against suicide were without weight and that the prospect of immortality was without probability.[3] These were printed for Millar before the end of 1755 and perhaps a dozen or more proof copies of what had now become *Five Dissertations* were circulated. One of these copies fell into the hands of Dr. William Warburton, 'the proud and insolent clerical and literary bully', who, not surprisingly, 'found it as abandoned of all virtuous principle, as of philosophic force'.[4] Securing assurance of government support, Warburton threatened Millar with a prosecution, and Millar urged Hume to withdraw the two essays. The force of Warburton's threat is difficult to assess; it was not, I think, by itself decisive. However, Hume had reason to believe that the General Assembly of the Church of Scotland proposed to investigate him as an infidel writer, and he must have recognized that to publish the two essays at that time would make it more difficult for his friends among the moderate clergy to quash the investigation. Further, his friend Adam Smith urged against publishing. Hume himself in his later years referred to his 'abundant Prudence' as having been a factor in the supression.[5] But if there was one decisive factor, as I suspect there was not, it would have been Hume's persuasion that the publication of the essays would cause more trouble than they were worth. In any event, Hume acceded to Millar's request, withdrew the two 'obnoxious Dissertations', and modified certain passages in the *Natural History*. It was these modifications that required the cancellation of the two

---

[3] J. Y. T. Greig, *David Hume* (London, 1934), p. 225; see also Mossner, *Life*, p. 325. The quality of the two essays suggests they may have been juvenile productions.

[4] Mossner, 'Hume's *Four Dissertations*', p. 40.

[5] Hume to Strahan, 25 Jan. 1772; *Letters*, ii. 252–4.

leaves mentioned above. Such modifications as can be established
have been recorded in their proper place in the text. (See below,
pp. 53, 54.) But, to the modern reader, they seem hardly to have
been worth the bother; certainly they did nothing to placate
Warburton, who wrote to Millar in a last-minute attempt to
suppress the modified version:

> Sir, I supposed you would be glad to know what sort of book it
> is which you are about to publish with Hume's name and yours to it.
> The design of the first essay is the very same with all Lord Boling-
> broke's, to establish *naturalism*, a species of atheism. . . .
>
> All the good his mutilation and fitting it up for the public has
> done, is only to add to its other follies, that of contradiction. He is
> establishing atheism; and in one single line of a long essay professes
> to believe Christianity. . . .[6]

What contradiction Warburton had in mind remains a mystery.
For of the two known changes Hume made, the first introduces an
irony that is more devastating than the descriptive passage it
replaced, and the second merely substitutes a generalization for
four specific biblical allusions, a generalization that, to anyone
who knew his Bible, would do little to blunt Hume's point. So
much, then, for the ability of Warburton to influence Hume, at
least on any matter he regarded as important.

With the withdrawal of the two essays a new gap appeared
which Hume filled by writing 'Of the Standard of Taste'. Finally,
in despite of Warburton's efforts to suppress it, the *Natural
History of Religion* was published on 7 February 1757 as the first
of the *Four Dissertations*. It had taken a year and a half from the
initial offer to the final publication.[7]

Given so involved a history, it will come as no surprise to the
reader to learn that the collation of the *Four Dissertations* is extremely
complex. This complexity, moreover, is exacerbated by binders'
errors which produced an untold number of variants. It would be
unrewarding to attempt to record them all, but the following may

---

[6] Warburton to Millar, 7 Feb. 1757; quoted by Mossner, 'Hume's *Four Dissertations*', p. 44.

[7] Although the *Four Dissertations* did not go into a second edition, each of them
was included in the 1758, and every subsequent, edition of the *Essays and Treatises on
Several Subjects*.

be taken as illustrative: the dedication is sometimes incorrectly bound after the preliminary, unsigned pair (A^2) on which is printed the title page and the fly title of the first dissertation—such is the state of my copy. The copy in the Rothschild collection (No. 1176) also exhibits this defect and, in addition, the unsigned pair (A^2) is folded the wrong way round so that the fly title to the first dissertation precedes the general title. Other variants will readily suggest themselves. The collation of a correctly bound copy, in which the dedication is present, would be as follows:

$$12^o, \pi 1 \; A^2 \, (A1 + a^4) \; B\text{–}C^{12} \, (\pm C12) \; D^{12} \, (\pm D1)$$
$$E\text{–}I^{12} \, K^8 \, (-K5\text{–}8) \; L^{12} \, M^8$$

$\pi 1$ is the half-title, with publisher's advertisements on the verso, and A^2 is a conjugate pair (title-page and fly title to the 'Natural History') between the leaves of which is bound a^4, the dedication. Cancels $C12$ and $D1$ contain the only modifications Hume made in the text of the 'Natural History'. In the proof copy of the *Five Dissertations*, the last two of which were the dissertations on suicide and immortality, $K5$ was the fly title to 'Dissertation IV: Of Suicide', the text of which began on $K6$. Hence the cancellation of leaves $K5\text{–}8$, and whatever additional leaves were required for the printing of the two withdrawn dissertations, and their replacement by the dissertation 'Of the Standard of Taste' which begins, in the finally published edition, on $L1$ and continues through to $M8$. The text of the 'Natural History of Religion' extends from $B1$ to $F11$ (pages 1–117). $F12$ is the fly title to 'Dissertation II: Of the Passions'.

With the composition of the *Natural History of Religion* and the *Dialogues* substantially completed before he was forty, Hume's career as an original philosopher was at an end. Apart from his history of England, the six volumes of which appeared between 1754 and 1762, he undertook no original work of any consequence. For the remainder of his life he devoted himself to what became an endless labour of revising and polishing his writings. It is thus a matter of some importance to the choice of a copy text to assess the nature of his revisions—and of some difficulty, since Hume himself was ambivalent towards them. On the one hand, he writes to Millar, urging him to discount the 1760 edition of his *Essays and Treatises* to make way for a new one: 'Such a considerable Number taken off your hand might enable you to bring the Book to a new Edition next Winter, when I propose to make some pretty considerable Improvements on it' [i. 378].[8] And as late as 1775 he felt impelled to enjoin Strahan that 'no new Editions shoud be made of any of my Writings, without mentioning it to me; I shall still have some Corrections to make' [ii. 302]. On the other hand, he is able to write of his corrections as a 'diversion' [i. 168]; to write: 'I can only say, that I do it for myself and that it amuses me' [ii. 188]; 'yet the corrections I make are not of Importance' [ii. 235]; 'I am sensible, it is an idle Amusement' [ii. 252]. A month before his death, while engaged in correcting his history, he writes: 'You will wonder, that, in my present Situation I employ myself about such Trifles, and you may compare me to the modern Greeks, who, while Constantinople was beseiged by the Turks and they themselves were threatened with total Destruction, occupyed themselves entirely in Disputes concerning the Procession of the holy Ghost. Such is the Effect of long Habit!' [ii. 329.]

The difficulties in taking Hume's revisions very seriously are increased when we come to examine them. The overwhelming majority are stylistic, as Hume himself occasionally observes. [See i. 265; ii. 243, 246.] Even with respect to style, it is disconcerting to note that after having changed a phrase or expression in one edition he would sometimes, an edition or two later, change it back to the original reading. At most we find an emphasis strengthened, or softened; a sentence inverted; a word changed— only rarely can we say for the better. While we must acknowledge that few authors ever laboured more diligently in their quest for perfection, we must also recognize that the perfection Hume sought was a perfection of expression; the substance had long since been settled in his mind. But although the changes Hume made are of little substantive importance, they are none the less interesting, and should certainly be recorded. The successive changes from edition to edition can be very much more easily followed if the

[8] All references in square brackets are to the volume and page of Greig's edition of the letters.

printed text is the earliest that can be found. In consequence, I
have adopted the text of the first edition as the copy text. The
reader with a different preference will discover that the critical
apparatus has been designed to make it possible for him to recon-
struct with ease the text of any later edition in which he might
chance to be interested.

Hume is an eighteenth-century writer, and he should be presented and read as one. It is pleasantly ironic to be able to invoke
the authority of Dr. Johnson to defend the editorial principles I
adopt, especially as they are applied to a project he would have
detested: 'An author's language, Sir, is a characteristical part of
his composition, and it is also characteristical of the age in which
he writes. Besides, Sir, when the language is changed we are not
sure that the sense is the same.' Accordingly I have, with exceptions
to be noted, retained the original spelling, punctuation, and capitalization of the first edition. The only departures from the text of
the first edition have been dictated by a desire to provide a text
that, while retaining the flavour of the original, does not present
gratuitous difficulties to the modern reader. Thus, neither the
long 's' nor catchwords have been retained. The eighteenth-
century convention of using repeated quotation marks, distracting
to us, has not been followed, but Hume's occasional use of italics
to indicate quotation has. Where the first edition uses double
quotes in the notes, this edition uses single quotes throughout.
The typographical convention, adopted only in the first three
editions, of printing the first word of each paragraph in small
capitals has not been followed. This necessitates another departure from the text of the first edition: in four instances the
words beginning a paragraph are to be emphasized in their own
right. In order to achieve conformity with Hume's manner of
indicating emphasis elsewhere in the first edition, I have printed
these words in italics. The five corrections listed in the errata have
been incorporated into the text without any indication in the
textual notes. Finally, a modern accented text has been used for the
two Greek quotations Hume makes.[9]

---

[9] A facsimile reproduction of p. 21 of the original text, containing the Euripides
quotation, may be consulted on facing page.

ANY of the human affections may lead us into the notion of invifible, intelligent power; hope as well as fear, gratitude as well as affliction: But if we examine our own hearts, or obferve what paffes around us, we fhall find, that men are much oftener thrown on their knees by the melancholy than by the agreeable paffions. Profperity is eafily received as our due, and few queftions are afked concerning its caufe or author. It engenders cheerfulnefs and activity and alacrity and a lively enjoyment of every focial and fenfual pleafure: And during this ftate of mind, men have little leifure or inclination to think of the unknown, invifible regions. On the other hand, every difaftrous accident alarms us, and fets us on enquiries concerning the principles whence it arofe: Apprehenfions fpring up with regard to futurity: And the mind, funk into diffidence, terror, and melancholy, has recourfe to every

Ουκ εςιν εδεν πιςον, ατ ευδοξια,
Ουτ' αν καλως πραοτον]α μη πραξειν κακως.
Φυρεσι δ'αυθ'οι θεοι παλιν τε και πρυσω,
Ταραγμον εντιθεν]ες, ως αγνωσια
Σεβωμεν αυθες.   HECUBA.

There is nothing fecure in the world; no glory, no profperity: The gods tofs all life into confufion; mix every thing with its reverfe; that all of us, from our ignorance and uncertainty, may pay them the more worfhip and reverence.

method

The interests of readability seem to justify a few other departures from the text of the first edition. With one exception they are readings that occur in *all* subsequent editions; they have, without exception, been indicated in the textual notes. First there are clear and obvious typographical errors. Next there are errors in punctuation that, if left standing, would puzzle the reader. And, finally, there is distracting spelling: thus, I have printed 'cloth' rather than 'cloath', 'passed' rather than 'past', and 'profane' rather than 'prophane'; I have retained 'fixt', 'profest', and their relations. Hume's (or his printer's) infrequent use of '&' and '&c' have been normalized to 'and' and 'etc.'

Finally, there is the problem of Hume's footnotes. I have lettered them consecutively in each section—in the first two editions Hume letters them, but by page—rather than adopting the asterisks, daggers, etc. he used in all later editions. In the last three editions Hume removes some of the longer notes from the foot of the page, letters them with capitals, and places them at the end of the volume. I have not thought it worthwhile to indicate these variations. More seriously, Hume's notes, in all editions, are frequently abbreviated beyond the recognition of most students. Further, many of his references are either mistaken, inexact, or insufficiently specific to permit ready verification. I can think of no useful purpose that would be served by preserving his abbreviations or perpetuating his errors in the text, only to expand the former and correct the latter immediately after. In consequence, I have modernized and expanded all of his references, and in most instances I have given the titles he cites in English translation. The reader interested in Hume's notes, exactly as they appear in the first edition, will find them reproduced in Appendix I. I have attempted to make all references sufficiently detailed so that they can be checked in any edition, but the actual editions I have used to verify Hume's references are given in the Bibliographical Index. Because of their accessibility, I have relied heavily on the editions of the Loeb Classical Library—only Manilius was missing from this useful series. An otherwise unidentified page or volume reference in square brackets is invariably to the relevant volume in this series. Translations in square brackets that are not in quotes are my own.

Occasionally Hume has either misinterpreted, over-generalized, or otherwise departed from a strict interpretation of the sources he cites. When this occurs, I have ventured to include a brief quotation from the source in question.

There are eight editions, each corrected by Hume, of the *Essays and Treatises on Several Subjects* in which the *Natural History* was reprinted: 1758, 1760, 1764, 1767, 1768, 1770, 1772, and 1777. These editions are always identified in the textual notes by date rather than by letter. A single date indicates that the variation occurs only in that edition; two dates separated by a hyphen, e.g. 60–68, indicate that the variation occurs in all editions between 1760 and 1768 inclusive; two (or more) dates separated by a comma e.g. 60, 68, indicate that the variation occurs *only* in those two editions and *not* in the intervening editions of 1764 and 1767. The first entry in a textual note repeats the key word(s) in the text and is followed by the variations in chronological order. Thus the textual note

10 concluded, that] 68 concluded that] 72–77 imagined, that

is to be interpreted as follows:

The two words 'concluded, that' which occur in line 10 of the reprinted text of the first edition, read, in the 1768 edition, 'concluded that', and in the two editions of 1772 and 1777, 'imagined, that'; in all other editions, viz. those of 1758, 1760, 1764, 1767, and 1770, the reading is the same as that of the first edition.

Editorial commentary has been kept to a minimum. I have not believed it desirable to contest or applaud Hume's account with a flurry of notes. Nor have I made any attempt to relate passages in this work to parallel or divergent passages in the *Dialogues* or other of his writings. My main concern has been to provide the reader with a text of the *Natural History of Religion* that is as accurate and complete as I could manage. Throughout I have assumed that the reader's interest is in Hume and not in what the editor thinks of him—or why. Where an editorial intrusion has seemed useful, it has either been placed within square brackets or occurs as a numbered note. All lettered notes are Hume's.

The editor's responsibility to identify and explain classical and Christian references is greatly reduced by the existence of two manuals that, between them, will enable the reader to identify virtually every classical author, god, goddess, hero, saint, sect, order, or Christian heresy mentioned by Hume: *The Oxford Companion to Classical Literature*, edited by Sir Paul Harvey, and *The Oxford Dictionary of the Christian Church*, edited by F. L. Cross. I urge the reader to have them by his side. With perhaps no more than three exceptions, I have not ventured to comment on any passage that could be illuminated by reference to either of these useful volumes.

FOUR

DISSERTATIONS.

I. THE NATURAL HISTORY OF RELIGION.
II. OF THE PASSIONS.
III. OF TRAGEDY.
IV. OF THE STANDARD OF TASTE.

BY

DAVID HUME, Efq.

LONDON,
Printed for A. MILLAR, in the Strand.
MDCCLVII.

TO

The Reverend Mr. Hume,[1]

Author of DOUGLAS, a Tragedy.

MY DEAR SIR,

It was the practice of the antients to address their compositions only to friends and equals, and to render their dedications monuments of regard and affection, not of servility and flattery. In those days of ingenuous and candid liberty, a dedication did honour to the person to whom it was addressed, without degrading the author. If any partiality appeared towards the patron, it was at least the partiality of friendship and affection.

Another instance of true liberty, of which antient times can alone afford us an example, is the liberty of thought, which engaged men of letters, however different in their abstract opinions, to maintain a mutual friendship and regard; and never to quarrel about principles, while they agreed in inclinations and manners. Science was often the subject of disputation, never of animosity. *Cicero*, an academic, addressed his philosophical treatises, sometimes to *Brutus*, a stoic; sometimes to *Atticus*, an epicurean.

I have been seized with a strong desire of renewing these laudable practices of antiquity, by addressing the following dissertations to you, my good friend: For such I will ever call and esteem you, notwithstanding the opposition, which prevails between us, with regard to many of our speculative tenets. These differences of opinion I have only found to enliven our conversation; while our

---

[1] John Home (1722–1808), a cousin and close friend of David Hume. He wrote several plays, of which *Douglas*, produced in December 1756, is the best known. The cool reception of his last play, *Alfred* (1778), led him to abandon play-writing. The only differences, 'concerning temporal Matters', that he had with Hume, were his indifference to port and his insistence on spelling his name with an 'o'. See *Letters*, ii. 333, n. 3.

The dedication was printed only in the first edition and, even there, because of Hume's being temporarily persuaded to withdraw it, 800 copies were sold without it before Hume could instruct Millar to restore it. For full details, see Hume's letter to William Mure, in *Letters*, i. 242–3.

common passion for science and letters served as a cement to our friendship. I still admired your genius, even when I imagined, that you lay under the influence of prejudice; and you sometimes told me, that you excused my errors, on account of the candor and sincerity, which, you thought, accompanied them.

But to tell truth, it is less my admiration of your fine genius, which has engaged me to make this address to you, then my esteem of your character and my affection to your person. That generosity of mind which ever accompanies you; that cordiality of friendship, that spirited honour and integrity, have long interested me strongly in your behalf, and have made me desirous, that a monument of our mutual amity should be publicly erected, and, if possible, be preserved to posterity.

I own too, that I have the ambition to be the first who shall in public express his admiration of your noble tragedy of DOUGLAS; one of the most interesting and pathetic pieces, that was ever exhibited on any theatre. Should I give it the preference to the *Merope* of *Maffei*,[2] and to that of *Voltaire*,[3] which it resembles in its subject; should I affirm, that it contained more fire and spirit than the former, more tenderness and simplicity than the latter; I might be accused of partiality: And how could I entirely acquit myself, after the professions of friendship, which I have made you? But the unfeigned tears which flowed from every eye, in the numerous representations which were made of it on this theatre; the unparalleled command, which you appeared to have over every affection of the human breast: These are incontestible proofs, that you possess the true theatric genius of *Shakespear* and *Otway*, refined from the unhappy barbarism of the one, and licentiousness of the other.

My enemies, you know, and, I own, even sometimes my friends, have reproached me with the love of paradoxes and singular opinions; and I expect to be exposed to the same imputation, on

---

[2] Francesco Scipione Maffei (Veronese, 1675–1755). His *Merope* was published at both Venice and Modena (1714) and a third edition was printed at Venice before the year was out; English translation, London, 1740.

[3] (1694–1778). The play was first published, Amsterdam and Leipzig, 1744; an English translation was printed at London the same year; it reached its third edition by 1753.

account of the character, which I have here given of your DOUGLAS.
I shall be told, no doubt, that I had artfully chosen the only time,
when this high esteem of that piece could be regarded as a paradox,
to wit, before its publication; and that not being able to contradict
in this particular the sentiments of the public, I have, at least, resolved to go before them. But I shall be amply compensated for all
these pleasantries, if you accept this testimony of my regard, and
believe me to be, with the greatest sincerity,

DEAR SIR,

Your most affectionate Friend,

and humble Servant,

EDINBURGH, 3,
Jan. 1757.

DAVID HUME.

DISSERTATION I.

NATURAL HISTORY

OF

RELIGION

DISSERTATION I

The Natural History of Religion

INTRODUCTION

As every enquiry, which regards Religion, is of the utmost impor-
tance, there are two questions in particular, which challenge our 5
principal attention, to wit, that concerning its foundation in
reason, and that concerning its origin in human nature. Happily,
the first question, which is the most important, admits of the most
obvious, at least, the clearest solution. The whole frame of nature
bespeaks an intelligent author; and no rational enquirer can, after 10
serious reflexion, suspend his belief a moment with regard to the
primary principles of genuine Theism and Religion. But the other
question, concerning the origin of religion in human nature, admits
of some more difficulty. The belief of invisible, intelligent power
has been very generally diffused over the human race, in all places 15
and in all ages; but it has neither perhaps been so universal as to
admit of no exceptions, nor has it been, in any degree, uniform in
the ideas, which it has suggested. Some nations have been dis-
covered, who entertained no sentiments of Religion, if travellers
and historians may be credited; and no two nations, and scarce 20
any two men, have ever agreed precisely in the same sentiments.
It would appear, therefore, that this preconception springs not
from an original instinct or primary impression of nature, such as
gives rise to self-love, affection betwixt the sexes, love of progeny,
gratitude, resentment; since every instinct of this kind has been 25
found absolutely universal in all nations and ages, and has always
a precise, determinate object, which it inflexibly pursues. The first
religious principles must be secondary; such as may easily be
perverted by various accidents and causes, and whose operation too,

4 enquiry,] 64–70 enquiry   Religion,] 58–70 religion] 72–77 religion,   6 its]
57 it's   9 solution. The] 72 solution, the   11 reflexion] 64–77 reflec-
tion   13–14 admits of] 58–77 is exposed to   24 betwixt] 60–77 between
27 precise,] 67–77 precise

in some cases, may, by an extraordinary concurrence of circumstances, be altogether prevented. What those principles are, which
give rise to the original belief, and what those accidents and causes
are, which direct its operation, is the subject of our present enquiry.

5

I

It appears to me, that if we consider the improvement of human
society, from rude beginnings to a state of greater perfection, polytheism or idolatry was, and necessarily must have been, the first
and most antient religion of mankind. This opinion I shall endeavour
10 to confirm by the following arguments.

'Tis a matter of fact uncontestable, that about 1700 years ago
all mankind were idolaters. The doubtful and sceptical principles
of a few philosophers, or the theism, and that too not entirely pure,
of one or two nations, form no objection worth regarding. Behold
15 then the clear testimony of history. The farther we mount up into
antiquity, the more do we find mankind plunged into idolatry. No
marks, no symptoms of any more perfect religion. The most antient
records of human race still present us with polytheism as the popular and established system. The north, the south, the east, the
20 west, give their unanimous testimony to the same fact. What can
be opposed to so full an evidence?

As far as writing or history reaches, mankind, in antient times,
appear universally to have been polytheists. Shall we assert, that,
in more antient times, before the knowledge of letters, or the dis-
25 covery of any art or science, men entertained the principles of pure
theism? That is, while they were ignorant and barbarous, they
discovered truth: But fell into error, as soon as they acquired
learning and politeness.

But in this assertion you not only contradict all appearance of
30 probability, but also our present experience concerning the principles
and opinions of barbarous nations. The savage tribes of *America*,

5 I] 58–77 SECT. I. *That Polytheism was the primary Religion of Men.*   6 that]
70–77 that,   9 antient] 70–77 ancient   11 'Tis] 70–77 It is   uncontest-
able] 60–77 incontestable   12 idolaters] 72–77 polytheists   16 idolatry]
72–77 polytheism   17 antient] 67, 70–77 ancient   18 polytheism] 72–77
that system   19 system] 72–77 creed   22 antient] 70–77 ancient   24 antient] 70–77 ancient

Africa, and *Asia* are all idolaters. Not a single exception to this rule. Insomuch, that, were a traveller to transport himself into any unknown region; if he found inhabitants cultivated with arts and sciences, tho' even upon that supposition there are odds against their being theists, yet could he not safely, till farther enquiry, 5 pronounce any thing on that head: But if he found them ignorant and barbarous, he might beforehand declare them idolaters; and there scarce is a possibility of his being mistaken.

It seems certain, that, according to the natural progress of human thought, the ignorant multitude must first entertain some 10 groveling and familiar notion of superior powers, before they stretch their conception to that perfect being, who bestowed order on the whole frame of nature. We may as reasonably imagine, that men inhabited palaces before huts and cottages, or studied geometry before agriculture; as assert that the deity appeared to them 15 a pure spirit, omniscient, omnipotent, and omnipresent, before he was apprehended to be a powerful, tho' limited being, with human passions and appetites, limbs and organs. The mind rises gradually, from inferior to superior: By abstracting from what is imperfect, it forms an idea of perfection: And slowly distinguishing the nobler 20 parts of its frame from the grosser, it learns to transfer only the former, much elevated and refined, to its divinity. Nothing could disturb this natural progress of thought, but some obvious and invincible argument, which might immediately lead the mind into the pure principles of theism, and make it overleap, at one bound, 25 the vast interval, which is interposed betwixt the human and the divine nature. But tho' I allow, that the order and frame of the universe, when accurately examined, affords such an argument; yet I can never think that this consideration could have an influence on mankind when they formed their first, rude notions of religion. 30

The causes of objects, which are quite familiar to us, never strike our attention or curiosity; and however extraordinary or surprizing

4 sciences] 72–77 science   tho'] 64–77 though   5 enquiry] 64–77 inquiry
8 scarce] 70–77 scarcely   12 being] 58–77 Being   15 deity] 58–77 Deity
17 tho'] 64–77 though   21 its frame] 67–77 its own frame   26 interval,]
64–77 interval   betwixt] 64–77 between   27 tho'] 64–77 though   30 mankind] 70–77 mankind,   first,] 58–77 first   31 of objects, which] 64–77 of such
objects, as   32 surprizing] 67–68, 77 surprising

these objects may be in themselves, they are passed over, by the
raw and ignorant multitude, without much examination or enquiry.
Adam, rising at once, in paradise, and in the full perfection of his
faculties, would naturally, as represented by *Milton*,[1] be astonished
5 at the glorious appearances of nature, the heavens, the air, the earth,
his own organs and members; and would be led to ask, whence this
wonderful scene arose. But a barbarous, necessitous animal (such
as man is on the first origin of society) pressed by such numerous
wants and passions, has no leisure to admire the regular face of
10 nature, or make enquiries concerning the cause of objects, to which,
from his infancy, he has been gradually accustomed. On the contrary, the more regular and uniform, that is, the more perfect,
nature appears, the more is he familiarized to it, and the less inclined to scrutinize and examine it. A monstrous birth excites his
15 curiosity, and is deemed a prodigy. It alarms him from its novelty;
and immediately sets him a trembling, and sacrificing, and praying.
But an animal compleat in all its limbs and organs, is to him an
ordinary spectacle, and produces no religious opinion or affection.
Ask him, whence that animal arose; he will tell you, from the
20 copulation of its parents. And these, whence? From the copulation
of theirs. A few removes satisfy his curiosity, and set the objects at
such a distance, that he entirely loses sight of them. Imagine not,
that he will so much as start the question, whence the first animal;
much less, whence the whole system or united fabric of the universe
25 arose. Of, if you start such a question to him, expect not, that he
will employ his mind with any anxiety about a subject, so remote,
so uninteresting, and which so much exceeds the bounds of his
capacity.

But farther, if men were at first led into the belief of one supreme
30 being, by reasoning from the frame of nature, they could never
possibly leave that belief, in order to embrace idolatry; but the same
principles of reasoning, which at first produced, and diffused over

---

1 objects may be in] 70–77 objects in   passed] 57 past   10–11 which, from
his infancy,] 77 which from his infancy   12–13 perfect, nature] 64–77 perfect
nature] 57 *the catchword* perfect *lacks the comma*   17 animal] 72–77 animal,
29 supreme] 70–77 Supreme   30 being] 60–77 Being   31 idolatry] 72–77
polytheism   32 reasoning] 70–77 reason   produced,] 60–77 produced

---

[1] *Paradise Lost,* viii. 250–82.

mankind, so magnificent an opinion, must be able, with greater facility, to preserve it. The first invention and proof of any doctrine is infinitely more difficult than the supporting and retaining it.

There is a great difference betwixt historical facts and speculative opinions; nor is the knowledge of the one propagated in the same 5 manner with that of the other. An historical fact, while it passes by oral tradition from eye-witnesses and contemporaries, is disguised in every successive narration, and may at last retain but very small, if any, resemblance of the original truth, on which it was founded. The frail memories of men, their love of exaggeration, their supine 10 carelessness; these principles, if not corrected by books and writing, soon pervert the account of historical events, where argument or reasoning has little or no place; nor can ever recal the truth, which has once escaped those narrations. 'Tis thus the fables of *Hercules, Theseus, Bacchus* are supposed to have been originally 15 founded in true history, corrupted by tradition. But with regard to speculative opinions, the case is far otherwise. If these opinions be founded in arguments so clear and obvious as to carry conviction with the generality of mankind, the same arguments, which at first diffused the opinions, will still preserve them in their 20 original purity. If the arguments be more abstruse, and more remote from vulgar apprehensions, the opinions will always be confined to a few persons; and as soon as men leave the contemplation of the arguments, the opinions will immediately be lost and be buried in oblivion. Which ever side of this dilemma we take, it must 25 appear impossible, that theism could, from reasoning, have been the primary religion of human race, and have afterwards, by its corruption, given birth to idolatry and to all the various superstitions of the heathen world. Reason, when very obvious, prevents these corruptions: When abstruse, it keeps the principles entirely 30 from the knowledge of the vulgar, who are alone liable to corrupt any principles, or opinions.

3 infinitely] 70–77 much 4 betwixt] 60–77 between 12 events,] 57, 70–77 events; 13 place;] 57, 70–77 place, 14 'Tis] 70–77 It is 16 founded in] 67–68 derived from 22 apprehensions] 70–77 apprehension 25 Which ever] 77 Whichever 28 idolatry] 72–77 polytheism 29 when very obvious] 70–77 when obvious 32 principles, or opinions.] 64–70 principles or opinions.] 72–77 principles or opinion.

II

If we would, therefore, indulge our curiosity, in enquiring concerning
the origin of religion, we must turn our thoughts towards idolatry
or polytheism, the primitive Religion of uninstructed mankind.

5   Were men led into the apprehension of invisible, intelligent
power by a contemplation of the works of nature, they could never
possibly entertain any conception but of one single being, who
bestowed existence and order on this vast machine, and adjusted
all its parts, according to one regular plan or connected system.
10 For tho', to persons of a certain turn of mind, it may not appear
altogether absurd, that several independent beings, endowed
with superior wisdom, might conspire in the contrivance and
execution of one regular plan; yet is this a mere arbitrary supposition, which, even if allowed possible, must be confessed neither
15 to be supported by probability nor necessity. All things in the
universe are evidently of a piece. Every thing is adjusted to every
thing. One design prevails thro' the whole. And this uniformity
leads the mind to acknowledge one author; because the conception
of different authors, without any distinction of attributes or opera-
20 tions, serves only to give perplexity to the imagination, without
bestowing any satisfaction on the understanding.[a]

On the other hand, if, leaving the works of nature, we trace the
footsteps of invisible power in the various and contrary events of
human life, we are necessarily led into polytheism, and to the
25 acknowledgment of several limited and imperfect deities. Storms

[a] The statue of *Laocoon*, as we learn from *Pliny*,[1] was the work of three artists:
But 'tis certain, that, were we not told so, we should never have concluded, that a
groupe of figures, cut from one stone,[2] and united in one plan, was not the work and
contrivance of one statuary. To ascribe any single effect to the combination of
several causes, is not surely a natural and obvious supposition.

---

1 II] 58–77 SECT. II. *Origin of Polytheism*.   2 in enquiring] 64 enquiring] 67–
68 and enquire   3–4 towards idolatry or polytheism] 72–77 towards polytheism
4 Religion] 70–77 religion   10 tho'] 64–77 though   13 plan;] 68 plan,
17 thro'] 64 through] 67–77 throughout   20 serves] 68 serve   24 polytheism,] 58–77 polytheism   [a]1–5 *Footnote* [a] *incorporated into the text,* 70–77.
[a]2 'tis] 70–77 it is   concluded,] 68 concluded] 72–77 imagined,   [a]3 groupe]
67–68 group

1 *Natural history*, Bk. XXXVI, Ch. 4, § 37.
2 The editor of the Loeb edition notes that the Laocoon 'is composed of five
blocks'. x. 30, n.a.

and tempest ruin what is nourished by the sun. The sun destroys what is fostered by the moisture of dews and rains. War may be favourable to a nation, whom the inclemency of the seasons afflicts with famine. Sickness and pestilence may depopulate a kingdom, amidst the most profuse plenty. The same nation is not, 5 at the same time, equally successful by sea and by land. And a nation, which now triumphs over its enemies, may anon submit to their more prosperous arms. In short, the conduct of events, or what we call the plan of a particular providence, is so full of variety and uncertainty, that, if we suppose it immediately ordered by any 10 intelligent beings, we must acknowledge a contrariety in their designs and intentions, a constant combat of opposite powers, and a repentance or change of intention in the same power, from impotence or levity. Each nation has its tutelar deity. Each element is subjected to its invisible power or agent. The province of each god 15 is separate from that of another. Nor are the operations of the same god always certain and invariable. To day, he protects: To morrow, he abandons us. Prayers and sacrifices, rites and ceremonies, well or ill performed, are the sources of his favour or enmity, and produce all the good or ill fortune, which are to be found amongst mankind. 20

We may conclude, therefore, that, in all nations, which have embraced polytheism or idolatry, the first ideas of religion arose not from a contemplation of the works of nature, but from a concern with regard to the events of life, and from the incessant hopes and fears, which actuate the human mind. Accordingly, we find, that 25 all idolaters, having separated the provinces of their deities, have recourse to that invisible agent, to whose authority they are immediately subjected, and whose province it is to superintend that course of actions, in which they are, at any time, engaged. *Juno* is invoked at marriages; *Lucina* at births. *Neptune* receives the 30 prayers of seamen; and *Mars* of warriors. The husbandman cultivates his field under the protection of *Ceres*; and the merchant acknowledges the authority of *Mercury*. Each natural event is supposed to be governed by some intelligent agent; and nothing prosperous

---

3 favourable] 58 favorable   6 and by land] 64–70 and land   8 events,] 57 events   10 that,] 64–68 that   17 invariable.] 60–64 invariable: To day,] 60–68 To day] 70–77 To-day   To morrow,] 60–68 To morrow] 70–77 To-morrow 21 that,] 58–68 that   22 polytheism or idolatry,] 72–77 polytheism,

or adverse can happen in life, which may not be the subject of peculiar prayers or thanksgivings.[b]

It must necessarily, indeed, be allowed, that, in order to carry men's attention beyond the visible course of things, or lead them 5 into any inference concerning invisible intelligent power, they must be actuated by some passion, which prompts their thought and reflection; some motive, which urges their first enquiry. But what passion shall we here have recourse to, for explaining an effect of such mighty consequence? Not speculative curiosity 10 surely, or the pure love of truth. That motive is too refined for such gross apprehensions, and would lead men into enquiries concerning the frame of nature; a subject too large and comprehensive for their narrow capacities. No passions, therefore, can be supposed to work upon such barbarians, but the ordinary affections 15 of human life; the anxious concern for happiness, the dread of future misery, the terror of death, the thirst of revenge, the appetite for food and other necessaries. Agitated by hopes and fears of this nature, especially the latter, men scrutinize, with a trembling curiosity, the course of future causes, and examine the 20 various and contrary events of human life. And in this disordered scene, with eyes still more disordered and astonished, they see the first obscure traces of divinity.

---

[b] *Fragilis et laboriosa mortalitas in partes ista digessit, infirmitatis suæ memor, ut portionibus quisquis coleret, quo maxime indigeret.* Pliny, *Natural History*, Bk. II, Ch. 5, § 15.[3] So early as *Hesiod's* time there were 30,000 deities. *Works and Days*, lines 252–5.[4] But the task to be performed by these, seems still too great for their number. The provinces of the deities were so subdivided, that there was even a God of *Sneezing*. See Aristotle, *Problems*, Bk. XXXIII, Ch. 7.[5] The province of copulation, suitable to the importance and dignity of it, was divided amongst several deities.

---

4 visible] 58–77 present   11 apprehensions,] 72–77 apprehensions;
12 nature;] 72–77 nature,   20 various and contrary] 60 various contrary
[b]1 *et*] 64–77 &   [b]4 these,] 70–77 these   [b]5 *Sneezing*.] 57 *Sneezing*,
[b]7 amongst] 58–77 among

---

[3] 'Frail, toiling mortality, remembering its own weakness, has divided such deities into groups, so as to worship in sections, each the deity he is most in need of.' i. 179.

[4] 'For upon the bounteous earth Zeus has thrice ten thousand spirits, watchers of mortal men, and these keep watch on judgements and deeds of wrong as they roam, clothed in mist, all over the earth.' p. 21.

[5] 'Why do we consider that sneezing is of divine origin, but not coughing or running at the nose?' 962a 21–2; ii. 215.

III

We are placed in this world, as in a great theatre, where the true springs and causes of every event, are entirely unknown to us; nor have we either sufficient wisdom to foresee, or power to prevent those ills, with which we are continually threatened. We hang in 5 perpetual suspense betwixt life and death, health and sickness, plenty and want; which are distributed amongst the human species by secret and unknown causes, whose operation is oft unexpected, and always unaccountable. These *unknown causes*, then, become the constant object of our hope and fear; and while the passions are 10 kept in perpetual alarm by an anxious expectation of the events, the imagination is equally employed in forming ideas of those powers, on which we have so entire a dependance. Could men anatomize nature, according to the most probable, at least the most intelligible philosophy, they would find, that these causes are 15 nothing but the particular fabric and structure of the minute parts of their own bodies and of external objects; and that, by a regular and constant machinery, all the events are produced, about which they are so much concerned. But this philosophy exceeds the comprehension of the ignorant multitude, who can only conceive the 20 *unknown causes* in a general and confused manner; tho' their imagination, perpetually employed on the same subject, must labour to form some particular and distinct idea of them. The more they consider these causes themselves, and the uncertainty of their operation, the less satisfaction do they meet with in their research; and, how- 25 ever unwilling, they must at last have abandoned so arduous an attempt, were it not for a propensity in human nature, which leads into a system, that gives them some seeming satisfaction.

There is an universal tendency amongst mankind to conceive all beings like themselves, and to transfer to every object those 30 qualities, with which they are familiarly acquainted, and of which they are intimately conscious. We find human faces in the moon,

---

1. III] 58–77 SECT. III. *The same subject continued.*   3 unknown to] 72–77 concealed from   6 betwixt] 60–77 between   21 tho'] 64–77 though 22 labour] 58 labor   25 research] 72–77 researches   28 some seeming satisfaction] 70–77 some satisfaction   29 amongst] 67–68, 72–77 among 30 object] 60–77 object,

armies in the clouds; and by a natural propensity, if not corrected by experience and reflection, ascribe malice and good-will to every thing, that hurts or pleases us. Hence the frequency and beauty of the *prosopopœia* in poetry, where trees, mountains and streams are 5 personified, and the inanimate parts of nature acquire sentiment and passion. And tho' these poetical figures and expressions gain not on the belief, they may serve, at least, to prove a certain tendency in the imagination, without which they could neither be beautiful nor natural. Nor is a river-god or hama-dryad always 10 taken for a mere poetical or imaginary personage; but may sometimes enter into the real creed of the ignorant vulgar; while each grove or field is represented as possest of a particular *genius* or invisible power, which inhabits and protects it. Nay, philosophers cannot entirely exempt themselves from this natural frailty; but have oft 15 ascribed to inanimate matter the horror of a *vacuum*, sympathies, antipathies, and other affections of human nature. The absurdity is not less, while we cast our eyes upwards; and transferring, as is too usual, human passions and infirmities to the deity, represent him as jealous and revengeful, capricious and partial, and, in short, a 20 wicked and foolish man in every respect, but his superior power and authority. No wonder, then, that mankind, being placed in such an absolute ignorance of causes, and being at the same time so anxious concerning their future fortunes, should immediately acknowledge a dependence on invisible powers, possest of senti-25 ment and intelligence. The *unknown causes*, which continually employ their thought, appearing always in the same aspect, are all apprehended to be of the same kind or species. Nor is it long before we ascribe to them thought, and reason, and passion, and sometimes even the limbs and figures of men, in order to bring them nearer 30 to a resemblance with ourselves.

In proportion as any man's course of life is governed by accident, we always find, that he encreases in superstition; as may particularly be observed of gamesters and sailors, who, tho', of all mankind,

    4 poetry,] 72–77 poetry;   mountains] 57 *catchword reads* mountains,   6 tho']
64–77 though   9 hama-dryad] 77 hamadryad   12 possest] 64–77 possessed
20 man] 70–77 man,   respect,] 70–77 respect   23 fortunes] 72–77 fortune
24 possest] 58–77 possessed   28 thought, and reason,] 72–77 thought and
reason   33 tho',] 58–60 tho'] 64–70 though] 72–77 though,

the least capable of serious meditation, abound most in frivolous and superstitious apprehensions. The gods, says *Coriolanus* in *Dionysius,*[a] have an influence in every affair; but above all, in war; where the event is so uncertain. All human life, especially before the institution of order and good government, being subject to fortuitous accidents; 5 it is natural, that superstition should prevail every where in barbarous ages, and put men on the most earnest enquiry concerning those invisible powers, who dispose of their happiness or misery. Ignorant of astonomy and the anatomy of plants and animals, and too little curious to observe the admirable adjustment of final causes; they 10 remain still unacquainted with a first and supreme creator, and with that infinitely perfect spirit, who alone, by his almighty will, bestowed order on the whole frame of nature. Such a magnificent idea is too big for their narrow conceptions, which can neither observe the beauty of the work, nor comprehend the grandeur of its author. 15 They suppose their deities, however potent and invisible, to be nothing but a species of human creatures, perhaps raised from among mankind, and retaining all human passions and appetites, along with corporeal limbs and organs. Such limited beings, tho' masters of human fate, being, each of them, incapable of extending his influence every 20 where, must be vastly multiplied, in order to answer that variety of events, which happen over the whole face of nature. Thus every place is stored with a crowd of local deities; and thus idolatry has prevailed, and still prevails, among the greatest part of uninstructed mankind.[b]

---

[a] Dionysius of Halicarnassus, *Roman Antiquities*, Bk. VIII, Ch. 2, § 2.

[b] The following lines of *Euripides* are so much to the present purpose that I cannot forbear quoting them:

> οὐκ ἔστι πιστὸν οὐδέν, οὔτ' εὐδοξία
> οὔτ' αὖ καλῶς πράσσοντα μὴ πρᾶξειν κακῶς.
> φύρουσι δ' αὐτοὶ θεοὶ πάλιν τε καὶ πρόσω
> ταραγμὸν ἐντιθέντες, ὡς ἀγνωσίᾳ
> σέβωμεν αὐτούς   HECUBA. [956-60]

There is nothing secure in the world; no glory, no prosperity. The gods toss all life into confusion; mix every thing with its reverse; that all of us, from our ignorance and uncertainty, may pay them the more worship and reverence.[1]

---

1 meditation] 70 consideration] 72–77 reflection   18 along with] 58–77 together with   19 tho'] 68–77 though   23 idolatry] 72–77 polytheism [b]1 purpose] 60–77 purpose,   [b]8–10 *In quotes instead of italics,* 58–77.

---

[1] Hume's translation is ambiguous in a way that the Greek is not: 'There is nothing secure in the world, neither glory nor prosperity'. Hume also neglects to translate αὐτοὶ, 'the gods themselves'.

Any of the human affections may lead us into the notion of invisible, intelligent power; hope as well as fear, gratitude as well as affliction: But if we examine our own hearts, or observe what passes around us, we shall find, that men are much oftener thrown
5 on their knees by the melancholy than by the agreeable passions. Prosperity is easily received as our due, and few questions are asked concerning its cause or author. It engenders cheerfulness and activity and alacrity and a lively enjoyment of every social and sensual pleasure: And during this state of mind, men have little
10 leisure or inclination to think of the unknown, invisible regions. On the other hand, every disastrous accident alarms us, and sets us on enquiries concerning the principles whence it arose: Apprehensions spring up with regard to futurity: And the mind, sunk in diffidence, terror, and melancholy, has recourse to every method
15 of appeasing those secret, intelligent powers, on whom our fortune is supposed entirely to depend.

No topic is more usual with all popular divines than to display the advantages of affliction, in bringing men to a due sense of religion; by subduing their confidence and sensuality, which, in
20 times of prosperity, make them forgetful of a divine providence. Nor is this topic confined merely to modern religions. The ancients have also employed it. *Fortune has never liberally, without envy,* says a Greek historian,*c* *bestowed an unmixt happiness on mankind; but with all her gifts has ever conjoined some disastrous circumstance, in order to*
25 *chastize men into a reverence for the gods, whom, in a continued course of prosperity, they are apt to neglect and forget.*

c Diodorus Siculus, Bk. III, Ch. 47.[2]

---

7 engenders] 58–77 begets   10 unknown,] 58–77 unknown   11 sets] 67 set   15 secret, intelligent] 64–68, 72–77 secret intelligent] 70 sacred intelligent   19 which,] 64–70 which   21 ancients] 68 antients   23 *unmixt*] 58–77 *unmixed*   25 *whom,*] 58–60 *whom*

---

[2] Diodorus is more specific; he mentions only the Sabaeans, inhabitants of Arabia the Blest, and observes that 'fortune has not invested [them] with a felicity which is perfect and leaves no room for envy, but with such great gifts she has coupled what is harmful and may serve as a warning to such men as are wont to despise the gods because of the unbroken succession of their blessings'. He then goes on to retail some accompanying horrors: tiny venomous snakes whose bite is incurable and a mysterious wasting disease that afflicts the inhabitants. See ii. 227, 229. Hume used the edition of L. Rhodoman (Hanau, 1604), which added a Latin translation to the Greek text of Stephanus (Geneva, 1559).

What age or period of life is the most addicted to superstition? The weakest and most timid. What sex? The same answer must be given. *The leaders and examples of every kind of superstition, says Strabo,[d] are the women. These excite the men to devotion and supplications, and the observance of religious days. It is rare to meet with one that lives apart from 5 the females, and yet is addicted to such practises. And nothing can, for this reason, be more improbable, than the account given of an order of men amongst the* Getes, *who practised celibacy, and were notwithstanding the most religious fanatics.* A method of reasoning, which would lead us to entertain a very bad idea of the devotion of monks; did we not 10 know by an experience, not so common, perhaps, in *Strabo's* days,[3] that one may practice celibacy, and profess chastity; and yet maintain the closest connexions and more entire sympathy with that timorous and pious sex.

IV   15

The only point of theology, in which we shall find a consent of mankind almost universal, is, that there is invisible, intelligent power in the world: But whether this power be supreme or subordinate, whether confined to one being or distributed amongst several, what attributes, qualities, connexions or principles of 20 action ought to be ascribed to those beings; concerning all these points, there is the widest difference in the popular systems of theology. Our ancestors in *Europe*, before the revival of letters, believed, as we do at present, that there was one supreme God, the author of nature, whose power, tho', in itself, uncontrolable, yet 25 was often exerted by the interposition of his angels and subordinate ministers, who executed his sacred purposes. But they also believed, that all nature was full of other invisible powers; fairies, goblins, elves, sprights; beings, stronger and mightier than men, but much

---

[d] *Geography*, Bk. VII, Ch. 4. [Hume's quotation is somewhat abridged.]

---

5 one] 57 one,   8 amongst] 67–68, 72–77 among   Getes] 58–77 GETES
10 very bad] 58–77 bad   15 IV] 58–67, 70–77 SECT. IV. *Deities not considered as creators or formers of the world.*] 68 . . . reformers . . .   19 being] 58–68, 72–77 being,   amongst]58–77 among   25–6 tho', in itself, uncontrolable, yet was] 60 . . . uncontroulable, was yet] 64–77 though in itself uncontroulable, was yet

---

[3] *c.* 64 B.C.–A.D. 19.

inferior to the celestial natures, who surround the throne of God. Now suppose, that any one, in those ages, had denied the existence of God and of his angels; would not his impiety justly have deserved the appellation of atheism, even tho' he had still allowed, by 5 some odd capricious reasoning, that the popular stories of elves and fairies were just and well-grounded? The difference, on the one hand, betwixt such a person and a genuine theist is infinitely greater, than that, on the other, betwixt him and one, that absolutely excludes all invisible, intelligent power. And it is a fallacy, merely from the 10 casual resemblance of names, without any conformity of meaning, to rank such opposite opinions under the same denomination.

To any one, who considers justly of the matter, it will appear, that the gods of all polytheists or idolaters are no better than the elves or fairies of our ancestors, and merit as little any pious wor-15 ship or veneration. These pretended religionists are really a kind of superstitious atheists, and acknowledge no being, that corresponds to our idea of a deity. No first principle of mind or thought: No supreme government and administration: No divine contrivance or intention in the fabric of the world.

20 The *Chinese*, when[a] their prayers are not answered, beat their idols. The deities of the *Laplanders* are any large stone which they

---

[a] Père Le Comte.[1]

---

2 Now] 64–77 Now,   one,] 64–68 one   4 tho'] 64–77 though
7 betwixt] 60–77 between   greater,] 58–77 greater   8 betwixt] 60–77
between   one,] 64–77 one   9 invisible,] 60–77 invisible   13 polytheists
or idolaters] 72–77 polytheists

---

[1] *Nouveaux Mémoires sur l'état présent de la Chine* (Amsterdam, 1698), ii. 104. 'It is true they sometimes do not pay to these Gods all that respect which seems due to their Quality. For it often happens that if the People after worshipping them a great while do not obtain what they desire, they turn them off, and look upon them as impotent Gods; others use them in the most reproachful manner: some load them with hard names, others with hard blows.' *Memoires and Observations . . . made in a late Journey Through the Empire of China.* Translated from the Paris edition (London, 1697), p. 326.
Louis Daniel Le Comte, S.J., was one of six missionaries sent to China in 1685. In the course of his stay, 1687–92, he travelled over 5,000 miles observing the people and their customs. His account of Chinese civilization was first published at Paris in 1696 and proved enormously popular—there were five Paris and two Amsterdam editions by 1701—and within three years of its first publication it was translated into Italian, English, Dutch, and German. His sympathetic treatment of Chinese religion could not fail to give offence: '. . . they have preserved the knowledge of

meet with of an extraordinary shape.*b* The *Egyptian* mythologists, in order to account for animal worship, said, that the gods, pursued by the violence of earth-born men,[3] who were their enemies, had formerly been obliged to disguise themselves under the semblance of beasts.*c* The *Caunii*, a nation in the lesser *Asia*, resolving to 5

---

b Jean-François Regnard, *Voiage de Lapponie.*[2]

c Diodorus Siculus, Bk. I, Ch. 86. [This is only one of three causes mentioned by Diodorus and is declared by him to belong 'entirely to the realm of fable'. See i. 293.] Lucian, 'On Sacrifices', § 14. *Ovid* alludes to the same tradition, *Metamorphoses*, Bk. V, lines 321–31. So also Manilius, Bk. IV. [Hume may have had reference to lines 793–4 where Venus is described as assuming the form of a fish and plunging into the river to escape the attentions of Typhon.]

---

5 lesser] 64–77 Lesser   *c*3 Ovid] 57 Ovid.

---

the true God for near two thousand years, and did honour their Maker in such a manner as may serve both for an Example and Instruction to Christians themselves'. Ibid., p. 317. And a few pages later he notes that they 'have practised the most pure Morality, while *Europe* and almost all the World wallowed in Error and Corruption'. Ibid., p. 320. The first of these propositions was condemned by order of 'Messieurs les Doyens et Docteurs de la Faculté de Theologie de Paris' as 'false, reckless, scandalous, erroneous, [and] injurious to the holy Christian Religion'; the second proposition was found, in addition, to be 'impious, contrary to the word of God, heretical, [and] subversive of the Faith'. An account of the deliberations of the learned doctors and the complete condemnation can be found in *Journal historique des assemblées, tenues en Sorbonne, Pour Condamner les Memoires de la Chine, etc.* ([Paris], 1701). See especially pp. 261–70. The work was also condemned in 1700 by the Seminary of Foreign Missions and in 1762 (long after Le Comte's death 'at an advanced age' in 1729) the *Nouvelle Mémoires* was condemned to be burnt by the *Parlement* of Paris. See Michaud's *Biographie Universelle Ancienne et Modern* (Paris, 1843–65), s.v. Le Compte. For a full account of all the editions see Henri Cordier's *Bibliotheca Sinica*, 12th edn. (Paris, 1904). (Reprinted by Burt Franklin, New York, 1968.)

[2] In vol. i of *Les Oeuvres* (Paris, 1731). An English translation occurs in John Pinkerton, *Voyages and Travels*, vol. i (London, 1808). Hume's assertion is only partially true; see p. 179: '. . . they mix Jesus Christ indifferently with their false gods, and they make only one being of God and the devil, whom they believe they may worship in the manner most agreeably to their taste. . . They have three principal gods; the first is called Thor, or the god of thunder; the second Storiunchar; and the third *Parjutte*, which means the sun.

'These three gods are worshipped only by the Laplanders of Lula and Pitha; for those of Kimiet and of Torno, among whom I have lived, know of one only, whom they call Seyta, and who is the same among them, as Storiunchar among the others. These gods are made of a long stone, destitute of any other figure than that which nature has given it, and such as they find it on the borders of the lakes. So that, every stone made in a peculiar manner, rough, or full of holes and concavities, is with them a god; and the more remarkable its structure is, the greater is their veneration for it.'

The main source of information about Lapland in Hume's day was John Scheffer's *History of Lapland*, first published in Latin in 1670, but soon translated into English (Oxford, 1674, and London, 1703). Hume probably happened on the recently published *Oeuvres* of Regnard while working on his *Treatise* in France, became engrossed in his fascinating account, and here turns it to good use.

[3] The giants. See i. 293.

admit no strange gods amongst them, regularly, at certain seasons, assembled themselves compleatly armed, beat the air with their lances, and proceeded in that manner to their frontiers; in order, as they said, to expel the foreign deities.*d Not even the immortal gods,* 5 said some *German* nations to *Cæsar, are a match for the Suevi.e*

Many ills, says *Dione* in *Homer* to *Venus* wounded by *Diomede,* many ills, my daughter, have the gods inflicted on men: And many ills, in return, have men inflicted on the gods.*f* We need but open any classic author to meet with these gross representations of the 10 deities; and *Longinus*g with reason observes, that such ideas of the divine nature, if literally taken, contain a true atheism.

Some writersh have been surprised, that the impieties of *Aristophanes* should have been tolerated, nay publickly acted and applauded, by the *Athenians*; a people so superstitious and so jealous 15 of the public religion, that, at that very time, they put *Socrates* to death for his imagined incredulity. But these writers consider not, that the ludicrous, familiar images, under which the gods are

---

d Herodotus, Bk. I, Ch. 172.   *e* Cæsar, *Gallic War*, Bk. IV, § 7.
f *Iliad*, Bk. V, lines 381–4.   *g* Longinus, *On the Sublime*, Ch. 9, § 7.
h Pierre Brumoy, *Théâtre des Grecs*;4 and Fontenelle, *Histoire des Oracles* (Paris, 1687), pp. 102–5.5

---

1 amongst] 58–77 among   12 surprised] 58–77 surprized   13 publickly 64–77 publicly   16 consider not] 72–77 do not consider

---

4 'Discours sur la comédie Grecques', v. 247 ff. See also his discussion of the part played by Aristophanes' *Clouds* in the condemnation of Socrates, ibid., pp. 446–59. Hume would have consulted either of the Paris editions of 1730 or 1749, or the Amsterdam edition of 1732.
5 'It is not very easie, to tell what kind of regard the *Pagans* had for their Religion: For we said a little while ago, that they contented themselves with the outward Respect, which their *Philosophers* paid to the *Oracles*; but this was not always so; for I am not certain, that *Socrates* refused to offer Incense to the *Gods*, or behaved himself like other People at the Publick Festivals; but this I am sure of, that the Rabble accused him of Atheism, though they could only guess at his Opinion in this Point; for he never openly explained himself. The People knew well enough what was taught publickly in the Schools of *Philosophers*; how then could they suffer Opinions, contrary to the Established Worship (and often-times even against the Existence of the *Gods*) to be there maintained? At least, they knew perfectly well, what was play'd upon the Theaters; for those shows were made for them: and it is sure the *Gods* were never treated with less Respect, than in the *Comedies* of *Aristophanes.*' *The History of Oracles, and the Cheats of the Pagan Priests* (London, 1688), Pt. I, Ch. 8, pp. 69–70. This was a very popular work; there were two editions in 1687 and others in 1697, 1701, 1707, and 1713. English translations appeared in 1688, 1699, and 1750.]

represented by that comic poet, instead of appearing impious, were the genuine lights, in which the ancients conceived their divinities. What conduct can be more criminal or mean, than that of *Jupiter* in the *Amphitryon?* Yet that play, which represented his gallant exploits, was supposed so agreeable to him, that it was always 5 acted in *Rome* by public authority, when the State was threatened with pestilence, famine, or any general calamity.*ⁱ* The *Romans* supposed, that, like all old letchers, he would be highly pleased with the rehearsal of his former feats of activity and vigour, and that no topic was so proper, upon which to flatter his pride and 10 vanity.

The *Lacedemonians*, says *Xenophon,ʲ* always, during war, put up their petitions very early in the morning, in order to be beforehand with their enemies, and by being the first solicitors, pre-engage the gods in their favour. We may gather from *Seneca,ᵏ* that it was usual 15 for the votaries in the temples, to make interest with the beadles or sextons, in order to have a seat near the image of the deity, that they might be the best heard in their prayers and applications to him. The *Tyrians*, when besieged by *Alexander*, threw chains on the statue of *Hercules*, to prevent that deity from deserting to the 20 enemy.*ˡ* *Augustus*, having twice lost his fleet by storms, forbad

---

ⁱ Arnobius, *Seven Books Against the Heathen*, Bk. VII, Ch. 33.⁶
ʲ *Constitution of the Lacedaemonians*, § 13, 3.
ᵏ *Moral Letters to Lucilius*, Letter 41.⁷
ˡ Curtius Rufus, *History of Alexander*, Bk. IV, Ch. 3, §§ 21–2.⁸ Diodorus Siculus, Bk. XVII, Ch. 41, § 8.⁹

---

4 in the *Amphitryon*] 70 in AMPHITRION   gallant] 72–77 gallante   9 of activity and vigour] 58 of activity and vigor] 67–68 of vigour] 70–77 of prowess and vigour   14 and] 70, 77 and,   15 favour] 58 favor   16–17 beadles or sextons] 70–77 beadle and sexton   17 in order to have] 64–77 that they might have   17–18 that they might be] 64–77 in order to be

---

⁶ *The Ante-Nicene Fathers*, vi. 531b. Hume goes somewhat beyond the actual passage, which does no more than raise the question: 'Does Jupiter lay aside his resentment if the *Amphitryon* of Plautus is acted and declaimed? or if Europa, Leda, Ganymede, or Danæ is represented by dancing, does he restrain his passionate impulses?'

⁷ An inference on Hume's part, but a fair one: 'We do not need to uplift our hands towards heaven, or to beg the keeper of a temple to let us approach his idol's ear, as if in this way our prayers were more likely to be heard.' i. 273.

⁸ More accurately, Hercules was restrained in the hope that he would prevent Apollo from deserting. i. 195.

⁹ In this passage the Tyrians 'tied the image of Apollo to its base with golden cords, preventing, as they thought, the god from leaving the city'. viii. 237.

Neptune to be carried in procession along with the other gods; and fancied, that he had sufficiently revenged himself by that expedient.[m] After *Germanicus's* death, the people were so enraged at their gods, that they stoned them in their temples; and openly
5 renounced all allegiance to them.[n]

To ascribe the origin and fabric of the universe to these imperfect beings never enters into the imagination of any polytheist or idolater. *Hesiod*, whose writings, along with those of *Homer*, contained the canonical system of the heathens;[o] *Hesiod*, I say, supposes
10 gods and men to have sprung equally from the unknown powers of nature.[p] And thro' the whole theogony of that author, *Pandora* is the only instance of creation or a voluntary production; and she too was formed by the gods merely from despight to *Prometheus*, who had furnished men with stolen fire from the celestial regions.[q]
15 The ancient mythologists, indeed, seem throughout to have rather embraced the idea of generation than that of creation, or formation; and to have thence accounted for the origin of this universe.

Ovid, who lived in a learned age, and had been instructed by philosophers in the principles of a divine creation or formation of
20 the world; finding, that such an idea would not agree with the popular mythology, which he delivers, leaves it, in a manner, loose and detached from his system. *Quisquis fuit ille Deorum:*[r] Whichever of the gods it was, says he, that dissipated the chaos, and introduced order into the universe. It could neither be *Saturn*, he knew, nor
25 *Jupiter*, nor *Neptune*, nor any of the received deities of paganism. His theological system had taught him nothing upon that head, and he leaves the matter equally undetermined.

[m] Suetonius, 'The Deified Augustus', Ch. 16.
[n] Ibid., 'Gaius Caligula', Ch. 5.
[o] Herodotus, Bk. II, Ch. 53. Lucian, 'Zeus Catechized', 'On Funerals', *etc.*
[p] ὡς ὁμόθεν γεγάασι θεοὶ θνητοί τ' ἄνθρωποι. Hesiod, *Works and Days*, line 108. ['how the gods and mortal men sprang from one source.' p. 11.]
[q] Hesiod, *Theogony*, lines 570 ff. ['Forthwith he made an evil thing for men as the price of fire; for the very famous Limping God formed of earth the likeness of a shy maiden as the son of Cronos willed.' p. 121.]
[r] *Metamorphoses*, Bk. I, line 32.

---

8 along with] 58–77 with   11 thro'] 64–68 through] 70–77 throughout
16 creation,] 64–77 creation   20 finding,] 58 finding   22 *Deorum:*] 58–77
Deorum?   Whichever] 58–68 Which-ever   26 head,] 70–77 head;

Didorus Siculus,[s] beginning his work with an enumeration of the most reasonable opinions concerning the origin of the world, makes no mention of a deity or intelligent mind; tho' it is evident from his history, that that author had a much greater proneness to superstition that to irreligion. And in another passage,[t] talking of the Ichthyophages, a nation in *India*, he says, that there being so great difficulty in accounting for their descent, we must conclude them to be *aborigines*, without any beginning of their generation, propagating their race from all eternity; as some of the physiologers, in treating of the origin of nature, have justly observed. 'But in such subjects as these,' adds the historian, 'which exceed all human capacity, it may well happen, that those, who discourse the most, know the least; reaching a specious appearance of truth in their reasonings, while extremely wide of the real truth and matter of fact.'

A strange sentiment in our eyes, to be embraced by a profest and zealous religionist.[u] But it was merely by accident, that the question concerning the origin of the world did ever in antient times enter into religious systems, or was treated of by theologers. The philosophers alone made profession of delivering systems of this nature; and it was pretty late too before these bethought themselves of having recourse to a mind or supreme intelligence, as the first cause of all. So far was it from being esteemed profane in those days to account for the origin of things without a deity, that *Thales, Anaximenes, Heraclitus*, and others, who embraced that

---

[s] Bk. I, Chs. 6–7.   [t] Ibid., Bk. III, Ch. 20.

[u] The same author, who can thus account for the origin of the world without a Deity, esteems it impious to explain from physical causes, the common accidents of life, earthquakes, inundations, and tempests; and devoutly ascribes these to the anger of *Jupiter* or *Neptune*. A plain proof, whence he derived his ideas of religion. See Bk. XV, Ch. 48.[10]

---

3 tho'] 64–77 though   4 that author] 70–77 he   6 *Ichthyophages*] 72–77
ICHTHYOPHAGI   that] 70–77 that,   16 profest] 58–77 professed
18 antient] 70–77 ancient   21 nature] 70–77 kind   23 profane] 57 prophane

---

[10] The original is more neutral: 'Natural scientists make it their endeavour to attribute responsibility in such cases [i.e. earthquakes, etc.] not to divine providence, but to certain natural circumstances determined by necessary causes, whereas those who are disposed to venerate the divine power assign certain plausible reasons for the occurrence, alleging that the disaster was occasioned by the anger of the gods at those who had committed sacrilege.' vii. 83, 85.

system of cosmogony, past unquestioned; while *Anaxagoras*, the first undoubted theist among the philosophers, was perhaps the first that ever was accused of atheism.[v]

We are told by *Sextus Empiricus*,[w] that *Epicurus*, when a boy, 5 reading with his preceptor these verses of *Hesiod*:

> Eldest of beings, *chaos* first arose;
> Next *earth*, wide-stretcht, the *seat* of all.

the young scholar first betrayed his inquisitive genius, by asking, *And chaos whence?* But was told by his preceptor, that he must 10 have recourse to the philosophers for a solution of such questions. And from this hint, *Epicurus* left philology and all other studies, in order to betake himself to that science, whence alone he expected satisfaction with regard to these sublime subjects.

The common people were never likely to push their researches 15 so far, or derive from reasoning their systems of religion; when philologers and mythologists, we see, scarce ever discovered so much penetration. And even the philosophers, who discoursed of such topics, readily assented to the grossest theory, and admitted the joint origin of gods and men from night and chaos; from fire, 20 water, air, or whatever they established to be the ruling element.

Nor was it only on their first origin, that the gods were supposed dependent on the powers of nature. Thro' the whole period of their

---

[v] It will be easy to give a reason, why *Thales*, *Anaximander*, and those early philosophers, who really were atheists, might be very orthodox in the pagan creed; and why *Anaxagoras* and *Socrates*, tho' real theists, must naturally, in ancient times, be esteemed impious. The blind, unguided powers of nature, if they could produce men, might also produce such beings as *Jupiter* and *Neptune*, who being the most powerful, intelligent existences in the world, would be proper objects of worship. But where a supreme intelligence, the first cause of all, is admitted, these capricious beings, if they exist at all, must appear very subordinate and dependent, and consequently be excluded from the rank of deities. *Plato* (*Laws*, Bk. X. [886 A–E]) assigns this reason of the imputation thrown on *Anaxagoras*, viz. his denying the divinity of the stars, planets, and other created objects.

[w] *Against the Physicists*, Bk. II, §§ 18–19.

---

1 unquestioned;] 70 unquestioned: 5 *Hesiod*:] 58–77 HESIOD,   7 wide-stretcht] 64–66 wide-strech'd   all.] 77 all: 9 *chaos*] 57 *choas*   11 hint,] 70–77 hint   16 scarce] 72–77 scarcely   17 And even] 67–68 Even 19 from fire] 68 and from fire   22 Thro'] 64–68 Through] 70–77 Throughout [v]3 tho'] 64–77 though   antient] 70–77 ancient   [v]7 of all,] 67 of all [v]10 viz. his] 67–68 his] 77 namely his

existence, they were subjected to the dominion of fate or destiny. *Think of the force of necessity,* says *Agrippa* to the *Roman* people, *that force, to which even the gods must submit.*[x] And the younger *Pliny,*[y] suitable to this way of reasoning, tells us, that, amidst the darkness, horror, and confusion, which ensued upon the first eruption of *Vesuvius,* several concluded, that all nature was going to wrack, and that gods and men were perishing in one common ruin.

It is great complaisance, indeed, if we dignify with the name of religion such an imperfect system of theology, and put it on a level with latter systems, which are founded on principles more just and more sublime. For my part, I can scarce allow the principles even of *Marcus Aurelius, Plutarch,* and some other *Stoics* and *Academics,* tho' infinitely more refined than the pagan superstition, to be worthy of the honourable denomination of theism. For if the mythology of the heathens resemble the antient *European* system of spiritual beings, excluding God and angels, and leaving only fairies and sprights; the creed of these philosophers may justly be said to exclude a deity, and to leave only angels and fairies.

V

But it is chiefly our present business to consider the gross polytheism and idolatry of the vulgar, and to trace all its various appearances, in the principles of human nature, whence they are derived.

Whoever learns, by argument, the existence of invisible, intelligent power, must reason from the admirable contrivance of natural objects, and must suppose the world to be the workmanship of that divine being, the original cause of all things. But the vulgar polytheist, so far from admitting that idea, deifies every part of the

---

[x] Dionysius of Halicarnassus, *Roman Antiquities,* Bk. VI, Ch. 54.
[y] *Letters,* Bk. VI, Letter 20, § 15.

---

1 existence,] 64–77 existence   3 younger] 64–77 Younger   3–4 suitable] 64–67 agreeable] 68–77 agreeably   4 reasoning] 72–77 thinking   5 horror,] 58–68 horror   10 latter] 72–77 later   13 tho'] 64–77 though   infinitely] 70–77 much   14 honourable] 58 honorable   denomination] 72–77 appellation   15 antient] 70–77 ancient   19 V] 58–60 *Various Forms of Polytheism; Allegory, Hero-Worship.*] 64–77 . . . *Poly-theism:* . . .   20–1 polytheism and idolatry] 72–77 polytheism   24 invisible,] 64–77 invisible

universe, and conceives all the conspicuous productions of nature to be themselves so many real divinities. The sun, moon, and stars are all gods, according to his system: Fountains are inhabited by nymphs, and trees by hamadryads: Even monkies, dogs, cats, and 5 other animals often become sacred in his eyes, and strike him with a religious veneration. And thus, however strong men's propensity to believe invisible, intelligent power in nature, their propensity is equally strong to rest their attention on sensible, visible objects; and in order to reconcile these opposite inclinations, they 10 are led to unite the invisible power with some visible object.

The distribution also of distinct provinces to the several deities is apt to cause some allegory, both physical and moral, to enter into the vulgar systems of polytheism. The god of war will naturally be represented as furious, cruel, and impetuous: The god of 15 poetry as elegant, polite, and amiable: The god of merchandise, especially in early times, as thievish and deceitful. The allegories, supposed in *Homer* and other mythologists, I allow, have been often so strained, that men of sense are apt entirely to reject them, and to consider them as the product merely of the fancy and conceit 20 of critics and commentators. But that allegory really has place in the heathen mythology is undeniable even on the least reflection. *Cupid* the son of *Venus*; the Muses the daughters of memory; *Prometheus* the wise brother, and *Epimetheus* the foolish; *Hygieia* or the goddess of health descended from *Æsculapius* or the god of 25 physic: Who sees not, in these, and in many other instances, the plain traces of allegory? When a god is supposed to preside over any passion, event, or system of actions; it is almost unavoidable to give him a genealogy, attributes, and adventures, suitable to his supposed powers and influence; and to carry on the similitude and 30 comparison, which is naturally so agreeable to the mind of man.

Allegories, indeed, entirely perfect, we ought not to expect as the products of ignorance and superstition; there being no work of genius, that requires a nicer hand, or has been more rarely executed with success. That *Fear* and *Terror* are the sons of *Mars* is just;

1 nature] 58–77 nature,   2 stars] 58–77 stars,   3 gods,] 64–77 gods
6 thus,] 70 thus   15 merchandise] 67–68 merchandize   19 product]
64–77 production   22 memory] 64–77 Memory   23 *Prometheus*] 58–77
PROMETHEUS,   27 actions;] 58–77 actions,   32 products] 72–77 productions

but why by *Venus?ᵃ* That *Harmony* is the daughter of *Venus* is regular; but why by *Mars?ᵇ* That *Sleep* is the brother of *Death* is suitable; but why describe him as enamoured of one of the Graces?ᶜ And since the ancient mythologists fall into mistakes so gross and obvious, we have no reason surely to expect such refined and long- 5 spun allegories, as some have endeavoured to deduce from their fictions.ᵈ

The deities of the vulgar are so little superior to human creatures, that where men are affected with strong sentiments of veneration or gratitude for any hero or public benefactor; nothing can be more 10 natural than to convert him into a god, and fill the heavens, after this manner, with continual recruits from amongst mankind. Most of the divinities of the antient world are supposed to have once been men, and to have been beholden for their *apotheosis* to the admiration and affection of the people. And the real history of their 15 adventures, corrupted by tradition, and elevated by the marvellous, became a plentiful source of fable; especially in passing thro' the hands of poets, allegorists, and priests, who successively improved upon the wonder and astonishment of the ignorant multitude. 20

Painters too and sculptors came in for their share of profit in the sacred mysteries; and furnishing men with sensible representations of their divinities, whom they cloathed in human figures, gave great encrease to the public devotion, and determined its object.

ᵃ Hesiod, *Theogony*, lines 933–5.

ᵇ Ibid., lines 936–7, and Plutarch, 'Pelopidas', Ch. 19. [The Greek text of Hesiod has 'Ares' (= Mars) and 'Cytherea', one of the titles of Aphrodite (= Venus) derived from the island of Cythera, at which she is supposed first to have landed.]

ᶜ Homer, *Iliad*, Bk. XIV, lines 263 ff.

ᵈ *Lucretius* was plainly seduced by the strong appearance of allegory, which is observable in the pagan fictions. He first addresses himself to *Venus* as to that generating power, which animates, renews, and beautifies the universe: But is soon betrayed by the mythology into incoherencies, while he prays to that allegorical personage to appease the furies of her lover, *Mars*: An idea not drawn from allegory, but from the popular religion and which *Lucretius*, as an *Epicurean*, could not consistently admit of. [*On the Nature of the Gods*, Bk. I, lines 1–40.]

---

5 obvious] 72–77 palpable   9 that] 70–77 that,   10 benefactor;] 64–77 benefactor,   12 amongst] 67–68, 72–77 among   13 antient] 70–77 ancient 15 And the] 68–77 The   17 thro'] 64–77 through   ᵈ1–7 Note ᵈ *incorporated into the main text*, 70–77.   ᵈ3 renews,] 60–72 renews   ᵈ5 lover, *Mars*:] 64–77 lover ᴹᴬʀˢ:

It was probably for want of these arts in rude and barbarous ages, that men deified plants, animals, and even brute, unorganized matter; and rather than be without a sensible object of worship, affixed divinity to such ungainly forms. Could any statuary of
5 *Syria*, in early times, have formed a just figure of *Apollo*, the conic stone, *Heliogabalus*, had never become the object of such profound adoration, and been received as a representation of the solar deity.*e*

Stilpo was banished by the council of *Areopagus* for affirming that the *Minerva* in the citadel was no divinity; but the workmanship of
10 *Phidias*, the sculptor.*f* What degree of reason may we expect in the religious belief of the vulgar in other nations; when *Athenians* and *Areopagites* could entertain such gross conceptions?

These then are the general principles of polytheism, founded in human nature, and little or nothing dependent on caprice and
15 accident. As the *causes*, which bestow on us happiness or misery, are, in general, very unknown and uncertain, our anxious concern endeavours to attain a determinate idea of them; and finds no better expedient than to represent them as intelligent, voluntary agents, like ourselves; only somewhat superior in power and
20 wisdom. The limited influence of these agents, and their great

---

e Herodian, Bk. V, Ch. 3, §§ 3–5.[1] *Jupiter Ammon* is represented by *Curtius* as a deity of the same kind, Bk. IV, Ch. 7, § 23.[2] The *Arabians* and *Pessinuntians* adored also shapeless, unformed stones as their deity. Arnobius, *Seven Books Against the Heathen*, Bk. VI, Ch. 11 [vi. 510b]. So much did their folly exceed that of the *Egyptians*.

f Diogenes Laertius, *Lives of Eminent Philosophers*, Bk. II, Ch. 11, 'Stilpo', § 116.

---

8 *Areopagus*] 58–77 AREOPAGUS,   10 may] 67–68 might] 70–77 must
11 in other] 67–68 among other   16 unknown] 64–77 little known   un-
certain] 64–77 very uncertain   17 endeavours] 58 endeavors   18 intelligent,] 77 intelligent   *e*2 *Pessinuntians*] 72–77 PERSINUNTIANS   *e*3 shapeless,]
60–77 shapeless

---

[1] '. . . two boys, Bassianus, aged about fourteen, and Alexianus, just turned nine, were being raised by their mothers and grandmother. Both boys were dedicated to the service of the sun god whom the local inhabitants worship under its Phoenician name of Elagabalus. There was a huge temple built there, richly ornamented with gold and silver and valuable stones. . . . There was no actual man-made statue of the god, the sort Greeks and Romans put up; but there was an enormous stone, rounded at the base and coming to a point on the top, conical in shape and black. This stone is worshipped as though it were sent from heaven; on it there are some small projecting pieces and markings that are pointed out, which the people would like to believe are a rough picture of the sun, because this is how they see them.' ii. 19, 21.

[2] 'What is worshipped as the god does not have the same form that artificers have commonly given to the deities; its appearance is very like that of a navel fastened in a mass of emeralds and other gems.' *History of Alexander*, i. 233.

proximity to human weakness, introduce the various distribution and division of their authority; and thereby give rise to allegory. The same principles naturally deify mortals, superior in power, courage, or understanding, and produce hero-worship; along with fabulous history and mythological tradition, in all its wild and [5] unaccountable forms. And as an invisible spiritual intelligence is an object too refined for vulgar apprehension, men naturally affix it to some sensible representation; such as either the more conspicuous parts of nature, or the statues, images, and pictures, which a more refined age forms of its divinities. [10]

Almost all idolaters, of whatever age or country, concur in these general principles and conceptions; and even the particular characters and provinces, which they assign to their deities, are not extremely different.[g] The *Greek* and *Roman* travellers and conquerors, without much difficulty, found their own deities every where; and [15] said, this is *Mercury*, that *Venus*; this *Mars*, that *Neptune*; by whatever titles the strange gods may be denominated. The goddess *Hertha* of our *Saxon* ancestors seems to be no other, according to *Tacitus*,[h] than the *Mater Tellus* of the *Romans*; and his conjecture was evidently just. [20]

VI

The doctrine of one supreme deity, the author of nature, is very antient, has spread itself over great and populous nations, and among them has been embraced by all ranks and conditions of persons: But whoever thinks that it has owed its success to the [25] prevalent force of those invincible reasons, on which it is undoubtedly founded, would show himself little acquainted with the ignorance and stupidity of the people, and their incurable prejudices

---

[g] See Cæsar of the religion of the Gauls, *The Gallic War*, Bk. 6, §§ 16–17.

[h] *Germany*, § 40. ['These tribes are protected by forests and rivers, nor is there anything noteworthy about them individually, except that they worship in common Nerthus, or Mother Earth (*Nerthum, id est Terram matrem*), and conceive her as intervening in human affairs, and riding in procession through the cities of men.' p. 321.]

---

4 along with] 58–77 together with   13 deities,] 57 deities   16 this is] 60–77 This is   17 titles] 70–77 title   may be] 64–77 might be   21 VI] 58–77 Sect. vi. *Origin of Theism from Polytheism.*   23 antient] 70–77 ancient 25 persons] 72–77 men   [g]1 Cæsar] 58–77 Cæsar

in favour of their particular superstitions. Even at this day, and in *Europe*, ask any of the vulgar, why he believes in an omnipotent creator of the world; he will never mention the beauty of final causes, of which he is wholly ignorant: He will not hold out his 5 hand, and bid you contemplate the suppleness and variety of joints in his fingers, their bending all one way, the counterpoise which they receive from the thumb, the softness and fleshy parts of the inside of his hand, with all the other circumstances, which render that member fit for the use, to which it was destined. To 10 these he has been long accustomed; and he beholds them with listlessness and unconcern. He will tell you of the sudden and unexpected death of such a one: The fall and bruise of such another: The excessive drought of this season: The cold and rains of another. These he ascribes to the immediate operation of providence: And 15 such events, as, with good reasoners, are the chief difficulties in admitting a supreme intelligence, are with him the sole arguments for it.

Many theists, even the most zealous and refined, have denied a *particular* providence, and have asserted, that the Sovereign mind 20 or first principle of all things, having fixt general laws, by which nature is governed, gives free and uninterrupted course to these laws, and disturbs not, at every turn, the settled order of events, by particular volitions. From the beautiful connexion, say they, and rigid observance of established rules, we draw the chief argu-25 ment for theism; and from the same principles are enabled to answer the principal objections against it. But so little is this understood by the generality of mankind, that, wherever they observe any one to ascribe all events to natural causes, and to remove the particular interposal of a deity, they are apt to suspect 30 him of the grossest infidelity. *A little philosophy*, says my Lord *Bacon, makes men atheists: A great deal reconciles them to religion.*[1] For

---

1 favour] 58 favor   3 he will] 57 he would   19 Sovereign] 58 sovereign
20 things,] 67–68 things   fixt] 58–77 fixed   22 events,] 58–77 events
29 interposal] 64–77 interposition   30 my Lord] 68 Lord] 70 my lord] 72–77 lord

---

[1] 'Of Atheisme': 'Certainely a little *Philosophie* inclineth mans minde to *Atheisme*, but depth in *Philosophie* bringeth men about to Religion.' Between 1597 and 1742, thirty-two editions of Bacon's *Essays* appeared. The above is the text of the 1612 edition. *Works*, xii. 337–8.

men, being taught, by superstitious prejudices, to lay the stress on a wrong place; when that fails them, and they discover, by a little reflection, that the course of nature is regular and uniform, their whole faith totters, and falls to ruin. But being taught, by more reflection, that this very regularity and uniformity is the strongest 5 proof of design and of a supreme intelligence, they return to that belief, which they had deserted; and they are now able to establish it on a firmer and more durable foundation.

Convulsions in nature, disorders, prodigies, miracles, tho' the most opposite to the plan of a wise superintendent, impress man- 10 kind with the strongest sentiments of religion; the causes of events seeming then the most unknown and unaccountable. Madness, fury, rage, and an inflamed imagination, tho' they sink men nearest the level of beasts, are, for a like reason, often supposed to be the only dispositions, in which we can have any immediate communica- 15 tion with the deity.

We may conclude, therefore, upon the whole, that since the vulgar, in nations, which have embraced the doctrine of theism, still build it upon irrational and superstitious opinions, they are never led into that opinion by any process of argument, but by a 20 certain train of thinking, more suitable to their genius and capacity.

It may readily happen, in an idolatrous nation, that, tho' men admit the existence of several limited deities, yet may there be some one god, whom, in a particular manner, they make the object of their worship and adoration. They may either suppose, that, in 25 the distribution of power and territory among the gods, their nation was subjected to the jurisdiction of that particular deity; or reducing heavenly objects to the model of things below, they may represent one god as the prince or supreme magistrate of the rest, who, tho' of the same nature, rules them with an authority, like 30 that which an earthly sovereign exercises over his subjects and vassals. Whether this god, therefore, be considered as their peculiar patron, or as the general sovereign of heaven, his votaries will endeavour, by every act, to insinuate themselves into his favour;

9 tho'] 70–77 though   13 tho'] 72–77 though   16 deity] 58–77 Deity
17 that] 70–77 that,   22 tho'] 68–77 though   24 god] 58–77 God   30 tho']
68–77 though   34 endeavour] 58 endeavor   act] 64–77 art   favour] 58 favor

and supposing him to be pleased, like themselves, with praise and
flattery, there is no eulogy or exaggeration, which will be spared in
their addresses to him. In proportion as men's fears or distresses
become more urgent, they still invent new strains of adulation;
5 and even he who out-does his predecessors, in swelling up the
titles of his divinity, is sure to be out-done by his successors, in
newer and more pompous epithets of praise. Thus they proceed;
till at last they arrive at infinity itself, beyond which there is no
farther progress: And it is well, if, in striving to get farther, and to
10 represent a magnificent simplicity, they run not into inexplicable
mystery, and destroy the intelligent nature of their deity; on which
alone any rational worship or adoration can be founded. While they
confine themselves to the notion of a perfect being, the creator of
the world, they coincide, by chance, with the principles of reason
15 and true philosophy; tho' they are guided to that notion, not by
reason, of which they are in a great measure incapable, but by the
adulation and fears of the most vulgar superstition.

We often find amongst barbarous nations, and even sometimes
amongst civilized, that, when every strain of flattery has been
20 exhausted towards arbitrary princes; when every human quality
has been applauded to the utmost; their servile courtiers represent
them, at last, as real divinities, and point them out to the people
as objects of adoration. How much more natural, therefore, is it,
that a limited deity, who at first is supposed only the immediate
25 author of the particular goods and ills in life, should in the end be
represented as sovereign maker and modifier of the universe?

Even where this notion of a supreme deity is already established;
tho' it ought naturally to lessen every other worship, and abase
every object of reverence, yet if a nation has entertained the opinion
30 of a subordinate tutelar divinity, saint, or angel; their addresses to
that being gradually rise upon them, and encroach on the adoration due to their supreme deity. The virgin *Mary*, ere checkt by

    5 predecessors,] 58–70 predecessors] 72–77 predecessor   6 successors,] 58–70
successors] 72–77 successor   11 deity;] 64–77 deity,   15 tho'] 68–77
though   16 incapable,] 67–68 incapable   18 find amongst] 58–64, 70–77
find, amongst] 67–68 find, among   18–19 sometimes amongst] 67–68 sometimes among   20 princes;] 58–77 princes,   28 tho'] 68–77 though
32 virgin] 58–77 Virgin   checkt] 58–77 checked

the reformation, had proceeded, from being merely a good woman to usurp many attributes of the Almighty:*a* God and St. *Nicholas* go hand in hand, in all the prayers and petitions of the *Muscovites*.

Thus the deity, who, from love, converted himself into a bull, in order to carry off *Europa*; and who, from ambition, dethroned his father, *Saturn*, became the *Optimus Maximus* of the heathens. Thus, notwithstanding the sublime ideas suggested by *Moses* and the inspired writers, many vulgar *Jews* seem still to have conceived the supreme Being as a mere topical deity or national protector.

Rather than relinquish this propensity to adulation, religionists, in all ages, have involved themselves in the greatest absurdities and contradictions.

Homer,[5] in one passage, calls *Oceanus* and *Tethys* the original parents of all things, conformable to the established mythology

---

a The *Jacobins*,[2] who denied the immaculate conception, have ever been very unhappy in their doctrine, even tho' political reasons have kept the Romish church from condemning it. The *Cordeliers*[3] have run away with all the popularity. But in the fifteenth Century, as we learn from *Boulainvilliers*, an *Italian Cordelier* maintained, that, during the three days, when *Christ* was interred, the hypostatic union was dissolved, and that his human nature was not a proper object of adoration, during that period. Without the art of divination, one might foretel, that so gross and impious a blasphemy would not fail to be anathematized by the people. It was the occasion of great insults on the part of the *Jacobins*; who now got some recompence for their misfortunes in the war about the immaculate conception. See Histoire abrégée, pag. 499.[4]

1 woman] 64–77 woman,   5 ambition,] 70 ambition   6–9 Thus, . . . protector.] 64–77 Thus, the God of ABRAHAM, ISAAC, and JACOB, became the supreme deity or JEHOVAH of the JEWS.] *in the proof*: Thus the deity, whom the vulgar Jews conceived only as the God of *Abraham, Isaac*, and *Jacob*, became their *Jehovah* and Creator of the world. [*from Green and Grosse's edition of the Essays, iv. 331.*] 14 conformable] 70–77 conformably   *a*1–11 *This entire note, except the concluding reference, was incorporated into the text of editions 70–77 between the paragraphs beginning* 'Thus the deity' *and* 'Rather than relinquish'   *a*2 tho'] 68–77 though Romish] 60–77 ROMISH   *a*4 Century] 64–77 century   an *Italian*] 68 and ITALIAN   *a*5 that,] 68 that

2 'A name given originally to the Dominican friars in France.' For a brief account of the controversy see the entry 'Immaculate conception of the BVM' in the *Oxford Dictionary of the Christian Church*.
3 'A name sometimes given in France to the Franciscan Observatines', an order deriving its inspiration from the Spiritual Franciscans. See the appropriate entries in the *O.D.C.C.*
4 Perhaps Comte Henri de Boulainvilliers, *Abrégé chronologique de l'histoire de France*, 3 vols. (Paris, 1733). No one-volume edition is listed in any of the standard catalogues, American, British, or French.
5 *Iliad*, Bk. XIV, lines 200–4. See also Bk. XV, line 12.

and tradition of the *Greeks*: Yet, in other passages, he could not forbear complimenting *Jupiter*, the reigning deity, with that magnificent appellation; and accordingly denominates him the father of gods and men. He forgets, that every temple, every street
5 was full of the ancestors, uncles, brothers, and sisters of this *Jupiter*; who was in reality nothing but an upstart parricide and usurper. A like contradiction is observable in *Hesiod*;[6] and is so much the less excusable, that his professed intention was to deliver a true genealogy of the gods.

10   Were there a religion (and we may suspect Mahometanism of this inconsistence) which sometimes painted the deity in the most sublime colours, as the creator of heaven and earth; sometimes degraded him nearly to a level with human creatures in his powers and faculties; while at the same time it ascribed to him suitable
15 infirmities, passions, and partialities of the moral kind: That religion, after it was extinct, would also be cited as an instance of those contradictions, which arise from the gross, vulgar, natural conceptions of mankind, opposed to their continual propensity towards flattery and exaggeration. Nothing indeed would prove

---

8 that] 64–77 as   11 deity] 58–77 Deity   12 colours] 58 colors
12–14 sometimes . . . while] *in the proof*: sometimes degraded him so far to a level with human creatures as to represent him wrestling with a man,[7] walking in the cool of the evening,[8] showing his back parts,[9] and descending from heaven to inform himself of what passes on earth;[10] while [*from Green and Grosse, Essays, iv. 332*]
15 partialities] 72–77 partialities,   kind: That] 64 kind: that

---

[6] In the *Theogony*, Zeus is referred to as 'the father of gods and men' (line 47); subsequently Chaos is declared to be the first (line 116); moreover Cronos is represented as castrating his father before Zeus was born (lines 176 ff.); and so on.
[7] Genesis 32: 24–30. This passage is usually interpreted as Jacob wrestling with an angel, yet verse 30 would seem to confirm Hume's interpretation: 'And Jacob called the name of the place Peniel [that is, *The face of God*]: for I have seen God face to face, and my life is preserved.'
[8] Genesis 3: 8. 'And they heard the voice of the LORD God walking in the garden in the cool of the day.'
[9] Exodus 33: 22–3. 'And it shall come to pass, while my glory passeth by, that I will put thee in a clift of the rock, and will cover thee with my hand while I pass by: And I will take away mine hand, and thou shalt see my back parts: but my face shall not be seen.'
[10] Exodus 33: 9–11. 'And it came to pass, as Moses entered into the tabernacle, the cloudy pillar descended, and stood *at* the door of the tabernacle, and *the* LORD talked with Moses. And all the people saw the cloudy pillar stand *at* the tabernacle door: and all the people rose up and worshipped, every man *in* his tent door. And the LORD spake unto Moses face to face, as a man speaketh unto his friend.'

more strongly the divine origin of any religion, than to find (and happily this is the case with Christianity) that it is free from a contradiction, so incident to human nature.

VII

It appears certain, that, tho' the original notions of the vulgar 5 represent the Divinity as a very limited being, and consider him only as the particular cause of health or sickness; plenty or want; prosperity or adversity; yet when more magnificent ideas are urged upon them, they esteem it dangerous to refuse their assent. Will you say, that your deity is finite and bounded in his perfections; 10 may be overcome by a greater force; is subject to human passions, pains, and infirmities; has a beginning, and may have an end? This they dare not affirm; but thinking it safest to comply with the higher encomiums, they endeavour, by an affected ravishment and devotion, to ingratiate themselves with him. As a confirmation of 15 this, we may observe, that the assent of the vulgar is, in this case, merely verbal, and that they are incapable of conceiving those sublime qualities, which they seemingly attribute to the deity. Their real idea of him, notwithstanding their pompous language, is still as poor and frivolous as ever.   20

That original intelligence, say the *Magians*, who is the first principle of all things, discovers himself *immediately* to the mind and understanding alone; but has placed the sun as his image in the visible universe; and when that bright luminary diffuses its beams over the earth and the firmament, it is a faint copy of the 25 glory, which resides in the higher heavens. If you would escape the displeasure of this divine being, you must be careful never to set your bare foot upon the ground, nor spit into a fire, nor throw any water upon it, even tho' it were consuming a whole city.[a] Who

---

[a] Thomas Hyde, *Historia religionis veterum Persarum, earumque Magorum*; *Zoroastris vita, etc.*, Oxford, 1700. [History of the ancient Persian religion, and also of the Magian; life of Zoroaster, etc. A formidably thick quarto of 556 pages; a second edition was published, Oxford, 1760.]

---

4 VII] 58–77 SECT. VII. *Confirmation of this Doctrine.*   5 that, tho'] 68, 72–77 that, though] 70 that though   6 a very limited] 70–77 a limited   12 pains,] 58 pains   14 endeavour] 58 endeavor   15 devotion,] 70 devotion   18 qualities,]   64–68 qualities   deity] 58–77 Deity   29 tho'] 68–77 though

can express the perfections of the Almighty, say the *Mahometans*? Even the noblest of his works, if compared to him, are but dust and rubbish. How much more must human conception fall short of his infinite perfections? His smile and favour renders men for ever 5 happy; and to obtain it for your children, the best method is to cut off from them, while infants, a little bit of skin, about half the breadth of a farthing. Take two bits of cloth,[b] say the *Roman catholics*, about an inch or an inch and a half square, join them by the corners with two strings or pieces of tape about sixteen inches 10 long, throw this over your head, and make one of the bits of cloth lie upon your breast, and the other upon your back, keeping them next your skin. There is not a better secret for recommending yourself to that infinite Being, who exists from eternity to eternity.

The *Getes*, commonly called immortal, from their steddy belief 15 of the soul's immortality, were genuine theists and unitarians. They affirmed *Zamolxis*, their deity, to be the only true god; and asserted the worship of all other nations to be addressed to mere fictions and chimeras. But were their religious principles any more refined, on account of these magnificent pretensions? Every fifth 20 year they sacrificed a human victim, whom they sent as a messenger to their deity, in order to inform him of their wants and necessities. And when it thundered, they were so provoked, that, in order to return the defiance, they let fly arrows at him, and declined not the combat as unequal. Such at least is the account, 25 which *Herodotus* gives of the theism of the immortal *Getes*.[c]

VIII

It is remarkable, that the principles of religion have a kind of flux and reflux in the human mind, and that men have a natural tendency

[b] Called the Scapulaire.

[c] Bk. IV, Ch. 94. [ii. 295, 297: 'Moreover when there is thunder and lightning these same Thracians shoot arrows skyward as a threat to the god, believing in no other god but their own.']

1 Almighty, say the *Mahometans*?] 60–77 Almighty? say the Mahometans. 4 favour] 58 favor   7 cloth] 57 cloath   10 cloth] 57 cloath   12 skin. There] 58–68 skin, there] 70 skin; there] 72–77 skin: There   14 steddy] 64–77 steady 17 nations] 58–60 nations,   20 sacrificed] 57 sacrified   22 that,] 68 that 26 VIII] 58–67, 70–77 SECT. VIII. *Flux and reflux of polytheism and theism*.] 68 . . . *Polytheism and Theism*.

to rise from idolatry to theism, and to sink again from theism into idolatry. The vulgar, that is, indeed, all mankind, a few excepted, being ignorant and uninstructed, never elevate their contemplation to the heavens, or penetrate by their disquisitions into the secret structure of vegetable or animal bodies; so as to discover a 5 supreme mind or original providence, which bestowed order on every part of nature. They consider these admirable works in a more confined and selfish view; and finding their own happiness and misery to depend on the secret influence and unforeseen concurrence of external objects, they regard, with perpetual attention, 10 the *unknown causes*, which govern all these natural events, and distribute pleasure and pain, good and ill, by their powerful, but silent, operation. The unknown causes are still appealed to, at every emergence; and in this general appearance or confused image, are the perpetual objects of human hopes and fears, wishes and 15 apprehensions. By degrees, the active imagination of men, uneasy in this abstract conception of objects, about which it is incessantly employed, begins to render them more particular, and to clothe them in shapes more suitable to its natural comprehension. It represents them to be sensible, intelligent beings, like mankind; 20 actuated by love and hatred, and flexible by gifts and entreaties, by prayers and sacrifices. Hence the origin of religion: And hence the origin of idolatry or polytheism.

But the same anxious concern for happiness, which engenders the idea of these invisible, intelligent powers, allows not mankind 25 to remain long in the first simple conception of them; as powerful, but limited beings; masters of human fate, but slaves to destiny and the course of nature. Men's exaggerated praises and compliments still swell their idea upon them; and elevating their deities to the utmost bounds of perfection, at last beget the attributes of unity 30 and infinity, simplicity and spirituality. Such refined ideas, being somewhat disproportioned to vulgar comprehension, remain not long in their original purity; but require to be supported by the notion of inferior mediators or subordinate agents, which interpose

6 mind] 58–68 mind,   8 view;] 68 view: 13–14 at every] 64–77 on
every   16 degrees,] 67–68 degrees   18 clothe] 57 cloathe   21 flexible] 68
inflexible   24 engenders] 58–77 begets   28 exaggerated] 58 exaggerate
33 their] 67–68 the

betwixt mankind and their supreme deity. These demi-gods or
middle beings, partaking more of human nature, and being more
familiar to us, become the chief objects of devotion, and gradually
recal that idolatry, which had been formerly banished by the
5 ardent prayers and panegyrics of timorous and indigent mortals.
But as these idolatrous religions fall every day into grosser and more
vulgar conceptions, they at last destroy themselves, and, by the
vile representations, which they form of their deities, make the
tide turn again towards theism. But so great is the propensity, in
10 this alternate revolution of human sentiments, to return back to
idolatry, that the utmost precaution is not able effectually to
prevent it. And of this, some theists, particularly the *Jews* and
Mahometans, have been sensible; as appears by their banishing all
the arts of statuary and painting, and not allowing the representa-
15 tions, even of human figures, to be taken by marble or colours; lest
the common infirmity of mankind should thence produce idolatry.
The feeble apprehensions of men cannot be satisfied with conceiving
their deity as a pure spirit and perfect intelligence; and yet their
natural terrors keep them from imputing to him the least shadow of
20 limitation and imperfection. They fluctuate betwixt these opposite
sentiments. The same infirmity still drags them downwards, from
an omnipotent and spiritual deity to a limited and corporeal one,
and from a corporeal and limited deity to a statue or visible representation. The same endeavour at elevation still pushes them
25 upwards, from the statue or material image to the invisible power;
and from the invisible power to an infinitely perfect deity, the
creator and sovereign of the universe.

IX

Polytheism or idolatrous worship, being founded entirely in vulgar
30 traditions, is liable to this great inconvenience, that any practice or
opinion, however barbarous or corrupted, may be authorized by

---

1 betwixt] 64–77 between   4 recal] 60–68 recall   idolatry,] 60–68 idolatry
15 colours] 58 colors   20 betwixt] 64–77 between   22 deity] 58–77 deity,
24 endeavour] 58 endeavor   28 IX] 58–77 SECT. IX. *Comparison of these Religions,
with regard to Perfection and Toleration.*

it; and full scope is left for knavery to impose on credulity, till morals and humanity be expelled from the religious systems of mankind. At the same time, idolatry is attended with this evident advantage, that, by limiting the powers and functions of its deities, it naturally admits the gods of other sects and nations to a share 5 of divinity, and renders all the various deities, as well as rites, ceremonies, or traditions, compatible with each other.[a] Theism is opposite both in its advantages and disadvantages. As that system supposes one sole deity, the perfection of reason and goodness, it should, if justly prosecuted, banish every thing frivolous, un- 10 reasonable, or inhuman from religious worship, and set before men the most illustrious example, as well as the most commanding motives of justice and benevolence. These mighty advantages are not indeed over-ballanced, (for that is not possible) but somewhat diminished, by inconveniencies, which, arise from the vices and 15 prejudices of mankind. While one sole object of devotion is ack-nowledged, the worship of other deities is regarded as absurd and impious. Nay, this unity of object seems naturally to require the unity of faith and ceremonies, and furnishes designing men with a pretext for representing their adversaries as prophane, and the 20 subjects of divine as well as human vengeance. For as each sect is positive that its own faith and worship are entirely acceptable to the deity, and as no one can conceive, that the same being should be pleased with different and opposite rites and principles; the several sects fall naturally into animosity, and mutually discharge on each 25

---

[a] *Verrius Flaccus*, cited by *Pliny*, affirmed, that it was usual for the *Romans*, before they laid siege to any town, to invocate the tutelar deity of the place, and by promis-ing him equal or greater honours than those he at present enjoyed, bribe him to betray his old friends and votaries. The name of the tutelar deity of *Rome* was for this reason kept a most religious mystery; lest the enemies of the republic should be able, in the same manner, to draw him over to their service. For without the name, they thought, nothing of that kind could be practised. *Pliny* says, that the common form of invocation was preserved to his time in the ritual of the pontifs. [*Natural History*, Bk. XXVIII, Ch. 4, §§ 18–19.] And *Macrobius* has transmitted a copy of it from the secret things of *Sammonicus Serenus*. [*The Saturnalia*, Bk. III, Ch. 9, p. 218.]

---

1 left] 77 given, 2 expelled from the] 72–77 expelled the 13 motives] 70–77 motives, 14 over-ballanced,] 64–72 over-balanced,] 77 over-balanced possible)] 77 possible 15 which,] 58–70, 77 which 20 pretext] 64–77 pretence prophane] 64–77 profane 21 subjects] 58–77 objects 22 positive] 57 positive, 23 deity,] 70 deity [a]3 honours] 58 honors

other, that sacred zeal and rancour, the most furious and implacable of all human passions.

The tolerating spirit of idolaters both in antient and modern times, is very obvious to any one, who is the least conversant in
5 the writings of historians or travellers. When the oracle of *Delphi* was asked, what rites or worship were most acceptable to the gods? Those legally established in each city, replied the oracle.[b] Even priests, in those ages, could, it seems, allow salvation to those of different communion. The *Romans* commonly adopted the gods of
10 the conquered people; and never disputed the attributes of those topical and national deities, in whose territories they resided. The religious wars and persecutions of the *Egyptian* idolaters are indeed an exception to this rule; but are accounted for by antient authors from reasons very singular and remarkable. Different species of
15 animals were the deities of the different sects of the *Egyptians*; and the deities being in continual war, engaged their votaries in the same contention. The worshipers of dogs could not long remain in peace with the adorers of cats or wolves.[c] And where that reason took not place, the *Egyptian* superstition was not so incompatible
20 as is commonly imagined; since we learn from *Herodotus*,[d] that very large contributions were given by *Amasis* towards rebuilding the temple of *Delphi*.

The intolerance of almost all religions, which have maintained the unity of god, is as remarkable as the contrary principle in
25 polytheists. The implacable, narrow spirit of the *Jews* is well known. *Mahometanism* set out with still more bloody principles; and even to this day, deals out damnation, tho' not fire and faggot, to all other sects. And if, amongst *Christians*, the *English* and *Dutch* have embraced the principles of toleration, this singularity has proceeded

---

[b] Xenophon, *Memorabilia*, Bk. I, Ch. 3, § 1.
[c] Plutarch, 'Isis and Osiris', Ch. 72.   [d] Bk. II, Ch. 180.

---

1 other,] 70–77 other   rancour] 58 rancor   3 idolaters] 70–77
idolaters,   antient] 70–77 ancient   6 were] 58–77 was   7 Those legally]
72–77 Those which are legally   10 people;] 67–68 people,   13 antient]
70–77 ancient   14 reasons very singular] 70–77 reasons singular   15 sects of
the] 58–77 sects among the   17 worshipers] 58–77 worshippers   18 And]
64–77 But   24 god,] 58–77 God,   24–5 in polytheists] 58–64, 70–77 of
polytheists] 67–68 of Polytheists   25 implacable,] 70–77 implacable   27 tho']
60–77 though   28 amongst] 70–77 among

from the steddy resolution of the civil magistrate, in opposition to the continued efforts of priests and bigots.

The disciples of *Zoroaster* shut the doors of heaven against all but the Magians.[e] Nothing could more obstruct the progress of the *Persian* conquests, than the furious zeal of that nation against the temples 5 and images of the *Greeks*. And after the overthrow of that empire, we find *Alexander*, as a polytheist, immediately re-establishing the worship of the *Babylonians*, which their former princes, as monotheists, had carefully abolished.[f] Even the blind and devoted attachment of that conqueror to the *Greek* superstition hindered not but he him- 10 self sacrificed according to the *Babylonish* rites and ceremonies.[g]

So sociable is polytheism, that the utmost fierceness and aversion, which it meets with in an opposite religion, is scarce able to disgust it, and keep it at a distance. *Augustus* praised extremely the reserve of his grandson, *Caius Cæsar*, when, passing by *Jerusalem*, he deigned 15 not to sacrifice according to the Jewish law. But for what reason did *Augustus* so much approve of this conduct? Only, because that religion was by the pagans esteemed ignoble and barbarous.[h]

I may venture to affirm, that few corruptions of idolatry and polytheism are more pernicious to political society than this cor- 20 ruption of theism,[i] when carried to the utmost height. The human sacrifices of the *Carthaginians*, *Mexicans*, and many barbarous nations,[j]

---

[e] Hyde, *Historia religionis veterum Persarum*. [See above, p. 55, n. *a*.]
[f] Arrian, *Anabasis of Alexander*, Bk. III, Ch. 16, §§ 3–5. See also Bk. VII, Ch. 17.
[g] Ibid., Bk. III, Ch. 16, § 5.   [h] Suetonius, 'The Deified Augustus', Ch. 93.
[i] *Corruptio optimi pessima*. [The corruption of the best is the worst.]
[j] Most nations have fallen into this guilt; tho' perhaps, that impious superstition has never prevailed very much in any civilized nation, unless we except the *Carthaginians*. For the *Tyrians* soon abolished it. A sacrifice is conceived as a present; and any present is delivered to the deity by destroying it and rendering it useless to men; by burning what is solid, pouring out the liquid, and killing the animate. For want of a better way of doing him service, we do ourselves an injury; and fancy that we thereby express, at least, the heartiness of our good will and adoration. Thus our mercenary devotion deceives ourselves, and imagines it deceives the deity.

---

1 steddy] 64–77 steady   6 empire,] 77 empire   12 aversion] 72–77 antipathy   13 scarce] 70–77 scarcely   15 when,] 60–68 when] 70–77 when this latter prince,   *Jerusalem*, he deigned] 70–77 JERUSALEM, deigned 16 according to the] 68 according to the custom of the   17 Only,] 67–68 Only 18 pagans] 58–77 PAGANS   *j*1 guilt; tho'] 60–68 guilt; though] 70–77 guilt of human sacrifices; though,   *j*4 the deity] 77 their deity   it and] 67–68 it, and   *j*7 good will] 58–70, 77 good-will

scarce exceed the inquisition and persecutions of *Rome* and *Madrid*. For besides, that the effusion of blood may not be so great in the former case as in the latter; besides this, I say, the human victims, being chosen by lot or by some exterior signs, affect not, in so
5 considerable a degree, the rest of the society. Whereas virtue, knowledge, love of liberty, are the qualities, which call down the fatal vengeance of inquisitors; and when expelled, leave the society in the most shameful ignorance, corruption, and bondage. The illegal murder of one man by a tyrant is more pernicious than the
10 death of a thousand by pestilence, famine, or any undistinguishing calamity.

In the temple of *Diana* at *Aricia* near *Rome*, whoever murdered the present priest, was legally entitled to be installed his successor.[k] A very singular institution! For, however barbarous and bloody
15 the common superstitions often are to the laity, they usually turn to the advantage of the holy order.

X

From the comparison of theism and idolatry, we may form some other observations, which will also confirm the vulgar observation,
20 that the corruption of the best things gives rise to the worst.

Where the deity is represented as infinitely superior to mankind, this belief, tho' altogether just, is apt, when joined with superstitious terrors, to sink the human mind into the lowest submission and abasement, and to represent the monkish virtues of mortification,
25 pennance, humility and passive suffering, as the only qualities, which are acceptable to him. But where the gods are conceived to be only a little superior to mankind, and to have been, many of them, advanced from that inferior rank, we are more at our ease in our addresses to them, and may even, without profaneness,
30 aspire sometimes to a rivalship and emulation of them. Hence

---

[k] Strabo, *Geography*, Bk. V, Ch. 3, § 12. Suetonius, 'Gaius Caligula', Ch. 35, § 3.

---

1 scarce] 70–77 scarcely   4 lot] 58–77 lot,   14 institution!] 64–68 institution: 17 X] 58–67, 70–77 SECT. X. *With regard to courage or abasement.*] 68 . . . *Courage or Abasement.*   22 tho'] 60–77 though   25 qualities,] 60–77 qualities

activity, spirit, courage, magnanimity, love of liberty, and all the virtues, which aggrandize a people.

The heroes in paganism correspond exactly to the saints in popery and holy dervises in *Mahometanism*. The place of *Hercules, Theseus, Hector, Romulus*, is now supplied by *Dominic, Francis,* 5 *Anthony*, and *Benedict*. And instead of the destruction of monsters, the subduing tyrants, the defence of our native country; celestial honours are obtained by whippings and fastings, by cowardice and humility, by abject submission and slavish obedience.

One great incitement to the pious *Alexander* in his warlike 10 expeditions was his rivalship of *Hercules* and *Bacchus*, whom he justly pretended to have excelled.[a] *Brasidas*, that generous and noble *Spartan*, after falling in battle, had heroic honours paid him by the inhabitants of *Amphipolis*, whose defence he had embraced.[b] And in general, all founders of states and colonies amongst the 15 Greeks were raised to this inferior rank of divinity, by those who reaped the benefit of their labours.

This gave rise to the observation of *Machiavel*,[c] that the doctrines of the *Christian* religion (meaning the catholic; for he knew no other) which recommend only passive courage and suffering, had 20 subdued the spirit of mankind, and had fitted them for slavery and subjection. And this observation would certainly be just, were there not many other circumstances in human society, which controul the genius and character of a religion.

Brasidas seized a mouse, and being bit by it, let it go. *There is* 25 *nothing so contemptible*, says he, *but what may be safe, if it has but courage to defend itself.*[d] *Bellarmine*, patiently and humbly allowed the fleas

---

[a] Arrian, *passim*. [See especially Bk. IV, Ch. 10, §§ 5–7.]

[b] Thucydides, *Peloponnesian War*, Bk. V, Ch. 11.

[c] *Discourses*, Bk. II, Ch. 2, §§ 6–7, pp. 363–4. [Machiavelli's observation is more qualified than Hume's summary leads us to believe.]

[d] Plutarch, *Moralia*, 'Sayings of Kings and Commanders', *Brasidas*, 1.

---

2 virtues,] 70–77 virtues   7 the defence] 68 and the defence
8 honours] 58 honors   7–9 celestial honours . . . slavish obedience.] 70–77
whippings and fastings, cowardice and humility, abject submission and slavish
obedience, are become the means of obtaining celestial honours among mankind.
13 honours] 58 honors   15 And in] 67–68 In   amongst] 72–77 among
17 labours] 58 labors   22 And this observation] 67–68 This observation] 70–77
An observation, which   [a] Arrian] 58–77 Arian

and other odious vermin to prey upon him. *We shall have heaven,* says he, *to reward us for our sufferings: But these poor creatures have nothing but the enjoyment of the present life.*[e] Such difference is there betwixt the maxims of a *Greek* hero and a *Catholic* saint.

XI

Here is another observation to the same purpose, and a new proof that the corruption of the best things begets the worst. If we examine, without prejudice, the antient heathen mythology, as contained in the poets, we shall not discover in it any such monstrous absurdity, as we may be apt at first to apprehend. Where is the difficulty of conceiving, that the same powers or principles, whatever they were, which formed this visible world, men and animals, produced also a species of intelligent creatures, of more refined substance and greater authority than the rest? That these creatures may be capricious, revengeful, passionate, voluptuous, is easily conceived; nor is any circumstance more apt, amongst ourselves, to engender such vices, than the licence of absolute authority. And in short, the whole mythological system is so natural, that, in the vast variety of planets and worlds, contained in this universe, it seems more than probable, that, somewhere or other, it is really carried into execution.

The chief objection to it with regard to this planet, is, that it is not ascertained by any just reason or authority. The antient tradition, insisted on by the heathen priests and theologers, is but a weak foundation; and transmitted also such a number of contradictory reports, supported, all of them, by equal authority, that it became absolutely impossible to fix a preference amongst them. A few volumes, therefore, must contain all the polemical writings of pagan

---

[e] Bayle, article 'Bellarmine'. [*A General Dictionary, Historical and Critical*, iii. 173–4, note z. The first volume of the original edition was published in 1695.]

---

2 says] 72–77 said   4 betwixt] 64–77 between   5 XI] 58–67, 70–77
SECT. XI. *With regard to reason or absurdity.*] 68 . . . *Reason or Absurdity.*
8 antient] 58, 70–77 ancient   16 amongst] 58–77 among   18 that,] 70 that
19 worlds] 77 words   20 that,] 58–68 that   23 antient] 70–77 ancient
24 by the heathen] 70–77 by heathen

priests. And their whole theology must consist more of traditional stories and superstitious practices than of philosophical argument and controversy.

But where theism forms the fundamental principle of any popular religion, that tenet is so conformable to sound reason, that philo- 5 sophy is apt to incorporate itself with such a system of theology. And if the other dogmas of that system be contained in a sacred book, such as the Alcoran, or be determined by any visible authority, like that of the *Roman* pontif, speculative reasoners naturally carry on their assent, and embrace a theory, which has been instilled into 10 them by their earliest education, and which also possesses some degree of consistence and uniformity. But as these appearances do often, all of them, prove deceitful, philosophy will soon find herself very unequally yoked with her new associate; and instead of regulating each principle, as they advance together, she is at every 15 turn perverted to serve the purposes of superstition. For besides the unavoidable incoherencies, which must be reconciled and adjusted; one may safely affirm, that all popular theology, especially the scholastic, has a kind of appetite for absurdity and contradiction. If that theology went not beyond reason and common sense, 20 her doctrines would appear too easy and familiar. Amazement must of necessity be raised: Mystery affected: Darkness and obscurity sought after: And a foundation of merit afforded the devout votaries, who desire an opportunity of subduing their rebellious reason, by the belief of the most unintelligible sophisms. 25

Ecclesiastical history sufficiently confirms these reflections. When a controversy is started, some people pretend always with certainty to foretell the issue. Which ever opinion, say they, is most contrary to plain sense is sure to prevail; even where the general interest of the system requires not that decision. Tho' the reproach 30 of heresy may, for some time, be bandied about amongst the disputants, it always rests at last on the side of reason. Any one, it is pretended, that has but learning enough of this kind to know the

1 priests. And] 67–70 priests: Their] 72–77 priests: And   9 *Roman*] 57 Roman   pontif] 72–77 pontiff   12–13 do often, all of them,] 64–77 are sure, all of them, to   17 incoherencies] 60–77 incoherences   23 afforded] 72–77 afforded to   28 foretell] 57 foretel   Which ever] 72–77 Whichever 30 Tho'] 64–77 Though   31 amongst] 67–77 among

definition of *Arian, Pelagian, Erastian, Socinian, Sabellian, Eutychian, Nestorian, Monothelite,* etc. not to mention *Protestant,* whose fate is yet uncertain, will be convinced of the truth of this observation. And thus a system becomes more absurd in the end, merely from
5 its being reasonable and philosophical in the beginning.

To oppose the torrent of scholastic religion by such feeble maxims as these, that *it is impossible for the same thing to be and not to be,* that *the whole is greater than a part,* that *two and three make five;* is pretending to stop the ocean with a bull-rush. Will you set up profane reason
10 against sacred mystery? No punishment is great enough for your impiety. And the same fires, which were kindled for heretics, will serve also for the destruction of philosophers.

XII

We meet every day with people so sceptical with regard to history,
15 that they assert it impossible for any nation ever to believe such absurd principles as those of *Greek* and *Egyptian* paganism; and at the same time so dogmatical with regard to religion, that they think the same absurdities are to be found in no other communions. *Cambyses* entertained like prejudices; and very impiously ridiculed,
20 and even wounded, *Apis,* the great god of the *Egyptians,* who appeared to his profane senses nothing but a large spotted bull. But *Herodotus*[a] judiciously ascribes this sally of passion to a real madness or disorder of the brain: Otherwise, says the historian, he would never have openly affronted any established worship. For
25 on that head, continues he, every nation are best satisfied with their own, and think they have the advantage over every other nation.

[a] Bk. III, Ch. 38. ['I hold it then in every way proved that Cambyses was very mad; else he would never have set himself to deride religion and custom.' ii. 51. The Apis incident is related earlier in Ch. 29 and, in Ch. 30, Herodotus observes about it: 'By reason of this wrongful deed, as the Egyptians say, Cambyses' former want of sense turned straightway to madness.' Ibid., p. 39.]

---

4 And] 67–68 'Tis] 70–77 It is　　　7 *the same thing*] 64–70 *the same*　　　13 XII]
58–60 SECT. XII. *With regard to doubt or conviction.*] 64–77 . . . *Doubt or Conviction.*
18 communions] 70–77 communion　　　24 would never] 58–77 never would

It must be allowed, that the *Roman* catholics are a very learned sect; and that no one communion, but that of the church of *England*, can dispute their being the most learned of all the christian churches: Yet *Averroes*,[1] the famous *Arabian*, who, no doubt, had heard of the *Egyptian* superstitions, declares, that, of all religions, 5 the most absurd and non-sensical is that, whose votaries eat, after having created, their deity.

I believe, indeed, that there is no tenet in all paganism, which would give so fair a scope to ridicule as this of the *real presence*: For it is so absurd, that it eludes the force of almost all argument. 10 There are even some pleasant stories of that kind, which, tho' somewhat profane, are commonly told by the Catholics themselves. One day, a priest, it is said, gave inadvertently, instead of the sacrament, a counter, which had by accident fallen among the holy wafers. The communicant waited patiently for some time, 15 expecting it would dissolve on his tongue: But finding, that it still remained entire, he took it off. *I wish*, cries he to the priest, *you have not committed some mistake: I wish you have not given me God the Father: He is so hard and tough there is no swallowing him.*

A famous general, at that time in the *Muscovite* service, having 20 come to *Paris* for the recovery of his wounds, brought along with him a young *Turk*, whom he had taken prisoner. Some of the doctors of the *Sorbonne* (who are altogether as positive as the *Dervises* of *Constantinople*) thinking it a pity, that the poor *Turk* should be damned for want of instruction, sollicited *Mustapha* very hard to 25 turn Christian, and promised him, for his encouragement, plenty of good wine in this world, and paradise in the next. These allurements

---

1 catholics] 64–77 Catholics   2 church] 64–68 Church   3 christian] 64–77 Christian   5 that, of] 64–68 that of   6 non-sensical] 68–77 nonsensical 7 created,] 67–68 created   10 of almost all] 70–77 of all   11 tho'] 60–77 though   16 But] 67–68 but   finding,] 67–77 finding   17 cries] 64–77 cried   23 *Dervises*] 58–77 dervises   26 him,] 70 him

---

[1] The last of the great Islamic philosophers, he was born at Cordova in 1126 and died, probably in Morocco, in 1198. He was an accomplished physician and jurist as well as philosopher. His commentaries on Aristotle's works earned him the title 'The Commentator' but his sturdy defence of the autonomy of philosophy did not endear him to the theologians of either the Islamic or Christian persuasion. The former accused him of heresy (1195) but the latter had to be content with officially condemning a number of propositions associated with his name. This was done under the auspices of Étienne Tempier, Bishop of Paris, in 1277.

were too powerful to be resisted; and therefore, having been well
instructed and catechized, he at last agreed to receive the sacra-
ments of baptism and the Lord's supper. The priest, however, to
make every thing sure and solid, still continued his instructions;
5 and began his catechism next day with the usual question, *How
many Gods are there? None at all*, replies *Benedict*; for that was his new
name. *How! None at all!* cries the priest. *To be sure*, said the honest
proselyte. *You have told me all along that there is but one God: And
yesterday I eat him.*

10   Such are the doctrines of our brethren, the Catholics. But to
these doctrines we are so accustomed, that we never wonder at
them: Tho', in a future age, it will probably become difficult to
persuade some nations, that any human, two-legged creature, could
ever embrace such principles. And it is a thousand to one, but these
15 nations themselves shall have something full as absurd in their own
creed, to which they will give a most implicite and most religious
assent.

I lodged once at *Paris* in the same *hotel* with an ambassador from
Tunis, who, having passed some years at *London*, was returning
20 home that way. One day, I observed his *Moorish* excellency diverting himself under the porch, with surveying the splendid equipages
that drove along; when there chanced to pass that way some
Capucin friars, who had never seen a *Turk*; as he, on his part, tho'
accustomed to the *European* dresses, had never seen the grotesque
25 figure of a *Capucin*: And there is no expressing the mutual admiration, with which they inspired each other. Had the chaplain of
the embassy entered into a dispute with these *Franciscans*, their
reciprocal surprize had been of the same nature. And thus all mankind stand staring at one another; and there is no beating it out of
30 their heads, that the turban of the *African* is not just as good or as
bad a fashion as the cowl of the *European*. *He is a very honest man,*

    2–3 sacraments] 67–68 sacrament   5 began his catechism next] 58–68 began
his catechism the next] 70–77 began the next   7 priest.] 67 priest,
10 brethren,] 70–77 brethren   Catholics] 68 Catholicks   12 Tho',] 60–72
Though,] 77 Though   13 human,] 67–68 human   creature,] 70–77 creature
16 implicite] 77 implicit   18 *Paris*] 67–72 PARIS,   19 passed] 57 past
20 day,] 67–77 day   23 tho'] 60–77 though   28 And thus] 70–77 Thus
29 out of] 72–77 into

said the prince of *Sallee*, speaking of *de Ruyter*, *It is a pity he were a Christian.*[2]

How can you worship leeks and onions, we shall suppose a *Sorbonnist* to say to a priest of *Sais*? If we worship them, replies the latter; at least, we do not, at the same time, eat them. But what 5 strange objects of adoration are cats and monkies, says the learned doctor? They are at least as good as the relicts or rotten bones of martyrs, answers his no less learned antagonist. Are you not mad, insists the Catholic, to cut one another's throat about the preference of a cabbage or a cucumber. Yes, says the pagan; I allow it, 10 if you will confess, that all those are still madder, who fight about the preference among volumes of sophistry, ten thousand of which are not equal in value to one cabbage or cucumber.[b]

---

[b] It is strange that the *Egyptian* religion, tho' so absurd, should yet have borne so great a resemblance to the *Jewish*, that antient writers even of the greatest genius were not able to observe any difference betwixt them. For it is very remarkable, that both *Tacitus* and *Suetonius*, when they mention that decree of the senate, under *Tiberius*, by which the *Egyptian* and *Jewish* proselytes were banished from *Rome*, expressly treat these religions as the same; and it appears, that even the decree itself was founded on that supposition. *Actum et de sacris Ægyptiis, Judaicisque pellendis; factumque patrum consultum, ut quatuor millia libertini generis* ea superstitione

---

3 onions,] 60–77 onions?   4 *Sais*?] 60–77 SAIS.   6 monkies,] 60–77 monkies?   7 doctor?] 60–77 doctor.   relicts] 77 relics   10 cucumber.] 64–77 cucumber?   [b]1 tho] 60–77 though   [b]2 antient] 70–77 ancient   [b]3 betwixt] 70–77 between   very remarkable,] 58–68 very remarkable] 70–77 remarkable   [b]5 *Tiberius*] 68 Tiberius

---

[2] 'One day Sidi Ali [ben Mohammed ben Moussa, a nominal vassal of the Sultan of Morocco,] offered for a piece of cloth a price far below its value. We have the story in De Ruyter's own words. He refused, and the potentate became so angry that he threatened to confiscate the cloth without further ceremony. Thereupon De Ruyter offered it him as a present, "For," said he, "if I sell it below its value I shall not be doing justice to my masters. But if I offer it to you, they will know that I do so for fear of worse." Sidi Ali threatened to seize De Ruyter's ship, but the Dutchman answered that his compatriots and other traders would then no longer trust the people of this country. As the ruler insisted, De Ruyter lost his temper, and exclaimed, "If I were on board my ship, you would not threaten me long!" Sidi Ali walked away, apparently in great fury, but he remarked to his attendants, as De Ruyter was afterwards told, that it was a pity such a man was a Christian.' P. Blok, *The Life of Admiral De Ruyter* (London, 1933), p. 27. Blok's source, although he does not tell us, is probably Geeraert Brandt's *Het leven en bedryf Van den heere Michiel de Ruiter* (Amsterdam, 1687). Hume would probably have consulted the French translation, *La Vie de Michel de Ruiter* (Amsterdam, 1698), but I have been unable to consult a copy.

Every by-stander will easily judge (but unfortunately the by-standers are very few) that, if nothing were requisite to establish any popular system, but the exposing the absurdities of other systems, every votary of every superstition could give a sufficient
5 reason for his blind and bigotted attachment to the principles, in which he has been educated. But without so extensive a knowledge, on which to ground this assurance, (and perhaps, better without it) there is not wanting a sufficient stock of religious zeal and faith amongst mankind. *Diodorus Siculus*[c] gives a remarkable instance to
10 this purpose, of which he was himself an eye-witness. While *Egypt* lay under the greatest terror of the *Roman* name, a legionary soldier having inadvertently been guilty of the sacrilegious impiety of killing a cat, the whole people rose upon him with the utmost fury; and all the efforts of their prince were not able to save him. The
15 senate and people of *Rome*, I am persuaded, would not, then, have been so delicate with regard to their national deities. They very frankly, a little after that time, voted *Augustus* a place in the celestial mansions; and would have dethroned every god in heaven, for his sake, had he seemed to desire it. *Præsens divus habebitur Augustus*,
20 says *Horace*.[3] That is a very important point: And in other nations

infecta, quîs idonea ætas, in insulam Sardiniam veherentur, coercendis illic latrociniis; et si ob gravitatem cæli interissent, vile damnum: *Ceteri cederent Italia, nisi certam ante diem profanos ritus exuissent.* Tacitus, *Annals*, Bk. II, Ch. 85. ['Another debate dealt with the proscription of the Egyptian and Jewish rites, and a senatorial edict directed that four thousand descendants of enfranchised slaves, tainted with that superstition and suitable in point of age, were to be shipped to Sardinia and there employed in suppressing brigandage: "if they succumbed to the pestilential climate, it was a cheap loss." The rest had orders to leave Italy, unless they had renounced their impious ceremonial by a given date.' ii. 517.] *Externas cæremonias, Ægyptios, Judaicosque ritus compescuit; coactis qui superstitione ea tenebantur, religosas vestes cum instrumento omni comburere, etc.* Suetonius, 'Tiberius', Ch. 36. ['He abolished foreign cults, especially the Egyptian and the Jewish rites, compelling all who were addicted to such superstitions to burn their religious vestments and all their paraphernalia.' i. 345.] These wise heathens, observing something in the general air, and genius, and spirit of the two religions to be the same, esteemed the differences of their dogmas too frivolous to deserve any attention.

[c] Bk. I, Ch. 83, §§ 8–9.

---

3 but the exposing] 70–77 but exposing　　　　5 principles,] 77 principles
7 it)] 77 it),　　　　9 amongst] 67–68, 72–77 among　　　　14 their] 58–77 the

---

[3] 'Augustus shall be deemed a god on earth.' *Odes*, Bk. III, Ode v, lines 2–3; p. 195.

and other ages, the same circumstance has not been esteemed alto-gether indifferent.[d]

Notwithstanding the sanctity of our holy religion, says *Tully*,[e] no crime is more common with us than sacrilege: But was it ever heard, that an *Egyptian* violated the temple of a cat, an ibis, or a crocodile? There is no torture, an *Egyptian* would not undergo, says the same author in another place,[f] rather than injure an ibis, an aspic, a cat, a dog, a crocodile. Thus it is strictly true, what *Dryden* observes,

> 'Of whatsoe'er descent their godhead be,
> Stock, stone, or other homely pedigree,
> In his defence his servants are as bold,
> As if he had been born of beaten gold.'
> ABSALOM and ACHITOPHEL.[4]

Nay, the baser the materials are, of which the divinity is composed, the greater devotion is he likely to excite in the breasts of his deluded votaries. They exult in their shame, and make a merit with their deity, in braving, for his sake, all the ridicule and con-tumely of his enemies. Ten thousand *Croises* inlist themselves under the holy banners, and even openly triumph in those parts of their religion, which their adversaries regard as the most reproachful.

There occurs, I own, a difficulty in the *Egyptian* system of theology; as indeed, few systems are entirely free from difficulties.

---

[d] When *Louis* the XIVth took on himself the protection of the Jesuites college of *Clermont*, the society ordered the king's arms to be put up over their gate, and took down the cross, in order to make way for it: Which gave occasion to the following epigram: Sustulit hinc Christi, posuitque insignia Regis:
    Impia gens, alium nescit habere Deum.[5]
[e] Cicero, *On the Nature of the Gods*, Bk. I, Ch. 29, §§ 81–2.
[f] Cicero, *Tusculan Disputations*, Bk. V, Ch. 27, § 78.

---

5 heard] 64–77 heard of   5 & 6 *Egyptian*] 67–68 ÆGYPTIAN   9 ob-serves,] 57 observes   10 *Kinsley's text*: 'whatsoe'r', 'Godhead'   11 *Ibid.*: 'Stone,'   12 *Ibid.*: 'Servants', *no comma after* 'bold'   19 *Croises*] 67–68 *Crusaders*] 70–77 Crusaders   20 banners,] 70–77 banners;   22 *Egyptian*] 68 ÆGYPTIAN   23 systems are] 72–77 systems of this kind are   [d]1 Jesuites] 58–68 Jesuits] 70–77 Jesuits'

---

[4] Lines 100–3.
[5]   Those who downed the cross of Christ, and upped the arms of Louis:
    A wicked folk they surely are who can't tell God from hooey.

It is evident, from their method of propagation, that a couple of cats, in fifty years, would stock a whole kingdom; and if that religious veneration were still paid them, it would, in twenty more, not only be easier in *Egypt* to find a god than a man, which *Petro-*
5 *nius*[6] says was the case in some parts of *Italy*; but the gods must at last entirely starve the men, and leave themselves neither priests nor votaries remaining. It is probable, therefore, that that wise nation, the most celebrated in antiquity for prudence and sound policy, foreseeing such dangerous consequences, reserved all their
10 worship for the full-grown divinities, and used the freedom to drown the holy spawn or little sucking gods, without any scruple or remorse. And thus the practice of warping the tenets of religion, in order to serve temporal interests, is not, by any means, to be regarded as an invention of these latter ages.

15 The learned, philosophical *Varro*,[7] discoursing of religion, pretends not to deliver any thing beyond probabilities and appearances: Such was his good sense and moderation! But the passionate, the zealous *Augustin*, insults the noble *Roman* on his scepticism and reserve, and professes the most thorough belief and assurance.[g]
20 A heathen poet, however, contemporary with the saint, absurdly esteems the religious system of the latter so false, that even the credulity of children, he says, could not engage them to believe it.[h]

Is it strange, when mistakes are so common, to find every one positive and dogmatical? And that the zeal often rises in propor-
25 tion to the error? *Moverunt*, says *Spartian*, *et ea tempestate Judæi bellum quod vetabantur mutilare genitalia.*[i]

If ever there was a nation or a time, in which the public religion

---

[g] *The City of God*, Bk. III, Ch. 17. [See especially vol. i, pp. 337 ff.]

[h] Claudius Rutilius Namatianus, *A Voyage Home to Gaul*, Bk. I, lines 391–4. ['Each seventh day is condemned to ignoble sloth, as 'twere an effeminate picture of a god fatigued. The other wild ravings from their lying bazaar methinks not even a child in his sleep could believe.' *Minor Latin Poets*, p. 799.]

[i] Aelius Spartianus, 'Life of Hadrian', Bk. XIV, § 2. [The Jews began war at this time because they were forbidden to mutilate their genitals.]

---

3 them, it would,] 60 them it would] 64–68 them, it would   7 that that]
70–77 that this

---

[6] *Satyricon*, § 17.
[7] *On the Latin Language*, Bk. V, Ch. 10, §§ 57–74.

lost all authority over mankind, we might expect, that infidelity in *Rome*, during the *Ciceronian* age, would openly have erected its throne, and that *Cicero* himself, in every speech and action, would have been its most declared abettor. But it appears, that, whatever sceptical liberties that great man might use, in his writings or in philosophical conversation; he yet avoided, in the common conduct of life, the imputation of deism and profaneness. Even in his own family, and to his wife, *Terentia*, whom he highly trusted, he was willing to appear a devout religionist; and there remains a letter, addrest to her, in which he seriously desires her to offer sacrifice to *Apollo* and *Æsculapius*, in gratitude for the recovery of his health.[j]

Pompey's devotion was much more sincere: In all his conduct, during the civil wars, he paid a great regard to auguries, dreams, and prophesies.[k] *Augustus* was tainted with superstition of every kind. As it is reported of *Milton*, that his poetical genius never flowed with ease and abundance in the spring;[9] so *Augustus* observed, that his own genius for dreaming never was so perfect during that season, nor was so much to be relied on, as during the rest of the year. That great and able emperor was also extremely uneasy when he happened to change his shoes, and put the right foot shoe on the left foot.[l] In short, it cannot be doubted, but the

---

[j] *Letters to His Friends*, Bk. XIV, Letter 7, § 1.
[k] Cicero, 'On Divination', Bk. II, Ch. 9, § 24.[8]
[l] Suetonius, Bk. II, 'The Deified Augustus', Chs. 90–92. Pliny, *Natural History*, Bk. II, Ch. 5, § 24.

---

2 age,] 70 age   5 use] 77 take   8 wife,] 60–77 wife   10 addrest]
58–77 addressed   15 prophesies] 58–60 prophecies   18 perfect] 67–68
perfect,   21 uneasy] 70–77 uneasy,   22 short,] 77 short

---

[8] The passage cited, although it mentions Pompey, is concerned only to argue that even if it were possible by means of divination to foretell one's end, no one would wish to know. A passage in Ch. 47, § 99, p. 483, does, by implication, associate Pompey with soothsayers: 'I recall a multitude of prophecies which the Chaldeans made to Pompey, to Crassus, and even to Caesar himself (now lately deceased), to the effect that no one of them would die except in old age, at home and in great glory.'

[9] By his nephew, Edward Phillips, in 'The Life of Milton', which he published in 1694 with his translation of Milton's *Letters of State*: '. . . his vein never happily flowed but from the autumnal equinoctial to the vernal.' See John Milton, *Complete Poems and Major Prose*, ed. Merritt Y. Hughes (New York, 1957), p. 1035.

votaries of the established superstition of antiquity were as numerous in every state, as those of the modern religion are at present.
Its influence was as universal; tho' it was not so great. As many
people gave their assent to it; tho' that assent was not seemingly
5 so strong, precise, and affirmative.

We may observe, that, notwithstanding the dogmatical, im-
perious style of all superstition, the conviction of the religionists, in
all ages, is more affected than real, and scarce ever approaches,
in any degree, to that solid belief and persuasion, which governs us
10 in the common affairs of life. Men dare not avow, even to their own
hearts, the doubts, which they entertain on such subjects: They
make a merit of implicite faith; and disguise to themselves their
real infidelity, by the strongest asseverations and most positive
bigotry. But nature is too hard for all their endeavours, and suffers
15 not the obscure, glimmering light, afforded in those shadowy
regions, to equal the strong impressions, made by common sense
and by experience. The usual course of men's conduct belies their
words, and shows, that the assent in these matters is some unaccountable operation of the mind betwixt disbelief and conviction,
20 but approaching much nearer the former than the latter.

Since, therefore, the mind of man appears of so loose and unsteddy
a contexture, that, even at present, when so many persons find an
interest in continually employing on it the chissel and the hammer,
yet are they not able to engrave theological tenets with any lasting
25 impression; how much more must this have been the case in
antient times, when the retainers to the holy function were so
much fewer in comparison? No wonder, that the appearances were
then very inconsistent, and that men, on some occasions, might
seem determined infidels, and enemies to the established religion,
30 without being so in reality; or at least, without knowing their
own minds in that particular.

Another cause, which rendered the antient religions much
looser than the modern, is, that the former were *traditional* and the

3 tho'] 68–77 though   4 tho'] 68–77 though   8 scarce] 70–77 scarcely
11 doubts,] 72–77 doubts   12 implicite] 60–77 implicit   14 en-
deavours] 58 endeavors   19 betwixt] 60–77 between   21 unsteddy]
64–77 unsteady   23 chissel] 68 chisel   26 antient] 70–77 ancient
32 antient] 70–77 ancient

latter are *scriptural*; and the tradition in the former was complex, contradictory, and, on many occasions, doubtful; so that it could not possibly be reduced to any standard and canon, or afford any determinate articles of faith. The stories of the gods were number-less like the popish legends; and tho' every one, almost, believed a part of these stories, yet no one could believe or know the whole: While, at the same time, all must have acknowledged, that no one part stood on a better foundation than the rest. The traditions of different cities and nations were also, on many occasions, directly opposite; and no reason could be found for preferring one to the other. And as there was an infinite number of stories, with regard to which tradition was no way positive; the gradation was insensible, from the most fundamental articles of faith, to those loose and precarious fictions. The pagan religion, therefore, seemed to vanish like a cloud, whenever one approached to it, and examined it piecemeal. It could never be ascertained by any fixt dogmas and principles. And tho' this did not convert the generality of mankind from so absurd a faith; for when will the people be reasonable? yet it made them faulter and hesitate more in maintaining their principles, and was even apt to produce, in certain dispositions of mind, some practices and opinions, which had the appearance of determined infidelity.

To which we may add, that the fables of the pagan religion were, of themselves, light, easy, and familiar; without devils or seas of brimstone, or any objects, that could much terrify the imagina-tion. Who could forbear smiling, when he thought of the loves of *Mars* and *Venus*, or the amorous frolics of *Jupiter* and *Pan*? In this respect, it was a true poetical religion; if it had not rather too much levity for the graver kinds of poetry. We find that it has been adopted by modern bards; nor have these talked with greater freedom and irreverence of the gods, whom they regarded as fictions, than the antient did of the real objects of their devotion.

The inference is by no means just, that, because a system of religion has made no deep impression on the minds of a people, it

5 tho'] 68–77 though   10 found] 64–77 assigned   11 stories,] 58–68 stories
12 no way] 64–77 nowise   16 fixt] 58–77 fixed   17 tho'] 68–77 though
24 devils] 70–77 devils,   25 objects,] 70 objects] 72–77 object   32 antient]
67–68 antients] 70–72 ancient] 77 ancients   33 that,] 58–68 that

must therefore have been positively rejected by all men of common sense, and that opposite principles, in spite of the prejudices of education, were generally established by argument and reasoning. I know not, but a contrary inference may be more probable. The 5 less importunate and assuming any species of superstition appears, the less will it provoke men's spleen and indignation, or engage them into enquiries concerning its foundation and origin. This in the mean time is obvious, that the empire of all religious faith over the understanding is wavering and uncertain, subject to all 10 varieties of humour, and dependent on the present incidents, which strike the imagination. The difference is only in the degrees. An antient will place a stroke of impiety and one of superstition alternately, thro' a whole discourse:[m] A modern often thinks in the same way, tho' he may be more guarded in his expressions.

15 *Lucian* tells us expressly,[n] that whoever believed not the most ridiculous fables of paganism was esteemed by the people profane and impious. To what purpose, indeed, would that agreeable author have employed the whole force of his wit and satyr against the national religion, had not that religion been generally believed 20 by his countrymen and contemporaries?

---

[m] Witness this remarkable passage of *Tacitus*: *Præter multiplices rerum humanarum casus, cælo terraque prodigia, et fulminum monitus, et futurorum præsagia, læta, tristia, ambigua, manifesta. Nec enim umquam atrocioribus populi Romani cladibus, magisque justis judiciis approbatum est, non esse curæ Diis securitatem nostram, esse ultionem.* Histories, Bk. I, Ch. 3. ['Besides the manifold misfortunes that befell mankind, there were prodigies in the sky and on the earth, warnings given by thunderbolts, and prophecies of the future, both joyful and gloomy, uncertain and clear. For never was it more fully proved by awful disasters of the Roman people or by indubitable signs that the gods care not for our safety, but for our punishment.' i. 7.] *Augustus's* quarrel with *Neptune* is an instance of the same kind. Had not the emperor believed *Neptune* to be a real being and to have dominion over the sea; where had been the foundation of his anger? And if he believed it, what madness to provoke still farther that deity? The same observation may be made upon *Quinctilian's* exclamations, on account of the death of his children. *Institutio Oratoria*, Bk. VI, Preface. [See especially § 4.]

[n] 'The Lover of Lies', § 3.

---

7 This] 68 This,　　8 time] 68 time,　　9–10 all varieties] 70–72 every variety　　10 humour] 58 humor　　12 antient] 70–77 ancient　　13 thro'] 68 through] 70–77 throughout　　14 tho'] 68–77 though　　16 esteemed] 70–77 deemed　　18 satyr] 67–68, 72–77 satire　　[m]11 being] 58–77 being,　　sea;] 64–77 sea,　　[m]13 *Quinctilian's*] 58–60, 77 QUINCTILIAN'S　　exclamations,] 64–77 exclamation,

Livy[o] acknowledges as frankly, as any divine would at present, the common incredulity of his age; but then he condemns it as severely. And who can imagine, that a national superstition, which could delude so great a man, would not also impose on the generality of the people? 5

The *Stoics* bestowed many magnificent and even impious epithets on their sage; that he alone was rich, free, a king, and equal to the immortal gods. They forgot to add, that he was not inferior in prudence and understanding to an old woman. For surely nothing can be more pitiful than the sentiments, which that sect 10 entertained with regard to all popular superstitions; while they very seriously agree with the common augurs, that, when a raven croaks from the left, it is a good omen; but a bad one, when a rook makes a noise from the same quarter. *Panætius* was the only *Stoic*, amongst the *Greeks*, who so much as doubted with regard to auguries 15 and divinations.[p] *Marcus Antonius*[q] tells us, that he himself had received many admonitions from the gods in his sleep. It is true; *Epictetus*[r] forbids us to regard the language of rooks and ravens; but it is not, that they do not speak truth: It is only, because they can foretel nothing but the breaking of our neck or the forfeiture of 20 our estate; which are circumstances, says he, that no way concern us. Thus the *Stoics* join a philosophical enthusiasm to a religious superstition. The force of their mind, being all turned to the side of morals, unbent itself in that of religion.[s]

Plato[t] introduces *Socrates* affirming, that the accusation of impiety 25 raised against him was owing entirely to his rejecting such fables,

---

[o] Bk. X, Ch. 40. [Thus, in one passage, Livy refers to the young man who solemnly investigated the chicken keepers as having 'been born before the learning that makes light of the gods'. iv. 515.]

[p] Cicero, 'On Divination', Bk. I, Ch. 3, § 6 and Ch. 7.

[q] Aurelius Antonnius, *Meditations*, Bk. I, Ch. 17, § 8.

[r] 'Encheiridion', § 18.

[s] The *Stoics*, I own, were not quite orthodox in the established religion; but one may see, from these instances, that they went a great way: And the people undoubtedly went every length.

[t] *Euthyphro*. [6 A–B.]

---

1 *Livy*] 68 LIVY,   4 great] 72–77 ingenious   11 all popular superstitions] 70–77 religious matters   12 very seriously] 70–77 seriously   15 amongst] 70–77 among   17 true;] 64–77 true,   20 foretel] 57 fortel   21 no way] 64–77 nowise

as those of *Saturn's* castrating his father, *Uranus*, and *Jupiter's* dethroning *Saturn*: Yet in a subsequent dialogue,[u] *Socrates* confesses, that the doctrine of the mortality of the soul was the received opinion of the people. Is there here any contradiction? Yes, surely:
5 But the contradiction is not in *Plato*; it is in the people, whose religious principles in general are always composed of the most discordant parts; especially in an age, when superstition sate so easy and light upon them.[v]

---

[u] *Phædo.*[10]

[v] *Xenophon's* conduct, as related by himself, is, at once, an incontestable proof of the general credulity of mankind in those ages, and the incoherencies, in all ages, of men's opinions in religious matters. That great captain and philosopher, the disciple of *Socrates*, and one who has delivered some of the most refined sentiments
5 with regard to a deity, gave all the following marks of vulgar, pagan superstition. By *Socrates's* advice, he consulted the oracle of *Delphi*, before he would engage in the expedition of *Cyrus*. *Anabasis*, Bk. III, Ch. 1, § 5. [Hume specifies the edition of Leunclavius, which accompanies the Greek text with a Latin translation. It was first published at Oxford in 1735; a second edition appeared in 1745.] Sees a dream
10 the night after the generals were seized; which he pays great regard to, but thinks ambiguous. Ibid., § 11 f. He and the whole army regard sneezing as a very lucky omen. Ibid., Ch. 2, § 9. Has another dream, when he comes to the river *Centrites*, which his fellow general, *Chirosophus*, also pays great regard to. Ibid., Bk. IV, Ch. 3, § 8. The *Greeks* suffering from a cold north wind, sacrifice to it, and the historian
15 observes, that it immediately abated. Ibid., Ch. 5, § 3 f. Xenophon consults the sacrifices in secret, before he would form any resolution with himself about settling a colony. Bk. V, Ch. 6, § 17. He himself a very skilful augur. Ibid., § 29. Is determined by the victims to refuse the sole command of the army, which was offered him. Bk. VI, Ch. 1, §§ 22–24. *Cleander*, the *Spartan*, tho' very desirous of it, refuses it for the
20 same reason. Ibid., Ch. 6, § 36. *Xenophon* mentions an old dream with the interpretation given him, when he first joined *Cyrus*. Ibid., Ch. 1, § 22. Mentions also the place of *Hercules's* descent into hell as believing it, and says the marks of it are still remaining. Bk. VI, Ch. 2, § 2. Had almost starved the army rather than lead to the field against the auspices. Ibid., Ch. 4, §§ 12–16. His friend, *Euclides*, the augur,

---

1 father, *Uranus*] 77 father URANUS   [v]13 *Chirosophus*] 70 CHEROSOPHUS
[v]14 it, and] 70–77 it; and   [v]17 He himself] 70–77 He was himself   [v]18 army, which] 70–77 army which   [v]19 tho'] 64–77 though   [v]23 army rather] 70–77 army, rather   lead to] 70–77 lead them to

---

[10] Both 64A and 65A might be interpreted as implying a common belief in the mortality of the soul, but it is later argued that the notion of death as the separation of the soul from the body 'leaves the average person with grave misgivings that when it is released from the body it may no longer exist anywhere, but may be dispersed and destroyed on the very day that the man himself dies, as soon as it is freed from the body, that as it emerges it may be dissipated like breath or smoke, and vanish away, so that nothing is left of it anywhere'. (Tredennick's translation.) See also 68B.

The same *Cicero*, who affected, in his own family, to appear a devout religionist, makes no scruple, in a public court of judicature, of treating the doctrine of a future state as a most ridiculous fable, to which no body could give any attention.[w] *Sallust*[x] represents *Cæsar* as speaking the same language in the 5 open senate.[y]

would not believe that he had brought no money from the expedition; till he 25 (*Euclides*) sacrificed, and then he saw the matter clearly in the *Exta*.[11] Bk. VII, Ch. 8, §§ 1–3. The same philosopher, proposing a project of mines for the encrease of the *Athenian* revenues, advises them first to consult the oracle. 'Ways and Means'. [See Chs. 4 and 5 for Xenophon's mine proposal; Ch. 6, § 2 for his advice to consult the oracle.] That all this devotion was not a farce, in order to serve a political purpose, 30 appears both from the facts themselves, and from the genius of that age, when little or nothing could be gained by hypocrisy. Besides, *Xenophon*, as appears from his *Memorabilia*, was a kind of heretic in those times, which no political devotee ever is. It is for the same reason, I maintain, that *Newton*, *Locke*, *Clarke*, etc. being *Arians* or *Socinians*, were very sincere in the creed they profest: And I always oppose this 35 argument to some libertines, who will needs have it, that it was impossible, but that these great philosophers must have been hypocrites.

[w] 'In Defence of Cluentius', Ch. 61, § 171.

[x] *The War with Catiline*, Ch. 51, §§ 16–20.

[y] *Cicero* (*Tusculan Disputations*, Bk. I, Chs. 5–6)[12] and *Seneca* (*Letter 24*)[13] as also *Juvenal* (*Satire 2*)[14] maintain that there is no boy or old woman so ridiculous as to believe the poets in their accounts of a future state. Why then does *Lucretius* so highly

---

3–4 a most ridiculous] 70–77 a ridiculous   [v]26 *Exta*.] 58–77 Exta.   [v]27 encrease] 64–77 increase   [v]32 Besides,] 58 Besides   [v]33 *Memorabilia*] 58–77 Memorabilia   [v]35 profest] 58–77 professed   [v]36 impossible,] 60–77 impossible

---

[11] The entrails of the sacrificial victim.

[12] See especially Ch. 6, § 10: 'A. Do you suppose me so crazy as to believe such tales? M. You don't believe them true? A. Certainly not. M. My word! that's a sad story. A. Why so? M. Because I could have been so eloquent in speaking against such tales.' p. 15.

[13] See especially § 18: 'I am not so foolish as to go through at this juncture the arguments which Epicurus harps upon, and say that the terrors of the world below are idle,—that Ixion does not whirl round on his wheel, that Sisyphus does not shoulder his stone uphill, that a man's entrails cannot be restored and devoured every day; no one is so childish as to fear Cerberus, or the shadows, or the spectral garb of those who are held together by naught but their unfleshed bones. Death either annihilates us or strips us bare. If we are then released, there remains the better part, after the burden has been withdrawn; if we are annihilated, nothing remains; good and bad are alike removed.' *Moral Letters*, i. 177.

[14] Not even children, unless they're not yet dry behind the ears, believe there are such things as ghosts and subterranean kingdoms, or black frogs in Stygian pools across which thousands are ferried. Lines 149–52.

But that all these freedoms implied not a total and universal infidelity and scepticism amongst the people, is too apparent to be denied. Tho' some parts of the national religion hung loose upon the minds of men, other parts adhered more closely to them: And
5 it was the great business of the sceptical philosophers to show, that there was no more foundation for one than for the other. This is the artifice of *Cotta*[16] in the dialogues concerning *the nature of the gods*. He refutes the whole system of mythology by leading the orthodox, gradually, from the more momentous stories, which
10 were believed, to the more frivolous, which every one ridiculed: From the gods to the goddesses; from the goddesses to the nymphs; from the nymphs to the fawns and satyrs. His master, *Carneades*, had employed the same method of reasoning.[z]

Upon the whole, the greatest and most observable differences
15 betwixt a *traditional*, *mythological* religion, and a *systematical*, *scholastic* one, are two: The former is often more reasonable, as

exalt his master for freeing us from these terrors?[15] Perhaps the generality of mankind
5 were then in the disposition of *Cephalus* in *Plato* (*Republic*, Bk. I [330D–331A]) who while he was young and healthful could ridicule these stories; but as soon as he became old and infirm, began to entertain apprehensions of their truth. This, we may observe, not to be unusual even at present.

[z] Sextus Empiricus, *Against the Physicists*, Bk. I, §§ 182–90.

---

3 Tho'] 64–77 Though   7 *the nature*] 58–77 the *nature*   9 orthodox,]
67–68, 72–77 orthodox   12 *Carneades*,] 68 CARNEADES   15 betwixt] 60–77
between   16 *scholastic*] 58–70 *scholastical*   [y]7–8 This, we may observe,] 77
This we may observe

---

[15] 'When man's life lay for all to see foully grovelling upon the ground, crushed beneath the weight of Religion, which displayed her head in the regions of heaven, threatening mortals from on high with horrible aspect, a man of Greece [Epicurus] was the first that dared to uplift mortal eyes against her, the first to make stand against her; for neither fables of the gods could quell him, nor thunderbolts, nor heaven with menacing roar, nay all the more they goaded the eager courage of his soul, so that he should desire, first of all men, to shatter the confining bars of nature's gates. Therefore the lively power of his mind prevailed, and forth he marched far beyond the flaming walls of the heavens, as he traversed the immeasurable universe in thought and imagination; whence victorious he returns bearing his prize, the knowledge what can come into being, what can not, in a word, how each thing has its powers defined and its deep-set boundary mark. Wherefore Religion is now in her turn cast down and trampled underfoot, whilst we by the victory are raised to heaven.' *On the Nature of Things*, Bk. I, lines 62–79; p. 7. See also Bk. II, lines 55–61.
[16] Upholds the Academic philosophy as against the Epicurean and Stoic in Cicero's *On the Nature of the Gods*. See especially Bk. III, Chs. 17–20.

consisting only of a multitude of stories, which, however groundless, imply no express absurdity and demonstrative contradiction; and sits also so easy and light on men's minds, that tho' it may be as universally received, it makes no such deep impression on the affections and understanding.

5

XIII

The primary religion of mankind arises chiefly from an anxious fear of future events; and what ideas will naturally be entertained of invisible, unknown powers, while men lie under dismal apprehensions of any kind, may easily be conceived. Every image of vengeance, severity, cruelty, and malice must occur and augment the ghastliness and horror, which oppresses the amazed religionist. A panic having once seized the mind, the active fancy still farther multiplies the objects of terror; while that profound darkness, or, what is worse, that glimmering light, with which we are invironed, represents the spectres of divinity under the most dreadful appearances imaginable. And no idea of perverse wickedness can be framed, which those terrified devotees do not readily, without scruple, apply to their deity.

10

15

This appears the natural state of religion, when surveyed in one light. But if we consider, on the other hand, that spirit of praise and eulogy, which necessarily has place in all religions, and which is the consequence of these very terrors, we must expect a quite contrary system of theology to prevail. Every virtue, every excellence must be ascribed to the divinity, and no exaggeration be esteemed sufficient to reach those perfections, with which he is endowed. Whatever strains of panegyric can be invented, are immediately embraced, without consulting any arguments or phænomena. And it is esteemed a sufficient confirmation of them,

20

25

---

3 tho'] 64–77 though   4 it makes] 70–77 it happily makes   6 XIII] 58–64, 70 Sect. XIII. *Impious conceptions of the divine nature in most popular religions of both kinds.*] 68 . . . *Conceptions . . . Nature . . . Religions . . .*] 72–77 *as* 58 *except 'in popular'* 11 and augment] 58–77 and must augment   12 ghastliness] 67–68 affright 15 invironed] 72–77 environed   24–5 excellence] 60–77 excellence,   25–6 be esteemed] 64–68 be deemed] 70–77 will be deemed   29 phænomena. And it] 70–77 phænomena: It

that they give us more magnificent ideas of the divine object of our worship and adoration.

Here therefore is a kind of contradiction betwixt the different principles of human nature, which enter into religion. Our natural 5 terrors present the notion of a devilish and malicious deity: Our propensity to praise leads us to acknowledge an excellent and divine. And the influence of these opposite principles are various, according to the different situation of the human understanding.

In very barbarous and ignorant nations, such as the *Africans* and 10 *Indians*, nay even the *Japonese*, who can form no extensive ideas of power and knowledge, worship may be paid to a being, whom they confess to be wicked and detestable; tho' they may be cautious, perhaps, of pronouncing this judgment of him in public, or in his temple, where he may be supposed to hear their reproaches.

15 Such rude, imperfect ideas of the divinity adhere long to all idolaters; and it may safely be affirmed, that the *Greeks* themselves never got entirely rid of them. It is remarked by *Xenophon*,[a] in praise of *Socrates*, that that philosopher assented not to the vulgar opinion, which supposed the gods to know some things, and be 20 ignorant of others: He maintained that they knew every thing; what was done, said, or even thought. But as this was a strain of philosophy[b] much above the conception of his countrymen, we need not be surprized, if very frankly, in their books and conversation, they blamed the deities, whom they worshiped in their 25 temples. It is observable, that *Herodotus* in particular scruples not,

---

[a] *Memorabilia*, Bk. I, Ch. 1, § 19.
[b] It was considered among the antients, as a very extraordinary, philosophical paradox, that the presence of the gods was not confined to the heavens, but was extended every where; as we learn from *Lucian*. 'Hermotimus'. [See especially § 81: 'We hear him say that God is not in heaven but pervades everything—sticks and stones and beasts right down to the meanest. And when his mother asks him why he talks such nonsense, he laughs at her and says: "If I learn this 'nonsense' properly, there will be nothing to stop me being the only rich man, the only king, and the rest slaves and scum compared with me."' vi. 409, 411.]

---

1 object] 77 objects   3 betwixt] 60–77 between   6 praise] 72–77 adulation   7 And the] 67–68 The   12 tho'] 64–77 though   15 divinity] 64–77 Divinity   18 that that] 70–77 that this   20 maintained] 70–77 maintained,   24 worshiped] 58–77 worshipped   [b]1 antients] 70–77 ancients

in many passages, to ascribe *envy* to the gods; a sentiment, of all others, the most suitable to a mean and devilish nature. The pagan hymns however, sung in public worship, contained nothing but epithets of praise; even while the actions ascribed to the gods were the most barbarous and detestable. When *Timotheus*, the poet, recited a hymn to *Diana*, where he enumerated, with the greatest eulogies, all the actions and attributes of that cruel, capricious goddess: *May your daughter,* said one present, *become such as the deity whom you celebrate.*[c]

But as men farther exalt their idea of their divinity; it is often their notion of his power and knowledge only, not of his goodness, which is improved. On the contrary, in proportion to the supposed extent of his science and authority, their terrors naturally augment; while they believe, that no secrecy can conceal them from his scrutiny, and that even the inmost recesses of their breast lie open before him. They must then be careful not to form expressly any sentiment of blame and disapprobation. All must be applause, ravishment, extacy. And while their gloomy apprehensions make them ascribe to him measures of conduct, which, in human creatures, would be highly blamed, they must still affect to praise and admire these measures in the object of their devotional addresses. And thus it may safely be affirmed, that many popular religions are really, in the conception of their more vulgar votaries, a species of dæmonism; and the higher the deity is exalted in power and knowledge, the lower of course is he frequently deprest in goodness and benevolence; whatever epithets of praise may be bestowed on him by his amazed adorers. Amongst idolaters, the words may be false, and belie the secret opinion: But amongst more exalted religionists, the opinion itself often contracts a kind of falshood, and belies the inward sentiment. The heart secretly detests such measures of cruel and implacable vengeance; but the judgment dares not but pronounce them perfect and adorable. And the

[c] Plutarch, 'Superstition', Ch. 10, 170A–B.

3 hymns] 64–77 hymns,   10 their idea] 67–68 the idea   21 these measures] 60–77 that conduct   22 And thus] 58–77 Thus   that many popular] 64–68 that most popular] 70–72 that popular   25 deprest] 58–77 depressed 27 Amongst] 70–77 Among   28 amongst] 70–77 among

additional misery of this inward struggle aggravates all the other terrors, by which these unhappy victims to superstition are for ever haunted.

Lucian[d] observes, that a young man, who reads the history of the gods in *Homer* or *Hesiod*, and finds their factions, wars, injustice, incest, adultery, and other immoralities so highly celebrated, is much surprized afterwards, when he comes into the world, to observe, that punishments are by law inflicted on the same actions, which he had been taught to ascribe to superior beings. The contradiction is still perhaps stronger betwixt the representations given us by some latter religions and our natural ideas of generosity, lenity, impartiality, and justice; and in proportion to the multiplied terrors of these religions, the barbarous conceptions of the divinity are multiplied upon us.[e] Nothing can preserve untainted

---

[d] 'Menippus', § 3.

[e] *Bacchus*, a divine being, is represented by the heathen mythology as the inventor of dancing and the theatre. Plays were antiently, even a part of public worship on the most solemn occasions, and often employed in times of pestilence, to appease the offended deities. But they have been zealously proscribed by the godly in latter ages; and the play-house, according to a learned divine, is the porch of hell.[1]

But in order to show more evidently, that it is possible for a religion to represent the divinity in still a more immoral unamiable light than the antient, we shall cite a long passage from an author of taste and imagination, who was surely no enemy to Christianity. It is the chevalier *Ramsay*, a writer, who had so laudable an inclination to be orthodox, that his reason never found any difficulty, even in the doctrines which freethinkers scruple the most, the trinity, incarnation, and satisfaction: His humanity alone, of which he seems to have had a great stock, rebelled against the doctrines of eternal reprobation and predestination. He expresses himself thus: 'What strange ideas', says he, 'would an Indian or a Chinese philosopher have of our holy religion, if they judged by the schemes given of it by our modern freethinkers,

---

1 struggle] 67–68 contest   7 surprized] 77 surprised   10 betwixt] 64–77 between   11 latter] 72–77 later   [e]2 antiently] 70–77 anciently   [e]4 latter] 72–77 later   [e]7 immoral unamiable] 58–77 immoral and unamiable   antient] 58–68 antients] 70–77 ancients   [e]9 chevalier] 64–77 Chevalier   [e]11 freethinkers] 60–77 free-thinkers   [e]15 freethinkers] 60–77 free-thinkers

---

1 The sentiment is a familiar one. Tertullian, in the first decades of the third century, tells of a woman who went to the theatre and was seized by a devil who justified his action, alleging 'I seized her upon my own ground.' (*De Spectaculis*, Ch. 26.) In the Elizabethan period, the stage was called 'the nest of the devil' and the 'consultatory of Satan', and plays were described as 'snares of the devil set to catch Souls'. (See E. K. Chambers, *Elizabethan Stage* (Oxford, 1923), i. 255.) The sentiment is also to be found in Jeremy Collier's *A Short View of the Immorality and Profaneness of the English Stage*, 3rd edn. (London, 1698). But Hume's source for the exact words he sets down continues to elude me.

the genuine principles of morals in our judgment of human
conduct, but the absolute necessity of these principles to the
and pharisaical doctors of all sects? According to the odious and too *vulgar* system
of these incredulous scoffers and credulous scriblers, "The God of the Jews is a most
cruel, unjust, partial and fantastical being. He created, about 6000 years ago, a man
and a woman, and placed them in a fine garden of *Asia*, of which there are no remains.
This garden was furnished with all sorts of trees, fountains, and flowers. He allowed 20
them the use of all the fruits of this beautiful garden, except of one, that was planted
in the midst thereof, and that had in it a secret virtue of preserving them in continual
health and vigor of body and mind, of exalting their natural powers and making
them wise. The devil entered into the body of a serpent, and solicited the first
woman to eat of this forbidden fruit; she engaged her husband to do the same. To 25
punish this slight curiosity and natural desire of life and knowledge, God not only
threw our first parents out of paradise, but he condemned all their posterity to
temporal misery, and the greatest part of them to eternal pains, tho' the souls of
these innocent children have no more relation to that of *Adam* than to those of
Nero and *Mahomet*; since, according to the scholastic drivellers, fabulists, and mytho- 30
logists, all souls are created pure, and infused immediately into mortal bodies, so
soon as the fœtus is formed. To accomplish the barbarous, partial decree of predestination and reprobation, God abandoned all nations to darkness, idolatry and superstition, without any saving knowledge or salutary graces; unless it was one particular
nation, whom he chose as his peculiar people. This chosen nation was, however, 35
the most stupid, ungrateful, rebellious, and perfidious of all nations. After God had
thus kept the far greater part of all the human species, during near 4000 years, in a
reprobate state, he changed all of a sudden, and took a fancy for other nations,
beside the *Jews*. Then he sent his only begotten Son to the world, under a human
form, to appease his wrath, satisfy his vindictive justice, and die for the pardon of 40
sin. Very few nations, however, have heard of this gospel; and all the rest, tho' left
in invincible ignorance, are damned without exception or any possibility of remis-
sion. The greatest part of those, who have heard of it, have changed only some
speculative notions about God, and some external forms in worship: For, in other
respects, the bulk of Christians have continued as corrupt, as the rest of mankind in 45
their morals; yea, so much the more perverse and criminal, that their lights were
greater. Unless it be a very small select number, all other Christians, like the pagans,
will be for ever damned; the great sacrifice offered up for them will become void and
of no effect. God will take delight for ever in their torments and blasphemies; and
tho' he can, by one *fiat*, change their hearts, yet they will remain for ever uncon- 50
verted and unconvertible, because he will be for ever unappeaseable and irrecon-
cileable. It is true, that all this makes God odious, a hater of souls, rather than a
lover of them; a cruel, vindictive tyrant, an impotent or a wrathful dæmon, rather
than an all-powerful, beneficent Father of spirits: Yet all this is a mystery. He has
secret reasons for his conduct, that are impenetrable; and tho' he appears unjust 55

---

*e*18 partial] 64–77 partial,   *e*19 *Asia*] 57 Asia   *e*23 vigor] 60–77 vigour
*e*28 tho'] 60–77 though   *e*29–30 *Adam . . . Nero* and *Mahomet*] 57 *no italics*
*e*30 drivellers] 58 driveller   *e*33 idolatry] 64–67, 70–77 idolatry,
*e*36 rebellious,] 70–77 rebellious   *e*38 nations,] 72–77 nations   *e*39 *Jews*] 57
Jews   a human] 67–68 the human   *e*41 tho'] 60–77 though   *e*42 excep-
tion] 58–77 exception,   *e*43 those,] 58–77 those   *e*45 corrupt,] 64–77
corrupt   *e*49 effect.] 70–77 effect;   ever] 70–77 ever,   *e*50 tho'] 60,
68–77 though *fiat*,] 70–77 *fiat*   *e*52 true,] 67–68 true   *e*53 rather] 77 rather,
*e*54 Father] 70–77 father   *e*55 tho'] 60–77 though

existence of society. If common conception can indulge princes in a system of ethics, somewhat different from that which should regulate private persons; how much more those superior beings, whose attributes, views, and nature are so totally unknown to us? 5 *Sunt superis sua jura;*[f] The gods have maxims of justice peculiar to themselves.

XIV

Here I cannot forbear observing a fact, which may be worth the attention of those, who make human nature the object of their 10 enquiry. It is certain, that, in every religion, however sublime the verbal definition, which it gives of its divinity, many of the votaries, perhaps the greatest number, will still seek the divine

and barbarous, yet we must believe the contrary, because what is injustice, crime, cruelty, and the blackest malice in us, is in him justice, mercy, and sovereign goodness." Thus the incredulous freethinkers, the judaizing Christians, and the fatalistic doctors, have disfigured and dishonoured the sublime mysteries of our holy faith; 60 thus, they have confounded the nature of good and evil; transformed the most monstrous passions into divine attributes, and surpassed the pagans in blasphemy, by ascribing to the eternal nature, as perfections, what makes the most horrid crimes amongst men. The grosser pagans contented themselves with divinizing lust, incest, and adultery; but the predestinarian doctors have divinized cruelty, 65 wrath, fury, vengeance, and all the blackest vices.' See the chevalier *Ramsay's* philosophical principles of natural and revealed religion, Part II. p. 401.[2]

The same author asserts, in other places, that the *Arminian* and *Molinist* schemes serve very little to mend the matter: And having thus thrown himself out of all received sects of Christianity, he is obliged to advance a system of his own, which is 70 a kind of *Origenism*, and supposes the pre-existence of the souls both of men and beasts, and the eternal salvation and conversion of all men, beasts, and devils. But this notion, being quite peculiar to himself, we need not treat of. I thought the opinions of this ingenious author very curious; but I pretend not to warrant the justness of them.

[f] Ovid, *Metamorphoses*, Bk. IX, line 500.

5 *jura*;] 60–77 *jura*.   7 XIV] 58–67, 70 SECT. XIV. *Bad influence of most popular religions on morality.*] 68 . . . *Influence . . . Religions on Morality.*] 72–77 *Bad influence of popular religion on morality.*   9 of those, who] 70–77 of such as   11 definition,] 64–77 definition   [e]56 barbarous,] 57 barbarous;   [e]58 freethinkers] 67–68, 72–77 free-thinkers] 70 free thinkers   [e]59 dishonoured] 58 dishonored   [e]60 thus,] 64–77 thus   [e]64 adultery] 57 adultry   [e]65 chevalier] 58–70 Chevalier   *Ramsay's*] 57 Ramsay's

[2] Andrew Michael Ramsay (usually styled the Chevalier, 1686–1743), *The Philosophical Principles of Natural and Revealed Religion, Unfolded in a Geometrical Order*, 2 Parts (Glasgow, 1748–9). The same sheets are sometimes found with an additional London title-page dated 1751.

favour, not by virtue and good morals, which alone can be acceptable to a perfect being, but either by frivolous observances, by
intemperate zeal, by rapturous extasies, or by the belief of
mysterious and absurd opinions. The least part of the *Sadder*,[1] as
well as of the *Pentateuch*, consists in precepts of morality; and we 5
may be assured, that that part was always the least observed and
regarded. When the old *Romans* were attacked with a pestilence,
they never ascribed their sufferings to their vices, or dreamed of
repentance and amendment. They never thought that they were
the general robbers of the world, whose ambition and avarice made 10
desolate the earth, and reduced opulent nations to want and
beggary. They only created a dictator,*a* in order to drive a nail into
a door; and by that means, they thought that they had sufficiently
appeased their incensed deity.

In *Ægina*, one faction entering into a conspiracy, barbarously 15
and treacherously assassinated seven hundred of their fellow-citi-
zens; and carried their fury so far, that, one miserable fugitive
having fled to the temple, they cut off his hands, by which he
clung to the gates, and carrying him out of holy ground, immediately
murdered him. *By this impiety*, says *Herodotus*,*b* (not by the other 20
many cruel assassinations) *they offended the gods, and contracted an
inexpiable guilt.*

Nay, if we should suppose, what seldom happens, that a popular
religion were found, in which it was expressly declared, that
nothing but morality could gain the divine favour; if an order of 25
priests were instituted to inculcate this opinion, in daily sermons,
and with all the arts of persuasion; yet so inveterate are the people's

---

a Called Dictator clavis figendæ causa. Livy, Bk. VII, Ch. 3, §§ 3–4. ['. . . it is said
that the elders recollected that a pestilence had once been allayed by the dictator's
driving a nail. Induced thereto by this superstition, the senate ordered the appoint-
ment of a dictator to drive the nail.' iii. 365.]

b *History*, Bk. VI, Ch. 91.

---

1 favour] 58 favor   6 assured] 64–77 assured also   9 thought] 72–77
thought,   15 Ægina] 67–68 EGINA   entering into] 70–77 forming
16–17 fellow-citizens] 58, 70 fellow citizens   25 favour] 58 favor

---

[1] *Seder*. Literally, 'order (of a ritual)'. A home or community service and ceremonial
dinner held on the first evening of the Passover. If Hume had in mind following
external forms without attention being given to their underlying meaning, the
passage makes perfectly good sense.

prejudices, that for want of some other superstition, they would make the very attendance on these sermons the essentials of religion, rather than place them in virtue and good morals. The sublime prologue of *Zaleucus's* laws[c] inspired not the *Locrians*, so far
5 as we can learn, with any sounder notions of the measures of acceptance with the deity, than were familiar to the other *Greeks*.

This observation, then, holds universally: But still one may be at some loss to account for it. It is not sufficient to observe, that the people, every where, degrade their deities into a similitude with
10 themselves, and consider them merely as a species of human creatures, somewhat more potent and intelligent. This will not remove the difficulty. For there is no *man* so stupid, as that, judging by his natural reason, he would not esteem virtue and honesty the most valuable qualities, which any person could possess. Why not
15 ascribe the same sentiment to his deity? Why not make all religion, or the chief part of it, to consist in these attainments?

Nor is it satisfactory to say, that the practice of morality is more difficult than that of superstition; and is therefore rejected. For, not to mention the excessive pennances of the *Brahmans* and *Tala-*
20 *poins*;[2] it is certain, that the *Rhamadan* of the *Turks*,[3] during which the poor wretches, for many days, often in the hottest months of the year, and in some of the hottest climates of the world, remain without eating or drinking from the rising to the setting of the sun; this *Rhamadan*, I say, must be more severe than the practice of
25 any moral duty, even to the most vicious and depraved of mankind. The four lents of the *Muscovites*,[4] and the austerities of some *Roman*

---

[c] To be found in Diodorus Siculus, Bk. XII, Chs. 20–21.

---

1 that] 70–77 that,	19 *Brahmans*] 58–77 *Brachmans*	23–4 setting of the
sun] 70–77 setting sun	24 severe] 57 severe,	

---

[2] 'A Buddhist monk or priest, properly of Pegu; extended by Europeans to those of Siam, Burmah, and other Buddhist countries.' *O.E.D.*

[3] *Ramadan*. Ninth month of the Islamic world; sacred because it was during this month that the Koran was revealed.

[4] Perhaps drawn from Richard Chancelor's 'Booke of the great and mighty Emperor of Russia . . . etc.' in Hakluyt's *Principall Navigations, Voiages and Discoveries of the English Nation* (London, 1589). 'They have foure Lents in the yeere, whereof our Lent is the greatest. Looke as we doe begin on the Wednesday, so they doe on the Munday before: And the weeke before that they call The Butter weeke: And in that weeke they eate nothing but Butter and milke. Howbeit I beleeve there

Catholics, appear more disagreable than meekness and benevolence. In short, all virtue, when men are reconciled to it by ever so little practice, is agreeable: All superstition is for ever odious and burthensome.

Perhaps, the following account may be received as a true solu- 5 tion of the difficulty. The duties, which a man performs as a friend or parent, seem merely owing to his benefactor or children; nor can he be wanting to these duties, without breaking thro' all the ties of nature and morality. A strong inclination may prompt him to the performance: A sentiment of order and moral beauty 10 joins its force to these natural tyes: And the whole man, if truly virtuous, is drawn to his duty, without any effort or endeavour. Even with regard to the virtues, which are more austere, and more founded on reflection, such as public spirit, filial duty, temperance, or integrity; the moral obligation, in our apprehension, removes all 15 pretence to religious merit; and the virtuous conduct is esteemed no more than what we owe to society and to ourselves. In all this, a superstitious man finds nothing, which he has properly performed for the sake of his deity, or which can peculiarly recommend him to the divine favour and protection. He considers not, 20 that the most genuine method of serving the divinity is by promoting the happiness of his creatures. He still looks out for some more

---

6 duties,] 60–68 duties   8 thro'] 60–77 through   10 beauty] 72–77
obligation   11 tyes] 58–77 ties   12 endeavour] 58 endeavor   16 pre-
tence] 72–77 pretension   esteemed] 70–77 deemed   20 favour] 58 favor

---

bee in no other countrey the like people for drunkennesse. The next Lent is called Saint Peters Lent, and beginneth alwayes the Munday next after Trinitie sunday, and endeth on Saint Peters even. If they should breake that fast, their beliefe is, that they should not come in at heaven gates. And when any of them die, they have a testimoniall with them in the Coffin, that when the soule commeth to heaven gates it may deliver the same to Saint Peter, which declareth that the partie is a true and holy Russian. The third Lent beginneth fifteene dayes before the later Lady day, and endeth on our Lady Eeven. The fourth Lent beginneth on Saint Martins day, and endeth on Christmas Eeven: which Lent is fasted for Saint Philip, Saint Peter, Saint Nicholas, and Saint Clement. For they foure be the principall and greatest Saints in that countrey. In these Lents they eate neither Butter, Egges, Milke, nor Cheese; but they are very straitely kept with Fish, Cabbages, and Rootes. And out of their Lents, they observe truely the Wednesdayes and Fridayes throughout the yeere: and on the Saturday they doe eate flesh.' See vol. ii of the Glasgow edition (1903–5), pp. 236–8; the passage quoted is from p. 237.

immediate service of the supreme being, in order to allay those terrors, with which he is haunted. And any practice recommended to him, which either serves to no purpose in life, or offers the strongest violence to his natural inclinations; that practice he will
5 the more readily embrace, on account of those very circumstances, which should make him absolutely reject it. It seems the more purely religious, that it proceeds from no mixture of any other motive or consideration. And if, for its sake, he sacrifices much of his ease and quiet, his claim of merit appears still to rise upon him,
10 in proportion to the zeal and devotion, which he discovers. In restoring a loan, or paying a debt, his divinity is no way beholden to him; because these acts of justice are what he was bound to perform, and what many would have performed, were there no god in the universe. But if he fast a day, or give himself a sound
15 whipping; this has a direct reference, in his opinion, to the service of God. No other motive could engage him to such austerities. By these distinguished marks of devotion, he has now acquired the divine favour; and may expect, in recompence, protection and safety in this world, and eternal happiness in the next.
20 Hence the greatest crimes have been found, in many instances, compatible with a superstitious piety and devotion: Hence it is justly regarded as unsafe to draw any certain inference in favour of a man's morals from the fervor or strictness of his religious exercises, even tho' he himself believe them sincere. Nay, it has been observed,
25 that enormities of the blackest dye, have been rather apt to produce superstitious terrors, and encrease the religious passion. *Bomilcar*, having formed a conspiracy for assassinating at once the whole senate of *Carthage*, and invading the liberties of his country, lost the opportunity, from a continual regard to omens and prophesies.
30 *Those who undertake the most criminal and most dangerous enterprizes are commonly the most superstitious*; as an antient historian[d] remarks on

[d] Didorus Siculus, Bk. XX, Ch. 43.

---

1 being] 64–77 Being   2 practice] 58–77 practice,   7 that] 67–77 because   11 no way] 64–77 nowise   18 favour] 58 favor   21 Hence it] 70–77 Hence, it   22 favour] 58 favor   23 fervor] 60–77 fervour   24 tho'] 60, 68–77 though   25 dye,] 67–68 die,] 70–77 dye   29 prophesies] 70–77 prophecies   31 antient] 70–77 ancient

this occasion. Their devotion and spiritual faith rise with their fears. *Catiline* was not contented with the established deities, and received rites of his national religion: His anxious terrors made him seek new inventions of this kind;*ᵉ* which he never probably had dreamed of, had he remained a good citizen, and obedient to the laws of his country.

To which we may add, that, even after the commission of crimes, there arise remorses and secret horrors, which give no rest to the mind, but make it have recourse to religious rites and ceremonies, as expiations of its offences. Whatever weakens or disorders the internal frame promotes the interests of superstition: And nothing is more destructive to them than a manly, steddy virtue, which either preserves us from disastrous, melancholy accidents, or teaches us to bear them. During such calm sunshine of the mind, these spectres of false divinity never make their appearance. On the other hand, while we abandon ourselves to the natural, undisciplined suggestions of our timid and anxious hearts, every kind of barbarity is ascribed to the supreme being, from the terrors, with which we are agitated; and every kind of caprice, from the methods which we embrace, in order to appease him. *Barbarity, caprice;* these qualities, however nominally disguised, we may universally observe, to form the ruling character of the deity, in popular religions. Even priests, instead of correcting these depraved ideas of mankind, have often been found ready to foster

---

ᵉ Cicero, 'First Speech Against Catiline'.⁵ Sallust, *The War with Catiline*, Ch. 22. ['It was said at the time that when Catiline, after finishing his address, compelled the participants in his crime to take an oath, he passed around bowls of human blood mixed with wine; that when after an imprecation upon traitors all had tasted it, as is usual in solemn rites, he disclosed his project; and his end in doing so was, they say, that they might be more faithful to one another because they shared the guilty knowledge of so dreadful a deed.' pp. 39, 41.]

---

3 his national] 60–77 the national   11 interests] 72 interest   And] 67–68 and   12 steddy] 64–77 steady   13 disastrous,] 67–68 disastrous 16 natural,] 58–77 natural   18 being] 64–77 Being   terrors,] 64–77 terrors 20 embrace,] 64–77 embrace   22 to form] 64, 68–77 form] 67 from   deity,] 64–77 deity

---

⁵ Although Cicero describes Catiline as a monster of corruption and depravity, it is difficult to find a passage supporting Hume's charge. Perhaps he had in mind Ch. 6, § 16 or Ch. 9, § 24.

and encourage them. The more tremendous the divinity is represented, the more tame and submissive do men become to his
ministers: And the more unaccountable the measures of acceptance required by him, the more necessary does it become to
5 abandon our natural reason, and yield to their ghostly guidance
and direction. And thus it may be allowed, that the artifices of
men aggravate our natural infirmities and follies of this kind, but
never originally beget them. Their root strikes deeper into the
mind, and springs from the essential and universal properties of
10 human nature.

XV

Tho' the stupidity of men, barbarous and uninstructed, be so great,
that they may not see a sovereign author in the more obvious works
of nature, to which they are so much familiarized; yet it scarce
15 seems possible, that any one of good understanding should reject
that idea, when once it is suggested to him. A purpose, an intention,
a design is evident in every thing; and when our comprehension is
so far enlarged as to contemplate the first rise of this visible system,
we must adopt, with the strongest conviction, the idea of some
20 intelligent cause or author. The uniform maxims too, which prevail
thro' the whole frame of the universe, naturally, if not necessarily,
lead us to conceive this intelligence as single and undivided, where
the prejudices of education oppose not so reasonable a theory.
Even the contrarieties of nature, by discovering themselves every
25 where, become proofs of some consistent plan, and establish one
single purpose or intention, however inexplicable and incomprehensible.

Good and ill are universally intermingled and confounded;
happiness and misery, wisdom and folly, virtue and vice. Nothing
30 is pure and entirely of a piece. All advantages are attended with
disadvantages. An universal compensation prevails in all conditions
of being and existence. And it is scarce possible for us, by our most

6 And thus] 67–77 Thus		11 XV] 58–64 SECT. XV. *General Corollary from
the whole.*] 67–77 *General Corollary.*		12 Tho'] 60–77 Though		14 scarce]
70–77 scarcely		21 thro'] 60–64 through] 67–77 throughout		32 is scarce
possible] 70–77 is not possible

chimerical wishes, to form the idea of a station or situation altogether desirable. The draughts of life, according to the poet's
fiction, are always mixed from the vessels on each hand of *Jupiter*:
Or if any cup be presented altogether pure, it is drawn only, as the
same poet tells us, from the left-handed vessel.[1]   5

The more exquisite any good is, of which a small specimen is
afforded us, the sharper is the evil, allied to it; and few exceptions
are found to this uniform law of nature. The most sprightly wit
borders on madness; the highest effusions of joy produce the deepest
melancholy; the most ravishing pleasures are attended with the   10
most cruel lassitude and disgust; the most flattering hopes make
way for the severest disappointments. And in general, no course of
life has such safety (for happiness is not to be dreamed of) as the
temperate and moderate, which maintains, as far as possible, a
mediocrity, and a kind of insensibility, in every thing.   15

As the good, the great, the sublime, the ravishing are found
eminently in the genuine principles of theism; it may be expected,
from the analogy of nature, that the base, the absurd, the mean,
the terrifying will be discovered equally in religious fictions and
chimeras.   20

The universal propensity to believe in invisible, intelligent
power, if not an original instinct, being at least a general attendant
of human nature, may be considered as a kind of mark or stamp,
which the divine workman has set upon his work; and nothing
surely can more dignify mankind, than to be thus selected from all 25
the other parts of the creation, and to bear the image or impression of the universal Creator. But consult this image, as it commonly appears in the popular religions of the world. How is the
deity disfigured in our representations of him! What caprice,

---

19 discovered equally] 77 equally discovered   23 may] 57 it may
26 creation] 67–68 universe   27 universal] 67–68 supreme   27–8 it
commonly appears] 70–77 it appears

---

[1] 'For two urns are set upon the floor of Zeus of gifts that he giveth, the one of
ills, the other of blessings. To whomsoever Zeus, that hurleth the thunderbolt,
giveth a mingled lot, that man meeteth now with evil, now with good; but to
whomsoever he giveth but of the baneful, him he maketh to be reviled of man, and
direful madness driveth him over the face of the sacred earth, and he wandereth
honoured neither of gods nor mortals.' *Iliad*, Bk. XXIV, lines 529–33; ii. 601, 603.

absurdity, and immorality are attributed to him! How much is he degraded even below the character which we should naturally, in common life, ascribe to a man of sense and virtue!

What a noble privilege is it of human reason to attain the know-
5 ledge of the supreme being; and, from the visible works of nature, be enabled to infer so sublime a principle as its supreme Creator? But turn the reverse of the medal. Survey most nations and most ages. Examine the religious principles, which have, in fact, prevailed in the world. You will scarcely be persuaded, that they are other
10 than sick men's dreams: Or perhaps will regard them more as the playsome whimsies of monkeys in human shape, than the serious, positive, dogmatical asseverations of a being, who dignifies himself with the name of rational.

Hear the verbal protestations of all men: Nothing they are so
15 certain of as their religious tenets. Examine their lives: You will scarcely think that they repose the smallest confidence in them.

The greatest and truest zeal gives us no security against hypocrisy: The most open impiety is attended with a secret dread and
20 compunction.

No theological absurdities so glaring as have not, sometimes, been embraced by men of the greatest and most cultivated understanding.[2] No religious precepts so rigorous as have not been adopted by the most voluptuous and most abandoned of men.

25 *Ignorance is the mother of Devotion*:[3] A maxim, that is proverbial, and confirmed by general experience. Look out for a people,

---

2 character] 70–77 character,   5 being] 58–77 Being   6 supreme
Creator] 67–68 sovereign Author   9–10 other than] 72–77 any thing but
10 Or] 67–68 or   11 monkeys] 70–77 monkies   14–15 they are so certain of
as] 72–77 so certain as   19 secret] 68 sacred   21 as] 72–77 that they
23 as] 72–77 that they   25 maxim,] 64–77 maxim

---

[2] Cicero, *On Divination*, Bk. II, Ch. 58: 'Somehow or other no statement is too absurd for some philosophers to make.' [p. 505.] See Hobbes, *Leviathan*, Pt. IV, § 46. (Molesworth edn., iii. 669.)

[3] The earliest occurrence of this maxim I have been able to locate is Henry Cole (Dean of St. Paul's), *Disputation at Westminster* (1559); it is also to be found in Robert Burton, Jeremy Taylor, and John Dryden, any one of whom is perhaps a more likely source for Hume.

entirely devoid of religion: If you find them at all, be assured, that they are but few degrees removed from brutes.[4]

What so pure as some of the morals, included in some theological systems? What so corrupt as some of the practices, to which these systems give rise?   5

The comfortable views, exhibited by the belief of futurity, are ravishing and delightful. But how quickly vanish, on the appearance of its terrors, which keep a more firm and durable possession of the human mind?

The whole is a riddle, an ænigma, an inexplicable mystery.   10 Doubt, uncertainty, suspence of judgment appear the only result of our most accurate scrutiny, concerning this subject. But such is the frailty of human reason, and such the irresistible contagion of opinion, that even this deliberate doubt could scarce be upheld; did we not enlarge our view, and opposing one species of super-   15 stition to another, set them a quarreling; while we ourselves, during their fury and contention, happily make our escape, into the calm, tho' obscure, regions of philosophy.

---

1 devoid] 57–70 void] 72–77 destitute   6 views,] 64–68 views   futurity,] 70 futurity   7 vanish,] 70–77 vanish   14 scarce] 70–77 scarcely   18 tho'] 60–77 though

---

4 J. V. Price remarks: 'The same phrase occurs in Bernard Mandeville's short essay of 1714, *An Enquiry into the Origin of Moral Virtue*. Speaking of alleged altruists Mandeville says, "those who wanted a sufficient Stock of either Pride or Resolution to buoy them up in mortifying of what was dearest to them, follow'd the sensual dictates of Nature, would yet be asham'd of confessing themselves to be those despicable Wretches, and were generally reckon'd to be so little remov'd from Brutes . . . ." (*The Fable of the Bees*, ed. by F. B. Kaye, i. 45).' *The Ironic Hume* (Austin, Tex., 1965), p. 107, n. 25.

APPENDIX

An exact transcription of Hume's references

See Introduction p. 14

II

a [As in text.]
b . . . Plin. lib. ii. cap. 7. . . . *Oper. & Dier.* lib. i. ver. 250 . . ., See *Arist. Probl.* Sect. 33. cap. 7. . . .

III

a Lib. viii.
b [As in text.]
c Diod. Sic. Lib. iii.
d Lib. vii.

IV

a Pere le Comte.
b Regnard, Voïage de Lapponie.
c Diod. Sic. lib. i. Lucian. de Sacrificiis. *Ovid.* alludes to the same tradition, Metam. lib. v. l. 321. So also Manilius, lib. iv.
d Herodot. lib. i.
e Cæs. Comment. de bell. Gallico, lib. iv.
f Lib. ix. 382.
g Cap. ix.
h Pere Brumoy, Theatre des Grecs; & Fontenelle, Histoire des Oracles.
i Arnob. lib. vii.
j De Laced. Rep.
k Epist. xli.
l Quint. Curtius, lib. iv. cap. 3. Diod. Sic. lib. xvii.
m Sueton. in vita Aug. cap. 16.
n Id. in vita Cal. cap. 5.
o Herodot. lib. ii. Lucian. *Jupiter confutatus, de luctu Saturn.* &c.
p . . . Hes. Opera & Dies l. 108.
q Theog. l. 570.
r Metamorph. lib. i. l. 32.
s Lib. i.
t Id. ibid.
u . . . See lib. xv. pag. 364. Ex edit. Rhodomanni
v . . . *Plato* (de Leg. lib. x.) . . .
w Adversus Mathem. lib. ix.

^x Dionys. Halic. lib. vi.
^y Epist. lib. vi.

V

^a Hesiod. Theog. l. 935.
^b Id. ibid. & Plut. in vita Pelop.
^c Iliad. xiv. 267.
^d [As in text.]
^e Herodian. lib. v. . . . , lib. iv. cap. 7. . . . Arnob. lib. vi. . . .
^f Diog. Laert. lib. ii.
^g . . . De bello Gallico, lib. vi.
^h De moribus Germ.

VI

^a [As in text.]

VII

^a Hyde de Relig. veterum Persarum.
^b [As in text.]
^c Lib. iv.

IX

^a . . . *Pliny*, lib. xxviii. cap. 2 . . .
^b Xenoph. Memor. lib. ii.
^c Plutarch. de Isid. & Osiride.
^d Lib. ii. sub fine.
^e Hyde de Relig. vet. Persarum.
^f Arrian. de Exped. lib. iii. Id. lib. vii.
^g Id. ibid.
^h Sueton. in vita Aug. c. 93.
ⁱ [As in text.]
^j [As in text.]
^k Strabo, lib. v. Sueton. in vita Cal.

X

^a Arrian. passim.
^b Thucyd. lib. v.
^c Discorsi, lib. vi.
^d Plut. Apophth.
^e Bayle, Article BELLARMINE.

XII

^a Lib. iii. c. 38.
^b . . . *Tacit. Ann.* lib. ii. c. 85. . . . *Sueton. Tiber.* c. 36. . . .

^c Lib. i.

^d [As in text.]

^e De nat. Deor. l. i.

^f Tusc. Quæst. lib. v.

^g De civitate Dei, l. iii. c. 17.

^h Claudii Rutilii Numitiani iter, lib. i. l. 386.

ⁱ In vita Adriani.

^j Lib. xiv. epist. 7.

^k Cicero de Divin. lib. ii. c. 24.

^l Sueton. Aug. cap. 90, 91, 92. Plin. lib. ii. cap. 7.

^m . . . *ultionem*, *Hist.* lib. i. . . . children, lib. vi. Præf.

ⁿ Philopseudes.

^o Lib. x. cap. 40.

^p Cicero de Divin. lib. i. cap. 3. & 7.

^q Lib. i. § 17.

^r Ench. § 17.

^s [As in text.]

^t Eutyphro.

^u Phædo.

^v . . . De exped. lib. iii. p. 294. ex edit. Leuncl. . . . [Hume gives page numbers instead of book, chapter, and section; 'Ways and Means' appears as De rat. red. p. 932. This reference is corrected in all subsequent editions to read 'p. 392'.]

^w Pro Cluentio, cap. 61.

^x De bello Catilin.

^y *Cicero* (Tusc. Quæst. lib. i. cap. 5, 6.) and *Seneca* (Epist. 24.) as also *Juvenal* (Satyr. 2.) . . . . *Plato* (de Rep. lib. i.) . . . .

^z Sext. Empir. advers. Mathem. lib. viii.

XIII

^a Mem. lib. i.

^b . . . *Hermotimus sive De sectis.*

^c Plutarch. de Superst.

^d Necyomantia.

^e [As in text.]

^f Ovid. Metam. lib. ix. 501.

XIV

^a . . . T. Livii, l. vii. c. 3.

^b Lib. vi.

^c To be found in Diod. Sic. lib. xii.

^d Diod. Sic. lib. xx.

^e Cic. Catil. i. Sallust. de bello Catil.

Dialogues concerning Natural Religion

BY

DAVID HUME

Edited from the original manuscript
by
JOHN VALDIMIR PRICE

TO

E. C. M.

ACKNOWLEDGEMENTS

EDITING the *Dialogues* has taken rather longer than I anticipated when I embarked on the project several years ago. During that time, however, I have had a number of profitable discussions with various scholars, philosophers, and ordinary readers about the work. As before, I owe a particular debt to Ernest Mossner, whose encouragement and advice have been unfailingly reliable. Various friends who unwittingly volunteered to read the typescript in one of its various stages have been good-humoured and informative when confronted with it. Among these, I have especially to thank Alan Bell, Gian Carlo Carabelli, Geoffrey Carnall, Ralph Cohen, Wayne Colver, Jack Gilbert, Ian Hilson, Warren McDougall, George Rousseau, and Bill Todd. I hope they are as pleased with the result as I was grateful for their advice and comments.

At the risk of repeating another cliché, I am constrained to acknowledge the help of scholars and writers with whom I have only corresponded, but who were courteous, prompt, and informative when approached about various matters. J. D. Fleeman was of considerable help in solving some of the problems presented by Hume's manuscript; Patricia Hernlund considerately provided details of William Strahan's ledgers; Donald R. Keyworth offered me details of his notes on some of Hume's revisions. Librarians in Edinburgh, Oxford, and London answered my inquiries with patience and skill, and my innumerable requests for yet one more photocopy were met promptly. E. N. Smith and P. P. Prech kindly helped me with proof-reading. The University of Edinburgh, by granting me two terms leave of absence in 1971, enabled me to sustain the kind of day-to-day routine that editing (and completing) a text requires. The greatest of my obligations is undoubtedly to the Royal Society of Edinburgh, for their kind permission to edit and publish the manuscript, and to their staff for many favours.

I finally ought to thank all those who have put up with my inability in the past five years to regard an edition of Hume's

Dialogues as anything other than a κτῆμα εἰς ἀει. Their relief at the completion of this task will be as great as mine. Relief at completion, however, does not absolve me from any errors in this edition, but is any book complete until Error has crept in and left his sly imprimatur?

CONTENTS

DAVID HUME'S
DIALOGUES CONCERNING NATURAL RELIGION:
COMPOSITION AND PUBLICATION

HUME'S interest in religion, natural or revealed, as a suitable subject for philosophical inquiry, appeared, according to his own account, at a very early age. His interest in the dialogue form cannot be precisely dated, but as early as 1743 he was reading dialogues on religious subjects. In a postscript to a letter of 30 June to William Mure of Caldwell, he stated, 'I have frequently in Edinburgh enquir'd for the Dialogues on Devotion publish'd at Glasgow some time ago; but coud not find them. If you have a Copy send it me, & I shall restore it with the first Occasion. It may be a means of my Conversion.'[1]

By 1748, he was ready to try his hand at a dialogue on natural religion when he published his *Philosophical Essays concerning Human Understanding*. The eleventh section of this book, entitled 'Of the Practical Consequences of Natural Religion', is in the form of a dialogue; Hume purports to have argued with a sceptical friend about the efficacy of the argument from design. In the second edition of the work, in 1750, Hume changed the title of this section to 'Of a Particular Providence and of a Future State'. The later title is misleading, and it is worth noting that Hume felt constrained to camouflage his conclusions both by adopting the dialogue form in order to attribute sceptical, if not heterodox, observations to 'a friend' and by later changing the ostensible subject of that section.

By 1751, Hume's interest in the dialogue form was even more emphatic. He was preparing for publication his *Enquiry concerning the Principles of Morals*, which appeared in December of that year; the final portion of this work is 'A Dialogue'. In this instance Hume brings the advantages of the dialogue form to bear upon the

---

[1] Printed both in *Letters*, i. 52, and *New Letters*, p. 14.

question of moral relativity. Yet in February, he had asked Sir Gilbert Elliot of Minto to examine this work, saying of it, 'I have scarcely wrote any thing more whimsical, or whose Merit I am more diffident of' (*Letters*, i. 145).

A month later, on 10 March 1751, his diffidence had completely disappeared. Once more asking Elliot for his advice and opinion, he makes the first known reference to the *Dialogues concerning Natural Religion*: 'You wou'd perceive by the Sample I have given you, that I make Cleanthes the Hero of the Dialogue. Whatever you can think of, to strengthen that Side of the Argument, will be most acceptable to me' (*Letters*, i. 153–4). Elliot drafted a long reply, but whether he sent it to Hume or not is unknown.[2]

It is difficult to guess how much of the *Dialogues* was completed when Hume wrote this letter. The draft of Elliot's reply does not refer to anything beyond Part III. Kemp Smith suggested that Hume had completed only a portion of the work and perhaps nothing beyond Part IV. That Hume sent Elliot only a 'Sample' would indicate that he was actively working on the *Dialogues*, but he must also have been composing the long essay, 'A Natural History of Religion', which was published in 1757, at about the same time. Certain similarities in example and word choice imply a similar time of composition, but these similarities occur in the early sections of the *Dialogues*. Hume may have temporarily abandoned the *Dialogues* for another project.

In January 1753, Hume wrote to John Clephane, 'As there is no happiness without occupation, I have begun a work which will employ me several years, and which yields me much satisfaction. 'Tis a History of Britain, from the Union of the Crowns to the present time. I have already finished the reign of King James' (*Letters*, i. 170). This work would and did in fact keep Hume occupied for several years, and it is unlikely that he gave much time to the *Dialogues*. Upon the completion of the *History of England* in early 1762, Hume would have been able to return to the *Dialogues*. Though he mentions the work to his friends, he gives no specific

---

[2] The whereabouts of this draft is now unknown, but at one time Dugald Stewart made a copy with the intention of printing it. It was in fact printed in *The Collected Works of Dugald Stewart*, edited by Sir William Hamilton (Edinburgh, 1854–60), i. 605–7, and is here reprinted in Appendix A.

indication that he is writing: 'I am engag'd in no work at present' he wrote to Elliot on 12 March 1763, 'But if I tire of Idleness, or more properly speaking, of reading for Amusement, I may probably continue my History.' Referring to the *Dialogues*, Hume adds, 'Is it not hard & tyrannical in you, more tyrannical than any Act of the Stuarts, not to allow me to publish my Dialogues? Pray, do you not think that a proper Dedication may atone for what is exceptional in them?' (*New Letters*, p. 71). Hume even had in mind a potential dedicatee: The Revd. Hugh Blair. In October 1763, just over a year after Blair had been appointed the first Regius Professor of Rhetoric and Belles-Lettres in the University of Edinburgh, Hume wrote, with tongue firmly in cheek, 'I have no present thoughts of publishing the work you mention; but when I do, I hope you have no objection of my dedicating it to you' (*New Letters*, p. 72).

Blair, like others Hume consulted, did not think the *Dialogues* should be published. Hume's letter had been in response to one Blair had written him on 29 September 1763, when Hume was on his way to France. Blair notes that Hume was regarded by the *philosophes* as being insufficiently heterodox on the subject of natural religion, an oversight easily rectified: 'I am well informed, in several Poker Clubs in Paris your Statue would have been erected. If you will show them the MSS of certain Dialogues perhaps that honour may still be done you. But for Gods sake let that be a posthumous work, if ever it shall see the light: Tho' I really think it had better not' (R.S.E., iii. 51; cited in *New Letters*, pp. 72 n.–73 n.). Blair's advice prevailed. Though Hume was definitely canvassing his friends and fellow authors during the period 1751–63 for advice and help on the *Dialogues*, he was actively engaged in so many other literary projects that he could forgo the publication of the *Dialogues*. There is no further mention of the work in Hume's correspondence until 1776. It is unlikely that he had forgotten it, even if Blair, Elliot, and others would have preferred to have it drop forever from sight.

Perhaps with an awareness of his approaching death, Hume prepared his Will in January 1776. It contains the following provision:

To my friend Dr Adam Smith, late Professor of Moral Philosophy in Glasgow, I leave all my manuscripts without exception, desiring him to publish my Dialogues concerning Natural Religion, which are comprehended in this present bequest; but to publish no other papers which he suspects not to have been written within these five years, but to destroy them all at his leisure. And I even leave him full power over all my papers, except the Dialogues above mentioned; and though I can trust to that intimate and sincere friendship, which has ever subsisted between us, for his faithful execution of this part of my will, yet, as a small recompense of his pains in correcting and publishing this work, I leave him two hundred pounds, to be paid immediately after the publication of it. (*Letters*, ii. 317 n.)

Adam Smith was not very happy with this responsibility and wrote to Hume about it. While Hume was travelling to Bath to take the waters for his ultimately fatal illness, he met Smith in Morpeth, on 23 April 1776. During this meeting, Smith apparently apprised Hume of his misgivings about being constrained to publish the *Dialogues* after Hume's death. To comply with Smith's request to publish the work at his discretion, Hume sent him an 'ostensible' letter from London on 3 May, stating:

My dear Sir

   After reflecting more maturely on that Article of my Will by which I left you the Disposal of all my Papers, with a Request that you shou'd publish my *Dialogues concerning natural Religion*, I have become sensible, that, both on account of the Nature of the Work, and of your Situation, it may be improper to hurry on that Publication. I therefore take the present Opportunity of qualifying that friendly Request: I am content, to leave it entirely to your Discretion at what time you will publish that Piece, or whether you will publish it at all. You will find among my Papers a very inoffensive Piece, called *My own Life*, which I composed a few days before I left Edinburgh, when I thought, as did all my Friends, that my Life was despaired of. There can be no Objection, that this small piece shoud be sent to Messrs Strahan and Cadell and the Proprietors of my other Works to be prefixed to any future Edition of them. (*Letters*, ii. 317–18.)

Hume's qualification is carefully worded. It does not enjoin Smith absolutely to publish the *Dialogues*, and Smith's 'Discretion' is to be exercised only in deciding if he, Smith, wishes to publish the work. If Smith should choose not to publish it, Hume's qualification leaves the field open for someone else to publish the *Dialogues*.

In a more familiar letter of the same date, addressed to 'My dear Friend', Hume tried to convince Smith that he was being unduly circumspect about accepting responsibility for publication of the *Dialogues*:

I send you enclosed an ostensible Letter, conformably to your Desire. I think, however, your Scruples groundless. Was Mallet any wise hurt by his Publication of Lord Bolingbroke? He received an Office afterwards from the present King and Lord Bute, the most prudish Men in the World; and he always justify'd himself by his sacred Regard to the Will of a dead Friend. At the same time, I own, that your Scruples have a specious Appearance. But my Opinion is, that, if, upon my Death, you determine never to publish these papers, you shoud leave them, seal'd up with my Brother and Family, with some Inscription, that you reserve to Yourself the Power of reclaiming them, whenever you think proper. If I live a few Years longer, I shall publish them myself. I consider an Observation of Rochefoucault, that a Wind, though it extinguishes a Candle, blows up a fire. (*Letters*, ii. 316.)

Hume was not convinced that the unhappy Smith would observe his wishes about publishing, and while in Bath began to make other plans. Just over a month later, on 8 June 1776, he wrote to William Strahan, his printer:

I am also to speak to you of another Work more important: Some Years ago, I composed a piece, which woud make a small Volume in Twelves. I call it *Dialogues on natural Religion*: Some of my Friends flatter me, that it is the best thing I ever wrote. I have hitherto forborne to publish it, because I was of late desirous to live quietly, and keep remote from all Clamour: For though it be not more exceptionable than some things I had formerly published; yet you know some of these were thought very exceptionable; and in prudence, perhaps, I ought to have suppressed them. I there introduce a Sceptic, who is indeed refuted, and at last gives up the Argument, nay confesses that he was only amusing himself by all his Cavils; yet before he is silenced, he advances several Topics, which will give

Umbrage, and will be deemed very bold and free, as well as much out of the Common Road. As soon as I arrive at Edinburgh, I intend to print a small Edition of 500, of which I may give away about 100 in Presents; and shall make you a Present of the Remainder, together with the literary Property of the whole, provided you have no Scruple, in your present Situation, of being the Editor: It is not necessary you shoud prefix your Name to the Title Page. I seriously declare, that after Mr Millar and You and Mr Cadell have publickly avowed your Publication of the *Enquiry concerning human Understanding*, I know no Reason why you shoud have the least Scruple with regard to these Dialogues. They will be much less obnoxious to the Law, and not more exposed to popular Clamour. Whatever your Resolution be, I beg you wou'd keep an entire Silence on this Subject. If I leave them to you by Will, your executing the Desire of a dead Friend, will render the publication still more excusable. Mallet never sufferd any thing by being the Editor of Bolingbroke's Works. (*Letters*, ii. 323–4.)

This letter was written the day before Hume found out the true state of his health. He learned on the next day, as is revealed in a letter to his brother,[3] that his illness was mortal. Knowing this, he must have begun to make yet further provision for the eventual publication of the *Dialogues*.

A month after he had returned to Edinburgh, he revoked the provision in his Will that left open the question of what would happen should Smith decide against publication. On 7 August, eighteen days before his death, he made the following Codicil to his Will:

In my later Will and Disposition I made some Destinations with regard to my Manuscripts: All these I now retract; and leave my Manuscripts to the Care of Mr William Strahan of London, Member of Parliament: Trusting to the Friendship that has long subsisted between us for his careful and faithful Execution of my Intentions. I desire, that my Dialogues concerning Natural Religion may be printed and published any time within two Years after my Death; to which, he may add, if he thinks proper, the two Essays formerly printed but not published. . . . I also ordain, that if my Dialogues

---

[3] 'You made me promise, that I shoud write you sincerely the true State of my Health, than which really nothing can be worse' (*Letters*, ii. 325).

from whatever Cause, be not published within two Years and a half after my Death, as also the Account of my Life, the Property shall return to my Nephew, David, whose Duty, in publishing them as the last Request of his Uncle, must be approved of by all the World. (R.S.E., ix. 24.)

The rebuke implied in this codicil must have given Hume some uneasiness, as he wrote to Smith on 15 August a further letter about the *Dialogues*. At the same time, he had taken the opportunity to see that the one extant copy of the manuscript did not run the risk of accidental disappearance:

I have orderd a new Copy of my Dialogues to be made besides that which will be sent to Mr Strahan, and to be kept by my Nephew. If you will permit me, I shall order a third Copy to be made, and consignd to you. It will bind you to nothing, but will serve as a Security. On revising them (which I have not done these 15 Years) I find that nothing can be more cautiously and more artfully written. You had certainly forgotten them. Will you permit me to leave you the Property of the Copy, in case they shoud not be published in five Years after my Decease? Be so good as to write me an answer soon. My State of Health does not permit me to wait Months for it. (*Letters*, ii. 334.)

Smith's answer to Hume was delayed because the letter was sent by carrier and not by post and lay in the carrier's quarters for eight days. In his reply, Smith is content to accept whatever Hume thinks fit, adding that Hume 'should not menace Strahan with the loss of anything in case he does not publish your work within a certain time' (R.S.E., vii. 39). In proof of Strahan's willingness to publish the work, he enclosed a letter from Strahan, adding at the same time that he wishes to append a few words as a postscript to Hume's autobiography.

The letter to which Smith refers is probably one of 10 June 1776 in which Strahan, after noting how Hume is bearing his poor health with 'Magnanimity and Resignation' adds, 'Some Particulars he has communicated, and some Directions he has given about his Works, in case of his Death, which shall be duly attended to and religiously observed. You already know all, so I need not say more of this to you till I see you. My Instructions are to keep an entire Silence upon the Subject to every body else' (R.S.E., viii. 48). This letter was written before Hume's of 12 June from Bath, in which Hume expressed his obligation to Strahan and gave him the property of his manuscripts. Thus, it would appear at this stage that Hume was relatively satisfied that Strahan would publish or at least print the *Dialogues* but later was revising his decision virtually to the moment before his death. Hume's last extant letter, to Adam Smith, leaves open various possibilities:

> There is No Man in whom I have a greater Confidence than Mr Strahan, yet have I left the property of that Manuscript to my Nephew David in case by any accident it should not be published within three years after my decease. The only accident I could forsee, was one to Mr Strahans Life, and without this clause My Nephew would have had no right to publish it. Be so good as to inform Mr Strahan of this Circumstance. (*Letters*, ii. 335–6.)

This letter is in the holograph of Hume's nephew, Hume being too ill to write himself.

The close relationship that Hume developed with his brother, John, and the rest of his family doubtless played an important role in securing the eventual publication of the *Dialogues*. Of David's religious inclinations and general character, his brother is alleged to have said, 'My brother Davie is a good enough sort of man, *but rather narrow minded*.'[4] Whatever his opinion of his brother's scepticism, he was nevertheless as solicitous of Hume's literary reputation and his last work as David himself had been. Barely a week after Hume's death, John Home wrote to Adam Smith, on 2 September, about *My own Life* and the *Dialogues*:

> The Copys of the Dialogues are finished and of the life, and will be sent to Mr Strahan to morrow; and I will mention to him your intention of adding to the last, something to finish so valuable a life, and will leave you at liberty, to look into the correction of the first, as it either answers your leisure, or ideas with regard to the composition, or what effects you think it may have with regard to your self. The two copys intended for you, will be left with my sister, when you please to require them. . . . (R.S.E., viii. 17.)

---

[4] [Samuel Jackson Pratt], *Supplement to the Life of David Hume* (London, 1777), pp. 33–4.

If John Home kept the original holograph of the *Dialogues*, and it seems highly likely that he did, there would have been in addition to Smith's two copies the one for Strahan. Hume's family were also taking no chances that the manuscript might be lost or forgotten.

John Home had been in touch with Strahan very soon after Hume's death. Apparently he had asked Strahan whether he intended to carry out Hume's request to publish the *Dialogues*. Strahan's reply, dated 9 September 1776, is as emphatic in its assurances to the brother as if he had been writing to the philosopher:

If your deceased Brother, and my most worthy Friend, whose Loss I shall sincerely lament as long as I live, shewed you the Letters that lately passed between us relating to his MSS., or if he left them behind him, you will see that I there promise to fulfill his Intentions most exactly; a Promise I shall most assuredly perform. I see no Sort of Objection to their Publication this ensuing Winter; but it is unnecessary to come to any fixed Resolution about them till I return to Town, and till I see Mr. Adam Smith, whose *Addition* to *the Life* will, I doubt not, be a very proper one; for he knew him well, and loved him much. (R.S.E., viii. 43.)

At this stage, of course, the various parties were interested in publishing both *My own Life* and the *Dialogues*, and Strahan concentrated his immediate attention on the former. It is one of the ironies surrounding the posthumous publications of Hume's writings that the zealots took far more umbrage with Adam Smith for his addition to *My own Life* than they raised about the publication of the *Dialogues*; yet Smith's apprehensions about the effect of the *Dialogues* was greater than his awareness of the stir his eulogy would provoke.

Three weeks after Hume's death, most of Edinburgh seems to have been aware of the gossip about Hume's literary property, if we are to judge from the various printed reports and private letters. For example, one W.G., writing to the young Dugald Stewart, on 15 September 1776, reports:

You must have heard long before this time of David Hume's death. He was sensible to the last, & died with the greatest compusure.

He has left Memoirs of his own life and Dialogues on Natural Religion, which he desired to be published. I have heard that he once had left them to Adam Smith for that purpose, but that Mr. Smith had refused to have any concern in the matter.[5]

The allusion to Smith's refusal is clearly to the *Dialogues*, since Smith was very emphatic about the addition he wanted to make to *My own Life*. He even submitted his original draft to Hume's brother for suggestions and emendations.[6]

It is not difficult to suspect that Hume perceived his friend's reluctance to have anything to do with publishing the *Dialogues*. Were there any doubts at all on this matter, Smith extinguished them in a letter he wrote to Strahan about the middle of September. A surviving rough draft of the letter leaves no doubt that he would never have given his imprimatur:

By a codicil to the will of our late most valuable friend Mr Hume the care of his manuscripts is left to you. Both from his will and from his conversation I understand that there are only two which he meant should be published, *an account of his own life*, and, *Dialogues concerning natural religion*. The latter, tho' finely written, I could have wished had remained in manuscript to be communicated only to a few people. When you read the work, you will see my reasons without my giving you the trouble of reading them in a Letter. But he has ordered it otherwise. In case of their not being published within three years after his decease he has left the property of them to his Nephew. Upon my objecting to this clause as unnecessary and improper, he wrote to me by his Nephews hand in the following terms. 'There is no man in whom I have a greater confidence than Mr Strahan; yet have I left the property of that Manuscript to my Nephew David in case by any accident they should not be published within three years after my decease. The only accident I could foresee was one to Mr Strahans Life; and without this clause my nephew would have had no right to publish it. Be so good as to inform Mr Strahan of this circumstance.' Thus far his letter which was dated on the 23 of August. He dyed on the 25 at 4 o'clock afternoon. I once had

---

[5] Edinburgh University Library, MS. Dc. 6. 111, fols. 46–7.
[6] In a letter of 7 October 1776, he included a draft of his proposed addition to *My own Life* (R.S.E., viii. 39). John Home replied a week later suggesting some minor alterations, which Smith accepted (R.S.E., viii. 18).

perswaded him to leave it entirely to my discretion either to publish them at what time I thought proper, or not to publish them at all. Had he continued of this mind the manuscript should have been most carefully preserved and upon my decease restored to his family; but it never should have been published in my lifetime. When you have read it, you will perhaps, think it not unreasonable to consult some prudent friend about what you ought to do.

I propose to add to his Life a very well authenticated account of his behaviour during his last Illness. I must however, beg that his life and those dialogues may not be published together as I am resolved for many reasons to have no concern in the publication of the dialogues. His Life I think ought to be prefixed to the next edition of his former works upon which he has made many very proper corrections chiefly in what concerns the Language. (R.S.E., viii. 41.)

A letter from Strahan to Smith dated 16 September 1776 may not be a direct reply to this one, but it does take cognizance of Smith's misgivings:

I had a Letter from the Brother of our late excellent Friend, a few Days before I received yours, and my Son writes me that the MSS. are also come to hand; but the Parcel will not be opened till my Return. All therefore that I can say just now, is, that I shall do nothing precipitately, and without the Advice of my Friends, to whose Opinion, and particularly to yours, I shall pay great Regard. I will likewise give the *Dialogues* a very attentive Perusal, before I consult any body, that I may at once see how far their Judgments coincide with my own. I own I did not expect to hear they were so very exceptionable, as in one of his late Letters to me, he tells me *there is nothing in them worse than what I have already published*, or Words to that Effect.—But at any Rate they shall certainly be published distinct from the *Life*; which I think we may throw out this Winter, and afterwards prefix to the Edition of his History now printing. I have not the least doubt that your Addition to it will be highly proper, and if it is ready, I beg you would transmit it to me without Delay; for I long myself very much to see it.—Every Particular respecting that great and good Man I would wish to know and to remember.—You see by his leaving the *Dialogues* ultimately to his Nephew in case of any Accident to me his extreme Solicitude that they should not be suppressed; so that if it is at all judged proper to

let them see the Light, I should wish to execute his Intentions.—
But of this, as I said before, I shall not hastily determine. (R.S.E.,
viii. 49.)

Strahan's proposal to read the *Dialogues* in order to see 'how far
their Judgments coincide with my own' suggests a criterion for
printing the *Dialogues* that perhaps could not have been applied
to all the works submitted to him. But it does seem that he would
not suppress them, which is clearly what Adam Smith intended
to do.

Smith was probably not made any happier by a letter he received from John Home dated 14 October. Writing from Ninewells, Hume's brother records that he has had a letter from Strahan
about having received the manuscripts of both *My own Life* and the
Dialogues, 'which last he makes no difficulty of publishing, as he had
promised . . .' (R.S.E., viii. 18). A surviving draft of a letter from
Smith to Strahan, written sometime in October 1776, contains the
following deleted passage:

You certainly judge right in publishing the new Edition of Mr Humes
works before you publish the dialogues. They might prevent the
sale of this Edition; and it is not impossible that they may hereafter
occasion the sale of another. I am still uneasy about the clamour which,
I forsee, they will excite. . . . (R.S.E., viii. 42.)

The ambiguity in this fragment must have been obvious to Smith,
and in the succeeding paragraph, he suggests other reasons why
it might be a good idea to publish the *Dialogues* later:

I am much obliged to you for so readily agreeing to print the
life, together with my additions, separate from the Dialogues. I even
flatter myself that this arrangement will contribute, not only to my
quiet, but to your interest. The clamour against the dialogues, if
published first, might hurt the sale of the new edition of his works;
and when that Clamour has a little subsided, the dialogues may hereafter occasion a quicker sale of another edition.

The appeal to Strahan's commercial instincts is a new wrinkle in
Smith's attempts to forestall, if not prevent, publication of the
Dialogues. Strahan did not print the *Dialogues* in an edition of

Hume's collected *Essays and Treatises on Several Subjects* until 1788; it was omitted from the editions of 1779 and 1784.

Two months after Hume's death, Strahan was thus as determined to print the *Dialogues* as Adam Smith was determined not to have anything to do with the publication. From the surviving letters, it is evident that Hume's family were keeping up the pressure on Strahan to carry out his promise. Early next year, just before *My own Life* was published, young David Hume, the nephew, began to add his voice to those inquiring about the *Dialogues*. In a letter of 30 January 1777 (unlocated) to Strahan, he asked about both *My own Life* and the *Dialogues*. He was at the time living in Glasgow, and Strahan wrote to him there on 13 February 1777, announcing the imminent publication of *My own Life*, copies of which were being sent to Scotland by the first ship sailing for Leith. Strahan then adds,

As for his *Dialogues on Natural Religion*, I am not yet determined whether I shall publish them or not.—I have all possible Regard to the Will of the Deceased: But as that can be as well fulfilled by you as by me, and as the Publication will probably make some Noise in the World, and its Tendency be considered in different Lights by different Men, I am inclined to think it had better be made by you. From you some will conclude it comes with Propriety, as done *in Obedience to the last Request of your Uncle*, as he himself expresses it;— from me, it might be suspected to proceed from Motives of Interest. —But in this Matter I hope you will do me the Justice to believe I put Interest wholly out of the Question. However, you shall not, at any rate, be kept long in Suspence, as you shall soon have my final Resolutions. (R.S.E., viii. 46.)

A fortnight later, Strahan had made up his mind: he would not publish the *Dialogues*. He wrote to John Home of Ninewells on 3 March 1777 informing him of this decision:

I am favoured with yours of the 17th and 25th ult. the first of which I should have sooner answered, had I not, in effect, done so before, in my Letter of the 13th to your Son at Glasgow, in reply to one he wrote me, dated the 30th of January, and which I did indeed conceive he would have communicated to you.—Probably he has, by this time, done so.

But lest he has not, I beg leave to acquaint you, without farther Delay (tho' your Brother allowed me a much longer Time to determine) that I decline publishing the *Dialogues on Natural Religion*.— My Reasons are, That the Work will probably make some Noise in the World, and be considered in various Lights by different Readers; and that therefore the Publication may be made with more Propriety by your Son, as done *in obedience to the last Request of his Uncle*, as your Brother himself expresses it: Whereas if the Book was published by me, I might be suspected of doing it from interested Motives, which, on this Occasion, have no Place with me, I do assure you.—The Copy you sent me I suppose I need not return to you, as you are possessed of the Original. Indeed, the Copy I have is, in general, very carelessly written, and in some Places quite unintelligible. (R.S.E., viii. 44.)

It is just possible to detect the slightest tone of relief in this letter. That the work was likely to 'be considered in various Lights by different Readers' is hardly the most astute observation in the world, and Strahan, in offering it as a serious pretext for not publishing the work, is totally unconvincing. He could have made the same observation, with equal accuracy, about any number of books he printed or published. His reluctance is amplified later in the same letter when he refers to the two essays on suicide and immortality, which had originally formed part of the *Four Dissertations* but which were suppressed; these he proposes should 'never more see the Light', but in fact they were published in 1777 anonymously and clandestinely.[7]

Early in 1777, then, it is obvious that neither Smith nor Strahan would superintend the publication of the *Dialogues*, and the task thus fell to Hume's nephew. A fragment of a letter or memorandum from John Home to Strahan (or perhaps vice versa), about the publication of the work, does indicate some of the considerations that young David bore in mind in deciding when to publish. The fragment appears to be from Home to Strahan in which he seems to

---

[7] The two essays were 'Of Suicide' and 'Of the Immortality of the Soul' which Hume had originally planned to include in a volume of 'Five Dissertations'. These essays were suppressed, another one added, and *Four Dissertations* appeared in 1757. An unauthorized edition of these essays, simply entitled *Two Essays*, was published in London in 1777 with no author or publisher indicated. In 1783, they appeared as *Essays on Suicide, and The Immortality of the Soul, Ascribed to the late David Hume, Esq.* See Professor Colver's introduction in this volume, pp. 8–11.

apologize to Strahan for not answering his letter sooner 'till he had consulted his son, and laid it before him as he was materially concerned, and tho a young man only just 20 and able to come to a sound and rational determination . . .' (R.S.E., viii. 45). As David Hume the younger was born on 27 February 1757, this would date the letter some time after that of Strahan's declining to publish the work. The reasons are outlined for David's wishing to press ahead with publication even though his father has advised against it:

> my oppinion was that he should delay the publication till the end of two years that he had a title by his uncles settlement, upon your next publication of it. Otherwise it was being too forward, & more than he was called upon in duty. & if a clamour rose against him it might be difficult to support himself against it almost in the commencement of his life. What weighes with him, is that his publishing it as early as he could, would looke more like obedience, than a voluntary deed, & of judgement, & as such exculpate him in the eyes of the world, as well as that the publick being in expectation of the publication, would receive it much better, than after some time when it might be almost forgotten. As it [is] a question of great importance & the young man will not be here from Glasgow for near 2 months, he will advise with his uncles & his own friends, & will then inform you, whether he accepts of your offer of immediate surrender of the title & in which case, may possibly desire from you a more formal resignation if such is requisite, after what you have wrote me. Copy to be kept as I am posesed of the original, which it seems has not been correctly taken, as it was taken in a hurry & among the last things done by my brother. . . . (R.S.E., viii. 45.)

Strahan's copy of the *Dialogues* has not survived, but it is difficult to say whether he surrendered his title to publication or not. If, however, he decided not to do so, for whatever reasons, the codicil of Hume's will meant that the property of the *Dialogues* was his until 25 February 1779, when it reverted to Hume's nephew. In view of the date of eventual publication of the *Dialogues*, it is not altogether impossible that Strahan decided not to relinquish his interest in the work. A shrewd and commercially successful printer, he perhaps did not believe in burning bridges until he had crossed them.

At this stage, however, an 'entire Silence' descends on the proceedings and negotiations for publication. The lamentable paucity of evidence and documents, printed or manuscript, between February 1777 and the appearance of two editions of the *Dialogues* in 1779 prompts some speculation. Strahan, in conformity with Adam Smith's wishes, did not relinquish his ownership of the publication rights; he may have possibly considered including the *Dialogues* in the posthumous 1777 edition of the *Essays and Treatises on Various Subjects* but decided against doing so when *My own Life* stirred up such a controversy. The furore was provoked by Smith's 'letter' to him as an addendum to *My own Life*; it was sufficiently heated to make him think twice about printing a work regarded by Smith, Blair, Elliot, and others of his acquaintance as pernicious or dangerous. If so innocuous a letter, in praise of the worthiness of Hume's life and his personal goodness, could create so much turmoil and acrimony, then a work continuing the themes of the controversial discussion of religion in Hume's other writings would doubtless encourage a public outcry and a condemnation of the printer or publisher. Strahan, who had been elected to Parliament in 1774, perhaps did not wish to be involved in another vitriolic and pointless controversy; thus, he temporized.

For two years very little is known about the fortunes or misfortunes of the manuscript of the *Dialogues*. The next important mention that I have been able to find is concerned with its actual publication: the entry in the Stationer's Register for 10 May 1779. The work is entered for 'The Author' with 'The Whole' of the shares assigned to him: 'Then entered For His Copy / Dialogues concerning Natural / Religion. By David Hume Esqr / Printed in 1779'.

To which of the 1779 editions does this entry refer? Of the two published in 1779, only one, that with 'The Second Edition' on its title-page, gives evidence of having been entered in the Stationer's Register. The imprint on the verso of the half-title reads: '*Entered in Stationers-Hall, according to / Act of Parliament.*' I have never seen a copy of the other edition with a half-title; it might conceivably have had a Stationer's Register entry, but no indication is given on any of the copies I have examined. The title-page of this edition (edition A, the first) is spartan enough to serve as a half-title:

DIALOGUES / CONCERNING / NATURAL RELIGION. / BY / DAVID HUME, Esq; / [*short swelled rule*] / Printed in 1779.
8°: π²A–T⁴; pp. [iv], 1–152.

The title-page of the 'Second Edition' (or edition B) is not much more informative:

DIALOGUES / CONCERNING / NATURAL RELIGION. / BY / DAVID HUME, Esq. / THE SECOND EDITION. / [*short swelled rule*] / LONDON: / M.DCC.LXXIX.
8°: π²A–Q⁸R²; pp. [5]6–264.

Though we have seen that Strahan eventually refused to publish the *Dialogues*, there is an enigmatic hint in a letter from Hugh Blair to Strahan, dated 3 August 1779, that Strahan may have had some role in the publication: 'as to D. Hume's Dialogues, I am surprised that though they have been published for some time, they have made so little noise. They are exceedingly elegant. They bring together some of his most exceptionable reasonings; but the principles themselves were all in his former works. The Part you took, was I think in one of your character & situation well judged.'[8] There are no entries in Strahan's ledgers for 1779 that might refer to the *Dialogues*, but Blair's letter does hint at something other than Strahan's outright refusal to publish the work. In view of the clamour raised by the publication of *My own Life*, Blair might reasonably have expected the *Dialogues* to provoke even more noise. For the same reason, Strahan might have decided to give what assistance he could to the publication of the *Dialogues* but to keep quiet about it. He was a master of the Stationers' Company and could thus have been responsible for the entry in the Register.

Towards the end of 1779, the *Dialogues* began to make a 'little noise'; it was reviewed in at least four journals, two in Edinburgh and two in London. *The Gentleman's Magazine* for October 1779

---

[8] Edinburgh University Library, MS. Dc. 2. 76¹⁰.

carried a brief notice (pp. 507–8) which named 'Robinson' as the publisher, or at least the distributor. This is doubtless George Robinson of Paternoster Row, a jobbing publisher with a very large wholesale trade. The longest review appeared in the November 1779 issue of *The Monthly Review; or, Literary Journal* (pp. 343–55); here too Robinson is listed as the publisher. A three-part review came out in an Edinburgh journal, *The Weekly Magazine, or Edinburgh Amusement*. Beginning in the Wednesday, 27 October 1779 issue (xlvi. 113–15), the review continued for another two issues, 3 and 10 November (xlvi. 136–8, 162–4), with Robinson named as the publisher. Another brief notice appeared in the *Edinburgh Eighth-Day Magazine* for Thursday, 28 October 1779, p. 243. Here the publisher is listed as 'Cadell', i.e., Thomas Cadell the younger, who had been associated with Scottish authors as early as 1769, when he published William Robertson's *Charles V* and who, with Strahan, published the first edition of Hume's autobiography.

The mention of both Cadell and Robinson as publisher is, to say the least, confusing; it is possible that the reviews refer to different editions, but as no publisher is specified on the title-page of either edition A or B, no certain identification can be made. Robinson had never published any of Hume's works in the author's lifetime, nor have I found him associated with the publication of any posthumous editions of Hume's works. Thomas Cadell, the successor to Hume's publisher Andrew Millar, was mentioned by Hume in a letter to Strahan in October 1766 (*Letters*, ii. 96) and appears in the imprint to the 1770 edition of Hume's *Essays and Treatises on Several Subjects*; he continued to be associated with the publication of Hume's works for some time. He could thus be considered as a likely candidate for the publisher of at least one of the editions. But which one?

Contemporary advertisements, as well as other new information, may offer a clue. In the *Caledonian Mercury* for 19 June 1779, published in Edinburgh, there is an advertisement announcing the imminent publication of the *Dialogues*—but 'The Second Edition'. In the same journal for 23 June 1779 appears an advertisement from John Balfour and Co. announcing the availability of the *Dialogues* 'just arrived from London . . .'. A similar notice was inserted by Charles Elliot in the issues of 26 June, 17 July, and 24 July, specifying 'The Second Edition'. Other advertisements for the same appear in the *Edinburgh Evening Courant* for 19 June, 23 June, 3 July, 17 July, and 31 July. Elliot, in his notice for 23 June, advertises the *Dialogues* as '*arrived this day from London . . .*'.

John Balfour's long association with Strahan and later with Cadell could easily suggest a surreptitious publication of 'The Second Edition' of Hume's *Dialogues*. What, then, of the first edition? It was also available in Scotland at this time.

James Beattie, one of Hume's most prominent critics, had received a copy of edition A and wrote to Mrs. Montagu on 25 June 1779,

An extraordinary Book has just now appeared in this country. . . . The copy, which I have, was sent me two days ago, by my friend and neighbour Dr Campbell . . . who accompanied it with a note in the following words. 'You have probably not yet seen this posthumous performance of David Hume. As the publisher, with whom I am not acquainted, has favoured me with a copy, I have sent it to you for your perusal, and shall be glad to have your opinion of it, after you have read it.'[9]

This observation clearly excludes Strahan and Cadell as publishers of the edition sent to Beattie, as they, along with William Creech of Edinburgh, had published Campbell's *The Philosophy of Rhetoric* in 1776.

Beattie, then, owned the book by 23 June 1779, and George Campbell had it even earlier. A clue to its source is offered by a letter of Beattie to the Duchess of Gordon, dated 15 July 1779. Forbes, in his biography of Beattie, printed part of this letter but omitted the following paragraph:

I know not whether your Grace has heard, that David Hume's Posthumous Dialogues are at last published. My neighbour Dr Campbel lately sent me a copy of them, with a card to the following purpose:—'that he had read them—that they seemed too dry and

⁹ Sir William Forbes, *An Account of the Life and Writings of James Beattie* (Edinburgh, 1806), ii. 52–3.

metaphysical to do much hurt;—that he did not discover any thing
new or very curious in them, they being only a sort of commentary
to the dialogues on *Natural Religion* and *providence* published in his
life time. What most astonishes me, says the Principal, is the zeal
which he shows for disseminating his sceptical principles.' I answered
the Doctor's card in these words 'that I was glad to hear on so good
authority, that this book was not likely to do so much harm, as the
author and publisher intended;—that I would acquiesce in his judgement, which I was sure was just, for that my spirits were not at
present in such a state as would permit me to read any writings of
that kind.'—I have been assured, that Mr Hume, when he knew
that he was dying, took such precautions in regard to the Manuscript,
as that it was not even in the power of his Executors to prevent the
publication. Adam Smith, to do him justice, refused to have any thing
to do with it. Mr Strahan refused to print it. The King was said to
have signified his desire, that it might be suppressed. But Mr Hume's
nephew, to whom his uncle had bequeathed his whole fortune both
in money and atheism, and who, it seems, is a brisk young man,
declared that the world should not be deprived of such a treasure,
though he should be obliged to print it in Holland. The copy I have
seen has no name of place or printer. But I know enough of the
business to see, that it is printed in Edinburgh.—And so the world is
now in possession of Mr Hume's Legacy. Dr Gregory left a Legacy
too, but a very different one. Was Dr Gregory known to Your Grace?
He and Mr Hume were well acquainted for many years; but at last
the Doctor's partiality to me produced a total separation. If my mind
were more at ease, I would try my hand on a *Dialogue* of the dead
between Dr Gregory & Mr Hume. . . .[10]

How Beattie came by this information is unknown, but it can to
some extent be confirmed by other facts. His disclosure that
Hume's nephew would have had the work printed in Holland if
necessary is another measure of just how little inclined publishers
were to be associated with the publication of the *Dialogues*. The
possibility of foreign publication, though it may sound a bit like

[10] Quoted from the Forbes (Fettercairn) papers (now in the National Library of
Scotland) by the permission of Mrs. P. G. C. Somervell and the Trustees of the
National Library of Scotland.
   The 'Dr Gregory' to whom Beattie refers is John Gregory (1724–73), Professor
of Medicine at Edinburgh University, 1766–73; the book to which Beattie refers is
his posthumous *A Father's Legacy to his Daughters* (London, 1774).

adolescent bravado, suggests that Hume's nephew was finding it difficult to publish the work.

Beattie's copy is clearly edition A, even though he received it from Campbell at the same time that edition B was beginning to appear in Edinburgh. He describes the work as having 'no name of place or printer', and this confirms his allegation about the place of publication. Edition B at least gives an ostensible place of publication. If we accept as accurate the advertisement in the *Edinburgh Eighth-Day Magazine*, then Cadell could have been associated with Robinson in publishing edition B. Robinson could have distributed the work for Cadell and thus have blurred responsibility for publication of the work in case public reaction was as inflammatory and outraged as expected.

Beattie's contention that edition A was published in Edinburgh can be further corroborated by examining Hume's holograph of the *Dialogues*, of which Hume's nephew had the original and a copy. Beattie's mention of young Hume's determination to carry out his uncle's wishes and the statement that the work was printed in Edinburgh clarify one of the few notes (in this case the longest) that the nephew made on the holograph of Part XI: 'I have sent two Leaves of the original Manuscript, as I have not been able to get the Copy compared with it.' It would be difficult to think that he might have sent these two leaves to a printer in London and then have got them back, but local printing would make the retrieval of two leaves easy. Compositorial marks appear in the last fifth of the manuscript, and they correspond to the gatherings and pagination of edition A (see below, pp. 131–5). In other respects as well, chiefly that of punctuation, edition A more closely resembles Hume's holograph than edition B, though both leave much to be desired in the way of fidelity to Hume's text. Edition B seems to have been set either from one of the manuscript copies Hume had made or from edition A. The greater closeness of the text of edition A to Hume's holograph indicates further support for Beattie's contention that the work was published in Edinburgh, since Hume's nephew would have been able to read proof against Hume's holograph.

Neither edition A nor edition B has press figures or printer's ornaments. It was more characteristic of Scottish printing than of English in the latter half of the eighteenth century to be without press figures; a few books with London imprints are free of press figures, but not many. The absence of press figures in both is, however, only negative evidence and does not necessarily support the conclusion that edition A was published in Edinburgh. Though the title-page of edition B indicates that it was published in London, it could just possibly have been printed in Edinburgh, since it was not unknown for Edinburgh printers to issue books with a London imprint. In addition, I must note that edition A *looks* Scottish, from its austere title-page to the arrangement of words on the page. The style is far more representative of Scottish printing at this time than of English. Edition B, though more spaciously and in some ways more attractively printed, does not look Scottish.

There are over five hundred differences between punctuation and capitalization in editions A and B; the differences are even more marked between either text and Hume's holograph. By comparing texts quoted in the reviews with the passages in A and B, it might have been possible to infer which edition the reviewer was quoting. This is a vain hope, as the punctuation sometimes follows that of edition A, sometimes that of B, and all too frequently that of neither. None of the reviews gives page references, so the considerable differences in pagination (152 pages *v.* 264 pages) between A and B cannot be used to check which text is being quoted.

One of the first discussions of Hume's book was Thomas Hayter's *Remarks on Mr. Hume's Dialogues, concerning Natural Religion* (Cambridge, 1780). It is clear from the first page reference that he is using edition B, and on several occasions he refers to a page number higher than 152. The same is true of Joseph Milner's book *Gibbon's Account of Christianity considered: Together with some Strictures on Hume's Dialogues concerning Natural Religion* (London, 1781). Edition A, having been printed in Edinburgh, might not have been widely available in England. Moreover, edition B could have been rushed into print by the London trade to prevent the Scots from having any commercial advantage.

From these various facts, both old and new, several conclusions may with reasonable probability be inferred. Edition A, correctly described as the first edition, was published in Edinburgh, not London, and before May 1779. The difficulty that Hume's nephew had in getting it published is greater than hitherto supposed, when we know that he considered the possibility of printing the work in Holland. This would be true *a fortiori* if the King did signify 'a desire that it might be suppressed', but in the absence of any supporting evidence I find it difficult to take seriously this bit of Beattie's tittle-tattle.

In a footnote appended to Beattie's letter of 25 June 1776, Forbes noted 'the "Dialogues concerning natural Religion" are now never heard of'.[11] He could not have seen the so-called 'third edition' of 1804, which consists only of the sheets of the 'second edition' with a new title-page.[12] Moreover, the work had been available since 1788 in collected editions of Hume's works, and a separate edition might be expected to sell poorly. Considering the difficulty Hume had in ensuring that the work was published and the problems in discovering the exact identity of the publisher(s), I have to report two further ironies. One is a Dublin edition of 1782, *Dialogues concerning Natural Religion. By David Hume, Esq. To which is added, Divine Benevolence asserted, and vindicated from The Objections of Ancient and Modern Sceptics. By Thomas Balguy*. . . . Hume would surely have been amused to see himself gathered into such company. But divinity can never hope to correct the failings of bibliography. An edition of 1821, styling itself 'A New Edition, with Additions' prefixes the following advertisement to the text:

The following Dialogues concerning Natural Religion, were first Published at Edinburgh in 1742, and at London in 1744, and have, since that period, gone through several editions. To render this Edition more worthy of

---

[11] Forbes, ii. 53 n.

[12] The title-page of this 'third edition' (merely a reissue of sheets of edition B with a new title-page) is 'printed by and for Thomas Hughes'. As the title-page is the only thing new, the inescapable implication is that Thomas Hughes printed the second edition. If so, this would seem to be the only work he ever printed. He is not listed in William B. Todd's *Directory of Printers and Others in Allied Trades, London and Vicinity, 1800–1840* (London: Printing Historical Society, 1972), pp. 102–3, and I have been unable to find any other reference to him or to his printing activities from 1779 to 1804.

Public approbation several essays have been added, by Hume and Voltaire, some of which were never before printed.

In the face of such confident assertion, Hume scholars can only marvel that the work's publishing history is no more complicated than it is.

HUME'S MANUSCRIPT

THE manuscript of Hume's *Dialogues concerning Natural Religion* in the Royal Society of Edinburgh (volume 12 of the thirteen bound volumes of Hume manuscripts and other manuscripts relating to Hume) consists of 42 leaves, paginated as follows: 1–14; 17–38; 41–87; [88]. (The last page is not numbered.) The measurements of the leaves vary between 21·8 cm. × 30·8 cm. and 20·5 cm. × 31 cm.[13] The leaves are written on recto and verso, with the exception of pages 4 and 32, which are blank.

In order to avoid having the pagination even more irregular than it is, Hume has renumbered some of the pages:

Page 27	was formerly	29
Page 28	was formerly	30
Page 29	was formerly	31
Page 30	was formerly	32
Page 31	was formerly	27, then 32
Page 32	was formerly	28, then 33

The introduction and twelve sections are paginated as follows: Introduction, 1–3. (p. 4, verso of second leaf, is blank.) I, 5–14. II, 17–26. III, 27–31. (p. 32 is blank.) IV, 33–8. V, 41–4. VI, 45–8. VII, 49–52. VIII, 53–6. IX, 57–60. X, 61–8. XI, 69–76. XII, 77–[88]. The renumbering affects only the third section. There had been gaps in the pagination between sections I and II as well as between II and III; the latter gap was removed by renumbering the pages but left the gap between I and II. Kemp Smith regards these three sections as existing 'substantially in their present form' in 1751.[14] The renumbering of the pages, however, points to some revision.

Kemp Smith's examination of the watermarks enabled him to strengthen his conjectures and conclusions about the dating of

---

[13] The latter measurement is that given by J. Y. T. Greig and Harold Beynon in their *Calendar of Hume MSS. in the Possession of the Royal Society of Edinburgh* (Edinburgh, 1932), p. 136.

[14] Norman Kemp Smith, ed., *Hume's Dialogues concerning Natural Religion* (New York, 1948), p. 87.

Hume's revisions. While I agree with some of the dating of the revisions he assigns, I find it difficult to draw any conclusions from the watermarks and think the changes in handwriting more reliable. I have distinguished the following watermarks:

A. A double circle surmounted by crown with lion rampant and crowned on plinth in centre. This is the Vryheit or Dutch Lion.[15]

B. The initials L V G. This is the countermark for A, originally standing for Lucius Van Gerrevink.

C. A lyre shape, with a curious tail, and PRO PATRIA clearly discernible—usually referred to as 'Pro Patria'.[16]

D. Small crown in centre, probably the countermark for C.

These occur on the following pages:

A: 7–8, 9–10, 13–14, 19–20, 23–4, 29–30, 31–2, 35–6, 41–2, 45–6, 51–2, 53–4, 57–8, 61–2, 67–8, 71–2, 73–4, 77–8, and 83–4.

B: 1–2, 5–6, 11–12, 17–18, 21–2, 25–6, 27–8, 33–4, 37–8, 43–4, 47–8, 49–50, 55–6, 59–60, 63–4, 65–6, 69–70, 75–6, 79–80, 81–2.

C: 3–4 and 85–6.

D: 87–8.

It is possible, if not likely, that these leaves represent one-half of a folded sheet measuring 32 × 42 cm., the normal size for paper watermarked with the Vryheit Lion. If Hume had in fact been folding these sheets down the middle to get something the size of the extant leaves of the manuscript, and if each of these half-sheets had two watermarks, such as A and B above, then one could expect a certain number of the extant leaves to be conjugate. For example, pages 5–8, 17–20, 21–4, 33–6, 49–52, 65–8, and 69–72 could originally have been a single sheet folded once. The present condition of the manuscript does not permit of such inferences, however, as each leaf has been tipped on to a binding stub, and it is thus impossible to determine whether two half-sheets are conjugate.

[15] Edward Heawood, *Watermarks, Mainly of the Seventeenth and Eighteenth Centuries* (Hilversum, 1950), No. 3149 (Pl. 400).

[16] Ibid., No. 3696 (Pl. 491).

Of less tantalizing and more tangible interest is that watermark C also appears on the codicil to Hume's will, dated 7 August 1776. Thus these leaves could be reasonably regarded as containing some final revisions. The watermark also appears on James Edmonstoune's last letter to Hume, coincidentally dated 7 August 1776, written to Hume from Linlithgow, eighteen miles west of Edinburgh. Watermarks A and B appear on several of Hume's letters written in 1752, 1757, and in 1765 from Paris. This paper is very common, however, and there is no mystery in finding it in so many places and used so often. Watermark C is considerably less common, but the coincidence of date and watermark between Hume's codicil, pages 3–4 and 85–6, and Edmonstoune's letter is nothing more than that.

In short, it seems to me that one would have to make a number of unjustifiable assumptions to conclude anything very exact from the watermarks. The evidence does suggest that the manuscript in the Royal Society of Edinburgh was not only Hume's fair copy, but his working copy as well, and the irregular sequence of the watermarks indicates that he may have revised various leaves or pages and destroyed their predecessors at some time or another. Complicated or lengthy additions or emendations almost certainly belong to 1776, as Hume would undoubtedly have preferred to leave an unambiguous, precisely ordered fair copy for the printer.

The last two sections of the manuscript are the most revised and amended. Part XI comprises pages 69–76. On page 69 of the manuscript, Hume's nephew has written, 'I have sent two Leaves of the Original Manuscript, as I have not been able to get the Copy compared with it.' In fact, all of gatherings P, Q, R, S, and T comprising pages 113–52 of the first edition may have been set from the holograph. Various pages of the manuscript are at any rate marked, probably by a compositor, as follows:

Page 69 of MS.: In the eighth line from the top of that page a left-hand bracket has been drawn in the word 'Conception' between the 'p' and the 't', with this notation in the margin: 113. P. This corresponds to the first edition's page 113, the recto of the first leaf of gathering P; the first letters on the page are 'tion', as also the catchword on page 112.

Page 72 of MS.: Seven lines from the bottom, a left-hand square bracket is drawn around the word 'with' and 121. Q in the margin. This corresponds to Q1ʳ, page 121 of the first edition, 'with' also being the catchword on page 120.

Page 75 of MS.: Thirteen lines from the top of the page the word 'Diffidence' has a left-hand square bracket drawn between the first and second 'f' and 129. R in the margin, corresponding to R1ʳ, page 129 of the first edition, beginning 'fidence' with that as the catchword on page 128.

Page 82 of MS.: Nine lines from the top of the page, the word 'greater' (which is itself added above the line) has a left-hand square bracket drawn around it and 145. T in the margin, corresponding to T1ʳ, page 145 of the first edition, with 'greater' as the first word on that page and the catchword on page 144.

Page 87 of MS.: Four lines from the bottom of the page the word 'much' has a left-hand square bracket drawn around it and 137. S in the margin, corresponding to S1ʳ, page 137 of the first edition, with 'much' as the first word on that page and the catchword on page 136.

Thus, at least five leaves of the manuscript are marked in a way that a compositor might have marked them. The handwriting, however, does faintly resemble that of Hume's nephew, in so far as one can judge from such a small specimen, and it is just possible (but most unlikely) that he was marking the sequence of gatherings himself, with the aid of the compositor. Because of the irregular sequence produced by the revisions in the manuscript, e.g. that of the last leaf, some additions that Hume wanted might not have appeared in their proper place.

Though I have little doubt that young David was conscientious about the publication of his uncle's manuscript, I think it unlikely that he was so interested in its printing that he was marking Hume's holograph copy for and with the compositor. He does say specifically that he sent two leaves of the original manuscript, but he may have sent others as well. The compositorial marks in sections XI and XII of the manuscript indicate that the printer had all these leaves, pages 69–88, at one time. The marks on the manuscript are those used by printers in the eighteenth century,[17] and it is only in these leaves that we find the names of the participants underlined twice, a convention for indicating small capitals and thus more likely to be compositorial rather than authorial. Furthermore, since these sections were the ones Hume revised the most, it is possible that the copies made by amanuenses were defective, or even out-of-date, in their transcriptions of these pages. They are the most difficult to follow, and only the instructions in the nephew's hand make clear the order of paragraphs in certain instances. Thus, if young David were reading proof derived from an amanuensis's copy against Hume's holograph, he would immediately have noted departures and would have had to send the original to the printer to ensure accuracy. We can be grateful that he took care to retrieve them, as we can learn from these leaves something about Hume's last-minute revisions in 1776.

The first eight pages of Part XII constitute pages 77–84 of the manuscript, and page 84 contains what would have been an earlier ending to the *Dialogues*. Hume always intended the work to end as it does, with Pamphilus's closing remark modelled on the conclusion of Cicero's *De Natura Deorum*. The original ending on page 84 of the manuscript was made up of this paragraph and the paragraph beginning 'It is contrary to common Sense . . .', i.e., what is now the last paragraph but three (p. 259). At an early stage, Hume apparently decided to add another paragraph, this one beginning '*To know God*, says *Seneca*' which is added on the margin of p. 84 of the manuscript and deleted. Kemp Smith regards this as Hume's new second ending, which would be difficult to date, although it appears from the handwriting to be a revision made in the early 1760s when Hume was finishing or had finished the *Dialogues*.

Unsatisfied with this revision, Hume, still at an early stage, added another leaf to his manuscript, constituting pages 85–6 (watermark C). On this leaf, he has recopied the paragraph beginning '*To know God*' and has added a further one: the paragraph beginning 'If the whole of natural Theology' (p. 260). Kemp Smith regards this paragraph as one of Hume's 1776 revisions. I do not

---

[17] Percy Simpson, *Proof-Reading in the Sixteenth, Seventeenth, and Eighteenth Centuries* (Oxford, 1935), pp. 88–107.

think either the watermark evidence or the handwriting supports this conclusion. The watermark on the leaf constituting pages 85–6 (the last leaf but one of the manuscript) appears on only one other leaf, pages 3–4, and there is no reason to think that pages 3–4 contain 1776 revisions. In addition, Hume has made almost no alterations when recopying the marginal paragraph ('*To know God*') on page 84 of the manuscript on to page 85, the new leaf. If a great interval of time had passed, it seems likely he would have made some changes in the wording.

On page 84 of the manuscript, at the end of the paragraph beginning 'It is contrary to common Sense', Hume's nephew has written the following instruction: 'all below and on the Margin not to be printed—go on to Page 85 *To know God*'. 'All below' consists of the last paragraph, which is deleted and rewritten, with alterations, on page 86 of the manuscript and what was initially intended as a note, marked 'AA', which was to be inserted on page 79 of the manuscript, as a note to the paragraph beginning 'And here I must acknowledge'. This would also seem to be part of an early revision. It is crowded on to the bottom of page 84 of the manuscript, and if Hume had been adding it in 1776, he might have preferred to do so at the bottom of page 86, the new leaf, where there is considerably more room. There are several corrections and additions made to the 'note' as it appears on the bottom of page 84, and these are quite likely to date from 1776. When Hume decided to add the important long paragraph beginning 'All men of sound reason' he must have decided that this addition ought to appear on the same page as the other addition, the note marked 'AA' on page 84 of the manuscript; otherwise, the correct sequence for the additions might not be clear. Both the note marked 'AA' and the long paragraph marked 'BB' are to be inserted in their proper place on page 79 of the manuscript. But 'BB' is to precede 'AA'. Without any clear indication as to the location of these additions, it is just possible that a printer might have regarded the note 'AA' as it originally appeared on page 84 as a note to that page. There is additional evidence to suggest that Hume in adding the long paragraph decided to make the note part of the text and thus put both these additions on the same leaf, recopied on to page 87 the revised version of the 'note' from page 84 and then added, on pages 87–8, the long paragraph.

One other slight bit of evidence can be adduced for regarding 'AA' as an early emendation with some modifications in 1776. One of the changes Hume has made has been from 'betwixt' to 'between'. Most of these minor embellishments probably date from 1776, both from the evidence of the handwriting and from the general change in Hume's attitude towards style.

Hume's most noticeable and most frequent emendations to the manuscript are additions or revisions above the line of text. I have recorded the revisions in the textual notes. The other interlineations, however, are a different matter, and they may often be late or even last-minute revisions. As they are part of the main body of the text, it would seem inappropriate to include them in the textual notes, but they are documented in an appendix. Where possible I have indicated whether they seem to be early or late additions.

One longer addition can with certitude be attributed to 1776: the paragraph beginning 'All men of sound reason' (p. 248). Hume had to add another leaf to the manuscript to make this addition, and the handwriting is clearly Hume's late hand. Doubtless a number of the other revisions also date from 1776; most are minor and are largely confined to stylistic nuances, though where the manuscript is modified, the changes are often significant. Thus, we have to treat with some caution the letter of 15 August 1776 to Adam Smith in which Hume says of the *Dialogues*, 'On revising them (which I have not done these 15 Years) I find that nothing can be more cautiously and more artfully written.' The last revisions would not seem to err on the side of caution.

THE TEXT

THE edition by Norman Kemp Smith in 1935 of David Hume's *Dialogues concerning Natural Religion* was the first attempt to provide an accurate modern text of any of Hume's philosophical works. Its immediate acceptance and success were entirely justified, and the edition was undoubtedly responsible for renewed interest in Hume and particularly in the *Dialogues*. Not the least of its attractions was Kemp Smith's introduction and analysis of Hume's religious temperament, an assessment that the passage of time has not significantly or convincingly altered.

Attitudes towards editing, however, have changed in forty years, and Kemp Smith's text can no longer be regarded as unexceptionable. Unlike previous editors of Hume, he had consulted the manuscript of the *Dialogues* in the Royal Society of Edinburgh and had based his revised text on that consultation. In addition, a number of Hume's alterations and emendations were noted. But not all. Kemp Smith printed some of these alterations as being of sufficient interest in one way or another while describing most of them as 'quite minor'. As scholars and critics read works ever more closely, what is minor and what is not begins to blur, and any change, emendation, addition, or deletion becomes important.

The decision to print what is primarily a diplomatic text may not meet with universal approbation. Kemp Smith, for example, chose not to follow the manuscript in its use of 'a capital initial letter for all substantives' on the grounds that Hume supervised for publication works by him in which nouns or substantives were not capitalized. What he would have done regarding capitalization —and punctuation and spelling for that matter—had he been able to see the *Dialogues* through the press cannot be known, but the evidence that he would have retained capital initial letters is at least as convincing as the evidence that he would not have. In any case, I have had to assume no higher authority than the author and have preserved his textual intentions as far as possible.

Moreover, there are not many eighteenth-century texts that can be edited from manuscripts. Editions of, say, *Gulliver's Travels* or *A Philosophical Enquiry into the Origin of our Ideas of the Sublime and Beautiful* would doubtless be different if holograph copies of them had survived. In Hume's case, where the work was published posthumously, and where the holograph has survived, an editor has a unique opportunity to present 'the true original' for the first time. In short, all editions of Hume's *Dialogues* hitherto have been filtered through a standardizing procedure. The result may be uniform and coherent, but it is not what the author wrote.

The text of the *Dialogues concerning Natural Religion* presented here is largely a diplomatic one. I have followed Hume's holograph as faithfully as possible, occasionally to the point of preserving inconsistencies.

The choice of italics for the names of the speakers runs counter to the first and all subsequent editions of the *Dialogues,* which use small capitals. In parts XI and XII of the manuscript, the markings indicate small capitals, but in the remainder the names are underlined once, to indicate italics. As the markings in sections XI and XII may be compositorial rather than authorial, I have chosen italics. When the characters are first introduced, on page 3 of the manuscript, Hume has written their names in large and small capitals, and I have preserved this. Elsewhere, the names are printed in italics, and in the very rare instances where Hume has neglected to underline the name, I have italicized it as well. Use of italics for the names of characters in a dialogue accords with other eighteenth-century printing practice.

The manuscript is liberally sprinkled with ampersands. In a few instances Hume has changed '&' to 'and'. I have not been able to infer any rule for 'and' one time and '&' another, but the changes Hume made I regarded as sufficient authority to change all ampersands to ands.

A similar problem arises in the use of the apostrophe as an elision, usually for 'e' or 'l', as in 'explored', 'explor'd', or even 'explord'; or 'cou'd' or 'wou'd'. Rules for such practice in the eighteenth century are not invariable. In writing of words with the suffix '-ed', one authority concludes, 'in the above cases, a Compositor uses the Apostrophe after his own discretion, and according as he finds what way the syllable *ed* runs smoothest'.[18] I have silently expanded the omission of either 'e' or an apostrophe in the instances where Hume has omitted one or the other but have not distinguished between '-ed' and ''d'. I have observed the same rule when there is neither apostrophe nor 'l' in 'would' or 'could'.

The copy-text is derived from a manuscript that was both Hume's fair and working copy, so it comes as no surprise that there are minor inconsistencies in spelling, punctuation, and capitalization. One of the most noticeable differences between this text and that of the first edition (indeed, that of all subsequent editions as well) will be in the capitalization. As the textual notes will indicate, Hume occasionally changed a word beginning with a lowercase letter to a capital. He clearly regarded capitalization as important and wrote to William Strahan in April 1757, 'Please only to tell the Compositor, that he always employ a Capital after the Colons' (*Letters*, i. 247). Since it was also standard practice in the eighteenth century to capitalize nouns, I have regarded Hume's habits and preferences as further authority to retain all capitalization as it appears in the manuscript. Ruthless decapitalization for the sake of a 'modernized' text is fashionable these days, but when there is even slight evidence to indicate that an author preferred a capital initial letter, the duty of an editor is to respect that preference. It is not necessarily the case that readers fifty years hence will have any more difficulty understanding a 'modernized' than an unmodernized text.

I have not supplied or changed any punctuation, though the stop after the section number in the manuscript has been omitted in printing. The chief problem with Hume's punctuation is to decide when clauses or phrases are set off by commas whether the clause is restrictive or not. In the case of an important philosophical text, I think this has to be the prerogative of the reader and scholar and not the duty of the editor. In general, however, Hume's punctuation in the manuscript of the *Dialogues* is less confusing than the punctuation in lifetime editions of his works.

---

[18] John Smith, *The Printer's Grammar* (London, 1755), pp. 106–7.

The Text is arranged as follows:

Text of *Dialogues*

Hume's notes (if any)

Textual Apparatus

Editor's notes and annotations

Hume's notes are only twelve in number. I have left them un-changed as part of the text, but have expanded or explained them, if necessary, in my own annotations.

The textual apparatus records changes (with the exception of interlineations) made by Hume in the text of the *Dialogues*. These changes consist of deletions, alterations, substitutions, additions, emendations, and so forth. I have used a right-hand square bracket to indicate Hume's alterations or substitutions. Thus

13 striven] strove

means that the word 'striven' in line 13 has been changed from or substituted for 'strove'. When Hume has deleted a word, a phrase, or a long series of words, I have enclosed it or them in square brackets, e.g.:

18 compensate [for]

This means simply that Hume has deleted 'for' after 'compensate'. My editorial notes in the textual apparatus are in italics.

Occasionally, Hume has amended his emendations. Thus, in some sense the textual apparatus itself has its own textual appara-tus. I have noted these alterations by line number preceded by superior '*n*' or note number, as on pages 184 and 256.

I have not regularized or changed the deletions or substitutions. However, in some instances in the text where I thought I had authority to do so I have regularized Hume's practice. Throughout the manuscript, for example, Hume has changed 'betwixt' to 'be-tween', 'scarce' to 'scarcely', and I have not recorded these changes in the textual apparatus. Hume has also changed ''tis' to 'it is' vir-tually every time it occurs; where he has not, I have kept the reading as he may have intended it as a stylistic embellishment. Hume had some trouble with the word 'throughout'; it appears as 'thoroughout' and 'throughout' as well as another version that cannot be deciphered because he has so effectively deleted the crucial letters. This inconsistency was probably due to eighteenth-century pronunciation of the word, but I have rendered it 'throughout' in all instances.

Since Hume had been dead for three years when the *Dialogues* appeared, the question of correcting in proof does not arise. He might very well have· altered the typography and punctuation had he been able to see proof. However, the very great trouble he went to regarding the publication indicates that he knew he would be dead before the work could be printed. Consequently he took some pains to ensure that his copy of the work would be as accurate as he could make it and would represent his final intentions.

Beyond the text lies the intellectual context of the *Dialogues*. Even the most casual perusal of books and essays on Hume's *Dialogues* will indicate a continuing and growing interest in the work. In our 'profane and irreligious Age', it is unlikely that any edition of any of Hume's works will raise the ecclesiastical eyebrow, and it is perhaps difficult for the reader born in the second half of the twentieth century to imagine, much less reproduce, the passions that the subject of natural religion could induce in the latter half of the eighteenth century. Equally, this putative reader may regard the dialogue form as having a certain archaeographical charm but otherwise being as extinct as the dodo. Such is the fate of a subject that inspired well over a thousand books and a form that in the eighteenth century numbers over two thousand instances.

Nevertheless, I have tried in the notes to give some hint of the context in which the *Dialogues* might have been written and read. The practice of supplying phrasal analogues, intellectual contexts, and parallel or opposing ideas is not common with philosophic texts, and I have kept these to a minimum. Only occasionally will they suggest sources, and their more important function is to suggest the currency of the topic, the heterodoxy in Hume's arguments, and the importance of the literary form he chose. I have identified specific allusions or quotations, without perfect success. No doubt enlightenment as to the source of certain allusions or quotations will reach me, by one means or another, in due course.

In quoting from possible sources, I have usually quoted from contemporary or earlier editions since the text Hume might have read would probably be different from a modern edition of that work. In quoting from the classics or works other than English, I have chosen wherever possible contemporary English translations. In the case of quotations from eighteenth-century editions of classical authors, I have also given a cross-reference to a modern edition (usually in the Loeb Classical Library series), when available. Hume doubtless read Cicero in Latin, Fénelon in French, and so forth, but it is unlikely that he was thinking in those languages when he was writing. Moreover, a great deal of the interest of the *Dialogues* lies in its style. English translations of classical or continental authors would indicate how eighteenth-century authors were in fact thinking and translating and, consequently, how Hume might have been formulating in English what he was reading in (say) Latin. More general sources are given in the bibliography. The annotations will reveal my indebtedness to other scholars and particularly to Kemp Smith.

DIALOGUES

concerning

NATURAL RELIGION

Pamphilus to Hermippus

IT has been remarked, my *Hermippus*, that, tho' the antient Philo- 5
sophers convey'd most of their Instruction in the form of Dialogue,[1]
this Method of Composition has been little practic'd in later Ages,
and has seldom succeeded in the hands of those, who have attempted
it. Accurate and regular Argument, indeed, such as is now expected
of philosophical Enquirers, naturally throws a man into the methodi- 10
cal and didactic manner; where he can immediately, without
Preparation, explain the Point, at which he aims; and thence proceed, without Interruption, to deduce the Proofs, on which it is
establish'd. To deliver a SYSTEM in Conversation scarcely appears
natural; and while the Dialogue-Writer desires, by departing from 15
the direct Style of Composition, to give a freer Air to his Performance, and avoid the Appearance of *Author* and *Reader*, he is apt to
run into a worse Inconvenience, and convey the Image of *Pedagogue*
and *Pupil*. Or if he carries on the Dispute in the natural Spirit of
Good-company, by throwing in a Variety of Topics, and preserving 20

---

[1] Anthony Ashley Cooper, Third Earl of Shaftesbury, *Characteristicks* (London,
1711), ii. 187–8: 'We Moderns . . . are so sparing in the way of DIALOGUE; which
heretofore was found the politest and best way of managing even the graver Subjects. . . . We need not wonder, therefore, that the sort of Moral Painting, by way
of *Dialogue*, is so out of fashion; and that we see no more of these Philosophical
Portraitures, now-a-days.'
  Matthew Tindal, *Christianity as Old as the Creation* (London, 1731), p. iv: 'The
Manner of debating a Subject Dialogue-wise, (as this between *A.* and *B.*) was
esteem'd by the Ancients the most proper, as well as most prudent Way of exposing
prevailing Absurdities; and Tully's two Discourses, *de Natura Deorum* and *de Divina-
tione* . . . are living Monuments of the Expediency, and Usefulness of this way of
Writing.'
  Richard Hurd, *Moral and Political Dialogues* (London, 1765), i. iv: 'WHEN THE
ANTIENTS had any thing to say to the world on the subject either of morals or government, they generally chose the way of DIALOGUE, for the conveyance of their instructions . . .'. Cf. the 1st edn. (London, 1764), pp. i–xii.

a proper Ballance among the Speakers; he often loses so much Time in Preparations and Transitions, that the Reader will scarcely think himself compensated, by all the Graces of Dialogue, for the Order, Brevity, and Precision, which are sacrific'd to them.

5   There are some Subjects, however, to which Dialogue writing is peculiarly adapted,[2] and where it is still preferable to the direct and simple Method of Composition.

Any Point of Doctrine, which is so *obvious*, that it scarcely admits of Dispute, but at the same time so *important*, that it cannot be too
10 often inculcated, seems to require some such Method of handling it; where the Novelty of the manner may compensate the Triteness of the Subject, where the Vivacity of Conversation may enforce the Precept, and where the Variety of Lights, presented by various Personages and Characters, may appear neither tedious nor
15 redundant.

Any Question of Philosophy, on the other hand, which is so *obscure* and *uncertain*, that human Reason can reach no fixt Determination with regard to it; if it should be treated at all; seems to lead us naturally into the Style of Dialogue and Conversation.
20 Reasonable Men may be allow'd to differ, where no-one can reasonably be positive: Opposite Sentiments, even without any Decision, afford an agreeable Amusement: And if the Subject be curious and interesting, the Book carries us, in a manner, into Company, and unites the two greatest and purest Pleasures of
25 human Life, Study and Society.[3]

Happily, these Circumstances are all to be found in the Subject of NATURAL RELIGION. What Truth so obvious, so certain, as the *Being* of a God, which the most ignorant Ages have acknowleg'd; for which the most refin'd Geniuses have ambitiously striven to
30 produce new Proofs and Arguments? What Truth so important as this, which is the Ground of all our Hopes, the surest Foundation

---

11 compensate [for]   29 striven] strove

---

[2] Hurd, *Dialogues*, i. vi: 'I have said, *where the subject is proper for familiar discourse*; for all subjects, I think, cannot, or should not be treated in this way.'

[3] John Jortin, *Discourses concerning the Truth of the Christian Religion* (London, 1746), p. v: 'The same truths may be placed in various views; and amongst men whose taste and fancy differ so widely, an argument shall seem persuasive, and a remark pertinent to one, which by another is slighted and rejected . . .'.

of Morality, the firmest Support of Society, and the only Principle, which ought never to be a Moment absent from our Thoughts and Meditations? But in treating of this obvious and important Truth; what obscure Questions occur, concerning the *Nature* of that divine Being; his Attributes, his Decrees, his Plan of Providence? 5 These have been always subjected to the Disputations of Men: Concerning these, human Reason has not reach'd any certain Determination: But these are Topics so interesting, that we cannot restrain our restless Enquiry with regard to them; tho' nothing but Doubt, Uncertainty and Contradiction have, as yet, been the 10 Result of our most accurate Researches.

This I had lately occasion to observe, while I passed, as usual, part of the Summer Season with CLEANTHES, and was present at those Conversations of his with PHILO and DEMEA, of which I gave you lately some imperfect Account. Your Curiosity, you then told 15 me, was so excited, that I must of Necessity enter into a more exact Detail of their Reasonings, and display those various Systems, which they advanc'd with regard to so delicate a Subject as that of natural Religion. The remarkable Contrast in their Characters still farther rais'd your Expectations; while you oppos'd the accurate 20 philosophical Turn of *Cleanthes* to the careless Scepticism of *Philo*, or compar'd either of their Dispositions with the rigid inflexible Orthodoxy of *Demea*. My Youth render'd me a mere Auditor of their Disputes; and that Curiosity natural to the early Season of Life, has so deeply imprinted in my Memory the whole Chain and 25 Connexion of their Arguments, that, I hope, I shall not omit or confound any considerable Part of them in the Recital.

PART 1

After I join'd the Company, whom I found sitting in *Cleanthes's* Library, *Demea* pay'd *Cleanthes* some Compliments, on the great 30 Care, which he took of my Education, and on his unweary'd Perseverance and Constancy in all his Friendships. The Father of *Pamphilus*, said he, was your intimate Friend: The Son is your

12 passed] past   19 in] of

Pupil, and may indeed be regarded as your adopted Son; were we to judge by the Pains which you bestow in conveying to him every useful Branch of Literature and Science.[1] You are no more wanting, I am perswaded, in Prudence than in Industry. I shall, therefore, 5 communicate to you a Maxim which I have observ'd with regard to my own Children, that I may learn how far it agrees with your Practice. The Method I follow in their Education is founded on the Saying of an Antient, *that Students of Philosophy ought first to learn Logics, then Ethics, next Physics, last of all, of the Nature of the Gods.*[a][2] 10 This Science of natural Theology, according to him, being the most profound and abstruse of any, requir'd the maturest Judgement in its Students; and none but a Mind, enrich'd with all the other Sciences, can safely be entrusted with it.

Are you so late, says *Philo*, in teaching your Children the Prin- 15 ciples of Religion? Is there no Danger of their neglecting or rejecting altogether those Opinions, of which they have heard so little, during the whole Course of their Education? It is only as a Science, reply'd *Demea*, subjected to human Reasoning and Disputation, that I post-pone the Study of natural Theology. To season 20 their Minds with early Piety is my chief Care; and by continual Precept and Instruction, and I hope too, by Example, I imprint deeply on their tender Minds an habitual Reverence for all the

[a] Chrysippus apud Plut: *de repug: Stoicorum.*

1 regarded as] said to be   2 which you bestow in conveying to him] you take of instructing him in   14 in teaching your Children] of instructing your Children in   16–17 of which . . . little] which . . . little of

[1] Philip Skelton, *Ophiomaches: or, Deism Revealed* (London, 1749), i. 11: 'As to my conscience, the late Mr. *Templeton*, father to this young Gentleman here, left him at the age of fifteen . . . to my care; and no one can say, I have not discharged this important trust like a man of honour. I have improved his fortune; I have given him a polite education . . .'. Hume had been the 'reader' of this book for Millar, the publisher, and recommended publication; written in dialogue form, it was also the first to notice 'Of Miracles'. Cf. Mossner, *Life*, p. 232.

[2] Hume is quoting from Plutarch's account of the Stoic philosophy of Chrysippus, *De Stoicorum repugnantiis* in Plutarch's *Moralia.* Cf. *The Philosophie, commonlie called, the Morals*, trans. Philemon Holland (London, 1657), p. 867 : '*Chrysippus* is of opinion that yo[u]ng Scholars and students should first learn those arts which concern speech, as Grammar, Logick, and Rhetorick; in the second place Morall Sciences; in the third Naturall Philosophy, and after all these, in the last place, to hear the doctrine as touching Religion and the Gods . . .'.

Principles of Religion. While they pass thro every other Science,
I still remark the Uncertainty of each Part, the eternal Disputations
of Men, the Obscurity of all Philosophy, and the strange, ridiculous
Conclusions, which some of the greatest Geniuses have derived
from the Principles of mere human Reason. Having thus tam'd 5
their Mind to a proper Submission and Self-Diffidence, I have no
longer any scruple of opening to them the greatest Mysteries of
Religion, nor apprehend any Danger from that assuming Arro-
gance of Philosophy, which may lead them to reject the most
establish'd Doctrines and Opinions.   10

Your Precaution, says *Philo*, of seasoning your Children's Minds
with early Piety, is certainly very reasonable; and no more than is
requisite, in this profane and irreligious Age.[3] But what I chiefly
admire in your Plan of Education is your Method of drawing
Advantage from the very Principles of Philosophy and Learning, 15
which, by inspiring Pride and Self-Sufficiency, have commonly, in
all Ages, been found so destructive to the Principles of Religion.
The Vulgar, indeed, we may remark, who are unacquainted with
Science and profound Enquiry, observing the endless Disputes of
the Learned, have commonly a thorough Contempt for Philosophy; 20
and rivet themselves the faster, by that means, in the great Points
of Theology, which have been taught them. Those, who enter a
little into Study and Enquiry, finding many Appearances of
Evidence in Doctrines the newest and most extraordinary, think
nothing too difficult for human Reason; and presumptuously 25
breaking thro all Fences, profane the inmost Sanctuaries of the
Temple. But *Cleanthes* will, I hope, agree with me, that, after we
have abandon'd Ignorance, the surest Remedy, there is still one
Expedient left to prevent this profane Liberty. Let *Demea's* Principles
be improv'd and cultivated: Let us become thoroughly sensible of 30

1 every] all the   Science] Sciences   2 each] every   6–7 I have
no longer any scruple of opening to them] no longer scruple to open to them
8 Danger] thing   12 than [what]   30 embrac'd *deleted after*
be   thoroughly] thorowly

[3] George Berkeley, *Alciphron* (London, 1732), I. 21: 'Then casting an Eye on the
Education of Children, from whence I can make a judgment of my own, I observe
they are instructed in religious matters before they can reason about them, and
consequently that all such instruction is nothing else but filling the tender mind of
a Child with prejudices.'

the Weakness, Blindness, and narrow Limits of human Reason:
Let us duely consider its Uncertainty and endless Contrarieties,
even in Subjects of common Life and Practice: Let the Errors and
Deceits of our very Senses be set before us; the insuperable Diffi-
5 culties, which attend first Principles in all Systems; the Contradictions, which adhere to the very Ideas of Matter, Cause and Effect,
Extension, Space, Time, Motion; and in a Word, Quantity of all
kinds, the Object of the only Science, that can fairly pretend to any
Certainty or Evidence. When these Topics are display'd in their
10 full Light, as they are by some Philosophers and almost all Divines;
who can retain such Confidence in this frail Faculty of Reason as to
pay any Regard to its Determinations in Points so sublime, so
abstruse, so remote from common Life and Experience? When the
Coherence of the Parts of a Stone, or even that Composition of Parts,
15 which renders it extended; when these familiar Objects, I say, are
so inexplicable, and contain Circumstances so repugnant and
contradictory; with what Assurance can we decide concerning the
Origin of Worlds, or trace their History from Eternity to Eternity?

While *Philo* pronounc'd these Words, I cou'd observe a Smile in
20 the Countenances both of *Demea* and *Cleanthes*. That of *Demea*
seem'd to imply an unreserv'd Satisfaction in the Doctrines deliver'd: But in *Cleanthes's* Features, I cou'd distinguish an Air of
Finesse; as if he perceiv'd some Raillery or artificial Malice in the
Reasonings of *Philo*.

25   You propose then, *Philo*, said *Cleanthes*, to erect religious Faith on
philosophical Scepticism; and you think, that if Certainty or
Evidence be expell'd from every other Subject of Enquiry, it will
all retire to these theological Doctrines, and there acquire a
superior Force and Authority. Whether your Scepticism be as
30 absolute and sincere as you pretend, we shall learn bye and bye,
when the company breaks up: We shall then see, whether you go
out at the Door or the Window; and whether you really doubt, if
your Body has Gravity, or can be injured by its Fall; according
to popular Opinion, deriv'd from our fallacious Senses and more

2 Uncertainty] Fallaciousness   4 Deceits] Uncertainty   5 all
[Sciences]   8 that] which   13 and [Practice]   23 Finesse [and
Raillery]   25 *Cleanthes*] he   31 breaks] shall break   33-4 according
to [pub(lic)]

fallacious Experience. And this Consideration, *Demea*, may, I think, fairly serve to abate our Ill-will to this humorous Sect of the Sceptics. If they be thoroughly in earnest, they will not long trouble the World with their Doubts, Cavils, and Disputes: If they be only in Jest, they are, perhaps, bad Raillyers, but can never be 5 very dangerous, either to the State, to Philosophy, or to Religion.

In reality, *Philo*, continu'd he, it seems certain, that tho' a Man, in a Flush of Humour, after intense Reflection on the many Contradictions and Imperfections of human Reason, may entirely renounce all Belief and Opinion; it is impossible for him to persevere 10 in this total Scepticism, or make it appear in his Conduct for a few Hours. External Objects press in upon him: Passions sollicit him: His philosophical Melancholy dissipates; and even the utmost Violence upon his own Temper will not be able, during any time, to preserve the poor Appearance of Scepticism.[4] And for what 15 Reason impose on himself such a Violence? This is a Point, in which it will be impossible for him ever to satisfy himself, consistent with his sceptical Principles: So that upon the whole nothing cou'd be more ridiculous than the Principles of the antient *Pyrrhonians*; if in reality they endeavour'd, as is pretended, to 20 extend throughout, the same Scepticism, which they had learn'd from the Declamations of their School, and which they ought to have confin'd to them.

In this View, there appears a great Ressemblance between the Sects of the *Stoics* and *Pyrrhonians*, tho' perpetual Antagonists: And 25 both of them seem founded on this erroneous Maxim, that what a Man can perform sometimes, and in some Dispositions, he can perform always, and in every Disposition. When the Mind, by stoical Reflections, is elevated into a sublime Enthusiasm of Virtue,

---

2 humorous] pleasant   4 with] by   16 Reason [shou'd he] in] concerning
21 extend throughout] introduce into common Life   21–2 which they had learn'd from the Declamations of their School] which they had learn'd from the Sciences] they had learn'd from the Declamation[s] in their Schools

---

[4] Cf. *Treatise*, I. iv. 7 (p. 316): 'Most fortunately it happens, that since reason is incapable of dispelling these clouds, nature herself suffices to that purpose, and cures me of this philosophical melancholy and delirium, either by relaxing this bent of mind, or by some avocation, and lively impression of my senses, which obliterate all these chimeras. I dine, I play a game of backgammon, I converse, and am merry with my friends . . .'.

and strongly smit with any *Species* of Honour or public Good, the utmost bodily Pain and Sufferance will not prevail over such a high Sense of Duty; and tis possible, perhaps, by its means, even to smile and exult in the midst of Tortures. If this sometimes may be
5 the Case in Fact and Reality, much more may a Philosopher, in his School, or even in his Closet, work himself up to such an Enthusiasm, and support in Imagination the acutest Pain or most calamitous Event, which he can possibly conceive. But how shall he support this Enthusiasm itself? The Bent of his Mind relaxes, and cannot be
10 recall'd at Pleasure: Avocations lead him astray: Misfortunes attack him unawares: And the *Philosopher* sinks by degrees into the *Plebeian*.

✓   I allow of your Comparison between the *Stoics* and *Sceptics*, reply'd
Philo. But you may observe, at the same time, that tho' the Mind cannot, in Stoicism, support the highest Flights of Philosophy, yet
15 even when it sinks lower, it still retains somewhat of its former Disposition; and the Effects of the Stoic's Reasoning will appear in his Conduct in common Life, and thro' the whole Tenor of his Actions. The antient Schools, particularly that of *Zeno*, produc'd Examples of Virtue and Constancy, which seem astonishing to present times.

20   Vain Wisdom all and false Philosophy.
          Yet with a pleasing Sorcery cou'd charm
          Pain, for a while, or Anguish, and excite
          Fallacious Hope, or arm the obdurate Breast
          With stubborn Patience, as with triple Steel.[5]

---

2 not prevail over] make small Impression, in opposition to   10 lead him astray] call him aside   12 *Sceptics*, [as just]   13 may] must   16 Stoic's Reasoning will appear in his] its Reasoning appear in its] his Reasoning appear in its   17 his] its   18 that of] the school of

---

[5] John Milton, *Paradise Lost*, ii. 565–9. Hume has changed Milton's 'obdured' to 'obdurate'. In his *History of England* (vi. 125), Hume had written of Milton, 'His Paradise Lost, his Comus, and a few others, shine out amidst some flat and insipid compositions: Even in the Paradise Lost, his capital performance, there are very long passages, amounting to near a third of the work, almost wholly devoid of harmony and elegance, nay of all vigor of imagination. The natural inequality in Milton's genius was much increased by the inequalities in his subject; of which some parts are of themselves the most lofty that can enter into human conception, others would have required the most labored elegance of composition to support them. It is certain, that this author, when in a happy mood, and employed on a noble subject, is the most wonderfully sublime of any poet in any language; Homer and Lucretius and Tasso not excepted.'

In like manner, if a man has accustom'd himself to sceptical Considerations on the Uncertainty and narrow Limits of Reason, he will not entirely forget them when he turns his Reflection on other Subjects; but in all his philosophical Principles and Reasoning, I dare not say, in his common Conduct, he will be found different 5 from those, who either never form'd any Opinions in the Case, or have entertain'd Sentiments more favourable to human Reason.

To whatever Length any-one may push his speculative Principles of Scepticism, he must act, I own, and live, and converse like other Men; and for this Conduct he is not oblig'd to give any other 10 Reason, than the absolute Necessity he lies under of so doing. If he ever carries his Speculations farther than this Necessity constrains him, and philosophizes, either on natural or moral Subjects, he is allur'd by a certain Pleasure and Satisfaction, which he finds in employing himself after that manner. He considers besides, that 15 every one, even in common Life, is constrain'd to have more or less of this Philosophy; that from our earliest Infancy we make continual Advances in forming more general Principles of Conduct and Reasoning; that the larger Experience we acquire, and the stronger Reason we are endow'd with, we always render our 20 Principles the more general and comprehensive; and that what we call *Philosophy* is nothing but a more regular and methodical Operation of the same kind. To philosophize on such Subjects is nothing essentially different from reasoning on common Life; and we may only expect greater Stability, if not greater Truth, from our 25 Philosophy, on account of its exacter and more scrupulous Method of proceeding.

But when we look beyond human Affairs and the Properties of the surrounding Bodies: When we carry our Speculations into the two Eternities, before and after the present State of things; into 30 the Creation and Formation of the Universe; the Existence and Properties of Spirits; the Powers and Operations of one universal Spirit, existing without Beginning and without End; omnipotent, omniscient, immutable, infinite, and incomprehensible: We must

---

1–2 Considerations] Reflections   3–4 turns his Reflection on other Subjects] leaves his Closet   8 It seems obvious, that *deleted before* To   17–18 make continual Advances] are continually advancing

be far removed from the smallest Tendency to Scepticism not to
be apprehensive, that we have here got quite beyond the Reach of
our Faculties. So long as we confine our Speculations to Trade or
Morals or Politics or Criticism, we make Appeals, every moment,
5 to common Sense and Experience, which strengthen our philosophical Conclusions, and remove (at least, in part) the Suspicion,
which we so justly entertain with regard to every Reasoning, that
is very subtile and refin'd. But in theological Reasonings, we have
not this Advantage; while at the same time we are employ'd upon
10 Objects, which, we must be sensible, are too large for our Grasp,
and of all others, require most to be familiariz'd to our Apprehension. We are like Foreigners in a strange Country, to whom every
thing must seem suspicious, and who are in danger every Moment
of transgressing against the Laws and Customs of the People, with
15 whom they live and converse. We know not how far we ought to
trust our vulgar Methods of Reasoning in such a Subject; since,
even in common Life and in that Province, which is peculiarly
appropriated to them, we cannot account for them, and are entirely
guided by a kind of Instinct or Necessity in employing them.
20   All Sceptics pretend, that, if Reason be consider'd in an abstract
View, it furnishes invincible Arguments against itself, and that
we cou'd never retain any Conviction or Assurance, on any Subject,
were not the sceptical Reasonings so refin'd and subtile, that they
are not able to counterpoize the more solid and more natural
25 Arguments, deriv'd from the Senses and Experience. But it is
evident, whenever our Arguments lose this Advantage, and run
wide of common Life, that the most refin'd Scepticism comes to be
on a Footing with them, and is able to oppose and counterballance
them. The one has no more Weight than the other. The Mind must
30 remain in Suspence between them; and it is that very Suspence or
Ballance, which is the Triumph of Scepticism.
      But I observe, says *Cleanthes,* with regard to you, *Philo,* and all

3 So] As   7 with regard to] concerning   13 must seem] seems
15 ought to] shou'd   16 a Subject] Subjects   19 *The following passage
indicated on the margin for inclusion at the end of this paragraph but deleted:* A very small
Part of this great System, during a very small time, is very imperfectly discovered
to us: And do we thence pronounce decisively concerning the Whole?   22 on
any Subject] even in the most common Affairs of Life   26 evident, [that]

speculative Sceptics, that your Doctrine and Practice are as much at Variance in the most abstruse Points of Theory as in the Conduct of common Life. Wherever Evidence discovers itself, you adhere to it, notwithstanding your pretended Scepticism; and I can observe too some of your Sect to be as decisive as those, who make greater Professions of Certainty and Assurance. In reality, would not a Man be ridiculous, who pretended to reject *Newton's* Explication of the wonderful Phænomenon of the Rainbow,[6] because that Explication gives a minute Anatomy of the Rays of Light; a Subject, forsooth, too refin'd for human Comprehension? And what wou'd you say to one, who having nothing particular to object to the Arguments of *Copernicus*[7] and *Galilaeo* for the Motion of the Earth, shou'd with-hold his Assent, on that general Principle, that these Subjects were too magnificent and remote to be explain'd by the narrow and fallacious Reason of Mankind?

There is indeed a kind of brutish and ignorant Scepticism, as you well observ'd, which gives the Vulgar a general Prejudice against what they do not easily understand, and makes them reject every Principle, which requires elaborate Reasoning to prove and establish it. This Species of Scepticism is fatal to Knowledge, not to Religion; since we find, that those who make greatest Profession of it, give often their Assent, not only to the great Truths of Theism, and natural Theology, but even to the most absurd Tenets, which a traditional Superstition has recommended to them. They firmly believe in Witches;[8] tho they will not believe nor attend to the

5 make] used   6 Assurance] Dogmatism [*This correction does not appear to be in Hume's hand*]   8 the[1]] that   11 object to] oppose to to the Arguments of   12 Arguments of *Copernicus* and *Galilaeo*] *Copernicus'* and *Galilaeo's* Arguments   16 brutish] brutal   16–17 as you well observ'd] as you observ'd very well   20 Knowledge, [but]   23 Theology] Religion   24 has recommended] can recommend

[6] Newton's *Opticks* (London, 1704). 'The First Book of Opticks', Pt. II, Prop. ix, Prob. iv (pp. 126–34).

[7] Nicholaus Copernicus, *De Revolutionibus Orbium Coelestrum, Libri VI* (Nuremberg, 1543), *passim*. Cf. the translation of the Preface and Book I by John F. Dobson and Selig Brodetsky, Occasional Note No. 10 of the Royal Astronomical Society (London 1947), pp. 10–11, 14–15, 20–1.

[8] Duncan Forbes, *Some Thoughts concerning Religion, Natural and Revealed* (Edinburgh, 1743), p. 13: 'It is impossible to believe any thing more firmly, than the vulgar do that the earth stands still, and that the sun moves round. . . . Where the common opinions about the devil, witches, witchcraft, &c. prevail, the belief is transmitted to posterity, and the children doubt as little as the fathers did.'

most simple Proposition of *Euclid*. But the refin'd and philosophical Sceptics fall into an Inconsistence of an opposite Nature. They push their Researches into the most abstruse Corners of Science; and their Assent attends them in every Step, proportion'd to the
5 Evidence, which they meet with. They are even oblig'd to acknowledge, that the most abstruse and remote Objects are those, which are best explain'd by Philosophy. Light is in reality anatomiz'd: The true System of the heavenly Bodies is discover'd and ascertain'd. But the Nourishment of Bodies by Food is still an
10 inexplicable Mystery: The Cohesion of the Parts of Matter is still incomprehensible. These Sceptics, therefore, are oblig'd, in every Question, to consider each particular Evidence apart, and proportion their Assent to the precise Degree of Evidence, which occurs. This is their Practice in all natural, mathematical, moral, and politi-
15 cal Science. And why not the same, I ask, in the theological and religious? Why must Conclusions of this Nature be alone rejected on the general Presumption of the Insufficiency of human Reason, without any particular Discussion of the Evidence? Is not such an unequal Conduct a plain Proof of Prejudice and Passion?
20 Our Senses, you say, are fallacious, our Understanding erroneous, our Ideas even of the most familiar Objects, Extension, Duration, Motion, full of Absurdities and Contradictions. You defy me to solve the Difficulties, or reconcile the Repugnancies, which you discover in them. I have not Capacity for so great an Undertaking:
25 I have not Leizure for it: I perceive it to be superfluous. Your own Conduct, in every Circumstance, refutes your Principles; and shows the firmest Reliance on all the receiv'd Maxims of Science, Morals, Prudence, and Behaviour.

I shall never assent to so harsh an Opinion as that of a celebrated
30 Writer,[b] who says that the Sceptics are not a Sect of Philosophers: They are only a Sect of Lyars. I may, however, affirm, (I hope,

---

[b] *L'Art de penser.*

---

2 fall into] are guilty of   3 Science] the Sciences   8 Bodies is [really]
9 Nourishment of Bodies by Food] falling of a Stone   10 the Parts of
Matter] its Parts   26 shows] masks *or* marks   [b]1 The Author of *deleted before*
L'Art de penser.

without Offence), that they are a Sect of Jesters or Railliers.[9] But for my Part, whenever I find myself dispos'd to Mirth and Amusement, I shall certainly choose my Entertainment of a less perplexing and abstruse Nature. A Comedy, a Novel, or at most a History, seems a more natural Recreation than such metaphysical Subtilities and Abstractions.

In vain wou'd the Sceptic make a Distinction between Science and common Life, or between one Science and another. The Arguments, employ'd in all, if just, are of a similar Nature, and contain the same Force and Evidence. Or if there be any Difference among them, the Advantage lies entirely on the Side of Theology and natural Religion. Many Principles of Mechanics are founded on very abstruse Reasoning; yet no Man, who has any Pretensions to Science, even no speculative Sceptic, pretends to entertain the least doubt with regard to them. The *Copernican* System contains the most surprizing Paradox, and the most contrary to our natural Conceptions, to Appearances, and to our very Senses: Yet even Monks and Inquisitors are now constrain'd to withdraw their Opposition to it. And shall *Philo*, a Man of so liberal a Genius, and extensive Knowledge, entertain any general undistinguish'd Scruples with regard to the religious Hypothesis, which is founded on the simplest and most obvious Arguments, and, unless it meet with artificial Obstacles, has such easy Access and Admission into the Mind of Man?

And here we may observe, continu'd he, turning himself towards *Demea*, a pretty curious Circumstance in the History of the Sciences. After the Union of Philosophy with the popular Religion, upon the first Establishment of Christianity, nothing was more usual, among all religious Teachers, than Declamations against Reason, against the Senses, against every Principle, deriv'd merely from human Research and Enquiry. All the Topics of the antient Academics were adopted by the Fathers; and thence propagated

2 to] for   3 Entertainment] Sports   18 constrain'd] oblig'd
30 merely] entirely   32 Academics [and Sceptics]

[9] Hume is referring to *La Logique ou l'art de penser* (1662), by Antoine Arnauld (1612–94) and Pierre Nicol (1625–95). Cf. the translation by John Ozell, *Logic; or the Art of Thinking* (London, 1723), p. 6: 'So that Pyrrhonism is not a Sect of People that are themselves convinced of what they teach, but a Sect of Lyars.'

for several Ages in every School and Pulpit throughout Christen-
dom. The Reformers embrac'd the same Principles of Reasoning, or
rather Declamation; and all Panegyrics on the Excellency of Faith
were sure to be interlarded with some severe Strokes of Satyre
5 against natural Reason. A celebrated Prelate*c* too, of the Romish
Communion, a Man of the most extensive Learning, who wrote
a Demonstration of Christianity, has also compos'd a Treatise,
which contains all the Cavils of the boldest and most determin'd
Pyrrhonism. Locke seems to have been the first Christian, who
10 ventur'd openly to assert, that *Faith* was nothing but a Species of
Reason, that Religion was only a Branch of Philosophy, and that a
Chain of Arguments, similar to that which establish'd any Truth
in Morals, Politics, or Physics, was always employ'd in discovering
all the Principles of Theology, natural and reveal'd.[10] The ill Use,
15 which *Bayle* and other Libertines made of the philosophical Scepticism of the Fathers and first Reformers, still farther propagated
the judicious Sentiment of Mr *Locke*: And it is now, in a manner,
avow'd, by all Pretenders to Reasoning and Philosophy, that Atheist
and Sceptic are almost synonimous. And as it is certain, that no
20 man is in earnest, when he professes the latter Principle; I wou'd
fain hope, that there are as few, who seriously maintain the former.

Don't you remember, said *Philo*, the excellent Saying of Lord
Bacon on this head. That a little Philosophy, reply'd *Cleanthes*,

---

c Mons.! Huet.[11]

---

3 all] every   4 were] was   5 Prelate] Writer   9 *Locke*] Mr
Locke   who] that   11 that a [liker]

---

[10] John Locke, *An Essay concerning Humane Understanding* (London, 1690), IV. xvii.
24, p. 347: 'Only I think it may not be amiss to take notice, that however Faith be
opposed to Reason, Faith is nothing but a firm Assent of the Mind; which if it be
regulated, as is our Duty, cannot be afforded to any thing but upon good Reason;
and so cannot be opposite to it.' Cf. Locke's *The Reasonableness of Christianity* (London,
1695), where the tenor of the argument maintains the compliance of faith and reason,
e.g.: '[God gave man] Reason, and with it a Law: That could not be otherwise than
what Reason should dictate . . .' (p. 301).
[11] Peter Daniel Huet (1630–1721), Bishop of Afranches. Hume refers to his *Traite
philosophique de la foiblesse de l'esprit humain* (1723); trans. by Edward Combe, *A
Philosophical Treatise concerning the Weakness of Human Understanding* (London, 1725).
The fourteenth chapter ('Proof XIII. *That the Law of doubting has been established by
many excellent Philosophers*') enumerates the ancients who lend historical validity to
the value of sceptical doubts.

makes a Man an Atheist: A great deal converts him to Religion.[12]
That is a very judicious Remark too, said *Philo*. But what I have in
my Eye is another Passage,[13] where, having mention'd *David*'s Fool,
who said in his Heart there is no God,[14] this great Philosopher observes, that the Atheists now a days have a double Share of Folly: 5
For they are not contented to say in their Hearts there is no God, but
they also utter that Impiety with their Lips, and are thereby guilty
of multiply'd Indiscretion and Imprudence. Such People, tho they
were ever so much in earnest, cannot, methinks, be very formidable.

But tho you shou'd rank me in this Class of Fools, I cannot forbear 10
communicating a Remark, that occurs to me from the History of
the religious and irreligious Scepticism, with which you have
entertain'd us. It appears to me, that there are strong Symptoms of
Priestcraft in the whole Progress of this Affair. During ignorant
Ages, such as those which follow'd the Dissolution of the antient 15
Schools, the Priests perceiv'd, that Atheism, Deism, or Heresy of
any kind cou'd only proceed from the presumptuous questioning
of receiv'd Opinions, and from a Belief, that human Reason was
equal to every thing. Education had then a mighty Influence over
the Minds of Men, and was almost equal in Force to those Sug- 20
gestions of the Senses and common Understanding, by which the
most determin'd Sceptic must allow himself to be govern'd. But
at present, when the Influence of Education is much diminish'd,
and Men, from a more open Commerce of the World, have learn'd
to compare the popular Principles of different Nations and Ages, 25
our sagacious Divines have chang'd their whole System of Philosophy, and talk the Language of *Stoics*, *Platonists*, and *Peripatetics*, not
that of *Pyrrhonians* and *Academics*. If we distrust human Reason, we ✓

 2–3 have in my Eye] mean   7 that] their   10 in] under   14 During] In
17 questioning] Questioning   23 when] that   27 Language of [the] not]
instead of   28 that of [the]

---

 [12] Francis Bacon, *Essays* (London, 1706), p. 42: 'It is true, that a little Philosophy
inclineth Man's mind to *Atheism*, but depth in Philosophy bringeth Mens minds
about to Religion . . .' (Essay 16). Cf. *Works*, ix. 132.
 [13] In Bacon's *Meditationes Sacrae* in the *Essays*, 'Of Atheism'.
 [14] Psalm 14: 1: 'The fool hath said in his heart, There is no God.' Cf. George
Cheyne, *Philosophical Principles of Religion, Natural and Revealed* (London, 1725), p. 178:
'The *Fool* indeed, *may have said in his Heart there is no God* . . .'.

have now no other Principle to lead us into Religion. Thus, Sceptics in one Age, Dogmatists in another;[15] which-ever System best
suits the Purpose of these reverend Gentlemen, in giving them an
Ascendant over Mankind, they are sure to make it their favorite
5 Principle, and establish'd Tenet.

It is very natural, said *Cleanthes*, for Men to embrace those
Principles, by which they find they can best defend their Doctrines;
nor need we have any Recourse to Priestcraft to account for so
reasonable an Expedient.[16] And surely, nothing can afford a
10 stronger Presumption, that any set of Principles are true, and
ought to be embrac'd, than to observe, that they tend to the Confirmation of true Religion, and serve to confound the Cavils of
Atheists, Libertines and Freethinkers of all Denominations.

PART 2

15 I must own, *Cleanthes*, said *Demea*, that nothing can more surprize
me, than the Light, in which you have, all along, put this Argument. By the whole Tenor of your Discourse, one wou'd imagine
that you were maintaining the Being of a God, against the Cavils
of Atheists and Infidels; and were necessitated to become a Cham-
20 pion for that fundamental Principle of all Religion. But this, I hope,
is not, by any means, a Question among us. No man; no man, at
least, of common Sense,[1] I am perswaded, ever entertain'd a serious

---

3 suits] serves   reverend Gentlemen] the Clergy   4 they are sure to make
it] is sure to be   5 Tenet] System   15 said] says   16 put] taken
18 were] was

[15] Cf. *Spectator*, 109 [Addison]: 'Hypocrisy in one Age is generally succeeded by
Atheism in another . . .'.

[16] Berkeley, *Alciphron*, I. 12: 'Priests of all Religion are the same, wherever there
are Priests there will be Priestcraft, and wherever there is Priestcraft there will be
a persecuting Spirit, which they never fail to exert to the utmost of their power
against all those who have the courage to think for themselves, and will not submit
to be hoodwinked and manacled by their Reverend leaders. . . . Cruelty and Ambition being the darling vices of Priests and Churchmen all the world over, they endeavour in all Countries to get an ascendant over the rest of mankind . . .'.

[1] Doubtless an allusion to Thomas Reid and his *Inquiry into the Human Mind, on
the Principles of Common Sense* (Edinburgh, 1764), where Reid had written (p. 26), 'It is
probable that the *Treatise of Human Nature* was not written in company; yet it contains manifest indications, that the author every now and then relapsed into the

Doubt with regard to a Truth so certain and self-evident. The
Question is not concerning the BEING, but the NATURE of GOD.
This I affirm, from the Infirmities of human Understanding, to be
altogether incomprehensible and unknown to us. The Essence of
that supreme Mind, his Attributes, the manner of his Existence, 5
the very Nature of his Duration; these and every particular, which
regards so divine a Being, are mysterious to Men. Finite, weak,
and blind Creatures, we ought to humble Ourselves in his august
Presence, and, conscious of our Frailties, adore in Silence his
infinite Perfections, which Eye hath not seen, Ear hath not heard, 10
neither hath it enter'd into the Heart of Man to conceive them.
They are covered in a deep Cloud from human Curiosity: It is
Profaneness to attempt penetrating thro' these sacred Obscurities:
And next to the Impiety of denying his Existence, is the Temerity
of prying into his Nature and Essence, Decrees and Attributes.[2] 15

But lest you should think, that my *Piety* has here got the better
of my *Philosophy*, I shall support my Opinion, if it needs any Support,
by a very great Authority. I might cite all the Divines almost, from
the Foundation of Christianity, who have ever treated of this or
any other theological Subject: But I shall confine myself, at present, 20
to one equally celebrated for Piety and Philosophy. It is Father
Malebranche, who, I remember, thus expresses himself.[a] 'One ought
not so much (says he) to call God a Spirit, in order to express
positively what he is, as in order to signify that he is not Matter.
He is a Being infinitely perfect: Of this we cannot doubt. But in 25
the same manner as we ought not to imagine, even supposing him

[a] *Recherche de la Verité.* Liv. 3. Chap. 9.

---

2 NATURE] Nature   4 The] His   5 supreme] divine   6 which] that
7 mysterious] mysterious and inconceivable   11 neither hath] nor has
12 They] These   13 thro'] into   23 express] signify

---

faith of the vulgar, and could hardly, for half a dozen pages, keep up the sceptical
character.' Reid had sent the manuscript of this book to Hume, via Hugh Blair, for
his opinion; Hume ironically corrected only the style. Cf. John Hill Burton, *Life
and Correspondence of David Hume* (Edinburgh, 1846), ii. 153–6; *Letters*, i. 375–6.

[2] Cf. Henry Home, Lord Kames, *Essays on the Principles of Morality and Natural
Religion* (Edinburgh, 1751), p. 335: 'The essence of the Deity is far beyond the reach
of our comprehension. Were he to exhibit himself to us, in broad day-light, it is not
a thing supposable, that he could be reached by any of our external senses . . . there
are no ordinary means to acquire any knowledge of the Deity, but by his works.'

corporeal, that he is cloath'd with a human Body, as the *Anthropo-morphites* asserted, under colour that that figure was the most perfect of any; so neither ought we to imagine, that the Spirit of God has human Ideas, or bears *any* Ressemblance to our Spirit; under colour
5 that we know nothing more perfect than a human Mind. We ought rather to believe, that as he comprehends the Perfections of Matter without being material . . . he comprehends also the Perfections of created Spirits, without being Spirit, in the manner we conceive Spirit: That his true Name is, *He that is*, or in other Words, Being
10 without Restriction, All Being, the Being infinite and universal.'[3]

After so great an Authority, *Demea*, reply'd *Philo*, as that which you have produc'd, and a thousand more, which you might produce, it wou'd appear ridiculous in me to add my Sentiment, or express my Approbation of your Doctrine. But surely, where reasonable
15 Men treat these Subjects, the Question can never be concerning the *Being* but only the *Nature* of the Deity.[4] The former Truth, as you well observe, is unquestionable and self-evident. Nothing exists without a Cause; and the original Cause of this Universe (whatever it be) we call GOD; and piously ascribe to him every
20 Species of Perfection. Who ever scruples this fundamental Truth

---

1 is] was   13 Sentiment] Testimony

---

[3] Nicolas Malebranche, *De Recherché de verité. Ou l'on traité de la nature de l'esprit de l'homme* (Paris, 1678), i. 427–8. Cf. *Malebranche's Search after Truth. Or a Treatise of the Nature of the Humane Mind*, trans. Richard Sault (London, 1694), pp. 75–6: 'Therefor we must not Judge rashly, that the word Spirit which we use to express what God is, and what we are, is an Equivocal Term, which signifies the same things, or things that are very like. God is more above Created Spirits, than those Spirits are above Bodies; and we ought not so much to call God a Spirit to shew positively what he is, as to signifie that he is not Material. He is a Being infinitely Perfect, no body can question it. But as we must not imagin with the *Anthropomorphites*, that he must have a Human Figure, because it seems to be most perfect, although we should suppose him Corporeal, neither must we imagin that the Spirit of God has any Human Thoughts: And that his Spirit is like unto ours, because we know nothing that is more perfect than our Spirit. We must rather believe, that as he possesses the Perfections of Matter without being Material, since it is certain that Matter has a relation to some Perfections that are in God; he also possesses the Perfections of Created Spirits, without being a Spirit in the manner as we conceive Spirits: That his Name is, *He that is*; that is, the unlimited Being, the All-Being, the Infinite and Universal Being.'
[4] Cf. Cicero, *De Natura Deorum*, trans. R. Francklin (London, 1741), p. 89: 'All Nations agree that there *are Gods*; the Opinion is innate, and as it were engraved in the Minds of all Men. The Difference amongst us is, *what they are*. Their Existence no one denies.'

deserves every Punishment, which can be inflicted among Philosophers, to wit, the greatest Ridicule, Contempt and Disapprobation. But as all Perfection is entirely relative, we ought never to
imagine, that we comprehend the Attributes of this divine Being,
or to suppose, that his Perfections have any Analogy or Likeness to 5
the Perfections of a human Creature. Wisdom, Thought, Design,
Knowledge; these we justly ascribe to him; because these Words
are honourable among Men, and we have no other Language or
other Conceptions, by which we can express our Adoration of him.
But let us beware, lest we think, that our Ideas any wise correspond 10
to his Perfections, or that his Attributes have any Ressemblance to
these Qualities among Men. He is infinitely superior to our limited
View and Comprehension; and is more the Object of Worship in
the Temple than of Disputation in the Schools.

In reality, *Cleanthes*, continu'd he, there is no need of having 15
recourse to that affected Scepticism, so displeasing to you, in order
to come at this Determination. Our Ideas reach no farther than our
Experience: We have no Experience of divine Attributes and Operations: I need not conclude my Syllogism: You can draw the
Inference yourself. And it is a Pleasure to me (and I hope to you too) 20
that just Reasoning and sound Piety here concur in the same
Conclusion, and both of them establish the adorably mysterious
and incomprehensible Nature of the supreme Being.

Not to lose any time in Circumlocutions, said *Cleanthes*, addressing
himself to *Demea*, much less in replying to the pious Declamations 25
of *Philo*; I shall briefly explain how I conceive this Matter. Look
round the World: Contemplate the Whole and every Part of it:
You will find it to be nothing but one great Machine, subdivided
into an infinite Number of lesser Machines, which again admit of
Subdivisions, to a degree beyond what human Senses and Faculties 30
can trace and explain. All these various Machines, and even their
most minute Parts, are adjusted to each other with an Accuracy,
which ravishes into Admiration all Men, who have ever contem-
plated them. The curious adapting of Means to Ends, throughout

1 which] that   2 to wit] *viz.*   2–3 Disapprobation] Censure   3 ought]
are   9 express] mark   10 us [here]   wise] way   15–16 having recourse
to] any of   24 said] reply'd   addressing] turning   26 explain [to you]
33 who] that

all Nature, resembles exactly, tho it much exceeds, the Productions
of human Contrivance; of human Design, Thought, Wisdom, and
Intelligence. Since therefore the Effects resemble each other, we
are led to infer, by all the Rules of Analogy, that the Causes also
5 resemble; and that the Author of Nature is somewhat similar to the
Mind of Man; tho' possessed of much larger Faculties, proportion'd
to the Grandeur of the Work, which he has executed. By this
Argument *a posteriori*, and by this Argument alone, do we prove at
once the Existence of a Deity, and his Similarity to human Mind and
10 Intelligence.[5]

I shall be so free, *Cleanthes*, said *Demea*, as to tell you, that from
the Beginning I cou'd not approve of your Conclusion concerning
the Similarity of the Deity to Men;[6] still less can I approve of the
Mediums, by which you endeavour to establish it. What! No
15 Demonstration of the Being of a God! No abstract Arguments! No
Proofs *a priori*! Are these, which have hitherto been so much insisted on by Philosophers, all Fallacy, all Sophism? Can we reach
no farther in this Subject than Experience and Probability? I will
not say, that this is betraying the Cause of a Deity: But surely, by
20 this affected Candour, you give Advantages to Atheists, which

---

1 much] extremely   5–6 to the Mind] to the human Mind   13 Men;
[but]   16 hitherto been] been hitherto   18 in] on   Experience *deleted
and* moral Evidence *added above line and then changed back to* Experience

---

[5] George Cheyne, *Philosophical Principles of Religion*, pp. 5–6: 'All the *Integral*
Parts of *Nature*, have a beautiful *Resemblance*, *Similitude*, and *Analogy* to one
another, and to their Almighty *Original*, whose images, more or less expressive
according to their several Orders and Gradations, in the *Scale* of Beings, they are;
and they who are Masters in the noble Art of just *Analogy*, may from a tolerable
Knowledge in any one of the *Integral* Parts of Nature, extend their Contemplations
more securely to the whole or any other *Integral* Part less known. Thus this great
Machine of the Universe has a Resemblance to the lesser One of a *humane Creature*;
for, as in the last, the vital Functions are perform'd by general and constant Laws ...'.
See R. H. Hurlbutt III, 'David Hume and Scientific Theism,' *Journal of the History
of Ideas*, xvii (1956), 486–96.
[6] Cf. Hume, 'Of the Dignity of Human Nature' in *Essays* (Edinburgh, 1741), pp.
161–2: 'Some exalt our Species to the Skies, and represent Man as a Kind of human
Demi-God, that derives his Origin from Heaven, and retains evident Marks of his
Lineage and Descent.' Compare Charles Gildon, *The Deist's Manual* (London, 1705),
p. viii: 'It is the Glory of the Protestant Religion (return'd *Christophil*) that, in it,
you must not cease to be a Man, to be a good *Christian*: But on the contrary you
become more a Man, exert the highest Efforts of *Reason*, and exalt it to almost a
Divine Perfection.'

they never cou'd obtain, by the mere Dint of Argument and Reasoning.

What I chiefly scruple in this Subject, said *Philo,* is not so much,   ✓ that all religious Arguments are by *Cleanthes* reduc'd to Experience, as that they appear not to be even the most certain and irrefragable 5 of that inferior kind.[7] That a Stone will fall, that Fire will burn, that the Earth has Solidity, we have observ'd a thousand and a thousand times; and when any new Instance of this Nature is presented, we draw without hesitation the accustom'd Inference. The exact Similarity of the Cases gives us a perfect Assurance of a similar 10 Event; and a stronger Evidence is never desir'd nor sought after. But wherever you depart, in the least, from the Similarity of the Cases, you diminish proportionably the Evidence; and may at last bring it to a very weak *Analogy,* which is confessedly liable to Error and Uncertainty.[8] After having experienc'd the Circulation of the 15 Blood in human Creatures, we make no Doubt, that it takes Place in *Titius* and *Mævius*: But from its Circulation in Frogs and Fishes, it is only a Presumption, tho' a strong one, from Analogy, that it takes place in Men and other Animals. The analogical Reasoning is much weaker, when we infer the Circulation of the Sap in 20 Vegetables from our Experience, that the Blood circulates in Animals; and those, who hastily follow'd that imperfect Analogy, are found, by more accurate Experiments, to have been mistaken.

If we see a House, *Cleanthes,* we conclude, with the greatest

---

5 appear] are asserted   9 Inference [without any Scruples or Hesitation]
13 proportionably] as much from   14 liable to [great]   19 analogical
Reasoning] Analogy   20 when we] to   24 If] When   conclude] infer

---

[7] Francis Atterbury, *Sermons and Discourses on Several Subjects and Occasions* (London, 1735), ii. 70: '... how very Strong and Irrefragable the first Evidences of Christianity must be, since they appear (both from Reason and Revelation) to be such, as that They who resisted them, would resist every thing besides them'.

[8] Kames, *Essays on ... Morality and Natural Religion*, pp. 337-8: 'But, laying aside perception and feeling, I should be utterly at a loss, by any sort of reasoning, to conclude the existence of any one thing, from that of any other thing.... But, where experience fails me, I desire to know, by what step, what link in the chain of reasoning, am I to connect my past experience with this inference, that in every case, I ought to form the same conclusion? If it be said, that nature prompts us to judge of similar instances, by former experience; this is giving up reason and demonstration, to appeal to that very feeling, on which, I contend, the evidence of this truth must entirely rest.'

Certainty, that it had an Architect or Builder; because this is precisely that Species of Effect, which we have experienc'd to proceed from that Species of Cause. But surely you will not affirm, that the Universe bears such a Ressemblance to a House, that we
5 can with the same Certainty infer a similar Cause, or that the Analogy is here entire and perfect. The Dissimilitude is so striking, that the utmost you can here pretend to is a Guess, a Conjecture, a Presumption concerning a similar Cause; and how that Pretension will be receiv'd in the World, I leave you to consider.[9]

10   It wou'd surely be very ill receiv'd, reply'd *Cleanthes*; and I shou'd be deservedly blam'd and detested, did I allow, that the Proofs of a Deity amounted to no more than a Guess or Conjecture. But is the whole Adjustment of Means to Ends in a House and in the Universe so slight a Resemblance? The Œconomy of final Causes?
15 The Order, Proportion, and Arrangement of every Part? Steps of a Stair are plainly contriv'd, that human Legs may use them in mounting; and this Inference is certain and infallible.[10] Human Legs are also contriv'd for walking and mounting; and this Inference, I allow, is not altogether so certain, because of the Dis-
20 similarity which you remark; but does it, therefore, deserve the Name only of Presumption or Conjecture?

Good God! cry'd *Demea*, interrupting him, where are we? Zealous Defenders of Religion allow, that the Proofs of a Deity fall short of perfect Evidence! And you, *Philo*, on whose Assistance I
25 depended, in proving the adorable Mysteriousness of the divine Nature, do you assent to all these extravagant Opinions of *Cleanthes*?

2 experienc'd] Experience   6 so] too   7 utmost . . . to] utmost to
which you can here pretend   10 receiv'd [to be sure]   15 Steps] The Steps
25 depended [on]

[9] François Salignac de la Mothe de Fénelon, *A Demonstration of the Existence, Wisdom and Omnipotence of God*, trans. A. Boyer (London, 1713), pp. 180–1: 'What would one say of a Man who should set up for a subtil Philosopher, or (to use the Modern Expression) a FREE-THINKER, and who entring a House should maintain it was made by Chance, and that Art had not, in the least, contributed to render it commodious to Men, because there are Caves somewhat like that House, which yet were never dug by the Art of Man?' Cicero, *De Natura Deorum*, p. 92: 'When you behold a large and beautiful House, surely no one can persuade you it was built for Mice and Weasels, though you do not see the Master . . .'.
[10] Fénelon, p. 181: '*This Stair-Case is made up of Low Steps, that one may ascend it with Ease; and turns according to the Apartments and Stories it is to serve.*'

For what other Name can I give them? Or why spare my Censure, when such Principles are advanc'd, supported by such an Authority, before so young a Man as *Pamphilus*?

You seem not to apprehend, reply'd *Philo*, that I argue with *Cleanthes* in his own way; and by shewing him the dangerous Conse- 5 quences of his Tenets, hope at last to reduce him to our Opinion. But what sticks most with you, I observe, is the Representation which *Cleanthes* has made of the Argument *a posteriori*; and finding, that that Argument is likely to escape your hold and vanish into Air, you think it so disguis'd that you can scarcely believe it to 10 be set in its true Light. Now, however much I may dissent, in other respects, from the dangerous Principles of *Cleanthes*, I must allow, that he has fairly represented that Argument; and I shall endeavour so to state the Matter to you, that you will entertain no farther Scruples with regard to it. 15

Were a Man to abstract from every thing which he knows or has seen, he wou'd be altogether incapable, merely from his own Ideas, to determine what kind of Scene the Universe must be, or to give the Preference to one State or Situation of things above another. For as nothing, which he clearly conceives, cou'd be esteemed 20 impossible or implying a Contradiction, every Chimera of his Fancy wou'd be upon an equal Footing; nor cou'd he assign any just Reason, why he adheres to one Idea or System, and rejects the others, which are equally possible.

Again; after he opens his Eyes, and contemplates the World, 25 as it really is, it wou'd be impossible for him, at first, to assign the Cause of any one Event; much less, of the Whole of things or of the Universe. He might set his Fancy a rambling; and she might bring him in an infinite Variety of Reports and Representations. These wou'd all be possible; but being all equally possible, 30 he wou'd never, of himself, give a satisfactory Account for his

7–8 the Representation which *Cleanthes* has made] that you will not allow *Cleanthes* to have made a just Representation   9 that Argument] it   11 set in its true Light] the same   12 *Cleanthes*, [in other Respects]   13 represented] stated   14 so to state the Matter to you] to set the Matter before you in such a Light   will] shall   17 seen [of the Universe]   18 the Universe] it   20 cou'd be esteemd] is   21 implying] implies   22 wou'd be] is   cou'd] can   28 a] on] a   31 for] of

preferring one of them to the rest. Experience alone can point out to him the true Cause of any Phænomenon.

Now according to this Method of Reasoning, *Demea*, it follows (and is, indeed, tacitly allow'd by *Cleanthes* himself) that Order, 5 Arrangement, or the Adjustment of final Causes is not, of itself, any Proof of Design; but only so far as it has been experienc'd to proceed from that Principle. For aught we can know *a priori*, Matter may contain the Source or Spring of Order originally, within itself, as well as Mind does; and there is no more Difficulty in 10 conceiving, that the several Elements, from an internal unknown Cause, may fall into the most exquisite Arrangement, than to conceive that their Ideas, in the great, universal Mind, from a like internal, unknown Cause, fall into that Arrangement. The equal Possibility of both these Suppositions is allow'd. But by Experience 15 we find (according to *Cleanthes*) that there is a Difference between them. Throw several Pieces of Steel together, without Shape or Form; they will never arrange themselves so as to compose a Watch: Stone, and Mortar, and Wood, without an Architect, never erect a House. But the Ideas in a human Mind, we see, by an 20 unknown, inexplicable Œconomy, arrange themselves so as to form the Plan of a Watch or House. Experience, therefore, proves, that there is an original Principle of Order in Mind, not in Matter. From similar Effects we infer similar Causes. The Adjustment of Means to Ends is alike in the Universe, as in a Machine of human 25 Contrivance. The Causes, therefore, must be resembling.

I was from the beginning scandaliz'd, I must own, with this Ressemblance, which is asserted, between the Deity and human Creatures; and must conceive it to imply such a Degradation of the supreme Being as no sound Theist cou'd endure. With your 30 Assistance, therefore, *Demea*, I shall endeavour to defend what you justly call the adorable Mysteriousness of the divine Nature, and shall refute this Reasoning of *Cleanthes*; provided he allows, that I have made a fair Representation of it.

1 one of them to the rest] any one of them   7 that Principle] Design   8 Source or Spring] Principle   11 than] that   13 But by Experience before, says he, that there is a Difference between these Cases *deleted before* The   15 find [says he] (according to *Cleanthes*)] says *Cleanthes* (as you affirm *Cleanthes*)   24 Means to Ends] final Causes   26 from the beginning] always   29 the] that

When *Cleanthes* had assented, *Philo*, after a short Pause, proceeded
in the following manner.

That all Inferences, *Cleanthes*, concerning Fact are founded on
Experience, and that all experimental Reasonings are founded on the
Supposition, that similar Causes prove similar Effects, and similar 5
Effects similar Causes; I shall not, at present, much dispute with
you. But observe, I entreat you, with what extreme Caution all
just Reasoners proceed in the transferring of Experiments to similar
Cases. Unless the Cases be exactly similar, they repose no perfect
Confidence in applying their past Observation to any particular 10
Phænomenon. Every Alteration of Circumstances occasions a Doubt
concerning the Event; and it requires new Experiments to prove
certainly, that the new Circumstances are of no Moment or
Importance. A Change in Bulk, Situation, Arrangement, Age,
Disposition of the Air, or surrounding Bodies; any of these par- 15
ticulars may be attended with the most unexpected Consequences:
And unless the Objects be quite familiar to us, it is the highest
Temerity to expect with Assurance, after any of these Changes,
an Event similar to that which before fell under our Observation.
The slow and deliberate Steps of Philosophers here, if any where, 20
are distinguish'd from the precipitate March of the Vulgar, who,
hurry'd on by the smallest Similitude, are incapable of all Discernment or Consideration.

But can you think, *Cleanthes*, that your usual Phlegm and Philosophy have been preserv'd in so wide a Step as you have taken, 25
when you compar'd to the Universe Houses, Ships, Furniture,
Machines; and from their Similarity in some Circumstances infer'd
a Similarity in their Causes? Thought, Design, Intelligence, such
as we discover in Men and other Animals, is no more than one of
the Springs and Principles of the Universe, as well as Heat or Cold, 30
Attraction or Repulsion, and a hundred others, which fall under
daily Observation. It is an active Cause, by which some particular
Parts of Nature, we find, produce Alterations on other Parts. But

---

8 the transferring] this Transference   10 in applying their] in their] in transferring   10–11 to any particular Phænomenon. Every] Any   11 occasions]
starts   22 hurry'd on] carry'd away   23 Consideration] Distinction]
Deliberation   27 Machines [etc. to the Universe]   their *deleted and then
restored*

can a Conclusion, with any Propriety, be transferr'd from Parts to the Whole? Does not the great Disproportion barr all Comparison and Inference? From observing the Growth of a Hair, can we learn any thing concerning the Generation of a Man? Wou'd the manner of a Leaf's blowing, even tho perfectly known, afford us any Instruction concerning the Vegetation of a Tree?

But allowing that we were to take the *Operations* of one part of Nature upon another for the Foundation of our Judgement concerning the *Origin* of the Whole (which never can be admitted) yet why select so minute, so weak, so bounded a Principle as the Reason and Design of Animals is found to be upon this Planet? What peculiar Privilege has this little Agitation of the Brain which we call Thought, that we must thus make it the Model of the whole Universe? Our Partiality in our own Favour does indeed present it on all Occasions: But sound Philosophy ought carefully to guard against so natural an Illusion.

So far from admitting, continu'd *Philo*, that the Operations of a Part can afford us any just Conclusion concerning the Origin of the Whole, I will not allow any one Part to form a Rule for another Part, if the latter be very remote from the former. Is there any reasonable Ground to conclude, that the Inhabitants of other Planets possess Thought, Intelligence, Reason, or any thing similar to these Faculties in Men? When Nature has so extremely diversify'd her manner of Operation in this small Globe; can we imagine, that she incessantly copies herself throughout so immense a Universe? And if Thought, as we may well suppose, be confin'd merely to this narrow Corner, and has even there so limited a Sphere of Action; with what Propriety can we assign it for the original Cause of all things? The narrow Views of a Peasant, who makes his domestic Œconomy the Rule for the Government of Kingdoms, is in Comparison a pardonable Sophism.

But were we ever so much assur'd, that a Thought and Reason, resembling the human, were to be found throughout the whole

2 Does not the great Disproportion] Do not the wide Disproportions   7 But allowing that we were] But were we   7–8 one part of Nature] Nature   9 admitted] allow'd] granted   19 Whole, [that]   31 is in Comparison a pardonable Sophism] is nothing in Comparison   pardonable] trivial   33 human, [that this Thought, I say,]   throughout] thro'

Universe, and were its Activity elsewhere vastly greater and more commanding than it appears in this Globe: Yet I cannot see, why the Operations of a World, constituted, arrang'd, adjusted, can with any Propriety be extended to a World, which is in its Embryo-State, and is advancing towards that Constitution and Arrange- 5 ment. By Observation, we know somewhat of the Œconomy, Action, and Nourishment of a finish'd Animal; but we must transfer with great Caution that Observation to the Growth of a Foetus in the Womb, and still more, to the Formation of an Animalcule in the Loins of its Male-Parent. Nature, we find, even 10 from our limited Experience, possesses an infinite Number of Springs and Principles, which incessantly discover themselves on every Change of her Position and Situation. And what new and unknown Principles wou'd actuate her in so new and unknown a Situation, as that of the Formation of a Universe, we cannot, 15 without the utmost Temerity, pretend to determine.

A very small Part of this great System, during a very short Time, is very imperfectly discover'd to us: And do we thence pronounce decisively concerning the Origin of the Whole?[11]

Admirable Conclusion! Stone, Wood, Brick, Iron, Brass, have 20 not, at this time, in this minute Globe of Earth, an Order or Arrangement without human Art and Contrivance: Therefore the Universe cou'd not originally attain its Order and Arrangement, without something similar to human Art. But is a Part of Nature a Rule for another Part very wide of the former? Is it a Rule 25 for the Whole? Is a very small Part a Rule for the Universe? Is Nature in one Situation, a certain Rule for Nature in another Situation, vastly different from the former?

And can you blame me, *Cleanthes*, if I here imitate the prudent Reserve of *Simonides*, who, according to the noted Story, being 30 ask'd by *Hiero what God was?* desir'd a day to think of it, and then two days more; and after that manner continually prolong'd the

1 elsewhere] thoroughout   2 appears] is   10 Animalcule [or of the
Senses]   10 we find, [for]   17–19 A . . . Whole? *added*   17 short]
small   21 minute] small   25 the former] it   26 Whole] World
27 a certain rule for] precisely similar to   32 after] in] after

11 This paragraph added in margin of p. 23 of manuscript with marks to indicate place of insertion and the notation 'A separate Paragraph' not apparently in Hume's hand.

Term, without ever bringing in his Definition or Description?[12] Cou'd you even blame me, if I had answer'd at first, *that I did not know*, and was sensible that this Subject lay vastly beyond the Reach of my Faculties? You might cry out Sceptic and Raillyer as

5 much as you pleas'd: But having found, in so many other Subjects, much more familiar, the Imperfections and even Contradictions of human Reason, I never shou'd expect any Success from its feeble Conjectures, in a Subject, so sublime, and so remote from the Sphere of our Observation. When two *Species* of Objects have

10 always been observ'd to be conjoin'd together, I can *infer*, by Custom, the Existence of one, wherever I *see* the Existence of the other: And this I call an Argument from Experience. But how this Argument can have place, where the Objects, as in the present Case, are single, individual, without Parralel, or specific Ressem-

15 blance, may be difficult to explain. And will any Man tell me with a serious Countenance, that an orderly Universe must arise from some Thought and Art, like the human; because we have Experience of it? To ascertain this Reasoning, it were requisite, that we had Experience of the Origin of Worlds; and it is not sufficient

20 surely, that we have seen Ships and Cities arise from human Art and Contrivance . . .

Philo was proceeding in this vehement manner, somewhat between Jest and Earnest, as it appear'd to me; when he observ'd some Signs of Impatience in *Cleanthes*, and then immediately stopped

25 short. What I had to suggest, said *Cleanthes*, is only that you wou'd not abuse Terms, or make Use of popular Expressions to subvert philosophical Reasoning. You know, that the Vulgar often distinguish Reason from Experience, even where the Question relates only to Matter of Fact and Existence; tho' it is found, where that

---

3 and [that I] lay] was	4 my] our	11 of [the]	14 Case, [concern-
ing the Origin of the World]	are] is	24 stopped] stopt	27 Reasoning]
Reasonings			

---

12 Cicero, *De Natura Deorum*, p. 38: 'If you should ask me what God is, or what his Essence, I should follow the Example of *Simonides*; who, when *Hiero* the Tyrant proposed the same Question to him, desired a Day to consider of it. When he required his Answer the next Day, *Simonides* beg'd two Days more; and often desiring double the Number, instead of giving his Answer, *Hiero* with Surprise ask'd him his Meaning in doing so; *because*, says he, *the longer I meditate on it, the more obscure it appears to me.*'

Reason is properly analyz'd, that it is nothing but a Species of Experience. To prove by Experience the Origin of the Universe from Mind is not more contrary to common Speech than to prove the Motion of the Earth from the same Principle. And a Caviller might raise all the same Objections to the *Copernican* System, which you have urg'd against my Reasonings. Have you other Earths, might he say, which you have seen to move? Have . . .

Yes! cry'd *Philo*, interrupting him, we have other Earths. Is not the Moon another Earth, which we see to turn round its Center? Is not Venus another Earth, where we observe the same Phænomenon? Are not the Revolutions of the Sun also a Confirmation, from Analogy, of the same Theory? All the Planets, are they not Earths, which revolve about the Sun? Are not the Satellites Moons, which move round Jupiter and Saturn, and along with these primary Planets, round the Sun? These Analogies and Ressemblances, with others, which I have not mention'd, are the sole Proofs of the *Copernican* System: And to you it belongs to consider, whether you have any Analogies of the same kind to support your Theory.

In reality, *Cleanthes*, continu'd he, the modern System of Astronomy is now so much receiv'd by all Enquirers, and has become so essential a Part even of our earliest Education,[13] that we are not commonly very scrupulous in examining the Reasons, upon which it is founded. It is now become a Matter of mere Curiosity to study the first Writers on that Subject, who had the full Force of Prejudice to encounter, and were oblig'd to turn their Arguments on every Side, in order to render them poupular and convincing. But if we peruse *Galilæo's* famous Dialogues concerning the System of the World,[14] we shall find, that that great Genius, one of the

---

7 Have . . . *deleted twice and then restored*   13 revolve] move   14 round] about] around   15 primary] original   round] about] around   18 whether] if   21 so much] much   27 every Side] all Sides

---

[13] As in, for example, '*Tom Telescope*', *The Newtonian System of Philosophy adapted to the Capacities of Young Gentlemen* (London, 1761), thought to be by John Newbery.
[14] Galilei Galileo, *Dialogo . . . sopra i due Massimi Sistemi del Mondo Tolemaico, e Copernicano* (Florence, 1632). Translated by Thomas Salusbury, *Dialogue on the Great World Systems* (London, 1661). It is likely that Hume hoped his *Dialogues* would have the same effect on the design argument as Galileo's arguments did on Pythagorean astronomy.

sublimest that ever existed, first bent all his Endeavours to prove, that there was no Foundation for the Distinction commonly made between elementary and celestial Substances. The Schools, proceeding from the Illusions of Sense, had carry'd this Distinction
5 very far; and had establish'd the latter Substances to be ingenerable, incorruptible, inalterable, impassible; and had assign'd all the opposite Qualities to the former. But *Galilæo*, beginning with the Moon, prov'd its Similarity in every particular to the Earth; its convex Figure, its natural Darkness when not illuminated,
10 its Density, its Distinction into solid and liquid, the Variations of its Phazes, the mutual Illuminations of the Earth and Moon, their mutual Eclipses, the Inequalities of the lunar Surface etc.[15] After many Instances of this kind, with regard to all the Planets, Men plainly saw, that these Bodies became proper Objects of Experience;
15 and that the Similarity of their Nature enabled us to extend the same Arguments and Phænomena from one to the other.

In this cautious Proceeding of the Astronomers, you may read your own Condemnation, *Cleanthes*; or rather may see, that the Subject in which you are engag'd exceeds all human Reason and
20 Enquiry. Can you pretend to show any such Similarity between the Fabric of a House, and the Generation of an Universe? Have you ever seen Nature in any such Situation as resembles the first Arrangement of the Elements? Have Worlds ever been form'd under your Eye?[16] And have you had Leizure to observe the whole
25 Progress of the Phænomenon, from the first Appearance of Order to its final Consummation? If you have, then cite your Experience, and deliver your Theory.

PART 3

How the most absurd Argument, reply'd *Cleanthes*, in the hands of
30 a Man of Ingenuity and Invention, may acquire an Air of Probability!

4 carry'd] stretch'd   14 these Bodies] they] the Planets   15 Nature]
Natures   16 from [the]   19 in which . . . engag'd] you are engag'd in
21 an] a   23 ever been] been ever   30 Air of [Truth and]

[15] In the dialogue 'The First Day', trans. Salusbury, pp. 48–54.
[16] Gildon, *Deist's Manual*, p. 5: 'Who was present at the Foundation of the Universe?'

Are you not aware, *Philo*, that it became necessary for *Copernicus* and his first Disciples to prove the Similarity of the terrestrial and celestial Matter; because several Philosophers, blinded by old Systems, and supported by some sensible Appearances, had deny'd this Similarity? But that it is by no means necessary, 5 that Theists shou'd prove the Similarity of the Works of Nature to those of Art; because this Similarity is self-evident and undeniable? The same Matter, a like Form: What more is requisite to show an Analogy between their Causes, and to ascertain the Origin of all things from a divine Purpose and Intention? Your 10 Objections, I must freely tell you, are no better than the abstruse Cavils of those Philosophers, who deny'd Motion; and ought to be refuted in the same manner, by Illustrations, Examples, and Instances, rather than by serious Argument and Philosophy. 15

Suppose, therefore, that an articulate Voice were heard in the Clouds, much louder and more melodious than any which human Art cou'd ever reach: Suppose, that this Voice were extended in the same Instant over all Nations, and spoke to each Nation in its own Language and Dialect: Suppose, that the Words deliver'd 20 not only contain a just Sense and Meaning, but convey some Instruction altogether worthy of a benevolent Being, superior to Mankind: Cou'd you possibly hesitate a Moment concerning the Cause of this Voice?[1] And must you not instantly ascribe to it some Design or Purpose? Yet I cannot see but all the same Objections 25 (if they merit that Appellation) which lie against the System of Theism, may also be produc'd against this Inference.

4 some sensible Appearances] the Illusions of Sense   9 show] prove
16 Suppose] Supposing   21 convey] convey'd   some *deleted and then restored*

---

[1] Berkeley, *Alciphron*, I. 240: 'Hence a common Man, who is not used to think and make Reflexions, wou'd probably be more convinced of the Being of a God, by one single Sentence heard once in his life from the Sky, than by all the Experience he has had of this visual Language, contrived with such exquisite skill, so constantly addressed to his Eyes, and so plainly declaring the Nearness, Wisdom, and Providence of him with whom we have to do.' Cf. also, Tindal, *Christianity as Old as the Creation*, p. 22: 'Had God, from time to time, spoke to all Mankind in their several Languages, and his Words had miraculously convey'd the same Ideas to all Persons; yet he cou'd not speak more plainly than he has done by the Things themselves, and the Relation which Reason shews there is between them . . .'.

Might you not say, that all Conclusions concerning Fact were founded on Experience: That when we hear an articulate Voice in the Dark, and thence infer a Man, it is only the Ressemblance of the Effects, which leads us to conclude that there is a like Ressemblance
5 in the Cause: But that this extraordinary Voice, by its Loudness, Extent, and Flexibility to all Languages, bears so little Analogy to any human Voice, that we have no Reason to suppose any Analogy in their Causes: And consequently, that a rational, wise, coherent Speech proceeded, you knew not whence, from some accidental
10 whistling of the Winds, not from any divine Reason or Intelligence? You see clearly your own Objections in these Cavils; and I hope too, you see clearly, that they cannot possibly have more Force in the one Case than in the other.[2]

But to bring the Case still nearer the present one of the
15 Universe, I shall make two Suppositions, which imply not any Absurdity or Impossibility. Suppose, that there is a natural, universal, invariable Language, common to every individual of human Race;[3] and that Books are natural Productions, which perpetuate themselves in the same manner with Animals and Vege-
20 tables, by Descent and Propagation. Several Expressions of our Passions contain a universal Language: All brute Animals have a natural Speech, which, however limited, is very intelligible to their own Species.[4] And as there are infinitely fewer Parts and less Contrivance in the finest Composition of Eloquence than in the
25 coarsest organiz'd Body, the Propagation of an *Illiad* or *Æneid* is an easier Supposition than that of any Plant or Animal.[5]

23 are] is

---

[2] The paragraph on pp. 177–8, 'Some Beauties . . . Design and Intention' was initially marked for inclusion here.

[3] Perhaps suggested by Lucretius, *De Rerum Natura*, V. 1011–90.

[4] Kames alluded to the idea in *Sketches of the History of Man* (Edinburgh, 1774), i. 40 n.: 'The Orang Outang has the external organs of speech in perfection; and many are puzzled to account why it never speaks.' Cf. James Beattie, *Dissertations Moral and Critical* (London, 1783), p. 234: '. . . the natural voices of one animal are in some degrees intelligible, or convey particular feelings, or impulses, to others of the same species.'

[5] A much-used example. Cf. Cicero, *De Natura Deorum*, pp. 138–9: 'He . . . may as well believe that if a great Quantity of the one and twenty Letters, composed either of Gold, or any other Matter, were thrown upon the Ground, they would fall into

Suppose, therefore, that you enter into your Library, thus peopled by natural Volumes, containing the most refin'd Reason and most exquisite Beauty: Cou'd you possibly open one of them, and doubt, that its original Cause bore the strongest Analogy to Mind and Intelligence? When it reasons and discourses; when it expostulates, argues, and inforces its Views and Topics; when it applies sometimes to the pure Intellect, sometimes to the Affections; when it collects, disposes, and adorns every Consideration suited to the Subject: Cou'd you persist in asserting, that all this, at the bottom, had really no Meaning, and that the first Formation of this Volume in the Loins of its original Parent proceeded not from Thought and Design?[6] Your Obstinacy, I know, reaches not that degree of Firmness: Even your sceptical Play and Wantonness wou'd be abash'd at so glaring an Absurdity.

---

2 vegetating *then* animal *added after* natural *and then deleted*   9 asserting] maintaining

---

such Order as legibly to form the *Annals of Ennius.*' Montaigne, *Apology for Raimond de Sebonde* in *Essays*, trans. Charles Cotton (London, 1743), ii. 247: 'Why at the same rate should we not believe, that as infinite Number of *Greek* Letters, strow'd all over a certain Place, might possibly fall into the Contexture of the *Illiad*?' Fénelon, p. 7: 'Who will believe that so perfect a Poem as Homer's *Illiad*, was not the Product of the Genius of a great Poet, and that the Letters of the Alphabet being confusedly jumbled and mix'd, were by Chance, as it were by the Cast of a Pair of Dice, brought together in such an Order as is necessary to describe, in Verses full of Harmony and Variety, so many great Events . . .?' Richard Bentley's Sermons, 'The Folly of Atheism, and . . . Deism' (5 Sept. 1692) and 'A Confutation of Atheism' (5 Dec. 1692) in *A Defence of Natural and Revealed Religion: Being a Collection of the Sermons Preached at the Lecture founded by . . . Robert Boyle* (London, 1739), i. 49, 87: '. . . to attribute such admirable Structures to blind Fortune or Chance, is no less than to suppose, That, if innumerable Figures of the twenty-four Letters be cast abroad at random, they might constitute in due Order the whole *Æneis* of *Virgil*, or the *Annales of Ennius* . . . . The *Æneis* of *Virgil*, or any other long Poem with good Sense and just Measures, could [not] be composed by the casual Combinations of Letters. Now, to pursue this Comparison; as it is utterly impossible to be believed, that such a Poem may have been eternal, transcribed from Copy to Copy without any first Author and Original; so it is equally incredible and impossible, that the Fabric of human Bodies, which hath such excellent and Divine Artifice . . . should be propagated and transcribed from the Father to Son without a first Parent and Creator of it.'

[6] William Wollaston, *The Religion of Nature Delineated* (London, 1726), p. 82: '. . . who can view the *structure* of a plant or animal; the *indefinite* number of their fibres and fine vessels, the *formation* of larger vessels and the several members out of them, and the apt *disposition* of all these . . . who can take notice of the several *faculties* of animals . . . and not see a *design*, in such *regular* pieces, so nicely wrought, and *so* preserved?'

But if there be any Difference, *Philo*, between this suppos'd Case and the real one of the Universe, it is all to the Advantage of the latter. The Anatomy of an Animal affords many stronger Instances of Design than the Perusal of *Livy* or *Tacitus*: And any Objection 5 which you start in the former Case, by carrying me back to so unusual and extraordinary a Scene as the first Formation of Worlds, the same Objection has place on the Supposition of our vegetating Library. Choose, then, your Party, *Philo*, without Ambiguity or Evasion: Assert either that a rational Volume is no Proof of a 10 rational Cause, or admit of a similar Cause to all the Works of Nature.

Let me here observe too, continu'd *Cleanthes*, that this religious Argument, instead of being weaken'd by that Scepticism, so much affected by you, rather acquires Force from it, and becomes more 15 firm and undisputed. To exclude all Argument or Reasoning of every kind is either Affectation or Madness. The declar'd Profession of every reasonable Sceptic is only to reject abstruse, remote and refin'd Arguments; to adhere to common Sense and the plain Instincts of Nature; and to assent, wherever any Reasons strike 20 him with so full a Force, that he cannot, without the greatest Violence, prevent it. Now the Arguments for natural Religion are plainly of this kind; and nothing but the most perverse, obstinate Metaphysics can reject them. Consider, anatomize the Eye:[7] Survey its Structure and Contrivance; and tell me, from your own

4 *Livy* or *Tacitus*] the *Iliad*   17 abstruse, remote] remote, abstruse,   21 Now
[all]   23 reject] refuse

_____

[7] Fénelon, p. 97: 'The two Eyes are equal, being placed about the Middle, on the two Sides of the Head, that they may, without Trouble, discover afar off, both on the Right and Left, all Strange Objects; and that they may commodiously watch for the Safety of all Parts of the Body. . . . And He that made them, has kindled in them, I know not what Celestial Flame, the like of which all the rest of Nature does not afford.' Gildon, pp. 34–5: 'What a Stupendious Machine is the Eye, if we survey the Muscles, Membranes and Humours of which it is compos'd? . . . Oh! *Philalethes*! could'st thou be incredulous to the forming this House and Gardens by CHANCE, and yet doubt that the Former of the Eye, so infinitely more curious and difficult, should be the Work of an intelligent, and most *Wise Cause*.' William Derham, *Physico-Theology* (London, 1713), p. 95: 'And here indeed we cannot but stand amazed, when we view [the eye's] admirable Fabrick, and consider the prodigious Exactness, and the exquisite skill employed in every Part ministring to this noble and necessary Sense.'

Feeling, if the Idea of a Contriver does not immediately flow in upon you with a Force like that of Sensation. The most obvious Conclusion surely is in favour of Design; and it requires Time, Reflection and Study to summon up those frivolous, tho' abstruse, Objections, which can support Infidelity. Who can behold the 5 Male and Female of each Species, the Correspondence of their Parts and Instincts, their Passions and whole Course of Life before and after Generation, but must be sensible, that the Propagation of the Species is intended by Nature?[8] Millions and Millions of such Instances present themselves thro every Part of the Universe; 10 and no Language can convey a more intelligible, irresistible Meaning, than the curious Adjustment of final Causes. To what Degree, therefore, of blind Dogmatism must one have attain'd, to reject such natural and such convincing Arguments?

Some Beauties in Writing we may meet with, which seem con- 15 trary to Rules, and which gain the Affections, and animate the Imagination, in opposition to all the Precepts of Criticism, and to the Authority of the establish'd Masters of Art.[9] And if the Argument for Theism be, as you pretend, contradictory to the Principles of Logic; its universal, its irresistible Influence proves clearly, 20 that there may be Arguments of a like irregular Nature. Whatever

4 those [abstruse]   15–(178)3 Some . . . Intention *added*

---

[8] Cf. Colin Maclaurin: *An Account of Sir Isaac Newton's Philosophical Discoveries* (London, 1748), p. 381: 'The plain argument for the existence of the Deity, obvious to all and carrying irresistible conviction with it, is from the evident contrivance and fitness of things for one another, which we meet with throughout all parts of the universe. There is no need of nice or subtle reasonings in this matter: a manifest contrivance immediately suggests a contriver. It strikes us like a sensation; and artful reasonings against it may puzzle us, but it is without shaking our belief. No person, for example, that knows the principles of optics and the structure of the eye, can believe that it was formed without skill in that science; or that the ear was formed without the knowledge of sounds; or that the male and female in animals were not formed for each other, and for continuing the species.' See R. H. Hurlbutt III, 'David Hume and Scientific Theism', *Journal of the History of Ideas*, xvii (1956), 492, and his book, *Hume, Newton, and the Design Argument* (Nebraska, 1965), pp. 40–2.

[9] Cf. *Spectator*, 592 (Addison): 'We may often take Notice of Men who are perfectly acquainted with all the Rules of good Writing, and notwithstanding choose to depart from them on extraordinary Occasions. I could give Instances out of all the Tragick Writers of Antiquity who have shewn their Judgment in this Particular, and purposely receded from an establish'd Rule of Drama, when it has made way for a much higher Beauty than the Observation of such a Rule would have been.'

Cavils may be urg'd; an orderly World, as well as a coherent, articulate Speech, will still be receiv'd as an incontestible Proof of Design and Intention.[10]

   It sometimes happens, I own, that the religious Arguments have 5 not their due Influence on an ignorant Savage and Barbarian; not because they are obscure and difficult, but because he never asks himself any Question with regard to them. Whence arises the curious Structure of an Animal? From the Copulation of its Parents. And these whence? From *their* Parents? A few Removes set the 10 Objects at such a Distance, that to him they are lost in Darkness and Confusion;[11] nor is he actuated by any Curiosity to trace them farther. But this is neither Dogmatism nor Scepticism, but Stupidity; a State of Mind very different from your sifting, inquisitive Disposition, my ingenious Friend. You can trace Causes 15 from Effects: You can compare the most distant and remote Objects: And your greatest Errors proceed not from Barrenness of Thought and Invention, but from too luxuriant a Fertility, which suppresses your natural good Sense, by a Profusion of unnecessary Scruples and Objections.

20   Here I cou'd observe, *Hermippus*, that *Philo* was a little embarrass'd and confounded: But while he hesitated in delivering an Answer, luckily for him, Demea broke in upon the Discourse, and sav'd his Countenance.

   Your Instance, *Cleanthes*, said he, drawn from Books and

---

4 the religious Arguments] these Arguments

---

   [10] This paragraph added on p. 30 of the manuscript (at the conclusion of Part III) and marked for insertion here. Hume has written in the margin of p. 29 of the manuscript. 'The Passage next Page at AA to be here taken in'.

   [11] Cicero, *De Natura Deorum*, p. 166: 'With Regard to Animals, do we not see with what Judgment they were made for the Propagation of their Species? Nature for this End created some Males and some Females. Their Parts are perfectly framed for Generation, and they have a wonderful Propensity to Copulation.' Gildon, p. 42: 'Who Produc'd you? Who made you? Who gave you that Being which you now enjoy? You will perhaps reply, that you deriv'd your Being from your Father and Mother, as they did theirs from their Parents; and so you must go on till you come to one first of the Race . . .'. Hume's wording in his *Natural History of Religion* is almost the same (p. 28 above): 'Ask him, whence that animal arose; he will tell you, from the copulation of its parents. And these, whence? From the copulation of theirs. A few removes satisfy his curiosity, and set the objects at such a distance, that he naturally loses sight of them.'

Language, being familiar, has, I confess, so much more Force on
that Account; but is there not some Danger too in this very Circumstance, and may it not render us presumptuous, by making us
imagine we comprehend the Deity, and have some adequate Idea
of his Nature and Attributes. When I read a Volume, I enter into 5
the Mind and Intention of the Author: I become him, in a manner,
for the Instant; and have an immediate Feeling and Conception of
those Ideas, which revolv'd in his Imagination, while employ'd in
that Composition. But so near an Approach we never surely can
make to the Deity. His ways are not our Ways. His Attributes are 10
perfect, but incomprehensible. And this Volume of Nature contains
a great and inexplicable Riddle, more than any intelligible Discourse or Reasoning.

The antient *Platonists*, you know, were the most religious and
devout of all the Pagan Philosophers: Yet many of them, particu- 15
larly *Plotinus*, expressly declare, that Intellect or Understanding is
not to be ascrib'd to the Deity, and that our most perfect Worship
of him consists, not in Acts of Veneration, Reverence, Gratitude or
Love; but in a certain mysterious Self Annihilation or total Extinction of all our Faculties.[12] These Ideas are, perhaps, too far stretch'd; 20
but still it must be acknowledg'd, that, by representing the Deity
as so intelligible, and comprehensible, and so similar to a human
Mind, we are guilty of the grossest and most narrow Partiality, and
make Ourselves the Model of the whole Universe.

All the *Sentiments* of the human Mind, Gratitude, Resentment, 25
Love, Friendship, Approbation, Blame, Pity, Emulation, Envy,
have a plain Reference to the State and Situation of Man, and are

---

1 Language, [by]   6 become *deleted and then restored*   8 in²] upon
13 Reasoning] reasoning   25–(180)23 All . . . Attributes *added*

---

[12] Maclaurin, p. 378: 'The abstruse nature of the subject gave occasion to the
later *Platonists*, particularly to *Plotinus*, to introduce the most mystical and unintelligible notions concerning the Deity and the worship we owe to him; as when he
tells us that intellect or understanding is not to be ascribed to the Deity, and that
our most perfect worship of him consists, not in acts of veneration, reverence,
gratitude or love; but in a certain mysterious self-annihilation, or total extinction
of all our faculties.' Cited in Hurlbutt, 'David Hume and Scientific Theism', p. 493.
Cf. Plotinus, *Enneads*, v. vi. 1; VI. vi. 8; VI. vii. 40; and VI. viii. *passim*. (for 'Intellect
. . . not to be ascrib'd to the Deity'); and III. vi. 6; VI. vii. 84–6; and VI. ix. 7–11 (for
'Worship . . . consists . . . in . . . Self Annihilation').

calculated for preserving the Existence, and promoting the Activity of such a Being in such Circumstances. It seems therefore unreasonable to transfer such Sentiments to a supreme Existence, or to suppose him actuated by them; and the Phænomena, besides, of
5 the Universe will not support us in such a Theory. All our *Ideas*, deriv'd from the Senses are confessedly false and illusive; and cannot, therefore, be suppos'd to have place in a Supreme Intelligence: And as the Ideas of internal Sentiment, added to those of the external Senses, compose the whole Furniture of human Under-
10 standing, we may conclude, that none of the *Materials* of Thought are in any respect similar in the human and in the divine Intelligence. Now as to the *Manner* of thinking; how can we make any Comparison between them, or suppose them any wise resembling? Our Thought is fluctuating, uncertain, fleeting, successive, and
15 compounded; and were we to remove these Circumstances, we absolutely annihilate its Essence, and it wou'd, in such a Case, be an Abuse of Terms to apply to it the Name of Thought or Reason. At least, if it appear more pious and respectful (as it really is) still to retain these Terms, when we mention the supreme Being, we
20 ought to acknowledge, that their Meaning, in that case, is totally incomprehensible; and that the Infirmities of our Nature do not permit us to reach any Ideas, which in the least correspond to the ineffable Sublimity of the divine Attributes.[13]

PART 4

25 It seems strange to me, said *Cleanthes*, that you, *Demea*, who are so sincere in the Cause of Religion, shou'd still maintain the

---

1 preserving] supporting   8 added] join] join'd   13 wise] way
20 ought to] should   21-2 do not permit us] permit us not

---

[13] This paragraph represents a new ending to Part III; it is added on pp. 30–1 of the manuscript and marked 'BB'. Immediately after the paragraph ending '. . . the Model of the whole Universe' Hume has written 'The Passage at BB at the Foot of the Page to be here taken in'.

mysterious, incomprehensible Nature of the Deity, and shou'd insist
so strenuously, that he has no manner of Likeness or Ressemblance
to human Creatures. The Deity, I can readily allow, possesses many
Powers and Attributes, of which we can have no Comprehension:
But if our Ideas, so far as they go, be not just, and adequate, and 5
correspondent to his real Nature, I know not what there is in this
Subject worth insisting on. Is the Name, without any Meaning, of
such mighty Importance? Or how do you *Mystics,* who maintain the
absolute Incomprehensibility of the Deity, differ from Sceptics or
Atheists, who assert, that the first Cause of All is unknown and un- 10
intelligible? Their Temerity must be very great, if, after rejecting the
Production by a Mind; I mean, a Mind, resembling the human (for
I know of no other) they pretend to assign, with Certainty, any
other specific, intelligible Cause: And their Conscience must be
very scrupulous indeed, if they refuse to call the universal, unknown 15
Cause a God or Deity; and to bestow on him as many sublime
Eulogies and unmeaning Epithets, as you shall please to require
of them.

Who cou'd imagine, reply'd *Demea,* that *Cleanthes,* the calm,   ✓
philosophical *Cleanthes,* wou'd attempt to refute his Antagonists, 20
by affixing a Nick-name to them; and like the common Bigots and
Inquisitors of the Age, have Recourse to Invective and Declama-
tion, instead of Reasoning? Or does he not perceive, that these
Topics are easily retorted, and that *Anthropomorphite* is an Appellation as invidious, and implies as dangerous Consequences, as the 25
Epithet of *Mystic,* with which he has honour'd us? In reality,
Cleanthes, consider what it is you assert, when you represent the
Deity as similar to a human Mind and Understanding. What is the
Soul of Man? A Composition of various Faculties, Passions, Senti-
ments, Ideas; united, indeed, into one Self or Person, but still 30
distinct from each other.[1] When it reasons, the Ideas, which are the

3 Creatures. [Are you unacquainted with / Reflect a moment on that Principle
of Philosophy, which you at present allege, that we have no Idea of any thing, which
[that *deleted*] has no Likeness to Ourselves, or to those Objects, which [that *deleted*]
have been expos'd to our Senses and Experience?]   8 how do you] wherein do
14 Cause:] Cause, distinct from it   15 the] this   19 cou'd] wou'd
20 wou'd] shou'd   26 he has] you have

[1] *Treatise,* p. 257 (I. iv. 2): '. . . what we call a *mind,* is nothing but a heap or

Parts of its Discourse, arrange themselves in a certain Form or Order; which is not preserv'd entire for a Moment, but immediately gives Place to another Arrangement. New Opinions, new Passions, new Affections, new Feelings arise, which continually
5 diversify the mental Scene, and produce in it the greatest Variety, and most rapid Succession imaginable. How is this compatible, with that perfect Immutability and Simplicity, which all true Theists ascribe to the Deity? By the same Act, say they, he sees past, present, and future: His Love and his Hatred, his Mercy and
10 his Justice are one individual Operation: He is entire in every Point of Space; and compleat in every Instant of Duration. No Succession, no Change, no Acquisition, no Diminution. What he is implies not in it any Shadow of Distinction or Diversity. And what he is, this moment, he ever has been, and ever will be, without any
15 new Judgement, Sentiment, or Operation. He stands fixt in one simple, perfect State; nor can you ever say, with any Propriety, that this Act of his is different from that other, or that this Judgement or Idea has been lately form'd, and will give place, by Succession, to any different Judgement or Idea.[2]
20   I can readily allow, said *Cleanthes*, that those who maintain the perfect Simplicity of the supreme Being, to the Extent in which you have explain'd it, are compleat *Mystics*, and chargeable with all the Consequences which I have drawn from their Opinion. They are, in a Word, Atheists, without knowing it. For tho' it be
25 allowed, that the Deity possesses Attributes, of which we have no Comprehension; yet ought we never to ascribe to him any Attributes, which are absolutely incompatible with that intelligent Nature, essential to him. A Mind, whose Acts and Sentiments and Ideas are not distinct and successive; one, that is wholly simple,

---

8 ascribe] agree to belong   19 Judgement] Opinion   22 compleat]
perfect   29 that is wholly] which is perfectly

---

collection of different perceptions, united together by certain relations, and suppos'd, tho' falsely, to be endow'd with a perfect simplicity and identity.'

[2] Demea's enunciation owes much to the arguments of Samuel Clarke's *Discourse concerning the Being and Attributes of God* (1704–6), not so much in actual phraseology but in tone and conduct of the argument. See particularly Clarke's first three propositions.

and totally immutable; is a Mind, which has no Thought, no Reason, no Will, no Sentiment, no Love, no Hatred; or in a Word, is no Mind at all. It is an Abuse of Terms to give it that Appellation; and we may as well speak of limited Extension without Figure, or of Number without Composition.   5

Pray consider, said *Philo*, whom you are at present inveighing against. You are honouring with the Appellation of Atheist all the sound, orthodox Divines almost, who have treated of this Subject; and you will, at last be, yourself, found, according to your Reckoning, the only sound Theist in the World. But if Idolaters be Atheists, 10 as, I think, may justly be asserted, and Christian Theologians the same; what becomes of the Argument, so much celebrated, derived from the universal Consent of Mankind?

But because I know you are not much sway'd by Names and Authorities, I shall endeavour to show you, a little more distinctly, 15 the Inconveniencies of that Anthropomorphism, which you have embrac'd; and shall prove, that there is no Ground to suppose a Plan of the World to be form'd in the divine Mind, consisting of distinct Ideas, differently arrang'd; in the same manner as an Architect forms in his Head the Plan of a House which he intends to 20 execute.

It is not easy, I own, to see, what is gain'd by this Supposition, whether we judge of the Matter by *Reason* or by *Experience*. We are still oblig'd to mount higher, in order to find the Cause of this Cause, which you had assign'd as satisfactory and conclusive.   25

If *Reason* (I mean abstract Reason, deriv'd from Enquiries *a priori*) be not alike mute with regard to all Questions concerning Cause and Effect; this Sentence at least it will venture to pronounce, that a mental World or Universe of Ideas requires a Cause as much as does a material World or Universe of Objects; and if similar in 30

---

1 immutable] inalterable   which] that   9 be, yourself,] be   11 may justly be asserted] you may justly assert   Christian Theologians] Christians 12–13 so much . . . Mankind?] the Argument from universal Consent?   17 Ground] Reason   suppose] think   18 to be] was   20 the] a   a] the   22 *The following sentence deleted at beginning of paragraph*: 'Tis evident, *Cleanthes*, when you assert, that the World arose from a Design, similar to the human, you do nothing but present us with a Mind or ideal World, consisting of similar Parts with the Universe or material World, and affirm the former to be the Cause of the latter. Supposition] Change   26–(184)5 If *Reason* . . . both of them. *added*.

its Arrangement must require a similar Cause. For what is there in this Subject, which should occasion a different Conclusion or Inference? In an abstract View, they are entirely alike; and no Difficulty attends the one Supposition, which is not common to 5 both of them.[3]

Again, when we will needs force *Experience* to pronounce some Sentence, even on these Subjects, which lie beyond her Sphere; neither can she perceive any material Difference in this particular, between these two kinds of Worlds, but finds them to be govern'd 10 by similar Principles, and to depend upon an equal Variety of Causes in their Operations. We have Specimens in Miniature of both of them. Our own Mind resembles the one: A vegetable or animal Body the other. Let Experience, therefore, judge from these Samples. Nothing seems more delicate with regard to its Causes 15 than Thought; and as these Causes never operate in two Persons after the same manner, so we never find two Persons, who think

4 the one Supposition] one   (183)26–5 If Reason . . . them] When we consult *Reason*, all Causes and Effects seem equally explicable *a priori*; nor is it possible to assign either of them, by the mere abstract Contemplation of their Nature, without consulting *Experience*, or considering what we have found to result from the Operation of Objects. And if this Proposition be true in general, that *Reason, judging a priori, finds all Causes and Effects alike explicable*, it must appear more so, when we compare the external World of Objects with that World of Thought, which is represented as its Cause. If *Reason* tell us, that the World of Objects requires a Cause, it must give us the same Information concerning the World of Thought: And if the one seems to Reason to require a Cause of any particular kind, the other must require a Cause of like kind. Any Proposition, therefore, which we can form concerning the Cause of the former, if it be consistent, or intelligible, or necessary, must also appear to Reason consistent or intelligible or necessary, when apply'd to the latter, such as you have describ'd it; and *vice versa*. 'Tis evident, then, that as far as abstract Reason can judge, tis perfectly indifferent, whether we rest on the Universe of Matter or on that of Thought; nor do we gain any thing by tracing the one into the other. 6 Again] On the other hand   8 neither can she] she cannot   9 Worlds] Systems   12 of them] these Worlds

[n]8 World of Objects] the former   [n]9 World of Thought] the latter World of Thought [which is represented as its Cause]   [n]12 former] Universe of Objects   Reason] be   [n]13 the latter] that of Thought

———

3 This paragraph, in Hume's mature hand, is a substitute for the one deleted on p. 35 of the Manuscript. The substituted paragraph is added at the end of Part IV of the manuscript on p. 38, and on p. 35 Hume has written in the margin 'The Passage at AA on p. 38 to be here taken in'. In addition, he had twice written on the margin of p. 35 'Print these Lines, tho eraz'd' but in both instances the instructions have been scored out, perhaps not by Hume. The revision, however, would appear to have been made by Hume in 1776.

exactly alike. Nor indeed does the same Person think exactly alike at any two different Periods of time. A Difference of Age, of the Disposition of his Body, of Weather, of Food, of Company, of Books, of Passions; any of these particulars or others more minute, are sufficient to alter the curious Machinery of Thought, and com- 5 municate to it very different Movements and Operations. As far as we can judge, Vegetables and animal Bodies are not more delicate in their Motions, nor depend upon a greater Variety or more curious Adjustment of Springs and Principles.

How therefore shall we satisfy Ourselves concerning the Cause 10 of that Being, whom you suppose the Author of Nature, or, according to your System of Anthropomorphism, the ideal World, into which you trace the material? Have we not the same Reason to trace that ideal World into another ideal World, or new intelligent Principle? But if we stop, and go no farther; why go so far? 15 Why not stop at the material World? How can we satisfy Ourselves without going on *in infinitum*? And after all, what Satisfaction is there in that infinite Progression? Let us remember the Story of the *Indian* Philosopher and his Elephant.[4] It was never more applicable than to the present Subject. If the material World rests upon 20 a similar ideal World, this ideal World must rest upon some other; and so on, without End. It were better, therefore, never to look beyond the present material World. By supposing it to contain the Principle of its Order within itself, we really assert it to be God; and the sooner we arrive at that divine Being so much the better. 25 When you go one Step beyond the mundane System, you only excite an inquisitive Humour, which it is impossible ever to satisfy.

To say, that the different Ideas, which compose the Reason of the supreme Being, fall into Order, of themselves, and by their own 30 Nature, is really to talk without any precise Meaning. If it has a

3 his] the   7 As] So] As   10–11 the Cause of that Being] the Deity
11 or, [in other Words]   21 similar [the]   26 you¹] we   mundane System]
Universe

---

[4] Locke, *Essay*, p. 80 (II. xiii. 19): 'Had the poor *Indian* Philosopher (who imagined that the Earth also wanted something to bear it up) but thought of this word *Substance*, he needed not to have been at the trouble to find an Elephant to support it, and a Tortoise to support his Elephant . . .'.

Meaning, I wou'd fain know, why it is not as good Sense to say, that the Parts of the material World fall into Order, of themselves, and by their own Nature? Can the one Opinion be intelligible, while the other is not so?

5   We have, indeed, Experience of Ideas, which fall into Order, of themselves, and without any *known* Cause: But, I am sure, we have a much larger Experience of Matter, which does the same; as in all Instances of Generation and Vegetation, where the accurate Analysis of the Cause exceeds all human Comprehension. We have also Experience of particular Systems of Thought and of Matter, which have no Order; of the first, in Madness, of the second, in Corruption. Why then shou'd we think, that Order is more essential to one than the other? And if it requires a Cause in both, what do we gain by your System, in tracing the Universe of Objects into a similar Universe of Ideas? The first Step, which we make, leads us on for ever. It were, therefore, wise in us to limit all our Enquiries to the present World, without looking farther. No Satisfaction can ever be attain'd by these Speculations, which so far exceed the narrow Bounds of human Understanding.

20   It was usual with the *Peripatetics*, you know, *Cleanthes*, when the Cause of any Phænomenon was demanded, to have Recourse to their *Faculties* or *occult Qualities*, and to say, for Instance, that Bread nourish'd by its nutritive Faculty, and Senna purg'd by its purgative: But it has been discover'd, that this Subterfuge was nothing but the Disguise of Ignorance; and that these Philosophers, tho less ingenuous, really said the same thing with the Sceptics or the Vulgar, who fairly confessed, that they knew not the Cause of these Phænomena. In like manner, when it is ask'd, what Cause produces Order in the Ideas of the supreme Being, can any other Reason be assign'd by you, Anthropomorphites, than that it is a *rational* Faculty, and that such is the Nature of the Deity? But why a similar Answer will not be equally satisfactory in accounting for the Order of the World, without having recourse to any such intelligent Creator, as you insist on, may be difficult to determine.

---

7 which] that   10 which] that   12 to [the]   16 It were, therefore, wise in us] Let us, therefore,   27 confessed] confest   30 be assign'd by] be given by

It is only to say, that *such* is the Nature of material Objects, and
that they are all originally possessed of a *Faculty* of Order and
Proportion. These are only more learned and elaborate ways of
confessing our Ignorance; nor has the one Hypothesis any real
Advantage above the other, except in its greater Conformity to 5
vulgar Prejudices.

You have display'd this Argument with great Emphasis, reply'd
Cleanthes: You seem not sensible, how easy it is to answer it. Even in
common Life, if I assign a Cause for any Event; is it any Objection,
Philo, that I cannot assign the Cause of that Cause, and answer 10
every new Question, which may incessantly be started? And what
Philosophers cou'd possibly submit to so rigid a Rule? Philosophers,
who confess ultimate Causes to be totally unknown, and are sensible,
that the most refin'd Principles, into which they trace the Phænomena, are still to them as inexplicable as these Phaenomena them- 15
selves are to the Vulgar. The Order and Arrangement of Nature,
the curious Adjustment of final Causes, the plain Use and Intention of every Part and Organ; all these bespeak in the clearest
Language an intelligent Cause or Author.[5] The Heavens and the
Earth join in the same Testimony: The whole Chorus of Nature 20
raises one Hymn to the Praises of its Creator: You alone, or almost
alone, disturb this general Harmony. You start abstruse Doubts,
Cavils, and Objections: You ask me, what is the Cause of this
Cause? I know not; I care not; That concerns not me. I have
found a Deity; and here I stop my Enquiry. Let those go farther, 25
who are wiser or more enterprizing.

I pretend to be neither, reply'd *Philo*: And for that very Reason,
I shou'd never perhaps have attempted to go so far; especially

2 possessed] possest   8 not [to be]   11 which] that   26 enterprizing [than me]   27–(188)12 I . . . itself.] Your Answer may, perhaps, be good,
said *Philo*, upon your Principles that the religious System can be prov'd by Experience,
and by Experience alone; and that the Deity arose from some external Cause. But
these Opinions, you know, will be adopted by very few. And as to all those, who
reason upon other Principles, and yet deny the mysterious Simplicity of the divine
Nature, my Objection still remains good.   [n]5 Opinions] System

[5] Hume, *The Natural History of Religion*, p. 25 above: 'The whole frame of nature
bespeaks an intelligent author . . .'. Forbes, p. 1: 'It is impossible to view the immen-
sity, the variety, the harmony, and the beauty of the Universe, without concluding
it to be the workmanship of a Being infinitely powerful, wise, and good.'

when I am sensible, that I must at last be contented to sit down with the same Answer, which, without farther Trouble, might have satisfy'd me from the Beginning. If I am still to remain in utter Ignorance of Causes, and can absolutely give an Explication 5 of nothing, I shall never esteem it any Advantage to shove off for a moment a Difficulty, which, you acknowlege, must immediately, in its full force, recur upon me. Naturalists indeed very justly explain particular Effects by more general Causes; tho' these general Causes themselves shou'd remain in the End totally inex- 10 plicable: But they never surely thought it satisfactory to explain a particular Effect by a particular Cause, which was no more to be accounted for than the Effect itself.[6] An ideal System, arrang'd of itself, without a precedent Design, is not a whit more explicable than a material one, which attains its Order in a like Manner; nor 15 is there any more Difficulty in the latter Supposition than in the former.

PART 5

But to show you still more Inconveniences, continu'd *Philo*, in your Anthropomorphism; please to take a new Survey of your Principles. 20 *Like Effects prove like Causes*.[1] This is the experimental Argument; and this, you say too, is the sole theological Argument.[2] Now it is certain, that the liker the Effects are, which are seen, and the liker the Causes, which are infer'd, the stronger is the Argument.[2] Every Departure on either Side diminishes the Probability, and

2–3 might have satisfy'd me from the Beginning] satisfy'd me from the first In- stant] content'd me at the Beginning   6 a Difficulty] any Difficulty   13 not a whit] no   14 which] that   18 to show you *deleted and then restored*   In- conveniences, [of y]   in] of   19 please to] pray   21 theological] religious

[6] The preceding three sentences ('I pretend ... Effect itself.') are added in Hume's mature hand at the bottom of p. 38 under the notation 'BB'. Hume has written in the margin of p. 38 'The Passage at BB to be here taken in' with the 'BB' marks in the text to indicate place of insertion. This, too, would appear to be one of Hume's 1776 revisions.

[1] Newton: *Principia, Rules of Reasoning*, Rule II: '*Therefore to the same natural effects we must, as far as possible, assign the same causes.*' Isaac Newton, *The Mathematical Principles of Natural Philosophy*, trans. Andrew Motte (London, 1729), ii. 202.

[2] Joseph Butler, *Fifteen Sermons Preached at the Rolls Chapel* (London, 1729), p. 301: 'What are the Laws by which Matters acts upon Matter, but certain Effects; which some, having observed to be frequently repeated, have reduced to general Rules?'

renders the Experiment less conclusive. You cannot doubt of this Principle: Neither ought you to reject its Consequences.

All the new Discoveries in Astronomy, which prove the immense Grandeur and Magnificence of the Works of Nature, are so many additional Arguments for a Deity, according to the true System of Theism: But according to your Hypothesis of experimental Theism they become so many Objections, by removing the Effect still farther from all Resemblance to the Effects of human Art and Contrivance. For if *Lucretius*[a] even following the old System of the World, cou'd exclaim,

> Quis regere immensi summam, quis habere profundi
> Indu manu validas potis est moderanter habenas?
> Quis pariter cœlos omnes convertere? et omnes
> Ignibus ætheriis terras suffire feraces?
> Omnibus inque locis esse omni tempore præsto?[3]

If *Tully*[b] esteem'd this Reasoning so natural as to put it into the Mouth of his *Epicurean. Quibus enim oculis animi intueri potuit vester* Plato *fabricam illam tanti operis, qua construi a deo atque ædificari mundum facit? quae molitio? quae ferramenta? qui vectes? quae machinae? qui ministri tanti muneris fuerunt? quemadmodum autem obedire et parere voluntati architecti aer, ignis, aqua, terra potuerunt?*[4] If this Argument, I say, had any Force in former Ages; how much greater must it have at present; when the Bounds of Nature are so infinitely enlarg'd, and

---

[a] Lib. II. 1094. [b] *De nat. Deor.* Lib. I.

---

1 doubt of] deny 2 reject] refuse 9 following] acceding to
22 greater must it have] more 23 enlarg'd] extended

---

[3] Lucretius, *De Rerum Natura*, II. 1094–9. In his translation (London, 1683), Thomas Creech paraphrased the passage as follows (p. 66): 'For, how, *good Gods*, can those that live in peace, / In undisturb'd and everlasting ease, / Rule this vast *All*? their labouring thoughts divide / 'Twixt Heaven and Earth, and all their motions guide . . .?' A modern translation takes no such liberties with the text: '. . . who is strong enough to rule the sum, who to hold in hand and control the mighty bridle of the unfathomable deep? who to run about all the heavens at one time and warm the fruitful worlds with ethereal fires, or to be present in all places and at all times . . .?' (Loeb trans., p. 163).

[4] Cicero, *De Natura Deorum*, pp. 14–15: 'For with what Eyes of the Mind was your *Plato* able to see that Workhouse of such stupendous Toil, in which he makes the World to be modell'd and built by God? What Materials, what Tools, what Bars, what Machines, what Servants, were employ'd in so vast a Work? How could the Air, Fire, Water, and Earth, pay Obedience and submit to the Will of the Architect?'

such a magnificent Scene is open'd to us? It is still more unreasonable to form our Idea of so unlimited a Cause from our Experience of the narrow Productions of human Design and Invention.

The Discoveries by Microscopes,[5] as they open a new Universe in Miniature, are still Objections, according to you; Arguments, according to me. The farther we push our Researches of this kind, we are still led to infer the universal Cause of All to be vastly different from Mankind, or from any Object of human Experience and Observation.

And what say you to the Discoveries in Anatomy, Chymistry, Botany?—These surely are no Objections, reply'd *Cleanthes*: They only discover new Instances of Art and Contrivance.[6] It is still the Image of Mind reflected on us as from innumerable Objects. Add, a Mind *like the human*, said *Philo*. I know of no other, reply'd *Cleanthes*. And the liker the better, insisted *Philo*. To be sure, said *Cleanthes*.

Now, *Cleanthes*, said *Philo*, with an Air of Alacrity and Triumph, Mark the Consequences. *First*. By this Method of Reasoning, you renounce all Claim to Infinity in any of the Attributes of the Deity. For as the Cause ought only to be proportion'd to the Effect, and the Effect, so far as it falls under our Cognizance, is not infinite; What Pretensions, have we, upon your Suppositions, to ascribe that Attribute to the divine Being? You will still insist, that, by removing him so much from all Similarity to human Creatures, we

---

1–2 It is still more unreasonable] We ought still less] It is still less reasonable   2 so] this   3 Productions] Effects   4 open [up]   10 to] of 18 Claim]Pretence   21 Pretensions, [you'll say / you will say]   22 Attribute] Epithet   You . . . by] By   23 we [will]

---

[5] Gildon, *Deist's Manual*, p. 30: 'We see, and can discourse distinctly of all from the *Elephant* to the *Mite*, but here our sight is bounded, and shuts from our Consideration infinite Numbers of *Living Creatures* less than a *Mite*, to which in some Proportion it is as big as an *Elephant* is to a *Mite*. And yet that there are such, how incredible soever it may seem, the Invention of *Microscopes* has discover'd.' Henry Baker published his popular and influential book, *The Microscope Made Easy*, in 1743; it went through several editions in the eighteenth century, and this treatise was supplemented in 1753 by his two-part *Employment for the Microscope*.

[6] Samuel Clarke, *A Discourse Concerning the Being and Attributes of God*, p. 69: 'I shall only observe this One thing; that the larger the Improvements and Discoveries are, which are daily made in Astronomy and Natural Philosophy; the more clearly is this Question [of design] continually determined, to the Shame and Confusion of Atheists.'

give into the most arbitrary Hypothesis, and at the same time, weaken all Proofs of his Existence.

Secondly. You have no Reason, on your Theory, for ascribing Perfection to the Deity, even in his finite Capacity; or for supposing him free from every Error, Mistake, or Incoherence in his Under- 5 takings. There are many inexplicable Difficulties in the Works of Nature, which, if we allow a perfect Author to be prov'd *a priori*, are easily solv'd, and become only seeming Difficulties, from the narrow Capacity of Man, who cannot trace infinite Relations. But according to your Method of Reasoning, these Difficulties become 10 all real; and perhaps will be insisted on, as new Instances of Likeness to human Art and Contrivance. At least, you must acknowledge, that it is impossible for us to tell, from our limited Views, whether this System contains any great Faults, or deserves any considerable Praise, if compar'd to other possible, and even real Systems. Cou'd 15 a Peasant, if the *Aneid* were read to him, pronounce that Poem to be absolutely faultless, or even assign to it its proper Rank among the Productions of human Wit; he, who had never seen any other Production?

But were this World ever so perfect a Production, it must still 20 remain uncertain, whether all the Excellencies of the Work can justly be ascrib'd to the Workman. If we survey a Ship, what an exalted Idea must we form of the Ingenuity of the Carpenter, who fram'd so complicated useful and beautiful a Machine? And what Surprize must we entertain, when we find him a stupid Mechanic, 25 who imitated others, and copy'd an Art, which, thro' a long Succession of Ages, after multiply'd Tryals, Mistakes, Corrections, Deliberations, and Controversies, had been gradually improving? Many Worlds might have been botch'd and bungled, throughout an Eternity, 'ere this System was struck out: Much Labour lost: 30 Many fruitless Tryals made: And a slow, but continu'd Improvment carry'd on during infinite Ages in the Art of World-making.

1 Hypothesis] Suppositions   2 weaken] destroy   3 on your Theory, for ascribing] according to your Hypothesis, to ascribe   4 for supposing] to suppose   5 Incoherence] Blunder   8 seeming] apparent   10 according to] in   11 on [by you]   14 contains] contain Faults [or not]   deserves] deserve   15 Praise] Praises   16 that Poem] the *Aneid*   20–(192)4 But ... imagin'd? *added*   26 which] that   which, [had been gradually improved]   32 during] thro'   World-making [thro' infinite Ages]

In such Subjects, who can determine, where the Truth; nay, who can conjecture where the Probability, lies; amidst a great Number of Hypotheses, which may be propos'd, and a still greater Number, which may be imagin'd?[7]

5   And what Shadow of an Argument, continu'd *Philo*, can you produce, from your Hypothesis, to prove the Unity of the Deity? A great Number of Men join in building a House or Ship,[8] in rearing a City, in framing a Commonwealth: Why may not several Deities combine in contriving and framing a World? This is only so much
10 greater Similarity to human Affairs. By sharing the Work among several, we may so much farther limit the Attributes of each, and get rid of that extensive Power and Knowledge, which must be suppos'd in one Deity, and which, according to you, can only serve to weaken the Proof of his Existence. And if such foolish, such
15 vicious Creatures as Man can yet often unite in framing and executing One Plan, how much more those Deities or Demons, whom we may suppose several Degrees more perfect?

To multiply Causes without Necessity is indeed contrary to true Philosophy: But this Principle applies not to the present
20 Case. Were one Deity antecedently prov'd by your Theory, who were possessed of every Attribute, requisite to the Production of the Universe; it wou'd be needless, I own (tho' not absurd) to suppose any other Deity existent. But while it is still a Question, whether all these Attributes are united in one Subject, or dispersed among

---

3 Hypotheses] Positions   9 much [a]   11 so much farther *deleted and then restored*   17 several] some   18–(193)12 To . . . Comprehension *added*   21 possessed] possest   24 dispersed among] disperst amongst

---

[7] This paragraph written on p. 44 of the manuscript at the end of Part V and marked with the symbol 'AA' for inclusion on p. 42 of the manuscript, where the marginal note in Hume's hand reads, 'The Passage marked AA on Page 44 to be here taken in'.

[8] Bernard Mandeville, *The Fable of the Bees* (London, 1729), ii. 149: 'What a Noble as well as Beautiful, what a glorious Machine is a First-Rate Man of War, when she is under Sail, well rigg'd, and well mann'd! As in Bulk and Weight it is vastly superior to any other moveable Body of human Invention, so there is no other that has an equal Variety of differently surprizing Contrivances to boast of. There are many Sets of Hands in the Nation, that, not wanting proper Materials, would be able in less than half a Year to produce, fit out, and navigate a First-Rate: yet it is certain, that this Task would be impracticable, if it was not divided and subdivided into a great Variety of different Labours. . .'.

several independent Beings: By what Phænomena in Nature can
we pretend to decide the Controversy? Where we see a Body rais'd
in a Scale, we are sure that there is in the opposite Scale, however,
concealed from Sight, some counterpoizing Weight equal to it:
But it is still allow'd to doubt, whether that Weight be an Aggre- 5
gate of several distinct Bodies, or one uniform united Mass. And
if the Weight requisite very much exceeds any thing which we
have ever seen conjoin'd in any single Body, the former Supposition
becomes still more probable and natural. An intelligent Being of
such vast Power and Capacity, as is necessary to produce the 10
Universe, or to speak in the Language of antient Philosophy, so prodigious an Animal, exceeds all Analogy and even Comprehension.[9]

But farther, *Cleanthes*; Men are mortal, and renew their Species
by Generation; and this is common to all living Creatures. The
two great Sexes of Male and Female, says *Milton*,[10] animate the 15
World. Why must this Circumstance, so universal, so essential, be
excluded from those numerous and limited Deities? Behold then
the Theogony of antient Times brought back upon us.

And why not become a perfect Anthropomorphite? Why not
assert the Deity or Deities to be corporeal, and to have Eyes, a Nose, 20
Mouth, Ears etc.[11] *Epicurus* maintain'd, that no Man had ever seen
Reason but in a human Figure; therefore the Gods must have a
human Figure.[12] And this Argument, which is deservedly so much

---

3 however] tho'   7 requisite] requir'd   9 An] So mighty an
10 necessary] requisite

---

[9] This paragraph added on p. 44 of the manuscript at the end of Part V and
marked with the symbol 'BB' for inclusion on p. 43 of the manuscript, where the
marginal note in Hume's hand reads, 'The Passage marked BB on Page 44 to be here
taken in'.

[10] *Paradise Lost*, VIII. 150–1: 'Communicating Male and Female Light, / Which two
great Sexes animate the World . . .'.

[11] Cicero, *De Natura Deorum*, p. 50: 'I return to the Gods. Can we suppose any of
them to be pink- or squint-eyed? Have they any Warts? Are any of them hook-nosed,
flap-ear'd, bettle-brow'd, or jolt-headed, as some of us are? Or are they free from
Imperfections?'

[12] Exact source untraced. Cf., however, Cicero's *Epicurus's Morals*, trans. John Digby
(London 1712), p. 114: 'He says in another place, That the Gods are imperceivable
to our Senses; that the Mind alone enjoys the Advantage of knowing 'em; that they
don't exist by a certain Solidity, nor by a distinction of Numbers, but that their Form
is like that of Men, by reason of the perpetual flux of Images, that affect the
Mind by the quality of their Nature.'

ridicul'd by *Cicero*, becomes, according to you, solid and philosophical.

   In a Word, *Cleanthes*, a Man, who follows your Hypothesis, is
able, perhaps, to assert, or conjecture, that the Universe, some
5 time, arose from some thing like Design: But beyond that Position
he cannot ascertain one single Circumstance, and is left afterwards
to fix every Point of his Theology, by the utmost Licence of Fancy
and Hypothesis. This World, for aught he knows, is very faulty
and imperfect, compar'd to a superior Standard; and was only the
10 first rude Essay of some Infant Deity, who afterwards abandon'd
it, asham'd of his lame Performance: It is the Work only of some
dependant, inferior Deity; and is the Object of Derision to his
Superiors: It is the Production of Old-Age and Dotage in some
superannuated Deity; and ever since his Death, has run on at
15 Adventures, from the first Impulse and active Force, which it
receiv'd from him—You justly give Signs of Horror, *Demea*, at
these strange Suppositions: But these, and a thousand more of
the same kind, are *Cleanthes*'s Suppositions, not mine. From the
Moment the Attributes of the Deity are suppos'd finite, all these
20 have Place. And I cannot, for my part, think, that so wild and un-
settled a System of Theology is, in any respect, preferable to none
at all.

   These Suppositions I absolutely disown; cry'd *Cleanthes*: They
strike me, however, with no Horror; especially, when propos'd in
25 that rambling way, in which they drop from you. On the contrary,
they give me Pleasure, when I see, that, by the utmost Indulgence
of your Imagination, you never get rid of the Hypothesis of Design
in the Universe; but are oblig'd, at every turn, to have Recourse
to it. To this Conception I adhere steadily; and this I regard as a
30 sufficient Foundation for Religon.

   1 *Cicero*] Divines   5 thing like] kind of   8 Hypothesis] Conjecture
8 knows] can know   11 lame Performance] Production   24 however . . .
Horror;] with no Horror, however;   Horror] Horrour   26–7 Indulgence of
your] Licence of

PART 6

It must be a slight Fabric, indeed, said *Demea*, which can be erected on so tottering a Foundation. While we are uncertain, whether there is one Deity or many; whether the Deity or Deities, to whom we owe our Existence, be perfect or imperfect, subordinate or supreme, dead or alive; what Trust or Confidence can we repose in them? What Devotion or Worship address to them? What Veneration or Obedience pay them? To all the Purposes of Life, the Theory of Religion becomes altogether useless: And even with regard to speculative Consequences, its Uncertainty, according to you, must render it totally precarious and unsatisfactory.[1]

To render it still more unsatisfactory, said *Philo*, there occurs to me another Hypothesis, which must acquire an Air of Probability from the Method of Reasoning so much insisted on by *Cleanthes*. That like Effects arise from like Causes: This Principle he supposes the Foundation of all Religion. But there is another Principle of the same kind, no less certain, and deriv'd from the same Source of Experience; that where several known Circumstances are *observ'd* to be similar, the unknown will also be *found* similar. Thus, if we see the Limbs of a human Body, we conclude, that it is also attended with a human Head, tho hid from us. Thus, if we see, thro a Chink in a Wall a small Part of the Sun, we conclude, that, were the Wall remov'd, we should see the whole Body. In short, this Method of Reasoning is so obvious and familiar, that no Scruple can ever be made with regard to its Solidity.

Now if we survey the Universe, so far as it falls under our Knowledge, it bears a great Ressemblance to an animal or organiz'd

2 which] that   6 supreme] superior   7 Worship [can we]   8 Obedience [can we]   17 Source of [Practice and]   19 will] must   21–3 Thus . . . Body.] Thus, if we hear in the Dark, Reason and Sense deliver'd in an articulate Voice, we infer, that there is also present a human Figure, which we shall discover on the Return of Light.   *This sentence deleted in margin:* If we see from a Distance the Buildings of a City, we infer that they contain Inhabitants, whom we shall discover on our Approach to them.

---

[1] *The Natural History of Religion*, p. 42 above: 'To ascribe the origin and fabric of the universe to these imperfect beings never enters into the imagination of any polytheist or idolater.'

Body, and seems actuated with a like Principle of Life and Motion. A continual Circulation of Matter in it produces no Disorder: A continual Waste in every Part is incessantly repair'd: The closest Sympathy is perceiv'd throughout the entire System: And each Part or Member, in performing its proper Offices, operates both to its own Preservation and to that of the Whole. The World, therefore, I infer, is an Animal, and the Deity is the SOUL of the World, actuating it, and actuated by it.

You have too much Learning, *Cleanthes*, to be at all surpriz'd at this Opinion, which, you know, was maintain'd by almost all the Theists of Antiquity, and chiefly prevails in their Discourses and Reasonings.[2] For tho' sometimes the antient Philosophers reason from final Causes, as if they thought the World the Workmanship of God; yet it appears rather their favourite Notion to consider it as his Body, whose Organization renders it subservient to him. And it must be confessed, that as the Universe resembles more a human Body than it does the Works of human Art and Contrivance; if our limited Analogy cou'd ever, with any Propriety, be extended to the Whole of Nature, the Inference seems juster in favour of the antient than the modern Theory.

There are many other Advantages too, in the former Theory, which recommended it to the antient Theologians. Nothing more repugnant to all their Notions, because nothing more repugnant to common Experience, than Mind without Body; a mere spiritual Substance, which fell not under their Senses nor Comprehension, and of which they had not observ'd one single Instance throughout all Nature. Mind and Body they knew, because they felt both: An Order, Arrangement, Organization, or internal Machinery in both they likewise knew, after the same manner: And it cou'd not but seem reasonable to transfer this Experience to the Universe, and to suppose the divine Mind and Body to be also co-eval, and to

16 confessed] confest   24 than [a]   without [a]   25 fell] falls   their Senses nor Comprehension] the Senses nor the Comprehension

---

[2] Cicero, *De Natura Deorum*, p. 23: '[Plato] likewise asserts, in his *Timaeus*, and in his *Laws*, that the *World*, the *Heavens*, the *Stars*, the *Earth*, the *Mind*, and *those Gods*, which are deliver'd down to us from our Ancestors, constitute the Deity.' Cf. Plato, *Timaeus*, 30–2; Loeb edn., VII. 54–61.

have, both of them, Order and Arrangement naturally inherent in them, and inseparable from them.

Here therefore is a new Species of Anthropomorphism, *Cleanthes*, on which you may deliberate; and a Theory, which seems not lyable to any considerable Difficulties. You are too much superior 5 surely to *systematical Prejudices*, to find any more Difficulty in supposing an animal Body to be, originally, of itself, or from unknown Causes, possessed of Order and Organization, than in supposing a similar Order to belong to Mind. But the *vulgar Prejudice*, that Body and Mind ought always to accompany each 10 other, ought not, one shou'd think, to be entirely neglected; since it is founded on *vulgar Experience*, the only Guide which you profess to follow in all these theological Enquiries. And if you assert, that our limited Experience is an unequal Standard, by which to judge of the unlimited Extent of Nature; you entirely abandon your 15 own Hypothesis, and must thenceforward adopt our Mysticism, as you call it, and admit of the absolute Incomprehensibility of the divine Nature.[3]

This Theory, I own, reply'd *Cleanthes*, has never before occur'd to me, tho a pretty natural one; and I cannot readily, upon so short 20 an Examination and Reflection, deliver any Opinion with regard to it. You are very scrupulous, indeed, said *Philo*; Were I to examine any System of Yours, I shou'd not have acted with half that Caution and Reserve, in starting Objections and Difficulties to it. However, if any thing occur to you, you will oblige us by proposing it. 25

Why then, reply'd *Cleanthes*, it seems to me, that, tho the World does, in many Circumstances, resemble an animal Body; yet is the Analogy also defective in many Circumstances, the most material: No Organs of Sense; no Seat of Thought or Reason; no-one precise Origin of Motion and Action. In short, it seems to bear a stronger 30

4 which] that   7 an animal Body] a Body   8 possessed] possest   8–9 in supposing] to suppose   9 Order to belong] Principle belonging   11–12 since it is] because   13–18 And . . . Nature. *deleted and then restored*   21 deliver any Opinion about it *deleted and transposed in altered form to end of sentence*   22 Were I to examine] And were I to start Objections and Difficulties *altered and moved to end of sentence*   25 you will] you'll   29 precise] distinct   30 bear a [much]

[3] Hume has written in the margin of the MS., 'Print this Sentence, tho eraz'd'.

Resemblance to a Vegetable than to an Animal; and your Inference wou'd be so far inconclusive in favour of the Soul of the World.

But in the next Place, your Theory seems to imply the Eternity of the World; and that is a Principle, which, I think, can be re-
5 futed by the strongest Reasons and Probabilities. I shall suggest an Argument to this Purpose, which, I believe, has not been insisted on by any Writer.[4] Those, who reason from the late Origin of Arts and Sciences, tho their Inference wants not Force, may perhaps be refuted by Considerations, deriv'd from the Nature of human
10 Society, which is in continual Revolution, between Ignorance and Knowledge, Liberty and Slavery, Riches and Poverty; so that it is impossible for us, from our limited Experience, to fortell with Assurance what Events may or may not be expected. Antient Learning and History seem to have been in greater danger of
15 entirely perishing after the Inundation of the barbarous Nations; and had these Convulsions continu'd a little longer or been a little more violent, we shou'd not probably have now known what passed in the World a few Centuries before us. Nay, were it not for the Superstition of the Popes, who preserv'd a little Jargon of
20 *Latin,* in order to support the Appearance of an antient and univer-sal Church, that Tongue must have been utterly lost: In which Case, the western World, being totally barbarous, wou'd not have been in a fit Disposition for receiving the *Greek* Language and Learning, which was convey'd to them after the Sacking of *Con-*
25 *stantinople.* When Learning and Books had been extinguish'd, even the mechanical Arts wou'd have fallen considerably to decay, and it is easily imagin'd that Fable or Tradition might ascribe to them a much later Origin than the true one. This vulgar Argument, there-fore, against the Eternity of the World, seems a little precarious.

---

5 an] a new   6 believe] think   8 Inference] Argument   10 is in [a]   Revolution, [and Uncertainty]   12 limited *deleted and then restored*
13 Antient] All antient   14–15 to have been in great danger of entirely perishing] to have been very near lost   18 passed] had past   were it not] had it not been   23 for receiving] to receive   24 after] upon   25 When] After   had been [totally]   27 imagin'd] suppos'd   28 later] better the true one] what is now suppos'd   vulgar] common

---

[4] Except, of course, by Hume in his essay 'Of the Rise and Progress of the Arts and Sciences' (1742).

But here appears to the Foundation of a better Argument. *Lucullus* was the first that brought Cherry-Trees from *Asia* to *Europe*;[5] tho' that Tree thrives so well in many *European* Climates, that it grows in the Woods without any Culture. It is possible, that, throughout a whole Eternity, no *European* had ever passed into 5 *Asia*, and thought of transplanting so delicious a Fruit into his own Country? Or if the Tree was once transplanted and propagated, how cou'd it ever afterwards perish? Empires may rise and fall; Liberty and Slavery succeed alternately; Ignorance and Knowledge give place to each other; but the Cherry-tree will still 10 remain in the Woods of *Greece*, *Spain* and *Italy*, and will never be affected by the Revolutions of human Society.

It is not two thousand Years, since Vines were transplanted into *France*; tho' there is no Climate in the World more favourable to them. It is not three Centuries since Horses, Cows, Sheep, Swine, 15 Dogs, Corn were known in *America*. It is possible, that, during the Revolutions of a whole Eternity, there never arose a *Columbus*, who might open the Communication between *Europe* and that Continent? We may as well imagine, that all Men wou'd wear Stockings for ten thousand Years, and never have the Sense to think of Garters 20 to tye them. All these seem convincing Proofs of the Youth, or rather Infancy of the World; as being founded on the Operation of Principles more constant and steady, than those by which human Society is govern'd and directed. Nothing less than a total Convulsion of the Elements will ever destroy all the *European* Animals and 25 Vegetables, which are now to be found in the Western World.

And what Argument have you against such Convulsions? reply'd

2 that]who   3 many] most   5 passed] past   6 and]or transplanting so delicious] transporting so agreeable   9 Liberty] Victory   11 *Greece*] *France* 13 since] that   14 no] not any   17 arose] was   20 Sense] Invention 21 Proofs of the [Freshness and]   26 which] that

---

[5] The Roman general Lucius Licinius Lucullus is credited with the introduction of the cherry-tree to Europe by Servius in his commentary on Virgil's *Georgic* (ii. 18): 'Sane Cerasus civitas est Ponti. Arbor "cerasus", pomum "cerasium" dicitur. Cerasos Lucullus capto oppido Cerasunte in Italiam primus attulit.' ('The name "Cerasus" is from the city of that name in Pontus. The tree is called "cerasus", the first "cerasium". These cherry-trees were first brought to Italy by Lucullus after he captured the town of Cerasus.') Cf. Virgil, *Works*, Loeb edn., i. 116–17. Servius Grammatici, *In Vergilii Bucolica et Georgica Commentarii*, Recensuit Georgius Thilo (Hildesheim, 1961), iii. 219.

Philo. Strong and almost incontestable Proofs may be trac'd over
the whole Earth, that every part of this Globe has continu'd for
many Ages entirely cover'd with Water.[6] And tho' Order were
suppos'd inseparable from Matter, and inherent in it; yet may
5 Matter be susceptible of many and great Revolutions, thro' the
endless Periods of eternal Duration. The incessant Changes, to
which every Part of it is subject, seem to intimate some such general
Transformations; tho' at the same time, it is observable, that all the
Changes, and Corruptions, of which we have ever had Experience,
10 are but Passanges from one State of Order to another; nor can Matter
ever rest in total Deformity and Confusion. What we see in the
Parts, we may infer in the Whole; at least, that is the Method of
Reasoning, on which you rest your whole Theory. And were I
oblig'd to defend any particular System of this Nature (which I
15 never willingly shou'd do) I esteem none more plausible, than that
which ascribes an eternal, inherent Principle of Order to the World;
tho attended with great and continual Revolutions and Alterations.
This at once solves all Difficulties; and if the Solution, by being so
general, is not entirely compleat and satisfactory, it is, at least,
20 a Theory, that we must, sooner or later, have recourse to,
whatever System we embrace. How cou'd things have been as
they are, were there not an original, inherent Principle of Order
somewhere, in Thought or in Matter? And it is very indifferent to
which of these we give the Preference. Chance has no place, on any
25 Hypothesis, sceptical or religious.[7] Every thing is surely govern'd

1 Strong] There are strong   may be trac'd] of a Deluge are to be found
2 this] that   2–3 that every part . . . Water *added*   15 do)] I [shou'd]
16 to the World] in Matter   18 solves all Difficulties] answers all Questions
19 is[1]] be   19–20 a Theory that] what   23 is very] seems   23–4 to which. . .
Preference.] which of them we prefer.

---

[6] Scientific theologians made much of this point, e.g., John Ray, *Three Physico-
Theological Discourses* (London, 1721), p. 121: '. . . it may rationally be supposed,
there were then great Mutations and Alterations made in the superficial Part of the
Earth . . .'.

[7] Butler, *Analogy of Religion*, p. 189: '. . . all reasonable Men know certainly, that
there cannot, in Reality, be any such thing as Chance; and conclude, that the things
which have this Appearance, are the Result of general Laws, and are resolveable
into them.' Hume had a little trouble with this sentence, writing first, 'Chance tis
ridiculous to mention on any Hypothesis', altering that to 'Chance, or, what is the
same thing, Liberty, seems not to have place on any Hypothesis', and finally
producing the above sentence.

by steady, inviolable Laws. And were the inmost Essence of things laid open to us, we shou'd then discover a Scene, of which, at present, we can have no Idea. Instead of admiring the Order of natural Beings, we shou'd clearly see, that it was absolutely impossible for them, in the smallest Article, ever to admit of any other Disposition.

Were any one inclin'd to revive the antient Pagan Theology, which maintain'd, as we learn from *Hesiod*, that this Globe was govern'd by 30,000 Deities, who arose from the unknown Powers of Nature:[8] You wou'd naturally object, *Cleanthes*, that nothing is gain'd by this Hypothesis, and that it is as easy to suppose all Men and Animals, Beings more numerous, but less perfect, to have sprung immediately from a like Origin. Push the same Inference a Step farther; and you will find a numerous Society of Deities as explicable as one Universal Deity, who possesses, within himself, the Powers and Perfections of the whole Society. All these Systems, then, of Scepticism, Polytheism, and Theism you must allow, on your Principles, to be on a like Footing, and that no-one of them has any Advantages over the others. You may thence learn the Fallacy of your Principles.[9]

PART 7

But here, continued *Philo*, in examining the antient System of the Soul of the World, there strikes me, all on a sudden, a new Idea, which, if just, must go near to subvert all your Reasoning, and destroy even your first Inferences, on which you repose such Confidence. If the Universe bears a greater Likeness to animal Bodies and to Vegetables, than to the Works of human Art, it is more

5 for them] they cou'd ever   7–20 Were . . . Principles *added*   8 which
. . . *Hesiod*] mention'd by *Varro*   18 to be [alike explicable]

[8] In both the *Works and Days* and *The Theogony*. Cf. the latter work in *The Works of Hesiod*, trans. Thomas Cooke (London, 1728), ii. 18: 'From *Earth*, and *Heav'n*, great Parents, first they trace / The Progeny of Gods, a bounteous Race . . .'. The figure 30,000 is used for any indefinite large number and is common occurrence in all periods of classical literature. Cf. *Works and Days*, 252–5; Loeb edn., pp. 20–2.
[9] This last paragraph added in Hume's mature hand and crowded on to the bottom of p. 48 of the manuscript.

probable, that its Cause resembles the Cause of the former than that of the latter, and its Origin ought rather to be ascrib'd to Generation or Vegetation than to Reason or Design. Your Conclusion, even according to your own Principles, is therefore lame 5 and defective.

Pray open up this Argument a little farther, said *Demea*. For I do not rightly apprehend it, in that concise manner, in which you have exprest it.

Our Friend, *Cleanthes*, reply'd *Philo*, as you have heard, asserts, 10 that since no Question of Fact can be prov'd otherwise than by Experience, the Existence of a Deity admits not of Proof from any other Medium. The World, says he, resembles the Works of human Contrivance: Therefore its Cause must also resemble that of the other. Here we may remark, that the Operation of one very small 15 part of Nature to wit Man, upon another very small Part, to wit, that inanimate Matter lying within his Reach, is the Rule, by which *Cleanthes* judges of the Origin of the Whole; and he measures Objects, so widely disproportion'd, by the same individual Standard. But to wave all Objections, drawn from this Topic; I affirm, that there are 20 other Parts of the Universe (besides the Machines of human Invention) which bear still a greater Ressemblance to the Fabric of the World, and which therefore afford a better Conjecture concerning the universal Origin of this System. These Parts are Animals and Vegetables. The World plainly resembles more an Animal or a 25 Vegetable than it does a Watch[1] or a Knitting Loom. Its Cause, therefore, it is more probable, resembles the Cause of the former. The Cause of the former is Generation or Vegetation. The Cause

---

6 up *deleted and then restored*   9 heard] seen   13–14 also resemble . . . other] be resembling   15 to wit] viz   to wit] viz   17 *Cleanthes*] he 23 this System] the Whole of Nature] the World

---

[1] Cf. William Derham, *The Artificial Clock-Maker* (London, 1696), p. 89: 'From this description it appeareth, that in this Sphere, the Sun, Moon, and other heavenly bodies, had their proper motion: and that this motion was effected by some enclosed *Spirit*. What this *enclosed Spirit* was, I cannot tell, but suppose it to be Springs, Wheels or Pullies, or some such means of Clock-work: Which being hidden from vulgar eyes, might be taken for Some Angel, Spirit, or Divine power; unless by Spirit here, you understand some aerious, subtiliz'd liquor, or vapours. But how this, or indeed any thing, but Clock-work, could give such true, and regular motions, I am not able to guess.'

therefore, of the World, we may infer to be something similar or analogous to Generation or Vegetation.

But how is it conceivable, said *Demea*, that the World can arise from any thing similar to Vegetation or Generation?

Very easily, reply'd *Philo*. In like manner as a Tree sheds its Seed into the neighbouring Fields, and produces other Trees; so the great Vegetable, the World, or this planetary System, produces within itself certain Seeds, which, being scatter'd into the surrounding Chaos, vegetate into new Worlds. A Comet, for Instance, is the Seed of a World; and after it has been fully ripen'd, by passing from Sun to Sun, and Star to Star, it is at last tost into the unform'd Elements, which every where surround this Universe, and immediately sprouts up into a new System.[2]

Or if, for the sake of Variety (for I see no other Advantage) we shou'd suppose this World to be an Animal; a Comet is the Egg of this Animal; and in like manner as an Ostrich lays its Egg in the Sand, which, without any farther Care, hatches the Egg, and produces a new Animal; so—

I understand you, says *Demea*: But what wild, arbitrary Suppositions are these? What *Data* have you for such extraordinary Conclusions? And is the slight, imaginary Ressemblance of the World to a Vegetable or an Animal sufficient to establish the same Inference with regard to both? Objects, which are in general so widely different; ought they to be a Standard for each other?

Right, cries *Philo*: This is the Topic on which I have all along insisted. I have still asserted, that we have no *Data* to establish any System of Cosmogony. Our Experience, so imperfect in itself, and so limited both in Extent and Duration, can afford us no probable

---

1 therefore of the World] of the Universe   6 and [thereby]   10 fully] duly   15 shou'd] will   21 *a word added above line but illegible and now torn from corner of MS.*   23–4 Objects . . . ought they] Ought Objects . . . to be 25–6 This . . . insisted.] This . . . insisted on.   28 so limited] so wonderfully limited

---

2 Pierre Bayle, *Miscellaneous Reflections, Occasion'd by the Comet* (London, 1708), ii. 540: 'I conclude . . . that [Comets] are Bodys as antient as the World, which by the Laws of Motion wherewith God governs the vast Machine of the Universe, are from time to time determin'd to pass within our view, and to reflect the Light of the Sun upon us, modify'd in such a manner as to make us perceive a long train of its golden Locks . . .'.

Conjecture concerning the Whole of things. But if we must needs fix on some Hypothesis; by what Rule, pray, ought we to determine our Choice? Is there any other Rule than the greater Similarity of the Objects compar'd? And does not a Plant or an Animal, which 5 springs from Vegetation or Generation, bear a stronger Ressemblance to the World, than does any artificial Machine, which arises from Reason and Design?

But what is this Vegetation and Generation, of which you talk, said *Demea*? Can you explain their Operations, and anatomize that 10 fine internal Structure, on which they depend?

As much, at least, reply'd *Philo,* as *Cleanthes* can explain the Operations of Reason, or anatomize that internal Structure, on which *it* depends. But without any such elaborate Disquisitions, when I see an Animal, I infer, that it sprang from Generation; and that with 15 as great Certainty as you conclude a House to have been rear'd by Design. These Words, *Generation, Reason,* mark only certain Powers and Energies in Nature, whose Effects are known, but whose Essence is incomprehensible; and one of these Principles, more than the other, has no Privilege for being made a Standard to the 20 whole of Nature.

In reality, *Demea,* it may reasonably be expected, that the larger the Views are which we take of things, the better will they conduct us in our Conclusions concerning such extraordinary and such magnificent Subjects. In this little Corner of the World alone, there 25 are four Principles, *Reason, Instinct, Generation, Vegetation,* which are similar to each other, and are the Causes of similar Effects. What a Number of other Principles may we naturally suppose in the immense Extent and Variety of the Universe, could we travel from Planet to Planet and from System to System, in order to examine 30 each Part of this mighty Fabric? Any one of these four Principles above-mention'd (and a hundred others, which lie open to our Conjecture) may afford us a Theory, by which to judge of the

---

1 must] will   6 than . . . Machine,] than any . . . Machine does,   11 As much, at least] Yes   14–15 and that with as great Certainty as you] as certainly as you would] as great as you would   15 rear'd by [Reason and]   19 no [more a]   to] for] of   20 Nature [than the other]   21–2 larger the Views are which we] the largest Views we can   the better will they] will probably 23 us [best/the better]   30 Fabric] Whole   32 Theory] Standard

Origin of the World; and it is a palpable and egregious Partiality to confine our View entirely to that Principle, by which our own Minds operate. Were this Principle more intelligible on that Account, such a Partiality might be somewhat excusable: But Reason, in its internal Fabric and Structure, is really as little known 5 to us as Instinct or Vegetation; and perhaps even that vague, undeterminate Word, Nature, to which the Vulgar refer every thing, is not at the bottom more inexplicable. The Effects of these Principles are known to us from Experience: But the Principles themselves, and their manner of Operation are totally unknown: 10 Nor is it less intelligible, or less conformable to Experience to say, that the World arose by Vegetation from a Seed shed by another World, than to say that it arose from a divine Reason or Contrivance, according to the Sense in which *Cleanthes* understands it.

But Methinks, said *Demea*, if the World had a vegetative Quality, 15 and cou'd sow the Seeds of new Worlds into the infinite Chaos, this Power wou'd be still an additional Argument for Design in its Author. For whence cou'd arise so wonderful a Faculty but from Design? Or how can Order spring from any thing, which perceives not that Order which it bestows?[3]   20

You need only look around you, reply'd *Philo*, to satisfy Yourself with regard to this Question. A Tree bestows Order and Organization on that Tree, which springs from it, without knowing the Order: An Animal, in the same manner, on its Offspring: a Bird, on its Nest: And Instances of this kind are even more frequent in the 25 World, than those of Order, which arise from Reason and Contrivance. To say that all this Order in Animals and Vegetables proceeds ultimately from Design is begging the Question; nor can that great Point be ascertain'd otherwise than by proving *a priori*, both that Order is, from its Nature, inseparably attach'd to 30

2–3 our own Minds] we Ourselves   3 this Principle] it   that] this
4 such a] this   6 Vegetation] Generation   7 undeterminate] undetermin'd
8 the *deleted and then restored*   12 by[1]] from   14 according to] in
26–7 Contrivance] Perception   28 proceeds] arises

---

[3] Shaftesbury, *Characteristicks*, ii. 284: 'STRANGE! That there shou'd be *in Nature* the Idea of an Order and Perfection, which NATURE her-self wants! That Beings which arise from *Nature* shou'd be so perfect, as to discover Imperfection in her Constitution; and be wise enough to correct that Wisdom by which they were made!'

Thought, and that it can never, of itself, or from original unknown Principles, belong to Matter.

But farther, *Demea*; this Objection, which you urge, can never be made Use of by *Cleanthes*, without renouncing a Defence, which 5 he has already made against one of my Objections. When I enquir'd concerning the Cause of that supreme Reason and Intelligence, into which he resolves every thing; he told me, that the Impossibility of satisfying such Enquiries cou'd never be admitted as an Objection in any Species of Philosophy. *We must stop somewhere*, says he; *nor is* 10 *it ever within the Reach of human Capacity to explain ultimate Causes, or show the last Connexions of any Objects. It is sufficient, if the Steps, so far as we go, are supported by Experience and Observation.* Now that Vegetation and Generation, as well as Reason, are experienc'd to be Principles of Order in Nature, is undeniable. If I rest my System of 15 Cosmogony on the former, preferably to the latter, 'tis at my Choice: The Matter seems entirely arbitrary. And when *Cleanthes* asks me what is the Cause of my great vegetative or generative Faculty, I am equally entitled to ask him the Cause of his great reasoning Principle. These Questions we have agreed to forbear on 20 both Sides; and it is chiefly his Interest on the present Occasion to stick to this Agreement. Judging by our limited and imperfect Experience, Generation has some Privileges above Reason: For we see every day the latter arise from the former, never the former from the latter.

25 Compare, I beseech you, the Consequences on both Sides. The World, say I, resembles an Animal, therefore it is an Animal, therefore it arose from Generation. The Steps, I confess, are wide; yet there is some small Appearance of Analogy in each Step. The World, says *Cleanthes*, resembles a Machine, therefore it is a Machine, 30 therefore it arose from Design. The Steps here are equally wide, and the Analogy less striking. And if he pretends to carry on *my* Hypothesis a Step farther, and to infer Design or Reason from the great Principle of Generation, on which I insist; I may, with better Authority, use the same Freedom to push farther his Hypothesis,

1 Thought] Perception   8 satisfying such Enquiries] answering such Questions   16 when] if   19 Principle] Faculty   23 former,[1] [but]   27 arose] arises   wide; [but]   30 arose] arises   33 on which I insist;] which [he insists] I insist on;

and infer a divine Generation or Theogony from his Principle of Reason. I have at least some faint Shadow of Experience, which is the utmost, that can ever be attain'd in the present Subject. Reason, in innumerable Instances, is observ'd to arise from the Principle of Generation, and never to arise from any other Principle.   5

Hesiod, and all the antient Mythologists, were so struck with this Analogy, that they universally explain'd the Origin of Nature from an animal Birth, and Copulation.[4] *Plato*,[5] too, so far as he is intelligible, seems to have adopted some such Notion in his *Timaeus*.[6]

The *Bramins* assert, that the World arose from an infinite Spider,   10 who spun this whole complicated Mass from his Bowels, and annihilates afterwards the whole or any Part of it, by absorbing it again, and resolving it into his own Essence. Here is a Species of Cosmogony, which appears to us ridiculous; because a Spider is a little contemptible Animal, whose Operations we are never likely to   15 take for a Model of the whole Universe.[7] But still here is a new Species of Analogy, even in our Globe. And were there a Planet wholly inhabited by Spiders, (which is very possible) this Inference wou'd there appear as natural and irrefragable as that which in our Planet ascribes the Origin of all things to Design and Intelligence,   20 as explain'd by *Cleanthes*. Why an orderly System may not be spun

---

6–9 *Hesiod* . . . *Timaeus. added*   6 *Hesiod*,] Also *Hesiod*, you know,   and all] as well as   7 Nature] all things   9 seems [also]   10–208(2) The *Bramins* . . . Reason. *added*   16 a¹] the   18 wholly] totally   19 our] this

---

[4] Hesiod, *Theogony*, 116–232 in *Works*, trans. Thomas Cooke, ii. 21–57: 'All Honours flow from him of Gods the God . . . [etc.].' Cf. Lucretius, *De Rerum Natura*, V. 783–820.

[5] Plato, *Timaeus*, 29d–31g.

[6] This paragraph added in margin and marked 'New Paragraph' on p. 52 of the manuscript.

[7] Cf. Pierre Bayle, *Dictionary Historical and Critical*, art. 'Spinoza' (London, 1734–8), v. 201 n.: 'Now those Cabalists, or Indian Pendets, carry the extravagance farther than all those philosophers, and pretend that God, or that Supreme Being, which they call Achar, immutable, immoveable, has not only produced or taken souls out of its own substance, but also whatever is material and corporeal in the universe, and that their production was not made in the way of efficient causes, but as a spider produces a cob-web out of its own bowels, and re-assumes it whenever it pleases. Creation therefore, say these imaginary doctors, is only an extraction or extension, which God makes of his own substance, of those webs which he draws, as it were, out of his own bowels. . . .'

from the Belly as well as from the Brain, it will be difficult for him to give a satisfactory Reason.[8]

I must confess, *Philo,* reply'd *Cleanthes,* that, of all Men living, the Task which you have undertaken, of raising Doubts and Objec-
5 tions, suits you best, and seems, in a manner, natural and unavoidable to you. So great is your Fertility of Invention, that I am not asham'd to acknowledge myself unable, on a sudden, to solve regularly such out-of-the-way Difficulties as you incessantly start upon me: Tho I clearly see, in general, their Fallacy and Error. And
10 I question not, but you are yourself, at present, in the same Case, and have not the Solution so ready as the Objection; while you must be sensible, that common Sense and Reason is entirely against you, and that such Whimsies, as you have deliver'd, may puzzle, but never can convince us.[9]

15 ## PART 8

What you ascribe to the Fertility of my Invention, reply'd *Philo,* is intirely owing to the Nature of the Subject. In Subjects, adapted to the narrow Compass of human Reason, there is commonly but one Determination, which carries Probability or Conviction with it;
20 and to a Man of sound Judgement, all other Suppositions, but that one, appear entirely absurd and chimerical. But in such Questions, as the present, a hundred contradictory Views may preserve a kind of imperfect Analogy; and Invention has here full Scope to exert itself. Without any great Effort of Thought, I believe that I cou'd,
25 in an Instant, propose other Systems of Cosmogony, which wou'd have some faint Appearance of Truth; tho it is a thousand, a Million to one, if either Yours or any-one of mine be the true System.

1 Brain] Brains	2 give . . . Reason]explain	4 raising] starting
11 while] tho	13 Whimsies] Whims	17 Subjects, [which are]
23 here] there	25 propose [many] Cosmogony, [all of]	27 mine] these

[8] This paragraph added at bottom of p. 52 of manuscript, with 'AA' markings to indicate that it is to follow the paragraph added in the margin (above, p. 207). These revisions appear to date from the 1760s; Cf. Hume's letters to Adam Smith, Hugh Blair, and William Strahan (Introduction, pp. 106–8).

[9] Berkeley, *Alciphron,* I. 208: 'This sort of Arguments I have always found dry and jejune; and, as they are not suited to my way of Thinking, they may perhaps puzzle, but never will convince me.'

For Instance; what if I shou'd revive the old *Epicurean* Hypothesis?[1] This is commonly, and I believe, justly, esteem'd the most absurd System, that has yet been proposed;[2] yet, I know not, whether, with a few Alterations, it might not be brought to bear a faint Appearance of Probability. Instead of supposing Matter infinite, as *Epicurus* did; let us suppose it finite. A finite Number of Particles is only susceptible of finite Transpositions: And it must happen, in an eternal Duration, that every possible Order or Position must be try'd an infinite Number of times. This World, therefore, with all its Events, even the most minute, has before been produc'd and destroy'd, and will again be produc'd and destroy'd, without any Bounds and Limitations.[3] No-one, who has a Conception of the Powers of Infinite, in comparison of finite, will ever scruple this Determination.

But this supposes, said *Demea*, that Matter can acquire Motion, without any voluntary Agent or first Mover.

And where is the Difficulty, reply'd *Philo*, of that Supposition? Every Event, before Experience, is equally difficult and incomprehensible; and every Event, after Experience, is equally easy and intelligible. Motion, in many Instances, from Gravity, from Elasticity, from Electricity, begins in Matter, without any known voluntary Agent; and to suppose always, in these Cases, an unknown voluntary Agent is mere Hypothesis; and Hypothesis attended with no Advantages. The Beginning of Motion in Matter itself is as conceivable *a priori* as its Communication from Mind and Intelligence.

Besides; why may not Motion have been propagated by Impulse thro all Eternity, and the same Stock of it, or nearly the same,

---

3 that] which] that   12 No-one] Nor can anyone   who] that

---

[1] Of an infinity of worlds. Cf. his *Letter to Herodotus*, 45, in *The Extant Remains*, ed. and trans. C. Bailey (Oxford, 1926), p. 9: 'There are infinite worlds both like and unlike this world of ours . . .'. Cf. Lucretius, *De Rerum Natura*, I. 958–1051.

[2] Clarke, *Discourse*, p. 59: 'And how ridiculous the Epicurean Hypothesis is, of the Earth producing them all at first by chance . . .'.

[3] Shaftesbury, *Characteristicks*, ii. 298: 'In length of time, amidst the infinite Hurry and Shock of Beings, this *single odd World*, by accident, might have been struck out, and cast into some Form (as among infinite *Chances*, what is three which may not happen?)'

be still upheld in the Universe? As much as is lost by the Composition of Motion, as much is gain'd by its Resolution. And whatever the Causes are, the Fact is certain, that Matter is, and always has been in continual Agitation, as far as human Experience or
5 Tradition reaches. There is not probably, at present, in the whole Universe, one Particle of Matter at absolute Rest.

And this very Consideration too, continu'd *Philo*, which we have stumbled on in the Course of the Argument, suggests a new Hypothesis of Cosmogony, that is not absolutely absurd and im-
10 probable. Is there a System, an Order, an Œconomy of things, by which Matter can preserve that perpetual Agitation, which seems essential to it, and yet maintain a Constancy in the Forms, which it produces? There certainly is such an Œconomy: For this is actually the Case with the present World. The continual Motion of
15 Matter, therefore, in less than infinite Transpositions, must produce this Œconomy or Order; and by its very Nature, that Order, when once establish'd, supports itself, for many Ages, if not to Eternity. But wherever Matter is so poiz'd, arrang'd, and adjusted as to continue in perpetual Motion, and yet preserve a Constancy in the
20 Forms its Situation must of Necessity have all the same Appearance of Art and Contrivance, which we observe at present. All the Parts of each Form must have a Relation to each other, and to the Whole: And the Whole itself must have a Relation to the other Parts of the Universe, to the Element, in which the Form subsists; to the
25 Materials, with which it repairs its Waste and Decay; and to every other Form, which is hostile or friendly. A Defect in any of these particulars destroys the Form; and the Matter, of which it is compos'd, is again set loose, and is thrown into irregular Motions and Fermentations, till it unite itself to some other regular Form. If
30 no such Form be prepar'd to receive it, and if there be a great Quantity of this corrupted Matter in the Universe, the Universe itself is entirely disorder'd; whether it be the feeble Embryo of a World in its first Beginnings, that is thus destroy'd, or the rotten

4 as[1]] so] as   9 Hypothesis] System   12 maintain [an
Uniformity and]   16–17 that Order . . . itself] it supports itself   18 But]
And   19 in] its   a Constancy] an Uniformity   20 Forms [which it
produces]   its Situation] it   21 Art] Artifice   22 Form] System
33 rotten] feeble

Carcass of one, languishing in old Age and Infirmity. In either case, a Chaos ensues; till finite, tho' innumerable Revolutions produce at last some Forms, whose Parts and Organs are so adjusted as to support the Forms amidst a continu'd Succession of Matter.

Suppose, (for we shall endeavour to vary the Expression) that Matter were thrown into any Position, by a blind, unguided Force; it is evident that this first Position must in all Probability be the most confus'd and most disorderly imaginable, without any Resemblance to those Works of human Contrivance, which, along with a Symmetry of Parts, discover an Adjustment of means to ends and a Tendency to Self-preservation. If the actuating Force cease after this Operation, Matter must remain for ever in Disorder, and continue an immense Chaos, without any Proportion or Activity. But suppose, that the actuating Force, whatever it be, still continues in Matter, this first Position will immediately give place to a second, which will likewise in all Probability be as disorderly as the first, and so on, thro' many Successions of Changes and Revolutions. No particular Order or Position ever continues a moment unaltered. The original Force, still remaining in Activity, gives a perpetual Restlessness to Matter. Every possible Situation is produc'd, and instantly destroy'd. If a Glimpse or Dawn of Order appears for a moment, it is instantly hurry'd away and confounded, by that never-ceasing Force, which actuates every part of Matter.

Thus the Universe goes on for many Ages in a continu'd Succession of Chaos and Disorder. But is it not possible that it may settle at last, so as not to lose its Motion and active Force (for that we have suppos'd inherent in it) yet so as to preserve an Uniformity of Appearance, amidst the continual Motion and Fluctuation of its Parts? This we find to be the Case with the Universe at present. Every Individual is perpetually changing, and every Part of every Individual, and yet the whole remains, in Appearance, the same. May we not hope for such a Position, or rather be assur'd of it, from the eternal Revolutions of unguided Matter, and may not this Account for all the appearing Wisdom and Contrivance, which is in the Universe? Let us contemplate the Subject a little, and we shall

---

2 finite, tho'] an   Revolutions] Succession of Forms and Changes   produce] produces   5–(212)4 Suppose . . . Difficulty *added*   29 with] of

find, that this Adjustment, if attain'd by Matter, of a seeming Stability in the Forms, with a real and perpetual Revolution or Motion of Parts, affords a plausible, if not a true Solution of the Difficulty.[4]

5   It is in vain, therefore, to insist upon the Uses of the Parts in Animals or Vegetables and their curious Adjustment to each other. I wou'd fain know how an Animal cou'd subsist, unless its Parts were so adjusted? Do we not find, that it immediately perishes whenever this Adjustment ceases, and that its Matter corrupting
10   tries some new Form? It happens, indeed, that the Parts of the World are so well adjusted, that some regular Form immediately lays claim to this corrupted Matter: And if it were not so, cou'd the World subsist? Must it not dissolve as well as the Animal, and pass thro' new Positions and Situations; 'till in a great, but finite Succes-
15   sion, it fall at last into the present or some such Order?

It is well, reply'd *Cleanthes*, you told us, that this Hypothesis was suggested on a sudden, in the Course of the Argument. Had you had Leizure to examine it, you wou'd soon have perceiv'd the insuperable Objections, to which it is expos'd. No Form, you say,
20   can subsist, unless it possess those Powers and Organs, requisite for its Subsistence: Some new Order or Œconomy must be try'd, and so on, without Intermission; till at last some Order, which can support and maintain itself, is fallen upon. But according to this Hypothesis, whence arise the many Conveniencies and Advantages,
25   which Men and all Animals possess? Two Eyes, two Ears are not absolutely necessary for the Subsistence of the Species. Human Race might have been propagated and preserv'd, without Horses, Dogs, Cows, Sheep, and those innumerable Fruits and Products, which serve to our Satisfaction and Enjoyment. If no Camels had been
30   created for the Use of Man in the sandy Desarts of *Africa* and

---

5 in] of   8 adjusted?] adjusted to each other?   perishes] dies   15 or some such Order] Order   18 wou'd] had   19 expos'd] liable   20 Organs] Members   22–3 till . . . upon.] till . . . Order, is fallen upon . . . itself. 26 necessary] requisite   30 sandy] dusty

---

4 This paragraph and the preceding one added in Hume's later hand on p. 56 of the manuscript, at the end of Part VIII, with the marking 'AA' on p. 54 of the manuscript and the marginal note 'The Passage at Mark AA on page 56 to be here taken in'.

Arabia, would the World have been dissolv'd? If no Loadstone had
been fram'd to give that wonderful and useful Direction to the
Needle, would human Society and the human kind have been
immediately extinguish'd? Tho the Maxims of Nature be in general
very frugal, yet Instances of this kind are far from being rare; and 5
any one of them is a sufficient Proof of Design, and of a benevolent
Design, which gave rise to the Order and Arrangement of the
Universe.

At least, you may safely infer, said *Philo*, that the foregoing
Hypothesis is so far incompleat and imperfect; which I shall not 10
scruple to allow. But can we ever reasonably expect greater Success
in any Attempts of this Nature? Or can we ever hope to erect a
System of Cosmogony, that will be liable to no Exceptions, and will
contain no Circumstance repugnant to our limited and imperfect
Experience of the Analogy of Nature? Your Theory itself cannot 15
surely pretend to any such Advantage; even tho you have run into
Anthropomorphism, the better to preserve a Conformity to common
Experience. Let us once more put it to Tryal. In all Instances which
we have ever seen, Ideas are copy'd from real Objects, and are
ectypal, not archetypal, to express myself in learned Terms: You 20
reverse this Order, and give Thought the Precedence. In all Instances which we have ever seen, Thought has no Influence upon
Matter, except where that Matter is so conjoin'd with it, as to have
an equal reciprocal Influence upon it. No Animal can move immediately any thing but the Members of its own Body; and indeed, the 25
Equality of Action and Re-action seems to be an universal Law of
Nature: But your Theory implies a Contradiction to this Experience.
These Instances, with many more, which it were easy to collect
(particularly the Supposition of a Mind or System of Thought that
is eternal, or in other words, an Animal ingenerable and immortal) 30
these Instances, I say, may teach, all of us, Sobriety in condemning
each other, and let us see, that as no System of this kind ought ever

1 would . . . been] had the World been   3 Needle] Compass   would
human . . . been] had human Society and human Kind been   7 which] that
11 expect [any]   12 erect] use   14–15 our limited . . . of the] the usual
16 Advantage] Privilege   18 Let . . . Tryal. *added in Hume's later hand*   all [the]
24 upon] over   27 this] that   29–31 (. . . the Supposition . . .) these
Instances, I say] the Creation from nothing   31 all of us] us all

to be receiv'd from a slight Analogy, so neither ought any to be rejected on Account of a small Incongruity. For that is an Inconvenience, from which we can justly pronounce no-one to be exempted.

5   All religious Systems, it is confest, are subject to great and insuperable Difficulties. Each Disputant triumphs in his Turn; while he carries on an offensive War, and exposes the Absurdities, Barbarities, and pernicious Tenets of his Antagonist. But all of them, on the Whole, prepare a compleat Triumph for the Sceptic,
10 who tells them, that no System ought ever to be embrac'd with regard to such Subjects: For this plain Reason, that no Absurdity ought ever to be assented to with regard to any Subject. A total Suspence of Judgement is here our only reasonable Ressource. And if every Attack, as is commonly observ'd, and no Defence, among
15 Theologians, is successful; how compleat must be *his* Victory, who remains always, with all Mankind, on the Offensive, and has himself no fixt Station or abiding City, which he is ever, on any Occasion, oblig'd to defend?

PART 9

20 But if so many Difficulties attend the Argument *a posteriori*, said Demea; had we not better adhere to that simple and sublime Argument *a priori*, which, by offering to us infallible Demonstration, cuts off at once all Doubt and Difficulty? By this Argument too, we may prove the INFINITY of the divine Attributes, which, I am afraid, can
25 never be ascertain'd with Certainy from any other Topic. For how can an Effect, which either is finite, or, for aught we know, may be so; how can such an Effect, I say, prove an infinite Cause? The Unity too of the divine Nature, it is very difficult, if not absolutely impossible, to deduce merely from contemplating the Works of
30 Nature; nor will the Uniformity alone of the Plan, even were it allow'd, give us any Assurance of that Attribute. Whereas the Argument *a priori*—

3–4 we can . . . exempted] no-one can justly be excepted   5 All] Every
are] is   8 Tenets] Consequences   11 For . . . that] because   13 our]
the   Ressource] Expedient   22 offering to us] producing

You seem to reason, *Demea*, interpos'd *Cleanthes*, as if those Advantages and Conveniencies in the abstract Argument were full Proofs of its Solidity. But it is first proper, in my Opinion, to determine what Argument of this Nature you choose to insist on; and we shall afterwards, from itself, better than from its *useful* Consequences, endeavour to determine what Value we ought to put upon it.

The Argument, reply'd *Demea*, which I wou'd insist on is the common one. Whatever exists must have a Cause or Reason of its Existence; it being absolutely impossible for any thing to produce itself, or be the Cause of its own Existence. In mounting up, therefore, from Effects to Causes, we must either go on in tracing an infinite Succession, without any ultimate Cause at all, or must at last have Recourse to some ultimate Cause, that is *necessarily* existent: Now that the first Supposition is absurd may be thus prov'd. In the infinite Chain or Succession of Causes and Effects, each single Effect is determin'd to exist by the Power and Efficacy of that Cause, which immediately preceded; but the whole eternal Chain or Succession, taken together, is not determin'd or caus'd by any thing: And yet it is evident that it requires a Cause or Reason, as much as any particular Object, which begins to exist in time. The Question is still reasonable, why this particular Succession of Causes existed from Eternity, and not any other Succession, or no Succession at all. If there be no necessarily existent Being, any Supposition, which can be form'd, is equally possible; nor is there any more Absurdity in Nothing's having existed from Eternity, than there is in that Succession of Causes, which constitutes the Universe. What was it then, which determin'd Something to exist rather than nothing, and bestow'd Being on a particular Possibility, exclusive of the rest? *External Causes*, there are suppos'd to be none. *Chance* is a Word without a Meaning. Was it *Nothing*? But that can never produce any thing. We must, therefore, have recourse to a necessarily existent Being, who carries the REASON of his Existence in himself; and who cannot be suppos'd not to exist without an express Contradiction. There is consequently such a Being, that is, there is a Deity.[1]

23 which] that   31 necessarily] necessary

[1] Clarke, *Discourse*, pp. 9–10: 'First then, it is Absolutely and Undeniably certain, that *Something has existed from all Eternity*. This is so evident and Undeniable

I shall not leave it to *Philo*, said *Cleanthes*, (tho I know that the starting Objections is his chief Delight) to point out the Weakness of this metaphysical Reasoning. It seems to me so obviously ill-grounded, and at the same time of so little Consequence to the Cause of true Piety and Religion, that I shall myself venture to show the Fallacy of it.

I shall begin with observing, that there is an evident Absurdity in pretending to demonstrate a Matter of Fact, or to prove it by any Arguments *a priori*. Nothing is demonstrable, unless the contrary implies a Contradiction. Nothing, that is distinctly conceivable, implies a Contradiction. Whatever we conceive as existent, we can also conceive as non-existent. There is no Being, therefore, whose Non-existence implies a Contradiction. Consequently there is no Being, whose Existence is demonstrable. I propose this Argument as entirely decisive, and am willing to rest the whole Controversy upon it.

It is pretended, that the Deity is a necessarily existent Being, and this Necessity of his Existence is attempted to be explain'd by asserting, that, if we knew his whole Essence or Nature, we shou'd perceive it to be as impossible for him not to exist as for twice two not to be four. But it is evident, that this can never happen, while our Faculties remain the same as at present. It will still be possible for us, at any time, to conceive the Non-existence of what we formerly conceiv'd to exist; nor can the Mind ever lie under a Necessity of supposing any Object to remain always in Being; in the same manner as we lie under a Necessity of always conceiving twice two to be four. The Words, therefore, *necessary Existence* have no Meaning; or which is the same thing, none that is consistent.

But farther; why may not the material Universe be the necessarily existent Being, according to this pretended Explication of Necessity? We dare not affirm that we know all the Qualities of Matter; and for aught we can determine, it may contain some

1–2 that . . . Objections] it   2–3 point out . . . of] start Objections to
7 I shall] We may   is] seems   8 a] any   22 It will] 'Twill   24 a] any
31 dare . . . we] pretend not to

a Proposition, that no Atheist in any Age has ever presumed to assert the contrary . . . [it] is one of the certainest and most evident Truths in the World. . . .'

Qualities, which, were they known, wou'd make its Non-existence appear as great a Contradiction as that twice two is five. I find only one Argument employ'd to prove, that the material World is not the necessarily existent Being; and this Argument is deriv'd from the Contingency both of the Matter and the Form of the World. 'Any Particle of Matter,' tis said, *a*'may be *conceiv'd* to be annihilated; and any Form may be *conceiv'd* to be alter'd. Such an Annihilation or Alteration, therefore, is not impossible.'[2] But it seems a great Partiality not to perceive, that the same Argument extends equally to the Deity, so far as we have any Conception of him; and that the Mind can at least imagine him to be non-existent, or his Attributes to be alter'd. It must be some unknown, inconceivable Qualities, which can make his Non-existence appear impossible, or his Attributes unalterable: And no Reason can be assigned, why these Qualities may not belong to Matter. As they are altogether unknown and inconceivable, they can never be prov'd incompatible with it.

Add to this, that in tracing an eternal Succession of Objects, it seems absurd to enquire for a general Cause or first Author. How can any thing, that exists from Eternity, have a Cause; since that Relation implies a Priority in time and a Beginning of Existence?

In such a Chain too, or Succession of Objects, each Part is caus'd by that which preceded it, and causes that which succeeds it. Where then is the Difficulty? But the WHOLE, you say, wants a Cause. I answer, that the uniting of these Parts into a Whole, like the uniting of several distinct Counties into one Kingdom, or several distinct Members into one Body, is perform'd merely by an arbitrary Act of the Mind, and has no Influence on the Nature of things.

a Dr Clarke.

11 imagine] conceive   14 unalterable] inalterable   assigned] shown
20 exists] is

[2] Clarke, *Discourse*, p. 23: 'For whether we consider the *Form* of the World, with the *Disposition* and *Motion* of its Parts; or whether we consider the *Matter* of it, as such, without respect to its present Form; every Thing in it, both the *whole* and every one of its *Parts*, their *Situation* and *Motion*, the *Form* and also the *Matter*, are the most Arbitrary and Dependent Things, and the farthest removed from Necessity that can possibly be imagined.' Clarke also attributes the assertion that the world is the necessarily existent being to Spinoza.

Did I show you the particular Causes of each Individual in a Collection of twenty Particles of Matter, I shou'd think it very unreasonable, shou'd you afterwards ask me, what was the Cause of the whole twenty. That is sufficiently explain'd in explaining the Cause
5 of the Parts.

Tho' the Reasonings, which you have urg'd, *Cleanthes*, may well excuse me, said *Philo*, from starting any farther Difficulties; yet I cannot forbear insisting still upon another Topic. Tis observ'd by Arithmeticians, that the Products of 9 compose always either 9 or
10 some lesser Product of 9; if you add together all the Characters, of which any of the former Products is compos'd. Thus, of 18, 27, 36, which are Products of 9, you make 9 by adding 1 to 8, 2 to 7, 3 to 6. Thus 369, is a Product also of nine; and if you add 3, 6, and 9 you make 18, a lesser Product of 9.[b3] To a superficial Observer, so
15 wonderful a Regularity may be admir'd as the Effect either of Chance or Design; but a skillful Algebraist immediately concludes it to be the Work of Necessity, and demonstrates, that it must for ever result from the Nature of these Numbers. Is it not probable, I ask, that the whole Œconomy of the Universe is conducted by a
20 like Necessity, tho' no human Algebra can furnish a Key, which solves the Difficulty? And instead of admiring the Order of natural Beings, may it not happen, that, cou'd we penetrate into the intimate Nature of Bodies, we shou'd clearly see why it was absolutely impossible, they cou'd ever admit of any other Disposition? So
25 dangerous is it to introduce this Idea of Necessity into the present

[b] *Republique des Lettres.* Août 1685.

6–219(2) Tho' . . . Hypothesis *added*   13 Thus [of]   15 may
[? seem]   18 Numbers] Figures

---

[3] Hume's reference is slightly inaccurate. He is citing the periodical *Nouvelles de la Republique des Lettres* for September 1685 (Amsterdam, 1685), Article II, pp. 944–5: 'Tout le monde sçait assez que les nombres multiples de 9. c'est à dire ceux qui contiennent 9. un certain nombre de fois juste, comme 18. 27. 36. jusqu'à 81. resont toûjours 9. lors qu'on met ensemble les nombres particuliers exprimez par les figures dont ces multiples sont composez. Ainsi mettez ensemble, un & huit, deux & sept, trois & six, nombres particuliers exprimez par les figures 1. & 8. 2. & 7. 3. & 6. dont sont composez ces multiples de 9. 18. 27. 36. vous retrouverez toûjours 9. . . . 126. est multiple de 9. vous voiez qu'un, deux, & six, mis ensemble sont 9. Dans 369. vous trouvez trois, six, & neuf, qui sont 18. multiple de 9. plus petit que 162.'

Question! And so naturally does it afford an Inference directly opposite to the religious Hypothesis![4]

But dropping all these Abstractions, continu'd *Philo*; and confining our Selves to more familiar Topics; I shall venture to add an Observation,[5] that the Argument *a priori* has seldom been found 5 very convincing, except to People of a metaphysical Head, who have accustom'd themselves to abstract Reasoning, and who finding from Mathematics, that the Understanding frequently leads to Truth, thro Obscurity and contrary to first Appearances, have transferr'd the same Habit of thinking to Subjects, where it ought 10 not to have Place. Other People, even of good Sense and the best enclin'd to Religion, feel always some Deficiency in such Arguments, tho they are not perhaps able to explain distinctly where it lies. A certain Proof, that Men ever did, and ever will derive their Religion from other Sources than from this Species of 15 Reasoning.

PART 10

It is my Opinion, I own, reply'd *Demea*, that each Man feels, in a manner, the Truth of Religion within his own Breast; and from a Consciousness of his Imbecillity and Misery, rather than from any 20 Reasoning, is led to seek Protection from that Being, on whom he and all Nature is dependent. So anxious or so tedious are even the best Scenes of Life, that Futurity is still the Object of all our Hopes and Fears. We incessantly look forward, and endeavour, by Prayers, Adoration, and Sacrifice, to appease those unknown Powers, whom 25

3–5 But . . . Observation] I shall venture, said *Philo*, to add to these Reasonings of *Cleanthes*,   5 Observation *used twice in error*   10 thinking to [other] 12 such [all]

---

[4] This paragraph added on p. 60 of the manuscript, with the mark 'AA' to indicate where it should go on p. 59 of the manuscript. Hume had at one time scored out this passage, but in the margin of p. 60 of the manuscript is the instruction, in Hume's hand, 'Print this Passage'.

[5] Hume amended this passage on p. 60 of the manuscript to take account of his new paragraph ('Tho' . . . Hypothesis.'). The same passage is also written in the margin of p. 59 and deleted.

we find, by Experience, so able to afflict and oppress us. Wretched Creatures that we are! What Ressource for us amidst the innumerable Ills of Life, did not Religion suggest some Methods of Atonement, and appease those Terrors, with which we are incessantly agitated and tormented?

I am indeed perswaded, said *Philo*, that the best and indeed the only Method of bringing every one to a due Sense of Religion is by just Representations of the Misery and Wickedness of Men. And for that Purpose a Talent of Eloquence and strong Imagery is more requisite than that of Reasoning and Argument. For is it necessary to prove, what every one feels within himself? Tis only necessary to make us feel it, if possible, more intimately and sensibly.

The People, indeed, reply'd *Demea*, are sufficiently convinc'd of this great and melancholy Truth. The Miseries of Life, the Unhappiness of Man, the general Corruptions of our Nature, the unsatisfactory Enjoyment of Pleasures, Riches, Honours; these Phrazes have become almost proverbial in all Languages. And who can doubt of what all Men declare from their own immediate Feeling and Experience?

In this Point, said *Philo*, the Learned are perfectly agreed with the Vulgar; and in all Letters, *sacred* and *profane*, the Topic of human Misery has been insisted on with the most pathetic Eloquence, that Sorrow and Melancholy cou'd inspire. The Poets, who speak from Sentiment, without a System, and whose Testimony has therefore the more Authority, abound in Images of this Nature. From *Homer* down to *Dr Young*, the whole inspir'd Tribe have ever been sensible, that no other Representation of things would suit the Feeling and Observation of each Individual.

As to Authorities, reply'd *Demea*, you need not seek them. Look round this Library of *Cleanthes*. I shall venture to affirm, that, except Authors of particular Sciences, such as Chymestry or Botany, who have no occasion to treat of human Life, there scarce is one of those innumerable Writers, from whom the Sense of human Misery has

---

1 oppress] torment   3 Ills] Evils   5 and tormented *added later*
7 every one] Men   10 is it necessary] what need is there   11 necessary]
requisite   22 that] which] that   26 inspir'd] poetic   27–8 Feeling and
Observation] Feelings and Observations   31 who] which   32 there scarce
is] there is scarce

not, in some Passage or other, extorted a Complaint and Confession of it. At least, the Chance is intirely on that Side; and no-one Author has ever, so far as I can recollect, been so extravagant as to deny it.

There you must excuse me, said *Philo*; *Leibnitz* has denyed it; and is perhaps the first,[a] who ventur'd upon so bold and paradoxical an 5 Opinion; at least, the first, who made it essential to his philosophical System.[2]

And by being the first, reply'd *Demea*, might he not have been sensible of his Error? For is this a Subject, in which Philosophers can propose to make Discoveries, especially in so late an Age? 10 And can any Man hope by a simple Denial (for the Subject scarcely admits of Reasoning) to bear down the united Testimony of Mankind, founded on Sense and Consciousness?

And why shou'd Man, added he, pretend to an Exemption from the Lot of all other Animals? The whole Earth, believe me, *Philo*, is 15 curst and polluted. A perpetual War is kindled amongst all living Creatures. Necessity, Hunger, Want stimulate the strong and courageous: Fear, Anxiety, Terror agitate the weak and infirm. The first Entrance into Life gives Anguish to the new-born Infant and to its wretched Parent: Weakness, Impotence, Distress attend each 20 Stage of that Life: And 'tis at last finish'd in Agony and Horror.[3]

Observe too, says *Philo*, the curious Artifices of Nature, in order to imbitter the Life of every living Being. The stronger prey upon the weaker, and keep them in perpetual Terror and Anxiety. The weaker too, in their turn, often prey upon the stronger, and vex and 25

[a] That Sentiment had been maintain'd by Dr King[1] and some few others before *Leibnitz*; tho by none of so great a Fame as that *German* philosopher.

---

3 so . . . recollect] yet   11 scarcely] scarce   13 founded on [their immediate]   16 amongst] betwixt   18 infirm] timid   [a]1 That . . . others] Dr. King and others had maintain'd that Sentiment

[1] William King, *De Origine Mali* (Dublin, 1702), *passim*; translated by Edmund Law (London, 1731). Hume's note occurs at the bottom of p. 61 of the manuscript, and in the margin Hume has written 'A Note to be plac'd at the bottom of the Page.'
[2] In his *Theodicée* (Amsterdam, 1710), *passim*. Cf. Samuel Clarke, *A Collection of Papers . . . between . . . Mr. Leibnitz, and Dr. Clarke* (London, 1717), *passim*.
[3] William King, *An Essay on the Origin of Evil* (Cambridge, 1739), p. 104: 'Whence so many *Inconveniences* in the Work of a most *good*, most *powerful God*? Whence that perpetual War between the very *Elements*, between *Animals*, between *Men*? Whence *Errors*, *Miseries* and *Vices*, the constant Companions of human Life from its Infancy? Whence Good to Evil Men, Evil to the Good?'

molest them without Relaxation. Consider that innumerable Race of Insects, which either are bred on the Body of each Animal, or flying about infix their Stings in him. These Insects have others still less than themselves, which torment them.⁴ And thus on each hand,
5 before and behind, above and below, every Animal is surrounded with Enemies, which incessantly seek his Misery and Destruction.

Man alone, said *Demea*, seems to be, in part, an Exception to this Rule. For by Combination in Society, he can easily master Lions, Tygers, and Bears, whose greater Strength and Agility naturally
10 enable them to prey upon him.

On the contrary, it is here chiefly, cry'd *Philo*, that the uniform and equal Maxims of Nature are most apparent. Man, it is true, can, by Combination, surmount all his *real* Enemies, and become master of the whole animal Creation: But does he not immediately raise up
15 to himself *imaginary* Enemies, the Dæmons of his Fancy, who haunt him with superstitious Terrors, and blast every Enjoyment of Life?⁵ His Pleasure, as he imagines, becomes, in their Eyes, a Crime: His Food and Repose give them Umbrage and Offence: His very Sleep and Dreams furnish new Materials to anxious Fear: And even Death,
20 his Refuge from every other Ill, presents only the Dread of endless and innumerable Woes. Nor does the Wolf molest more the timid Flock, than Superstition does the anxious Breast of wretched Mortals.

Besides, consider, *Demea*; this very Society, by which we surmount those wild Beasts, our natural Enemies; what new Enemies
25 does it not raise to us? What Woe and Misery does it not occasion?

3–4 others still . . . torment] others less . . . which still   17 imagines] may imagine   becomes . . . Eyes,] in their Eyes, becomes   19 to [his]   Fear] Fears even [the prospect of]   22 Breast] Breasts   23 *Demea*; [that]

---

⁴ Or, as Swift put it in 'On Poetry: A Rhapsody' (335–40):
The Vermin only teaze and pinch
Their Foes superior by an Inch.
So, Nat'ralists observe, a Flea
Hath smaller Fleas that on him prey,
And these have smaller Fleas to bite 'em,
And so proceed *ad infinitum* . . .

⁵ Kames, *Essays . . . on Morality and Natural Religion*, p. 311: 'For it is a well known truth, that passion has a wonderful effect upon the imagination. The less we know of a new object, the greater liberty we take, to dress it up in frightful colours. The object is forthwith conceived to have all those dreadful qualities, which are suggested by the imagination; and the same terror is raised, as if those qualities were real and not imaginary.'

Man is the greatest Enemy of Man. Oppression, Injustice, Contempt, Contumely, Violence, Sedition, War, Calumny, Treachery, Fraud; by these they mutually torment each other: And they wou'd soon dissolve that Society which they had form'd, were it not for the Dread of still greater Ills, which must attend their Separation. 5

But tho these external Insults, said *Demea*, from Animals, from Men, from all the Elements which assault us, form a frightful Catalogue of Woes, they are nothing in comparison of those, which arise within Ourselves, from the distemper'd Condition of our Mind and Body. How many lie under the lingering Torment of 10 Diseases. Hear the pathetic Enumeration of the great Poet.

> Intestine Stone and Ulcer, Colic Pangs,
> Dæmoniac Frenzy, moaping Melancholy,
> And moon-struck Madness, pining Atrophy,
> Marasmus and wide wasting Pestilence.   15
> Dire was the tossing, deep the Groans: DESPAIR
> Tended the Sick, busiest from Couch to Couch.
> And over them triumphant DEATH his Dart
> Shook, but delay'd to strike, tho oft invok'd
> With Vows, as their chief Good and final Hope.[6]   20

The Disorders of the Mind, continu'd *Demea*, tho' more secret, are not perhaps less dismal and vexatious. Remorse, Shame, Anguish, Rage, Dissappointment, Anxiety, Fear, Dejection, Despair; who has ever past thro' Life without cruel Inroads from these Tormentors? How many have scarcely ever felt any better Sensations? 25 Labour and Poverty, so abhorr'd by every one, are the certain Lot of the far greater Number: And those few privileg'd Persons, who enjoy Ease and Opulence, never reach Contentment or true Felicity. All the Goods of Life united wou'd not make a very happy Man: But all the Ills united wou'd make a Wretch indeed; and any one 30 of them almost (and who can be free from every one) nay often the Absence of one Good (and who can possess all) is sufficient to render Life ineligible.

5 which must] that wou'd   23 Dejection, Despair] Melancholy   24 thro'] a
26 are] is   30 Ills] Evils

6 Milton, *Paradise Lost*, XI. 485–93. Hume has omitted line 488: 'Dropsies, and asthmas, and joint-racking rheums.'

Were a Stranger to drop, on a sudden, into this World, I wou'd show him, as a Specimen of its Ills, an Hospital full of Deseases, a Prison crowded with Malefactors and Debtors, a Field of Battle strow'd with Carcasses, a Fleet foundering in the Ocean, a Nation
5 languishing under Tyranny, Famine, or Pestilence.[7] To turn the gay Side of Life to him, and give him a Notion of its Pleasures; whither shou'd I conduct him? to a Ball, to an Opera, to Court? He might justly think, that I was only showing him a Diversity of Distress and Sorrow.

10   There is no evading such striking Instances, said *Philo*, but by Apologies, which still farther aggravate the Charge. Why have all Men, I ask, in all Ages, complain'd incessantly of the Miseries of Life?—They have no just Reason, says one: These Complaints proceed only from their discontented, repining, anxious Disposition.—
15 And can there possibly, I reply, be a more certain Foundation of Misery, than such a wretched Temper?

But if they were really as unhappy as they pretend, says my Antagonist, why do they remain in Life?—

Not satisfy'd with Life, afraid of Death.[8]

20 This is the secret Chain, say I, that holds us. We are terrify'd, not brib'd to the Continuance of our Existence.

It is only a false Delicacy, he may insist, which a few refin'd Spirits indulge, and which has spread these Complaints among the

---

17–18 my Antagonist] he   20 say] says   21 of our] of

---

[7] Bayle, *Dictionary*, art. 'Manichees', iv. 94 n.: 'Travels afford perpetual lessons upon this subject: they show everywhere the monuments of mens misfortunes and wickednesses: this appears everywhere by the many prisons, hospitals, gibbets, and beggars.'

[8] Cf. Charles Churchill, *Gotham* (London, 1764), p. 11:

> OLD-AGE, a *second Child*, by Nature curs'd
> With more and greater evils than the first,
> Weak, sickly, full of pains; in ev'ry breath
> Railing at Life, and yet afraid of death . . . (I. 218–21.)

Though it seems unlikely that Hume would have had much sympathy for Churchill, given the latter's antagonism towards the Scots, the similarity of Hume's line to Churchill's words seems more than coincidence. Of course, the sentiments in both could have a common source in Book III of Lucretius, where the fear of death and the pain in life are remarked in almost every line. If Hume were alluding to Churchill it would suggest revisions of the *Dialogues* in the mid 1760s rather than earlier as implied in his letter of 15 Aug. 1776 to Adam Smith (Introduction, p. 111).

whole Race of Mankind—And what is this Delicacy, I ask, which you blame? Is it any thing but a greater Sensibility to all the Pleasures and Pains of Life? And if the Man of a delicate, refin'd Temper, by being so much more alive than the rest of the World, is only so much more unhappy; what Judgement must we form in general of 5 human Life?

Let Men remain at rest, says our Adversary; and they will be easy. They are willing Artificers of their own Misery.—No! reply I; An anxious Languor follows their Repose: Dissappointment, Vexation, Trouble, their Activity and Ambition.   10

I can observe something like what you mention in some others, reply'd *Cleanthes*: But I confess, I feel little or nothing of it in myself; and hope that it is not so common as you represent it.

If you feel not human Misery yourself, cry'd *Demea*, I congratulate you on so happy a Singularity. Others, seemingly the most pros- 15 perous, have not been asham'd to vent their Complaints in the most melancholy Strains. Let us attend to the great, the fortunate Emperor, *Charles* the fifth, when, tir'd with human Grandeur, he resigned all his extensive Dominions into the hands of his Son. In the last Harangue, which he made on that memorable Occasion, 20 he publickly avow'd, *that the greatest Prosperities which he had ever enjoy'd, had been mixt with so many Adversities, that he might truly say he had never enjoy'd any Satisfaction or Contentment.*[9] But did the retir'd Life, in which he sought for Shelter, afford him any greater Happiness? If we may credit his Son's Account, his Repentance com- 25 menc'd the very Day of his Resignation.

Cicero's Fortune, from small Beginnings, rose to the greatest Lustre and Renown; yet what pathetic Complaints of the Ills of Life do his familiar Letters, as well as philosophical Discourses, contain? And suitably to his own Experience, he introduces *Cato*, the great, 30

---

4 the World] Mankind   7 our Adversary] my Antagonist   10 Vexation, Trouble] Trouble and Vexation   16 to vent] of venting   18 Grandeur] Grandeurs   22 *Adversities*] *Adversaries*

---

[9] Bayle, *Dictionary*, ii. 438 n., art. 'Charles V': 'He confesses himself, in the Speech he made, when he resigned all his Dominions, *That the greatest Prosperities, he ever had in the World, were mixed with so many Adversities, that he could say he never had any Contentment.*'

the fortunate *Cato*, protesting in his Old-Age, that, had he a new Life in his Offer, he wou'd reject the Present.[10]

Ask Yourself, ask any of your Acquaintance, whether they wou'd live over again the last ten or twenty Years of their Life. No! But
5 the next twenty, they say, will be better.

> And from the Dregs of Life, hope to receive
> What the first sprightly Running cou'd not give.[11]

Thus at last they find (such is the Greatness of human Misery; it reconciles even Contradictions) that they complain, at once, of the
10 Shortness of Life, and of its Vanity and Sorrow.

And is it possible, *Cleanthes*, said *Philo*, that after all these Reflections, and infinitely more, which might be suggested, you can still persevere in your Anthropomorphism, and assert the moral Attributes of the Deity, his Justice, Benevolence, Mercy, and Recti-
15 tude, to be of the same Nature with these Virtues in human Creatures? His Power we allow infinite: Whatever he wills is executed: But neither Man nor any other Animal are happy: Therefore he does not will their Happiness. His Wisdom is infinite: He is never mistaken in choosing the Means to any End: But the Course
20 of Nature tends not to human or animal Felicity: Therefore it is not establish'd for that Purpose. Thro' the whole Compass of human Knowledge, there are no Inferences more certain and infallible than these. In what Respect, then, do his Benevolence and Mercy resemble the Benevolence and Mercy of Men?
25 *Epicurus*'s old Questions are yet unanswer'd. Is he willing to prevent Evil, but not able? then is he impotent. Is he able, but not

---

3 whether they] if th[ey]   23 Respect] Respects

[10] Cicero, 'Cato Major', *De Senectutute*. Cf. *Cato Major; or, A Treatise on Old Age*, trans. John Logan (Glasgow, 1751), pp. 165–6: 'For my part, I have a passionate desire to see your fathers again, whom I loved and honoured while here; and I not only long to meet those I knew and loved, but those illustrious souls also, of whom I have heard and read, and have with pleasure mentioned them in my writings. Nor would I now, on any terms, agree to be stopped in my passage to them; no, not on condition to be restored to the bloom and vigour of youth again: or should any heavenly power grant me the privilege of turning back, if I pleased, from this age to infancy, and to set out again from my cradle, I would absolutely refuse it; for, as I have now got well nigh to the end of my race, I should be extremely unwilling to be called back, and obliged to start again.' It is perhaps worth noting that Hume is using 'Present' in the sense of 'gift'. Cf. Loeb edn., pp. 94–7.

[11] John Dryden, *Aureng-Zebe* (London, 1676), IV. i. 41–2. Hume has written 'hope' for 'think'.

willing? then is he malevolent. Is he both able and willing? Whence then is Evil?[12]

You ascribe *Cleanthes*, (and I believe justly) a Purpose and Intention to Nature. But what, I beseech you, is the Object of that curious Artifice and Machinery, which she has display'd in all 5 Animals? The Preservation alone of Individuals and Propagation of the Species. It seems enough for her Purpose, if such a Rank be barely upheld in the Universe, without any Care or Concern for the Happiness of the Members, that compose it. No Ressource for this Purpose: No Machinery, in order merely to give Pleasure or Ease: 10 No Fund of pure Joy and Contentment: No Indulgence without some Want or Necessity, accompanying it. At least, the few Phænomena of this Nature are over-ballanc'd by opposite Phænomena of still greater Importance.

Our Sense of Music, Harmony, and indeed Beauty of all kinds 15 gives Satisfaction, without being absolutely necessary to the Preservation and Propogation of the Species. But what racking Pains, on the other hand, arise from Gouts, Gravels, Megrims, Toothakes, Rheumatisms; where the Injury to the Animal-Machinery is either small or incurable? Mirth, Laughter, Play, Frolic seem gratuitous 20 Satisfactions, which have no farther Tendency: Spleen, Melancholy, Discontent, Superstition are Pains of the same Nature. How then does the divine Benevolence display itself, in the Sense of you, Anthropomorphites? None but we Mystics, as you were pleas'd to call us, can account for this strange Mixture of Phænomena, by 25 deriving it from Attributes, infinitely perfect, but incomprehensible.

And have you at last, said *Cleanthes* smiling, betray'd your Intentions, *Philo*? Your long Agreement with *Demea* did indeed a little surprize me; but I find you were all the while erecting

3–4 you ascribe *Cleanthes* . . . Nature] you ascribe . . . Nature, *Cleanthes*.   4 that] her   9 Members . . . it] Individuals   16 necessary] requisite   21 which] that   22 How] Where   25 strange] odd   29 but I [now]   were] was

[12] Bayle, *Dictionary*, art. 'Paulicians' note E, iv. 513 n.: '*God, says Epicurus, is either willing to remove evil, and is not able: or he is able, and not willing: or he is neither willing, nor able: or else he is both willing and able. If he is willing and not able, he must then be weak, which cannot be affirmed of God. If he is able and not willing, he must be envious, which is likewise contrary to the nature of God. If he is neither willing nor able, he must be both envious and weak, and consequently not God. If he is both willing and able, which only can agree with the notions of God, whence then proceeds evil?*'

a conceal'd Battery against me. And I must confess, that you have now fallen upon a Subject, worthy of your noble Spirit of Opposition and Controversy. If you can make out the present Point, and prove Mankind to be unhappy or corrupted, there is an End at once 5 of all Religion. For to what Purpose establish the natural Attributes of the Deity, while the moral are still doubtful and uncertain?

You take Umbrage very easily, reply'd *Demea*, at Opinions the most innocent, and the most generally receiv'd even amongst the religious and devout themselves: And nothing can be more surpriz-10 ing than to find a Topic like this, concerning the Wickedness and Misery of Man, charg'd with no less than Atheism and Profaneness. Have not all pious Divines and Preachers, who have indulg'd their Rhetoric on so fertile a Subject; have they not easily, I say, given a Solution of any Difficulties, which may attend it? This World is but 15 a Point in Comparison of the Universe: This Life but a Moment in comparison of Eternity. The present Evil Phænomena, therefore, are rectify'd in other Regions, and in some future Period of Existence. And the Eyes of Men, being then open'd to larger Views of things, see the whole Connexion of general Laws, and trace, with Adoration, 20 the Benevolence and Rectitude of the Deity, thro' all the Mazes and Intricacies of his Providence.

No! reply'd *Cleanthes,* No! These arbitrary Suppositions can never be admitted contrary to Matter of Fact, visible and uncontroverted. Whence can any Cause be known but from its known 25 Effects? Whence can any Hypothesis be prov'd but from the apparent Phænomena? To establish one Hypothesis upon another is building entirely in the Air; and the utmost we ever attain, by these Conjectures and Fictions, is to ascertain the bare Possibility of our Opinion; but never can we, upon such terms, establish its Reality. 30 The only Method of supporting divine Benevolence (and it is what I willingly embrace) is to deny absolutely the Misery and Wickedness of Man. Your Representations are exaggerated: Your melancholy Views mostly fictitious: Your Inferences contrary to Fact and Experience. Health is more common than Sickness: 35 Pleasure than Pain: Happiness than Misery. And for one Vexation,

3 the] your   6 while] if   7 at [the]   14 which] that   17 rectify'd]
redrest   22 can never] never can   29 Opinion] Opinions   32 Man] Men

which we meet with, we attain, upon Computation, a hundred Enjoyments.

Admitting your Position, reply'd *Philo*, which yet is extremely doubtful; you must, at the same time, allow, that, if Pain be less frequent than Pleasure, it is infinitely more violent and durable. 5 One hour of it is often able to outweigh a day, a week, a month of our common insipid Enjoyments:[13] And how many days, weeks, and months are past by several in the most acute Torments? Pleasure, scarcely in one Instance, is ever able to reach Extasy and Rapture: And in no one Instance can it continue for any time at its 10 highest Pitch and Altitude. The Spirits evaporate; the Nerves relax; the Fabric is disorder'd; and the Enjoyment quickly degenerates into Fatigue and Uneasyness. But Pain often, Good God, how often! rises to Torture and Agony; and the longer it continues, it becomes still more genuine Agony and Torture. Patience is exhausted; 15 Courage languishes; Melancholy seizes us; and nothing terminates our Misery but the Removal of its Cause, or another Event, which is the Sole Cure of all Evil, but which, from our natural Folly, we regard with still greater Horror and Consternation.

But not to insist upon these Topics, continu'd *Philo*, tho' most 20 obvious, certain, and important; I must use the Freedom to admonish you, *Cleanthes*, that you have put this Controversy upon a most dangerous Issue, and are unawares introducing a total Scepticism into the most essential Articles of natural and revealed Theology. What! no Method of fixing a just Foundation for Religion, unless we 25 allow the Happiness of human Life, and maintain a continu'd Existence even in this World, with all our present Pains, Infirmities, Vexations, and Follies, to be eligible and desirable! But this is contrary to every one's Feeling and Experience: It is contrary to an Authority so establish'd as nothing can subvert: No decisive Proofs 30 can ever be produc'd against this Authority; nor is it possible for you to compute, estimate, and compare all the Pains and all the

---

3 extremely] more than] extremely   6 often] frequently   9 scarcely] but   able [even for a Moment]   25 fixing] ascertaining   28 Vexations, and [Sorrows]   31 produc'd] adduc'd

---

[13] Bayle, *Dictionary*, art. 'Xenophanes', v. 579 n.: 'One hour's grief contains more evil, than there is good in six or seven pleasant days.'

Pleasures in the Lives of all Men and of all Animals: And thus by your resting the whole System of Religion on a Point, which, from its very Nature, must for ever be uncertain, you tacitly confess, that that System is equally uncertain.

5   But allowing you, what never will be believ'd; at least, what you never possibly can prove, that animal, or at least, human Happiness in this Life exceeds its Misery; you have yet done nothing: For this is not, by any means, what we expect from infinite Power, infinite Wisdom, and infinite Goodness. Why is there any Misery at
10 all in the World? Not by Chance surely. From some Cause then. Is it from the Intention of the Deity? But he is perfectly benevolent. Is it contrary to his Intention? But he is Almighty. Nothing can shake the Solidity of this Reasoning, so short, so clear, so decisive; except we assert, that these Subjects exceed all human Capacity,
15 and that our common Measures of Truth and Falshood are not applicable to them; a Topic, which I have all along insisted on, but which you have, from the Beginning, rejected with Scorn and Indignation.

But I will be contented to retire still from this Retrenchment:
20 For I deny that you can ever force me in it: I will allow, that Pain or Misery in Man is *compatible* with infinite Power and Goodness in the Deity, even in your Sense of these Attributes: What are you advanc'd by all these Concessions? A mere possible Compatibility is not sufficient. You must *prove* these pure, unmixt, and uncontrole-
25 able Attributes from the present mixt and confus'd Phænomena, and from these alone. A hopeful Undertaking! Were the Phænomena ever so pure and unmixt, yet being finite, they wou'd be insufficient for that Purpose. How much more, where they are also so jarring and discordant?

30   Here, *Cleanthes*, I find myself at Ease in my Argument. Here I triumph. Formerly, when we argu'd concerning the natural Attributes of Intelligence and Design, I needed all my sceptical and metaphysical Subtility to elude your Grasp. In many Views of the Universe, and of its Parts, particularly the latter, the Beauty and
35 Fitness of final Causes strike us with such irresistible Force, that all

6 possibly *deleted and then restored*   7 its] human   14 Subjects [so far]
19 Retrenchment] Defense   26 hopeful] strange   33 Grasp] hold

Objections appear (what I believe they really are) mere Cavils and Sophysms; nor can we then imagine how it was ever possible for us to repose any Weight on them. But there is no View of human Life or of the Condition of Mankind, from which, without the greatest Violence, we can infer the moral Attributes, or learn that infinite 5 Benevolence, conjoin'd with infinite Power and infinite Wisdom, which we must discover by the Eyes of Faith alone. It is your turn now to tug the labouring Oar, and to support your philosophical Subtilities against the Dictates of plain Reason and Experience.

PART 11   10

I scruple not to allow, said *Cleanthes*, that I have been apt to suspect the frequent Repetition of the Word, Infinite, which we meet with in all theological Writers, to savour more of Panegyric than of Philosophy, and that any Purposes of Reasoning, and even of Religion, wou'd be better serv'd, were we to rest contented with more 15 accurate and more moderate Expressions. The Terms, *admirable, excellent, superlatively great, wise, and holy*; these sufficiently fill the Imaginations of Men; and any thing beyond, besides that it leads into Absurdities, has no Influence on the Affections or Sentiments. Thus, in the present Subject, if we abandon all human Analogy, as 20 seems your Intention, *Demea*, I am afraid we abandon all Religion, and retain no Conception[1] of the great Object of our Adoration. If we preserve human Analogy, we must for ever find it impossible to reconcile any mixture of Evil in the Universe with infinite Attributes; much less, can we ever prove the latter from the former. 25 But supposing the Author of Nature to be finitely perfect, tho far exceeding Mankind; a satisfactory Account may then be given of natural and moral Evil, and every untoward Phænomenon be explain'd and adjusted. A less Evil may then be chosen, in order to

1 I believe] perhaps   12 we meet] is to be met

---

[1] A left-hand bracket ([) is drawn in this word between 'p' and 't' with the marginal annotation [113. P. Just above this annotation is a note in the holograph of Hume's nephew (p. 69 of the manuscript), 'I have sent two Leaves of the original Manuscript, as I have not been able to get the Copy compared with it'. See textual introduction.

avoid a greater: Inconveniencies be submitted to, in order to reach
a desirable End: And in a Word, Benevolence, regulated by Wisdom,
and limited by Necessity, may produce just such a World as the
present. You, *Philo,* who are so prompt at starting Views, and
5 Reflections, and Analogies; I wou'd gladly hear, at length, without
Interruption, your Opinion of this new Theory; and if it deserve
our Attention, we may afterwards, at more Leizure, reduce it into
Form.

My Sentiments, reply'd *Philo,* are not worth being made a
10 Mystery of; and therefore, without any Ceremony, I shall deliver
what occurs to me, with regard to the present Subject. It must, I
think, be allow'd, that, if a very limited Intelligence, whom we shall
suppose utterly unacquainted with the Universe, were assur'd, that
it were the Production of a very good, wise, and powerful, Being,
15 however finite, he wou'd, from his Conjectures, form *beforehand* a
different Notion of it from what we find it to be by Experience; nor
wou'd he ever imagine, merely from these Attributes of the Cause of
which he is inform'd, that the Effect cou'd be so full of Vice and
Misery and Disorder, as it appears in this Life. Supposing now, that
20 this Person were brought into the World, still assur'd, that it was
the Workmanship of such a sublime and benevolent Being; he
might, perhaps, be surpriz'd at the Disappointment; but wou'd
never retract his former Belief, if founded on any very solid Argument; since such a limited Intelligence must be sensible of his own
25 Blindness and Ignorance, and must allow, that there may be many
Solutions of those Phænomena, which will for ever escape his
Comprehension. But supposing, which is the real Case with regard
to Man, that this Creature is not antecedently convinc'd of a
supreme Intelligence, benevolent, and powerful, but is left to
30 gather such a Belief from the Appearances of things; this entirely
alters the Case, nor will he ever find any Reason for such a Conclusion. He may be fully convinc'd of the narrow Limits of his
Understanding, but this will not help him in forming an Inference

---

7 reduce] lick   14 powerful [tho' finite]   15 a [very]   17 imagine
[that it]   Attributes] Conveniences   17–18 merely from . . . Effect *added in
margin*   19 appears] appear   21 sublime and benevolent] perfect   25 may
be] are   many [other]   26 those [untoward]   26–7 his Comprehension] him
29 benevolent] good, wise

concerning the Goodness of superior Powers, since he must form that Inference from what he knows, not from what he is ignorant of. The more you exaggerate his Weakness and Ignorance; the more diffident you render him, and give him the greater Suspicion, that such Subjects are beyond the Reach of his Faculties. You are oblig'd, 5 therefore, to reason with him merely from the known Phænomena, and to drop every arbitrary Supposition or Conjecture.

Did I show you a House or Palace, where there was not one Apartment convenient or agreeable; where the Windows, Doors, Fires, Passages, Stairs, and the whole Oeconomy of the Building 10 were the Source of Noise, Confusion, Fatigue, Darkness, and the Extremes of Heat and Cold; you wou'd certainly blame the Contrivance, without any farther Examination. The Architect wou'd in vain display his Subtility, and prove to you, that if this Door or that Window were altered, greater Ills wou'd ensue. What he says, 15 may be strictly true: The Alterations of one particular, while the other Parts of the Building remain, may only augment the Inconveniencies. But still you wou'd assert in general, that, if the Architect had had Skill and good Intentions, he might have form'd such a Plan of the Whole, and might have adjusted the Parts in such 20 a manner, as wou'd have remedy'd all or most of these Inconveniencies. His Ignorance or even your own Ignorance of such a Plan, will never convince you of the Impossibility of it. If you find many Inconveniencies and Deformities in the Building, you will always, without entering into any Detail, condemn the Architect. 25

In short, I repeat the Question: Is the World, consider'd in general, and as it appears to us in this Life, different from what a Man or such a Limited Being would, *beforehand*, expect from a very powerful, wise, and benevolent Deity? It must be strange Prejudice to assert the contrary. And from thence I conclude, that, however 30 consistent the World may be, allowing certain Suppositions and Conjectures, with the Idea of such a Deity, it can never afford us an Inference concerning his Existence. The Consistence is not

---

7 and to drop every] without any   Supposition or Conjecture] Suppositions or Conjectures   11 were] was   15 Ills] Inconveniencies   25 always...
Architect] always condemn the Architect . . . Detail.   30 conclude] infer
32 such a Deity] such a perfect Being   33 concerning his] of the   Existence
[of such a Being]

absolutely deny'd, only the Inference. Conjectures, especially where Infinity is excluded from the divine Attributes, may, perhaps, be sufficient to prove a Consistence; but can never be foundations for any Inference.

5   There seem to be *four* Circumstances, on which depend all, or the greatest Part of the Ills, that molest sensible Creatures; and it is not impossible but all these Circumstances may be necessary and unavoidable. We know so little beyond common Life, or even of common Life, that, with regard to the Oeconomy of a Universe,
10 there is no Conjecture, however wild, which may not be just; nor any one, however plausible, which may not be erroneous. All that belongs to human Understanding, in this deep Ignorance and Obscurity, is to be sceptical, or at least cautious; and not to admit of any Hypothesis, whatever; much less, of any which is supported
15 by no Appearance of Probability. Now this I assert to be the Case with regard to all the Causes of Evil, and the Circumstances, on which it depends. None of them appear to human Reason, in the least degree, necessary or unavoidable; nor can we suppose them such, without the utmost Licence of Imagination.

20   The *first* Circumstance, which introduces Evil, is that Contrivance or Oeconomy of the animal Creation, by which Pains, as well as Pleasures, are employ'd to excite all Creatures to Action, and make them vigilant in the great Work of Self-preservation. Now Pleasure alone, in its various Degrees, seems to human Under-
25 standing sufficient for this Purpose. All Animals might be constantly in a State of Enjoyment; but when urg'd by any of the Necessities of Nature, such as Thirst, Hunger, Wearyness; instead of Pain, they might feel a Diminution of Pleasure, by which they might be prompted to seek that Object, which is necessary to their
30 Subsistence. Men pursue Pleasure as eagerly as they avoid Pain; at least, might have been so constituted.[2] It seems, therefore,

1 deny'd [but]   14 Hypothesis] Conjecture   14–15 which . . .
Appearance] that is not supported by an Appearance   15 this I assert] I assert this
19 Imagination] Hypothesis   20 which] that   29 necessary] requisite

[2] Kames, *Essays on . . . Morality and Natural Religion*, p. 368: 'It is further to be observed in general, that aversion to pain, is not so great, at least in mankind, as to counterbalance every other appetite. Most men would purchase an additional share of happiness, at the expence of some pain.'

plainly possible to carry on the Business of Life without any Pain. Why then is any Animal ever render'd susceptible of such a Sensation? If Animals can be free from it an hour, they might enjoy a perpetual Exemption from it; and it requir'd as particular a Contrivance of their Organs to produce that Feeling, as to endow them with Sight, Hearing, or any of the Senses. Shall we conjecture, that such a Contrivance was necessary, without any Appearance of Reason? And shall we build on that Conjecture as on the most certain Truth?

But a Capacity of Pain wou'd not alone produce Pain, were it not for the *second* Circumstance, *viz*, the conducting of the World by general Laws; and this seems no wise necessary to a very perfect Being. It is true; if every thing were conducted by particular Volitions, the Course of Nature wou'd be perpetually broken, and no man cou'd employ his Reason in the Conduct of Life. But might not other particular Volitions remedy this Inconvenience? In short, might not the Deity exterminate all Ill, wherever it were to be found; and produce all Good, without any Preparation or long Progress of Causes and Effects?

Besides, we must consider, that, according to the present Oeconomy of the World, the Course of Nature, tho' suppos'd exactly regular, yet to us appears not so, and many Events are uncertain, and many dissappoint our Expectations. Health and Sickness, Calm and Tempest, with an infinite Number of other Accidents, whose Causes are unknown and variable, have a great Influence both on the Fortunes of particular Persons and on the Prosperity of public Societies: And indeed all human Life, in a manner, depends on such Accidents. A Being, therefore, who knows the secret Springs of the Universe, might easily, by particular Volitions, turn all these Accidents to the Good of Mankind, and render the whole World happy, without discovering himself in any Operation. A Fleet, whose Purposes were Salutary to Society, might always meet with a fair Wind: Good Princes enjoy sound Health and long Life: Persons, born to Power and Authority, be fram'd with good Tempers and virtuous Dispositions. A few such Events as these, regularly and wisely conducted, wou'd change the

5 their] the   12 wise] way   14 broken] broke   28 knows [all]

Face of the World; and yet wou'd no more seem to disturb the Course of Nature or confound human Conduct, than the present Oeconomy of things, where the Causes are secret, and variable, and compounded. Some small Touches, given to *Caligula*'s Brain in his
5 Infancy, might have converted him into a *Trajan*: One Wave, a little higher than the rest, by burying *Caesar* and his Fortune in the bottom of the Ocean, might have restor'd Liberty to a considerable Part of Mankind. There may, for aught we know, be good Reasons, why Providence interposes not in this Manner; but they are un-
10 known to us: And tho' the mere Supposition, that such Reasons exist, may be sufficient to *save* the Conclusion concerning the divine Attributes, yet surely it can never be sufficient to *establish* that Conclusion.

If every thing in the Universe be conducted by general Laws,
15 and if Animals be render'd susceptible of Pain, it scarcely seems possible but some Ill must arise in the various Shocks of Matter, and the various Concurrence and Opposition of general Laws: But this Ill wou'd be very rare, were it not for the *third* Circumstance which I propos'd to mention, *viz*, the great Frugality, with which all
20 Powers and Faculties are distributed to every particular Being. So well adjusted are the Organs and Capacities of all Animals, and so well fitted to their Preservation, that, as far as History or Tradition reaches, there appears not to be any single Species, which has yet been extinguish'd in the Universe. Every Animal has the requi-
25 site Endowments; but these Endowments are bestow'd with so scrupulous an Oeconomy, that any considerable Diminution must entirely destroy the Creature. Wherever one Power is encreas'd,

6 by burying] might have bury'd   7 might have] and   15 scarcely seems] seems scarce   23 which] that   24 Universe. [*Caesar*, speaking of the Woods in *Germany*, mentions some Animals as subsisting there, which are now utterly extinct. *De Bello Gall*: Lib. 6.[3] These, and some few more Instances, may be Exceptions to the Proposition here deliver'd. *Strabo* (Lib. 4)[4] quotes from *Polybius* an Account of an Animal about the *Tyrol*, which is not now to be found. If *Polybius* was not deceiv'd, which is possible, the Animal must have been then very rare, since *Strabo* cites but one Authority, and speaks doubtfully. *added in margin as note but then deleted*. speaking *substituted for* treating *in first line*]   24-5 Every Animal . . . Endowments are] But at the same time, it must be confest, that every Endowment is

3 Caesar, *The Gallic War*, Bk. VI, 26–8, tr. H. S. Edwards (Loeb edn.), pp. 351–5.
4 Strabo, *Geography*, Bk. IV, vi, 10, tr. H. L. Jones (Loeb edn.), p. 289.

there is a proportional Abatement in the others. Animals, which excell in Swiftness, are commonly defective in Force. Those, which possess both, are either imperfect in some of their Senses, or are oppressed with the most craving Wants. The human Species, whose chief Excellency is Reason and Sagacity, is of all others the 5 most necessitous, and the most deficient in bodily Advantages; without Cloaths, without Arms, without Food, without Lodging, without any Convenience of Life, except what they owe to their own Skill and Industry. In short, Nature seems to have form'd an exact Calculation of the Necessities of her Creatures; and like a 10 *rigid Master*, has afforded them little more Powers or Endowments, than what are strictly sufficient to supply those Necessities. An *indulgent Parent* wou'd have bestow'd a large Stock, in order to guard against Accidents, and secure the Happiness and Welfare of the Creature, in the most unfortunate Concurrence of Circum- 15 stances. Every Course of Life wou'd not have been so surrounded with[5] Precipices, that the least Departure from the true Path, by Mistake or Necessity, must involve us in Misery and Ruin. Some Reserve, some Fund wou'd have been provided to ensure Happiness; nor wou'd the Powers and the Necessities have been adjusted with so 20 rigid an Oeconomy. The Author of Nature is inconceivably power-ful: His Force is suppos'd great, if not altogether inexhaustible: Nor is there any Reason, as far as we can judge, to make him observe this strict Frugality in his Dealings with his Creatures. It wou'd have been better, were his Power extremely limited, to have created fewer 25 Animals, and to have endowed these with more Faculties for their Happines and Preservation. A Builder is never esteem'd prudent, who undertakes a Plan, beyond what his Stock will enable him to finish.[6]

1 which] that   4 oppressed] opprest   Wants] Necessities   5 Excell-ency] Endowment   is[2] are   8 they] we   their] our   11 little] no Endowments] Capacities   15–16 Circumstances] Adventures   16 surrounded] border'd   19 ensure [the Creature's]   21 is [suppos'd]   22 Force . . . altogether] Stock is   24–8 It . . . finish. *added*   25 better [for him] 26 Animals] of them   these [better]

---

[5] A left-hand bracket ([) is drawn between 'surrounded' and 'with' with the marginal annotation [211. Q. See textual introduction.

[6] The last two sentences of this paragraph are added on the margin of p. 72 of the manuscript, deleted, and rewritten at the end of section XI, on p. 76 of the manuscript. The mark 'BB' is used to indicate where the two sentences, as well as the succeeding paragraph, should be inserted.

In order to cure most of the Ills of human Life, I require not that
Man should have the Wings of the Eagle, the Swiftness of the Stag,
the Force of the Ox, the Arms of the Lion, the Scales of the Crocodile or Rhinoceros; much less do I demand the Sagacity of an Angel
5 or Cherubim. I am contented to take an Encrease in one single
Power or Faculty of his Soul. Let him be endow'd with a greater
Propensity to Industry and Labor; a more vigorous Spring and
Activity of Mind; a more constant Bent to Business and Applica-
tion. Let the whole Species possess naturally an equal Diligence
10 with that which many Individuals are able to attain by Habit and
Reflection; and the most beneficial Consequences, without any
Allay of Ill, is the most immediate and necessary Result of this
Endowment. Almost all the moral, as well as natural Evils of human
Life arise from Idleness; and were our Species, by the original Con-
15 stitution of their Frame, exempt from this Vice or Infirmity, the
perfect Cultivation of Land, the Improvement of Arts and Manu-
factures, the exact Execution of every Office and Duty, immediately
follow; and Men at once may fully reach that State of Society, which
is so imperfectly attain'd by the best regulated Government. But
20 as Industry is a Power, and the most valuable of any, Nature seems
determin'd, suitably to her usual Maxims, to bestow it on men with
a very sparing hand; and rather to punish him severely for his
Deficiency in it, than to reward him for his Attainments. She has
so contriv'd his Frame, that nothing but the most violent Necessity
25 can oblige him to labor, and she employs all his other Wants to
overcome, at least in part, the Want of Diligence, and to endow
him with some Share of a Faculty, of which she has thought fit
naturally to bereave him. Here our Demands may be allow'd
very humble, and therefore the more reasonable. If we requir'd the
30 Endowments of superior Penetration and Judgment, of a more
delicate Taste of Beauty, of a nicer Sensibility to Benevolence and
Friendship; we might be told, that we impiously pretend to break
the Order of Nature, that we want to exalt Ourselves into a higher
Rank of Being, that the Presents which we require, not being

1–(239)7 In order . . . Evils. *added*   1–2 that . . . have] to Man   10 with]
to   29 reasonable] legitimate   30 superior [of]   32 pretend] pretended
33 want] wanted

suitable to our State and Condition, wou'd only be pernicious to us.
But it is hard; I dare to repeat it, it is hard, that being plac'd in a
World so full of Wants and Necessities; where almost every Being
and Element is either our Foe or refuses us their Assistance; we
shou'd also have our own Temper to struggle with, and shou'd be 5
depriv'd of that Faculty, which can alone fence against these
multiply'd Evils.[7]

The *fourth* Circumstance, whence arises the Misery and Ill of the
Universe, is the inaccurate Workmanship of all the Springs and
Principles of the great Machine of Nature. It must be acknow- 10
ledg'd, that there are few Parts of the Universe, which seem not to
serve some Purpose, and whose Removal wou'd not produce a
visible Defect and Disorder in the Whole. The Parts hang all together; nor can one be touch'd without affecting the rest, in a
greater or less degree. But at the same time, it must be observ'd, 15
that none of these Parts or Principles, however useful, are so
accurately adjusted, as to keep precisely within those Bounds, in
which their Utility consists; but they are, all of them, apt, on every
Occasion, to run into the one Extreme or the other. One wou'd
imagine, that this grand Production had not receiv'd the last hand 20
of the Maker; so little finish'd is every part, and so coarse are the
Strokes, with which it is executed. Thus, the Winds are requisite
to convey the Vapours along the Surface of the Globe, and to assist
Men in Navigation: But how oft, rising up to Tempests and Hurri-
canes, do they become pernicious? Rains are necessary to nourish 25
all the Plants and Animals of the Earth: But how often are they
defective? how often excessive? Heat is requisite to all Life and
Vegetation; but is not always found in the due Proportion. On the
Mixture and Secretion of the Humours and Juices of the Body
depend the Health and Prosperity of the Animal: But the Parts 30
perform not regularly their proper Function. What more useful
than all the Passions of the Mind, Ambition, Vanity, Love, Anger?

17–18 in which] wherein   26 Plants] Vegetables   28 due] just   On the
[due]   31 regularly] always   Function] Functions

---

[7] This paragraph added on p. 76 of the manuscript, followed by this instruction
(not in Hume's holograph): 'Go back to the top of page 73 and begin with a new
Paragraph.' From the handwriting, I would judge this addition to date from 1776.

But how oft do they break their Bounds, and cause the greatest Convulsions in Society? There is nothing so advantageous in the Universe, but what frequently becomes pernicious, by its Excess or Defect; nor has Nature guarded, with the requisite Accuracy, against all Disorder or Confusion. The Irregularity is never, perhaps, so great as to destroy any Species; but is often sufficient to involve the Individuals in Ruin and Misery.

On the Concurrence, then of these *four* Circumstances does all, or the greatest Part of natural Evil depend. Were all living Creatures incapable of Pain, or were the World administer'd by particular Volitions, Evil never cou'd have found Access into the Universe: And were Animals endow'd with a large Stock of Powers and Faculties, beyond what strict Necessity requires; or were the several Springs and Principles of the Universe so accurately fram'd as to preserve always the just Temperament and Medium; there must have been very little Ill in comparison of what we feel at present. What then shall we pronounce on this Occasion? Shall we say, that these Circumstances are not necessary, and that they might easily have been alter'd in the Contrivance of the Universe? This Decision seems too presumptuous for Creatures, so blind and ignorant. Let us be more modest in our Conclusions. Let us allow, that, if the Goodness of the Deity (I mean a Goodness like the human) cou'd be establish'd on any tolerable Reasons *a priori*, these Phænomena, however untoward, wou'd not be sufficient to subvert that Principle; but might easily, in some unknown manner, be reconcilable to it. But let us still assert, that as this Goodness is not antecedently establish'd, but must be inferr'd from the Phænomena, there can be no Grounds for such an Inference, while there are so many Ills in the Unverse, and while these Ills might so easily have been remedy'd, as far as human Understanding can be allow'd to judge on such a Subject. I am Sceptic enough to allow, that the bad Appearances, notwithstanding all my Reasonings, may be compatible with such Attributes as you suppose: But surely they can never prove these Attributes. Such a Conclusion cannot result

---

1–2 greatest Convulsions] utmost Confusion frequently   4 the requisite] sufficient [to]   32 Appearances [may possibly]   3 frequently becomes] becomes   25 easily [be allow'd]   manner,   33–4 can never] never can

from Scepticism; but must arise from the Phænomena, and from our Confidence in the Reasonings, which we deduce from these Phænomena.

Look round this Universe. What an immense Profusion of Beings, animated and organiz'd, sensible and active! You admire this prodigious Variety and Fecundity. But inspect a little more narrowly these living Existences, the only Beings worth regarding. How hostile and destructive to each other! How insufficient all of them for their own Happiness! How contemptible or odious to the Spectator! The whole presents nothing but the Idea of a blind Nature, impregnated by a great vivifying Principle, and pouring forth from her Lap, without Discernment or parental Care, her maim'd and abortive Children.[8]

Here the *Manichæn* System occurs as a proper Hypothesis to solve the Difficulty: And no doubt, in some respects, it is very specious, and has more Probability than the common Hypothesis, by giving a plausible Account of the strange Mixture of Good and Ill, which appears in Life.[9] But if we consider, on the other hand, the perfect Uniformity and Agreement of the Parts of the Universe, we shall not discover in it any Marks of the Combat of a malevolent with a benevolent Being. There is indeed an Opposition of Pains

---

2 which we deduce] we draw   4–13 Look . . . Children. *added*   6 Fecundity] Fecund (*in the holograph of Hume's nephew*)   11 a great] an infinitely
14 System [of two Principles]   18 which] that

---

[8] This paragraph is apparently one of Hume's last additions. It is written on pp. 75–6 of the manuscript, with the mark 'AA' to indicate its sequence in the order of paragraphs on p. 74 of the manuscript. At the end of the paragraph is the instruction in the holograph of Hume's nephew, 'Go back to page 74, and begin a new paragraph, with the words *Here the Manichæn*'.

[9] The '*Manichæn* System' assumes the essential and eternal opposition of good and evil forces working within one unit of human being. Some Manichaens posited an eventual triumph of good, but with an implied acceptance of the necessity of evil to bring this about. Augustine, in *De Duabus Animabus*, implies that the Manichaeans represent man as having two souls, one good and one evil. Hume may have been familiar with the work of the French Hugenot, Isaac de Beausrobe, whose exhaustive *Histoire critique de Manichée et du Manicheisme* (Amsterdam, 1734–9) was the first modern discussion of the subject, and he doubtless had read Bayle's article in the *Dictionary*. In the *Enquiry concerning the Principles of Morals* (London, 1751), he writes (p. 96): 'Could we admit the two Principles of the *Manichæans*, 'tis an infallible Consequence, that their Sentiments of human Actions, as well of every Thing else must be totally opposite; and that every Instance of Justice and Humanity, from its necessary Tendency, must please the one Deity, and displease the other.'

and Pleasures in the Feelings of sensible Creatures: But are not all the Operations of Nature carry'd on by an Opposition of Principles, of Hot and Cold, Moist and Dry, Light and Heavy? The true Conclusion is, that the original Source of all things is entirely in-
5 different to all these Principles, and has no more Regard to Good above Ill than to Heat above Cold, or to Drought above Moisture, or to Light above Heavy.

There may *four* Hypotheses be fram'd concerning the first Causes of the Universe; *that* they are endow'd with perfect Goodness, *that*
10 they have perfect Malice, *that* they are opposite and have both Goodness and Malice, *that* they have neither Goodness nor Malice. Mixt Phænomena can never prove the two former unmixt Principles. And the Uniformity and Steadiness of general Laws seem to oppose the third. The fourth, therefore, seems by far the most
15 probable.

What I have said concerning natural Evil will apply to moral, with little or no Variation; and we have no more Reason to infer, that the Rectitude of the Supreme Being resembles human Rectitude than that his Benevolence resembles the human. Nay, it will be
20 thought, that we have still greater Cause to exclude from him moral Sentiments, such as we feel them; since moral Evil, in the Opinion of many, is much more predominant above moral Good than natural Evil above natural Good.

But even tho' this shou'd not be allow'd, and tho' the Virtue,
25 which is in Mankind, shou'd be acknowledg'd much superior to the Vice; yet so long as there is any Vice at all in the Universe, it will very much puzzle you Anthropomorphites, how to account for it. You must assign a Cause for it, without having Recourse to the first Cause. But as every Effect must have a Cause, and that Cause
30 another; you must either carry on the Progression *in infinitum*, or rest on that original Principle, who is the ultimate Cause of all things.—

Hold! Hold! cry'd *Demea*: Whither does your Imagination hurry

---

4 Source] Cause   6 Drought above Moisture] Moisture above Drought   7 or to Light above Heavy *added later*   8 fram'd] form'd   first] original   17 no more] the same   18 Supreme Being] First Cause   Being [no more]   19 resembles the human] does   20 greater Cause] more Reason   25 which] that   31 rest on] stop at

you? I join'd in Alliance with you, in order to prove the incomprehensible Nature of the divine Being, and refute the Principles of *Cleanthes*, who wou'd measure every thing by a human Rule and Standard. But I now find you running into all the Topics of the greatest Libertines and Infidels; and betraying that holy Cause, 5 which you seemingly espous'd. Are you secretly, then, a more dangerous Enemy than *Cleanthes* himself?

And you are so late in perceiving it? reply'd *Cleanthes*. Believe me, *Demea*; your Friend, *Philo*, from the beginning, has been amusing himself at both our Expence; and it must be confessed, that the 10 injudicious Reasoning of our vulgar Theology has given him but too just a handle of Ridicule. The total Infirmity of human Reason, the absolute Incomprehensibility of the divine Nature, the great and universal Misery and still greater Wickedness of Man; these are strange Topics surely to be so fondly cherish'd by Orthodox 15 Divines and Doctors. In Ages of Stupidity and Ignorance, indeed, these Principles may safely be espous'd; and perhaps, no Views of things are more proper to promote Superstition, than such as encourage the blind Amazement, the Diffidence,[10] and Melancholy of Mankind. But at present—   20

Blame not so much, interpos'd *Philo*, the Ignorance of these reverend Gentlemen. They know how to change their Style with the times. Formerly it was a most popular theological Topic to maintain, that human Life was Vanity and Misery, and to exaggerate all the Ills and Pains, which are incident to Men. But of late 25 Years, Divines, we find, begin to retract this Position, and maintain, tho' still with some Hesitation, that there are more Goods than Evils, more Pleasures than Pains, even in this Life. When Religion stood entirely upon Temper and Education, it was thought proper to encourage Melancholy; as indeed, Mankind 30 never have Recourse to superior Powers so readily as in that Disposition. But as Men have now learn'd to form Principles, and to

---

5 Infidels] Sceptics   8 in] of   10 confessed] confest   17 Principles]
Arguments] Doctrines   Principles [which]   29 it was] 'twas

---

[10] A left-hand bracket ([) is drawn between the second 'f' and the 'i' of this word, with the notation [129. R. in the margin. See textual introduction.

draw Consequences, it is necessary to change the Batteries, and
to make Use of such Arguments as will endure, at least, some Scrutiny and Examination. This Variation is the same (and from the
same Causes) with that which I formerly remark'd with regard to
5 Scepticism.

Thus *Philo* continu'd to the last his Spirit of Opposition, and his
Censure of establish'd Opinions. But I cou'd observe, that *Demea* did
not at all relish the latter Part of the Discourse; and he took Occasion
soon after, on some Pretence or other, to leave the Company.[11]

PART 12

10

After *Demea's* Departure, *Cleanthes* and *Philo* continu'd the Conversation, in the following Manner. Our Friend, I am afraid, said
Cleanthes, will have little Inclination to revive this Topic of Discourse, while you are in Company; and to tell Truth, *Philo*, I shou'd
15 rather wish to reason with either of you apart on a Subject, so
sublime and interesting. Your Spirit of Controversy, join'd to your
Abhorrence of vulgar Superstition, carries you strange Lengths,
when engag'd in an Argument; and there is nothing so sacred
and venerable, even in your own Eyes, which you spare on that
20 Occasion.

I must confess, reply'd *Philo*, that I am less cautious on the Subject of natural Religion than on any other; both because I know
that I can never, on that head, corrupt the Principles of any Man
of common Sense, and because no-one, I am confident, in whose
25 Eyes I appear a Man of common Sense, will ever mistake my Intentions.[1] You in particular, *Cleanthes*, with whom I live in unreserv'd

---

3 This Variation is the same] This is the same Variation   9 after] afterwards
Pretence] Pretext   12 in] after   14 shou'd] wou'd

---

11 Gildon, *Deist's Manual*, p. 301: 'They took leave of good *Christophorus*, and
return'd safe to the House of *Christophil*, whence *Pleonexus* departed the next Day, on
pretended earnest Business, least he shou'd be oblig'd to repeat a Conversation so
little agreeable to him.'
1 *Letters*, i. 173: 'Let us revive the happy times, when Atticus and Cassius the
Epicureans, Cicero the Academic, and Brutus the Stoic, could, all of them, live in
unreserved friendship together, and were insensible to all those distinctions, except
so far as they furnished agreeable matter to discourse and conversation.'

Intimacy; you are sensible, that, notwithstanding the Freedom of
my Conversation, and my Love of singular Arguments, no-one has
a deeper Sense of Religion impressed on his Mind, or pays more
profound Adoration to the divine Being, as he discovers himself to
Reason, in the inexplicable Contrivance and Artifice of Nature. A 5
Purpose, an Intention, a Design strikes every where the most
careless, the most stupid Thinker; and no man can be so harden'd
in absurd Systems, as at all times to reject it. *That Nature does nothing
in vain*, is a Maxim establish'd in all the Schools, merely from the
Contemplation of the Works of Nature, without any religious 10
Purpose; and, from a firm Conviction of its Truth, an Anatomist,
who had observ'd a new Organ or Canal, wou'd never be satisfy'd,
till he had also discover'd its Use and Intention. One great Foundation of the *Copernican* System is the Maxim, *that Nature acts by the
simplest Methods, and chooses the most proper Means to any End*; and 15
Astronomers often, without thinking of it, lay this strong Foundation of Piety and Religion. The same thing is observable in other
Parts of Philosophy: And thus all the Sciences almost lead us insensibly to acknowledge a first intelligent Author; and their
Authority is often so much the greater, as they do not directly 20
profess that Intention.

It is with Pleasure I hear *Galen* reason concerning the Structure
of the human Body. The Anatomy of a Man, says he,[a] discovers
above 600 different Muscles; and whoever duly considers these,
will find, that in each of them Nature must have adjusted at least 25
ten different Circumstances, in order to attain the End, which she
propos'd; proper Figure, just Magnitude, right Disposition of the
several Ends, upper and lower Position of the Whole, the due
Insertion of the several Nerves, Veins, and Arteries: So that in the
Muscles alone, above 6000 several Views and Intentions must have 30
been form'd and executed. The Bones he calculates to be 284: The

[a] *De formatione fœtus.*

2 Arguments] Opinions   Arguments, [there is]   no-one [who]   3 im-
pressed] imprest   or] nor   11 its] this   12 observ'd] discover'd
17–18 The same . . . And *added in margin*   18 all the Sciences] every Science
lead] leads   20 as] when] that   26–7 which she propos'd] she propos'd
30 several] different

distinct Purposes, aim'd at in the Structure of each, above forty.[2]
What a prodigious Display of Artifice, even in these simple and
homogeneous Parts? But if we consider the Skin, Ligaments, Vessels,
Glandules, Humours, the several Limbs and Members of the Body;
5 how must our Astonishment rise upon us, in Proportion to the
Number and Intricacy of the Parts so artificially adjusted? The
farther we advance in these Researches, we discover new Scenes of
Art and Wisdom: But descry still, at a Distance, farther Scenes
beyond our Reach; in the fine internal Structure of the Parts, in the
10 Oeconomy of the Brain, in the Fabric of the seminal Vessels. All
these Artifices are repeated in every different Species of Animal,
with wonderful Variety, and with exact Propriety, suited to the
different Intentions of Nature, in framing each Species. And if the
Infidelity of *Galen*, even when these natural Sciences were still
15 imperfect, cou'd not withstand such striking Appearances; to
what Pitch of pertinacious Obstinacy must a Philosopher in this
Age have attain'd, who can now doubt of a supreme Intelligence?

Cou'd I meet with one of this Species (who, I thank God, are very
rare) I wou'd ask him: Supposing there were a God, who did not
20 discover himself immediately to our Senses; were it possible for him
to give stronger Proofs of his Existence, than what appear on the
whole Face of Nature? What indeed cou'd such a divine Being do,
but copy the present Œconomy of things; render many of his
Artifices so plain, that no Stupidity cou'd mistake them; afford
25 Glimpses of still greater Artifices, which demonstrate his prodigious
Superiority above our narrow Apprehensions; and conceal altogether
a great many from such imperfect Creatures? Now according to all
Rules of just Reasoning, every Fact must pass for undisputed,
when it is supported by all the Arguments, which its Nature

7 advance] go   discover [still]   15 to *deleted and then restored*   15–16 to
what [a]   21 on] in   25 which demonstrate] that show   27 many [of them]
28 every] any

---

² *De Foetuum Formatione*, cap. vi (in *Galeni Operum* (Basle, 1549), I, 1248–54; or
Galen, *Medicoram Graecorum Opera Quae Exstant*, ed. D. Carolus Gottlob Kühn
(Leipzig, 1821–33), IV, 687–702). Cf. Clarke, *Discourse*, p. 111: 'If *Galen* so many Ages
since, could find in the Construction and Constitution of the parts of a Human
Body, such undeniable marks of Contrivance and Design, as forced *Them* to acknowledge and admire the Wisdom of its Author; What would he have said, if he had
known the *Late* Discoveries in Anatomy and Physick . . .?'

admits of; even tho these Arguments be not, in themselves, very numerous or forcible: How much more, in the present Case, where no human Imagination can compute their Number, and no Understanding estimate their Cogency?

I shall farther add, said *Cleanthes*, to what you have so well urg'd, 5 that one great Advantage of the Principle of Theism, is, that it is the only System of Cosmogony, which can be render'd intelligible and compleat, and yet can throughout preserve a strong Analogy to what we every day see and experience in the World. The Comparison of the Universe to a Machine of human Contrivance is so obvious 10 and natural, and is justify'd by so many Instances of Order and Design in Nature, that it must immediately strike all unprejudic'd Apprehensions, and procure universal Approbation. Whoever attempts to weaken this Theory, cannot pretend to succeed by establishing in its Place any other, that is precise and determinate: 15 It is sufficient for him, if he start Doubts and Difficulties; and by remote and abstract Views of Things, reach that Suspence of Judgement, which is here the utmost Boundary of his Wishes. But besides, that this State of Mind is in itself unsatisfactory, it can never be steadily maintain'd against such striking Appearances, 20 as continually engage us into the religious Hypothesis. A false, absurd System, human Nature, from the Force of Prejudice, is capable of adhering to, with Obstinacy and Perseverance: But no System at all, in opposition to a Theory, supported by strong and obvious Reason, by natural Propensity, and by early Education, I 25 think it absolutely impossible to maintain or defend.

So little, reply'd *Philo*, do I esteem this Suspence of Judgement in the present Case to be possible, that I am apt to suspect there enters somewhat of a Dispute of Words into this Controversy, more than is usually imagin'd. That the Works of Nature bear a 30 great Analogy to the Productions of Art is evident; and according to all the Rules of good Reasoning, we ought to infer, if we argue at all concerning them, that their Causes have a proportional Analogy. But as there are also considerable Differences, we have

1 of *deleted and then restored*   3–4 and no Understanding] or   6 Principle]
System] Principles   Theism [of The]   12 Design in Nature] Contrivance
all] the most   15 other, [Theory]   16 start] starts   21 Hypothesis]
Theory   32 argue] reason

reason to suppose a proportional Difference in the Causes; and in particular ought to attribute a much higher Degree of Power and Energy to the supreme Cause than any we have ever observ'd in Mankind. Here then the Existence of a DEITY is plainly ascertain'd
5 by Reason; and if we make it a Question, whether, on account of these Analogies, we can properly call him a *Mind* or *Intelligence*, notwithstanding the vast Difference, which may reasonably be suppos'd between him and human Minds; what is this but a mere verbal Controversy? No man can deny the Analogies between the
10 Effects: To restrain Ourselves from enquiring concerning the Causes is scarcely possible: From this Enquiry, the legitimate Conclusion is, that the Causes have also an Analogy: And if we are not contented with calling the first and supreme Cause a GOD or DEITY, but desire to vary the Expression; what can we call him
15 but MIND or THOUGHT, to which he is justly suppos'd to bear a considerable Ressemblance?

All men of sound Reason are disgusted with verbal Disputes, which abound so much in philosophical and theological Enquiries; and it is found, that the only remedy for this abuse must arise from
20 clear Definitions, from the Precision of those Ideas which enter into any Argument, and from the strict and uniform Use of those Terms which are employ'd. But there is a species of Controversy, which, from the very Nature of Language and of human Ideas, is involved in perpetual Ambiguity, and can never, by any precaution or any
25 definitions, be able to reach a reasonable Certainty or precision. These are the controversies concerning the degrees of any Quality or Circumstance. Men may argue to all Eternity, whether Hannibal be a great, or a very great, or a superlatively great man, what degree of beauty Cleopatra possess'd, what Epithet of praise Livy
30 or Thucydides is intitled to, without bringing the Controversy to any Determination. The Disputants may here agree in their Sense and differ in the terms, or *vice versa*; yet never be able to define their terms, so as to enter into each others meaning: Because the degrees of these qualities are not, like quantity or
35 number, susceptible of any exact mensuration, which may be the

---

1 proportional] proportionable   16 Ressemblance] Analogy   17–(250)3 All
. . . Animosity. *added*

Standard in the Controversy. That the Dispute concerning Theism is of this Nature, and consequently is merely verbal, or perhaps, if possible, still more incurably ambiguous, will appear upon the slightest Enquiry. I ask the Theist, if he does not allow, that there is a great and immeasurable, because incomprehensible, Difference 5 between the *human* and the *divine* mind: The more pious he is, the more readily will he assent to the Affirmative, and the more will he be dispos'd to magnify the Difference: He will even assert, that the Difference is of a Nature, which cannot be too[3] much magnify'd. I next turn to the Atheist, who, I assert, is only nominally so, and 10 can never possibly be in earnest; and I ask him, whether, from the coherence and apparent Sympathy in all the parts of this world, there be not a certain degree of analogy among all the operations of Nature, in every situation and in every age; whether the rotting of a Turnip, the generation of an animal, and the structure of human 15 thought be not energies that probably bear some remote analogy to each other: It is impossible he can deny it: He will readily acknowledge it. Having obtain'd this Concession, I push him still farther in his retreat; and I ask him, if it be not probable, that the Principle which first arrang'd, and still maintains order in this universe, 20 bears not also some remote inconceivable analogy to the other operations of Nature, and among the rest to the Oeconomy of human Mind and Thought. However reluctant, he must give his Assent. Where then, cry I to both these Antagonists, is the Subject of your dispute: The Theist allows, that the original Intelligence 25 is very different from human reason: The Atheist allows, that the original Principle of Order bears some remote Analogy to it. Will you quarrel, Gentlemen, about the degrees, and enter into a controversy, which admits not of any precise meaning, nor consequently of any determination. If you shou'd be so obstinate, I shou'd not be 30 surpriz'd to find you insensibly change sides; while the Theist on the one hand exaggerates the Dissimilarity between the supreme Being, and frail, imperfect, variable, fleeting, and mortal Creatures; and the Atheist on the other magnifies the Analogy among all the operations of Nature, in every period, every situation, and every 35

---

[3] A left-hand bracket ([) is drawn over 'much' with the notation [139. S. in the margin (not in Hume's hand). See textual introduction.

position. Consider then, where the real point of controversy lies, and if you cannot lay aside your Disputes, endeavour, at least, to cure yourselves of your Animosity.[4]

And here I must also acknowledge, *Cleanthes*, that, as the Works of Nature have a much greater Analogy to the Effects of *our* Art and Contrivance, than to those of *our* Benevolence and Justice; we have reason to infer that the natural Attributes of the Deity have a greater Ressemblance to those of Man, than his moral have to human Virtues. But what is the Consequence? Nothing but this, that the moral Qualities of Man are more defective in their kind than his natural Abilities. For as the Supreme Being is allow'd to be absolutely and entirely perfect, whatever differs most from him departs the farthest from the supreme Standard of Rectitude and Perfection.

It seems evident, that the Dispute between the Sceptics and Dogmatists is entirely verbal, or at least regards only the Degrees of Doubt and Assurance, which we ought to indulge with regard to all Reasoning: And such Disputes are commonly, at the bottom, verbal, and admit not of any precise Determination. No philosophical Dogmatist denies, that there are Difficulties both with regard to the Senses and to all Science, and that these Difficulties are in a regular, logical Method, absolutely insolveable. No Sceptic denies, that we lie under an absolute Necessity, notwithstanding these Difficulties, of thinking, and believing, and reasoning with regard to all Kind of Subjects, and even of frequently asserting with Confidence and Security. The only Difference, then, between these Sects, if they merit that Name, is, that the Sceptic, from Habit, Caprice, or Inclination, insists most on the Difficulties; the Dogmatist, for like Reasons, on the Necessity.[5]

5 have] bear   8 those of Man] the human] Men   10 Man] Men
his] their   13 the farthest] so far

[4] This paragraph, the longest in the *Dialogues*, is added at the end of Part 12, on pp. 87–8 of the manuscript with the mark 'BB' to indicate the point of insertion on p. 79 of the manuscript. This was one of Hume's last additions, made in 1776.
[5] This paragraph was initially intended to appear as a note. It first appeared on p. 84 of the manuscript as a note to be inserted on p. 79 of the manuscript as a note to the preceding paragraph, with the mark 'AA' to indicate point of insertion. In revising the ending of the *Dialogues*, Hume has deleted this note–paragraph and recopied it on p. 87 of the manuscript; in the margin of p. 79 is the instruction 'Vid. Page 87' (not in Hume's hand). The words 'a Note' also appear just above this recopied version, but not, I think, in Hume's hand. I have restored the 'Note' to

These, *Cleanthes*, are my unfeign'd Sentiments on this Subject; and these Sentiments, you know, I have ever cherish'd and maintained. But in proportion to my Veneration for true Religion, is my Abhorrence of vulgar Superstitions; and I indulge a peculiar Pleasure, I confess, in pushing such Principles, sometimes into Absur- 5 dity, sometimes into Impiety. And you are sensible, that all Bigots, notwithstanding their great Aversion to the latter above the former, are commonly equally guilty of both.

My Inclination, reply'd *Cleanthes*, lies, I own, a contrary way. Religion, however corrupted, is still better than no Religion at all. 10 The doctrine of a future State is so strong and necessary a Security to Morals, that we never ought to abandon or neglect it. For if finite and temporary Rewards and Punishments have so great an Effect, as we daily find: How much greater must be expected from such as are infinite and eternal? 15

How happens it then, said *Philo*, if vulgar Superstition be so salutary to Society, that all History abounds so much with Accounts of its pernicious Consequences on public Affairs? Factions, civil Wars, Persecutions, Subversions of Government, Oppression, Slavery; these are the dismal Consequences which always attend 20 its Prevalency over the Minds of Men. If the religious Spirit be ever mention'd in any historical Narration, we are sure to meet afterwards with a Detail of the Miseries, which attend it. And no Period of time can be happier or more prosperous, than those in which it is never regarded, or heard of. 25

The Reason of this Observation, reply'd *Cleanthes*, is obvious. The proper Office of Religion is to regulate the Heart of Men, humanize their Conduct, infuse the Spirit of Temperance, Order, and Obedience; and as its Operation is silent, and only inforces the Motives of Morality and Justice, it is in danger of being 30

---

5 I confess, in] of   12 never ought] ought never   16 Superstition] Religion   20 which] that   23 which] that   24 those] that   in *deleted and then restored*   25 regarded] mention'd or] nor   27 Heart] Hearts

---

the text on the grounds that Hume, in preparing a final draft of the work, was conscious of the incongruity of a discursive note in a dialogue. Pamphilus is ostensibly recounting a conversation he had heard, and it is unlikely that the participants would append discursive footnotes to a discussion.

overlooked, and confounded with these other Motives. When it distinguishes itself, and acts as a separate Principle over Men, it has departed from its proper Sphere, and has become only a Cover to Faction and Ambition.

5   And so will all Religion, said *Philo*, except the philosophical and rational kind. Your Reasonings are most easily eluded than my Facts. The Inference is not just, because finite and temporary Rewards and Punishments have so great Influence, that therefore such as are infinite and eternal must have so much greater.[6] Con-
10 sider, I beseech you, the Attachment, which we have to present things, and the little Concern which we discover for Objects, so remote and uncertain. When Divines are declaiming against the common Behaviour and Conduct of the World, they always represent this Principle the strongest imaginable (which indeed it is)
15 and describe almost all human kind as lying under the Influence of it, and sunk into the deepest Lethargy and Unconcern about their religious Interests. Yet these same Divines, when they refute their speculative Antagonists, suppose the Motives of Religion to be so powerful, that, without them, it were impossible for civil
20 Society to subsist; nor are they asham'd of so palpable a Contradiction. It is certain, from Experience, that the smallest Grain of

---

1 overlooked] overlookt   9 greater. [If indeed we consider the Matter merely in an abstract Light: If we compare only the Importance of the Motives, and then reflect on the natural Self-love of Mankind; we shall not only look for a great Effect from religious Considerations; but we must really esteem them absolutely irresistible and infallible in their Operation. For what other Motive can reasonably counter-ballance them even for a Moment? But this is not found to hold in Reality; and there-fore, we may be certain, that there is some other Principle of human Nature, which we have here overlookt, and which diminishes, at least, the Force of these Motives. This Principle is]   17 they [come to]   [n]1 Matter] Matters   merely] only [n]6 Reality] Fact

---

[6] Butler, *Analogy*, p. 136: '. . . it has been observed; that some Sort of moral Government is necessarily implied, in That natural Government of God, which we experience ourselves under: that good and bad Actions, at present, are naturally rewarded and published, not only as beneficial and mischievous to Society: but also as virtuous and vitious: and that there is, in the very Nature of the thing, a Tendency to their being rewarded and punished in a much higher Degree, than they are at present. . . . A moral Scheme of Government then, is visibly established, and, in some Degree, carried into Execution: And this, together with the essential Tenden-cies of Virtue and Vice duly considered, naturally raises in us an Apprehension, that it will be carried on farther towards Perfection, in a future State, and that every one shall there receive according to his Deserts.'

natural Honesty and Benevolence has more Effect on Men's Conduct, than the most pompous Views, suggested by theological Theories and Systems. A Man's natural Inclination works incessantly upon him; it is for ever present to the Mind; and mingles itself with every View and Consideration: Whereas religious Motives, where they act at all, operate only by Starts and Bounds; and it is scarcely possible for them to become altogether habitual to the Mind. The Force of the greatest Gravity, say the Philosophers, is infinitely small, in comparison of that of the least Impulse; yet it is certain, that the smallest Gravity will, in the End, prevail above a great Impulse; because no Strokes or Blows can be repeated with such Constancy as Attraction and Gravitation.

Another Advantage of Inclination: It engages on its Side all the Wit and Ingenuity of the Mind; and when set in opposition to religious Principles, seeks every Method and Art of eluding them: In which it is almost always successful. Who can explain the Heart of Man, or account for those strange Salvos and Excuses, with which People satisfy themselves, when they follow their Inclinations, in opposition to their religious Duty? This is well understood in the World; and none but Fools ever repose less Trust in a Man, because they hear, that, from Study and Philosophy, he has entertain'd some speculative Doubts with regard to theological Subjects. And when we have to do with a Man, who makes a great Profession of Religion and Devotion; has this any other Effect upon several, who pass for prudent, than to put them on their Guard, lest they be cheated and deceiv'd by him?

We must farther consider, that Philosophers, who cultivate Reason and Reflection, stand less in need of such Motives to keep them under the Restraint of Morals: And that the Vulgar, who alone may need them, are utterly incapable of so pure a Religion, as represents the Deity to be pleas'd with nothing but Virtue in human Behaviour. The Recommendations to the Divinity are

2 Views] Representations   3 A Man's] One's   6 act] operate   7 scarcely] scarce   10 yet it is] and yet 'tis   12 Constancy [and Perpetuity] as Attraction and Gravitation] as the Attraction of Gravity   13 Advantage of [natural]   23 makes] has   25 who [justly]   27–8 who cultivate . . . less] and Men of Education stand little   29–30 who alone . . . them *deleted and then restored*   32 Divinity] Deity

generally suppos'd to be either frivolous Observances, or rapturous Ecstasies, or a bigoted Credulity. We need not run back into Antiquity, or wander into remote Regions, to find Instances of this Degeneracy. Amongst ourselves, some have been guilty of that
5 Atrociousness, unknown to the *Aegyptian* and *Grecian* Superstitions, of declaiming, in express Terms, against Morality, and representing it as a sure Forfeiture of the divine Favour, if the least Trust or Reliance be laid upon it.[7]

But even tho' Superstition or Enthusiasm shou'd not put itself
10 in direct Opposition to Morality; the very diverting of the Attention, the raising up a new and frivolous Species of Merit, the preposterous Distribution, which it makes of Praise and Blame; must have the most pernicious Consequences, and weaken extremely Men's Attachment to the natural Motives of Justice and Humanity.
15 Such a Principle of Action likewise, not being any of the familiar Motives of human Conduct, acts only by Intervals on the Temper, and must be rouz'd by continual Efforts, in order to render the pious Zealot satisfy'd with his own Conduct, and make him fulfill his devotional Task. Many religious Exercises are enter'd into with
20 seeming Fervor, where the Heart, at the time, feels cold and languid: A Habit of Dissimulation is by degrees contracted: And Fraud and Falsehood become the predominant Principle. Hence the Reason of that vulgar Observation, that the highest Zeal in Religion and the deepest Hypocrisy, so far from being inconsistent,
25 are often or commonly united in the same individual Character.[8]

2 Credulity. [and tho' there may be Exceptions to this Rule with regard to particular Persons, yet these compose much the smaller Number.]   8 laid] made   10–11 Attention [of the Mind]   15 any of the [natural or]   17 in order to [give]   20 at] for   22 Hence] Thus we see   23 of] for vulgar Observation] common Phænomenon

---

[7] The last two sentences in this paragraph are deleted, but Hume has written 'Print this Passage' in the margin of p. 81 of the manuscript.

[8] Cf. *The Natural History of Religion*, p. 90 above: 'Hence the greatest crimes have been found, in many instances, compatible with a superstitious piety and devotion: Hence it is justly regarded as unsafe to draw any certain inference in favour of a man's morals from the fervor or strictness of his religious excercises, even tho' he himself believe them sincere. Nay, it has been observed, that enormities of the blackest dye, have been rather apt to produce superstitious terrors, and encrease the religious passion.' Also, *History of England*, vi. 118: 'The religious hypocrisy, it may be remarked, is of a singular nature; and being unknown to the person himself, tho'

The bad Effects of such Habits, even in common Life, are easily imagin'd: But where the Interests of Religion are concern'd, no Morality can be forcible enough to bind the enthusiastic Zealot. The Sacredness of the Cause sanctifies every Measure, which can be made use of to promote it.   5

The steady Attention alone to so important an Interest as that of eternal Salvation is apt to extinguish the benevolent Affections, and beget a narrow, contracted Selfishness. And when such a Temper is encourag'd, it easily eludes all the general Precepts of Charity and Benevolence.   10

Thus the Motives of vulgar Superstition have no great Influence on general Conduct; nor is their Operation very favourable to Morality in the Instances, where they predominate.

Is there any Maxim in Politics more certain and infallible, than that both the Number and Authority of Priests shou'd be confin'd 15 within very narrow Limits, and that the civil Magistrate ought, for ever, to keep his *Fasces and Axes* from such dangerous Hands? But if the Spirit of popular Religion were so salutary to Society, a contrary Maxim ought to prevail. The greater Number of Priests, and their greater Authority and Riches will always augment the 20 religious Spirit. And tho' the Priests have the Guidance of this Spirit; why may we not expect a superior Sanctity of Life, and greater[9] Benevolence and Moderation, from Persons, who are set apart for Religion, who are continually inculcating it upon others, and who must themselves imbibe a greater Share of it? Whence 25 comes it then, that, in fact, the utmost a wise Magistrate can pro-pose with regard to popular Religions, is, as far as possible, to make a saving Game of it, and to prevent their pernicious Consequences

3 Zealot] Zealots   4 which] that   9 encourag'd] engender'd   11 no great] little or no   13 in the [few]   15 Authority of [the]   shou'd be] ought to be   17 for ever, to keep] to keep, for ever,   23 Persons] those 25–6 Whence . . . then] But so it is, we find

---

more dangerous, it implies less falshood than any other species of insincerity.' This opinion was not limited just to sceptical Scots: Swift in 'On the Testimony of Conscience', *Irish Tracts 1720–1723*, ed. H. Davis (Oxford, 1963), p. 157, wrote, 'It is very possible for a Man who has the Appearance of Religion, and a great Pretender to Conscience, to be wicked and an Hypocrite. . . .'

[9] A left-hand bracket ([) is drawn around this word with the notation [145. T in the margin. See textual introduction.

with regard to Society. Every Expedient which he tries for so
humble a Purpose is surrounded with Inconveniencies. If he admits
only one Religion among his Subjects, he must sacrifice, to an
uncertain Prospect of Tranquillity, every Consideration of public
5 Liberty, Science, Reason, Industry, and even his own Independency.
If he gives Indulgence to several Sects, which is the wiser Maxim, he
must preserve a very philosophical Indifference to all of them, and
carefully restrain the Pretensions of the prevailing Sect; otherwise
he can expect nothing but endless Disputes, Quarrels, Factions,
10 Persecutions, and civil Commotions.

True Religion, I allow, has no such pernicious Consequences: But
we must treat of Religion, as it has commonly been found in the
World; nor have I any thing to do with that speculative Tenet of
Theism, which, as it is a Species of Philosophy, must partake of the
15 beneficial Influence, of that Principle, and at the same time must
lie under a like Inconvenience, of being always confin'd to very few
Persons.[10]

Oaths are requisite in all Courts of Judicature; but it is a Question whether their Authority arises from any popular Religion.
20 Tis the Solemnity and Importance of the Occasion, the Regard to
Reputation, and the reflecting on the general Interests of Society,
which are the chief Restraints upon Mankind. Custom-house Oaths
and political Oaths are but little regarded even by some who pretend to Principles of Honesty and Religion: And a Quaker's
25 Asseveration is with us justly put upon the same Footing with the
Oath of any other Person. I know, that *Polybius*[b][11] ascribes the

---

b Lib. 6 Cap. 54.

---

3 among] amongst   3–5 to an uncertain Prospect of Tranquillity *deleted after*
Independency *and transposed to earlier part of sentence*   12 commonly] always
13 Tenet] Principle   Tenet of [refin'd]   14 must [also]   the] its   19 whether]
if   22 which] that   23 who] that   [10]2 Since] if   [10]3 are] be

---

[10] The following sentence appears on the margin of p. 82 of the manuscript next
to this paragraph but is deleted: 'Since Government, Reason, Learning, Friendship,
Love, and every human Advantage are attended with Inconveniences, as we daily
find, what may be expected in all the various Models of Superstition; a Quality,
compos'd of whatever is the most absurd, corrupted, and barbarous of our Nature?
Were there any one Exception to that universal Mixture of Good and Ill, which is
found in Life, this might be pronounc'd thoroughly and entirely ill.' Beneath this
paragraph in the margin is written 'a separate Paragraph' but this too is deleted.
[11] Hume may have been using an edition of the *Histories* of Polybius whose

Infamy of *Greek* Faith to the Prevalency of the *Epicurean* Philosophy; but I know also, that *Punic* Faith had as bad a Reputation in antient Times, as *Irish* Evidence has in modern; tho' we cannot account for these vulgar Observations by the same Reason. Not to mention, that *Greek* Faith was infamous before the Rise of the *Epicurean* Philosophy; and *Euripides*,[c] in a Passage which I shall point out to you,[12] has glanc'd a remarkable Stroke of Satyre against his Nation, with regard to this Circumstance.

Take Care, *Philo*, reply'd *Cleanthes*, take Care: Push not Matters too far: Allow not your Zeal against false Religion to undermine your Veneration for the true. Forfeit not this Principle, the chief, the only great Comfort in Life; and our principal Support amidst all the Attacks of adverse Fortune. The most agreeable Reflection, which it is possible for human Imagination to suggest, is that of genuine Theism, which represents us as the Workmanship of a Being perfectly good, wise, and powerful; who created us for Happiness, and who, having implanted in us immeasurable Desires of Good, will prolong our Existence to all Eternity, and will transfer us into an infinite Variety of Scenes, in order to satisfy those Desires, and render our Felicity compleat and durable. Next to such a Being himself (if the Comparison be allow'd) the happiest Lot which we can imagine, is that of being under his Guardianship and Protection.

These Appearances, said *Philo*, are most engaging and alluring; and with regard to the true Philosopher, they are more than Appearances. But it happens here, as in the former Case, that, with regard to the greater Part of Mankind, the Appearances are deceitful, and that the Terrors of Religion commonly prevail above its Comforts.

[c] *Iphigenia in Tauride.*

---

2 *Punic* Faith] *Irish* Evidence   antient] modern   , 4 these vulgar Observations] it   7 you [when you please]   glanc'd a [very]   16 us for [our] 26 greater Part] Generality   the[2] these

---

numeration was not standard, as his reference is actually to Book 6, Chapter 56, where Polybius doubts the reliability of Greek statesmen. Cf. Loeb edn., iii. 392–7.

[12] Probably a reference to lines 1157–233 in *Iphigenia in Tauris*, a passage full of dramatic irony, in which Iphigenia warns Thoas to beware of Greeks and their deception, while at the same time contriving the deception of Thoas. See the translation by Gilbert West in *Odes of Pindar* (London, 1766), i. 224–30.

It is allow'd, that Men never have Recourse to Devotion so readily as when dejected with Grief or depressed with Sickness. Is not this a Proof, that the religious Spirit is not so nearly ally'd to Joy as to Sorrow?

5   But Men, when afflicted, find Consolation in Religion, reply'd *Cleanthes*. Sometimes, said *Philo*: But it is natural to imagine, that they will form a Notion of those unknown Beings, suitably to the present Gloom and Melancholy of their Temper, when they betake themselves to the Contemplation of them. Accordingly, we find the tremendous Images to predominate in all Religions; and we ourselves, after having employ'd the most exalted Expression in our Descriptions of the Deity, fall into the flatest Contradiction, in affirming, that the Damn'd are infinitely superior in Number to the Elect.

I shall venture to affirm, that there never was a popular Religion, which represented the State of departed Souls in such a Light, as wou'd render it eligible for human kind, that there shou'd be such a State. These fine Models of Religion are the mere Product of Philosophy. For as Death lies between the Eye and the Prospect of Futurity, that Event is so shocking to Nature, that it must throw a Gloom on all the Regions, which lie beyond it; and suggest to the Generality of Mankind the Idea of *Cerberus* and Furies; Devils, and Torrents of Fire and Brimstone.

It is true; both Fear and Hope enter into Religion; because both these Passions, at different times, agitate the human Mind, and each of them forms a Species of Divinity, suitable to itself. But when a Man is in a cheerful Disposition, he is fit for Business or Company or Entertainment of any kind; and he naturally applies himself to these, and thinks not of Religion. When melancholy, and dejected, he has nothing to do but brood upon the Terrors of the invisible World, and to plunge himself still deeper in Affliction. It may, indeed, happen, that after he has, in this manner ingrav'd the religious Opinions deep into his Thought and Imagination, there may arrive a Change of Health or Circumstances, which may restore his good Humour, and raising cheerful Propsects of Futurity,

2 as when [they are]   depressed] deprest   7 suitably] suitable   10 all] most   11 employ'd [all]   Expression] Expressions   14 Religion [in the World] 16 wou'd] to   17 These] Such   20 Gloom] Shadow   which] that 25 Species] Specter   28 When [he is]   29 nothing [else]   upon] over

make him run into the other Extreme of Joy and Triumph. But still it must be acknowledg'd, that, as Terror is the primary Principle of Religion, it is the Passion, which always predominates in it, and admits but of short Intervals of Pleasure.

Not to mention, that these Fits of excessive, enthusiastic Joy, by exhausting the Spirits, always prepare the way for equal Fits of superstitious Terror and Dejection; nor is there any State of Mind so happy as the calm and equable. But this State it is impossible to support, where a Man thinks, that he lies, in such profound Darkness and Uncertainty, between an Eternity of Happiness and an Eternity of Misery. No wonder, that such an Opinion disjoints the ordinary Frame of the Mind, and throws it into the utmost Confusion. And tho' that Opinion is seldom so steady in its Operation as to influence all the Actions; yet is it apt to make a considerable Breach in the Temper, and to produce that Gloom and Melancholy, so remarkable in all devout People.

It is contrary to common Sense to entertain Apprehensions or Terrors, upon account of any Opinion whatsoever, or to imagine that we run any Risque hereafter, by the freest Use of our Reason. Such a Sentiment implies both an *Absurdity* and an *Inconsistency*. It is an Absurdity to believe the Deity has human Passions, and one of the lowest of human Passions, a restless Appetite for Applause. It is an Inconsistency to believe, that, since the Deity has this human Passion, he has not others also; and in particular, a Disregard to the Opinions of Creatures, so much inferior.

To know God, says *Seneca, is to worship him.*[13] All other Worship is indeed absurd, superstitious, and even impious. It degrades him to the low Condition of Mankind, who are delighted with Entreaty, Sollicitation, Presents, and Flattery. Yet is this Impiety the smallest of which Superstition is guilty. Commonly, it depresses the Deity far below the Condition of Mankind, and represents him as a capricious Dæmon, who exercises his Power without Reason

---

3 which] that   always [most]   11 that] if   14 the] our   22 Appetite for [vulgar]   26–(260)11 *To know* . . . Subjects. *added in margin, then deleted and later rewritten on next-to-last sheet (p. 85) of MS.*

[13] *Epistulae Morales* 95. 50: 'Primus est deorum cultus deos credere . . .' ('The most important aspect of divine worship is to believe in God . . .'). Cf. Loeb edn., iii. 88–9.

and without Humanity. And were that divine Being dispos'd to be offended at the Vices and Follies of silly Mortals, who are his own Workmanship; ill would it surely fare with the Votaries of most popular Superstitions. Nor wou'd any of human Race merit his 5 Favor, but a very few, the philosophical Theists, who entertain, or rather indeed endeavor to entertain, suitable Notions of his divine Perfections: As the only Persons, intitled to his *Compassion* and *Indulgence*, wou'd be the philosophical Sceptics, a Sect almost equally rare, who, from a natural Diffidence of their own Capacity, 10 suspend, or endeavor to suspend all Judgement with regard to such Sublime and such extraordinary Subjects.[14]

If the whole of natural Theology, as some People seem to maintain, resolves itself into one simple, tho' somewhat ambiguous, at least undefin'd Proposition, *that the Cause or Causes of Order in the* 15 *Universe probably bear some remote Analogy to human Intelligence:* If this Proposition be not capable of Extension, Variation, or more particular Explication: If it affords no Inference that affects human Life, or can be the Source of any Action or Forbearance: And if the Analogy, imperfect as it is, can be carry'd no farther than to the 20 human Intelligence;[15] and cannot be transfer'd, with any Appearance of Probability, to the other Qualities of the Mind: If this really be the Case, What can the most inquisitive, contemplative, and religious Man do more than give a plain, philosophical Assent to the Proposition, as often as it occurs; and believe, that the Arguments, 25 on which it is establish'd, exceed the Objections, which lie against it? Some Astonishment indeed will naturally arise from the Greatness of the Object: Some Melancholy from its Obscurity: Some Contempt of human Reason, that it can give no Solution more

---

3 most] all   5 Theists, [those]   12–(261)17 If . . . Pupil. *added*
16 not capable] incapable   18 Forbearance] steady Sentiment] Forbearance
20 transfer'd] extended   28 of] for

---

[14] This paragraph was added, probably in the 1760s, by Hume in the margin of p. 84 of the manuscript. Kemp Smith suggests that Hume intended it to be a 'new, *second* ending' (p. 94). When Hume made his final revisions in 1776, he recopied this paragraph in his mature hand on p. 85 of the manuscript.
[15] Thomas Blacklock, *Paracelsis . . . in Two Dissertations* (Edinburgh, 1767), p. 356: 'Analogy will no longer conduct my wandering steps: its light was indeed ambiguous and uncertain whilst it remained, but now all is darkness and solitude; fancy and hypothesis must supply the rest.'

satisfactory with regard to so extraordinary and magnificent a
Question. But believe me, *Cleanthes*, the most natural Sentiment,
which a well dispos'd Mind will feel on this Occasion, is a longing
Desire and Expectation, that Heaven wou'd be pleas'd to dissipate,
at least alleviate this profound Ignorance, by affording some more 5
particular Revelation to Mankind, and making Discoveries of the
Nature, Attributes, and Operations of the divine Object of our
Faith[16]. A Person, season'd with a just Sense of the Imperfections
of natural Reason, will fly to reveal'd Truth with the greater
Avidity: While the haughty Dogmatist, perswaded, that he can 10
erect a compleat System of Theology by the mere Help of Philosophy, disdains any farther Aid, and rejects this adventitious In-
structor. To be a philosophical Sceptic is, in a man of Letters, the
first and most essential Step towards being a sound, believing
Christian;[17] a Proposition, which I would willingly recommend to 15
the Attention of *Pamphilus*: And I hope *Cleanthes* will forgive me for
interposing so far in the Education and Instruction of his Pupil.[18]

    Cleanthes and *Philo* pursu'd not this Conversation much farther;
and as nothing ever made greater Impression on me, than all the
Reasonings of that day; so, I confess, that, upon a serious Review of 20
the Whole, I cannot but think, that *Philo*'s Principles are more probable than *Demea*'s; but that those of *Cleanthes* approach still nearer
to the Truth.[19]

Finis.

---

 1 with regard to] of   8 Person *deleted and then restored*   11 Help of
[Theology]   13 in] for   21 are] were   22 approach] approach'd

[16] Maclaurin, *Account*, p. 392: 'Surely it is in his power to grant us a far greater
improvement of the faculties we already possess, or even to endow us with new
faculties, of which, at this time, we have no idea, for penetrating farther into the
scheme of nature, and approaching nearer to himself, the first and supreme cause.'
  [17] Shaftesbury, *Characteristicks*, ii. 209: 'I consider still that, in strictness, the Root
of all is THEISM; and that to be a settled Christian, it is necessary to be first of all
a *good* THEIST.'
  [18] This paragraph is one of Hume's 1776 revisions. It appears on pp. 85–6 of the
manuscript (the last two leaves) immediately following the paragraph beginning
'*To know God*', which is recopied on p. 85 immediately preceding this paragraph.
  [19] Cicero, *De Natura Deorum*, p. 268: 'The Conversation ended here and we parted.
Velleius judged that the Arguments of *Cotta* were truest; but Those of *Balbus* seem'd
to me to have the greater Probability.'
   This ending also appears on p. 84 of the manuscript; in redrafting the conclusion
Hume has changed the verb tense, from past to present.

APPENDIX A

The draft of Elliot's letter in reply to Hume's of 10 March 1751 (Introduction, p. 106) is at least of some historical interest. The location of this draft is now unknown, and it may possibly have been destroyed. At one time, Dugald Stewart had a copy, or the original, of this draft and intended to print it. Sir William Hamilton, in his edition of *The Collected Works of Dugald Stewart* (Edinburgh, 1854–60), printed a long portion of this draft (i. 605–7), and it is here reproduced.

Dear Sir,—Inclosed I return your papers, which, since my coming to town, I have again read over with the greatest care. The thoughts which this last perusal of them has suggested I shall set down, merely in compliance with your desire, for I pretend not to say anything new upon a question which has already been examined so often and so accurately. I must freely own to you, that to me it appears extremely doubtful if the position which Cleanthes undertakes to maintain can be supported, at least in any satisfactory manner, upon the principles he establishes and the concessions he makes. If it be only from effect exactly similar that experience warrants us to infer a similar cause, then I am afraid it must be granted, that the works of Nature resemble not so nearly the productions of man as to support the conclusions which Cleanthes admits can be built only on that resemblance. The two instances he brings to illustrate his argument are ingenious and elegant— the first, especially, which seemingly carries great weight along with it; the other, I mean that of the Vegetating Library, as it is of more difficult apprehension, so I think it is not easy for the mind either to retain or to apply it. But, if I mistake not, this strong objection strikes equally against them both. Cleanthes does no more than substitute two artificial instances in the place of natural ones: but if these bear no nearer a resemblance than natural ones to the effects which we have experienced to proceed from men, then nothing *can* justly be inferred from them; and if this resemblance be greater, then nothing farther *ought* to be inferred from them. In one respect, however, Cleanthes seems to limit his reasonings more than is necessary even upon his own principles. Admitting, for once, that experience is the only source of our knowledge, I cannot see how it follows, that, to enable us to infer a similar cause, the effects must not only be similar, but exactly and precisely so. Will not experience authorize me to conclude, that a machine or piece of mechanism was produced by human art, unless I have happened previously to see a machine or piece of mechanism exactly of the same sort? Point out, for instance, the contrivance and end of a watch to a peasant who had never before seen anything more curious than the coarsest instruments of husbandry, will he not immediately conclude, that this watch is an effect produced by human art and design? And I would still further ask, does a spade or plough much more resemble a watch than a watch does an organized animal? The result of our whole experience, if experience indeed be the only principle, seems rather to amount to this: There are but two ways in which we have ever observed the different parcels of matter to be thrown together; either at random, or with design and purpose. By the first we have never seen produced a regular complicated effect, corresponding to a certain end; by the second, we uniformly have. If, then, the works of nature, and the productions of man, resemble each other in this one general characteristic, will not even experience sufficiently warrant us to ascribe to both a similar though proportionable cause? If you answer, that abstracting from the experience we acquire in this world, order and adjustment of parts is no proof of design, my reply is, that no conclusions, drawn from the nature of so chimerical a being as man, considered abstracted from experience, can at all be listened to. The principles of the human mind are clearly so contrived as not to unfold themselves till the proper objects and proper opportunity and occasion be presented. There is no arguing upon the nature of man but by considering him as grown to maturity, placed in society, and become acquainted with surrounding objects. But if you should still farther urge, that, with regard to instances of which we have no experience, for aught we know, matter may contain the principles of order, arrangement, and the adjustment of final causes, I should only answer, that whoever can conceive this proposition to be true, has exactly the same idea of matter that I have of mind. I know not if I have reasoned justly upon Cleanthes's principles, nor is it indeed very material. The purpose of my letter is barely to point out what to me appears the fair and philosophical method of proceeding in this inquiry. That this universe is the effect of an intelligent designing cause, is a principle which has been most universally received in all ages and in all nations; the proof uniformly appealed to is, the admirable order and adjustment of the works of nature. To proceed, then, experimentally and philosophically, the first question in point of order seems to be, what is the effect which the contemplation of the universe, and the several parts of it, produces upon a considering mind? This is a question of fact; a popular question, the discussion of which depends not upon refinements and subtlety, but merely upon impartiality and attention. I ask, then, what is the sentiment which prevails in one's mind, after having considered not only the more familiar objects that surround him, but also all the discoveries of Natural Philosophy and Natural History; after having considered not only the general economy of the universe, but also the most minute parts of it, and the amazing adjustment of means to ends with a precision unknown to human art, and in instances innumerable? Tell me, (to use the words of Cleanthes,) does not the idea of a contriver flow in upon you with a force like that of sensation? Expressions how just! (yet in the mouth of Cleanthes you must allow me to doubt of their propriety.) Nor does this conviction only arise from the consideration of the inanimate parts of the creation, but still more strongly from the contemplation of the faculties of the understanding, the affections of the heart, and the various instincts discoverable both in men and brutes: all so properly adapted to the circumstances and situation both of the species and the individual. Yet this last observation, whatever may be in it, derives no force from experience. For who ever saw a mind produced? If we are desirous to push our experiments still farther, and inquire, whether the survey of the universe has regularly and uniformly led to the belief of an intelligent cause? Shall we not find, that, from the author of the book of Job to the preachers at Boyle's Lecture, the same language has been universally held? No writer, who has ever treated this subject, but has either applied himself to describe, in the most emphatical language, the beauty and order of the universe, or else to collect together and place in the most striking light, the many instances of contrivance and design which have been discovered by observation and experiment. And when they have done this, they seem to have imagined that their task was finished, and their demonstration complete; and indeed no wonder,—for it seems to me, that we are scarce more assured of our own existence, than that this well-ordered universe is the effect of an intelligent cause.

This first question, then, which is indeed a question of fact, being thus settled upon observations which are obvious and un-refined, but not on that account the less satisfactory, it becomes the business of the philosopher to inquire, whether the conviction arising from these observations be founded on the conclusions of reason, the reports of experience, or the dictates of feeling, or possibly upon all these together; but if his principles shall not be laid so wide as to account for the fact already established upon prior evidence, we may, I think, safely conclude, that his principles are erroneous. Should a philosopher pretend to demonstrate to me, by a system of optics, that I can only discern an object when placed directly opposite to my eye, I should certainly answer, your system must be defective, for it is contradicted by matter of fact. . . .

APPENDIX B

Interlineations

Hume's interlineations in the manuscript of the *Dialogues* are not so numerous as we might expect, if we consider how frequently he revised even minor details of his texts. The autograph copy in the Royal Society of Edinburgh was, as I have said, both his fair and his working copy, and he may have tried to keep emendations to a minimum. It has proved virtually impossible (if not pointless) to try to distinguish late from early interlineations, but I have distinguished between corrections above the line (coded as 'cal') and additions above the line ('aal'). I have regarded as a correction any alteration in which the original wording or phrasing has been changed, however slightly. Additions above the line are strictly that; whether they are omissions which Hume remembered to add, later after-thought, or other reconsiderations could only be guessed at.

The interlineations are arranged by page number, line number, wording, and kind of correction. Thus

151	1–2	Considerations		cal

means that on page 151, lines 1–2, the word 'Considerations' is a correction made above the line. (In this instance, Hume changed the word 'Reflections' to 'Considerations'; the textual notes record the rejected wordings.) Occasionally, Hume has changed his punctuation, and I have recorded this, though it has produced some typographically unattractive curiosities, viz.:

159	20	, at present,		aal

When a word occurs twice in the same line I have indicated its line position in round brackets after the word. I have not recorded interlineations consisting of corrections to a word only, as in 'opening' for 'open'. These changes, however, few in number, are in the textual notes.

146	1	regarded as	cal
146	2	which you bestow in conveying to	cal
146	5	which	aal
146	14	in teaching	cal
146	16	of	cal

147	1	every	cal
147	2	each	cal
147	6	have	cal
147	7	any	cal
147	7	of	cal
147	8	Danger	cal
147	17	found	aal
148	2	Uncertainty	cal
148	4	Deceits	cal
148	8	that	cal
148	23	Raillery	cal
148	25	*Cleanthes*	cal
148	27	from	aal
149	2	humorous	cal
149	4	with their Doubts, Cavils, and Disputes	aal
149	14	during any time	aal
149	16	in	cal
149	21	extend throughout	cal
149	21	had	aal
149	22	from the Declamations of their School	cal
150	2	not prevail over	cal
150	10	lead	cal
150	10	astray	cal
150	14	may	cal
150	17	the Stoic's	cal
150	17	will	aal
150	17	his	cal
151	1–2	Considerations	cal
151	3–4	turns his Reflection on other Subjects	cal
151	4	philosophical	aal
151	4–5	I dare not say, in his common Conduct, he	aal
151	9	I own	aal
151	10	Conduct	aal
151	17	make	cal
152	3	So	cal
152	7	with regard to	cal
152	13	must	cal
152	15	ought to	cal
152	16	a	cal
152	22	on any Subject	cal
152	27	that	aal
153	5	too	aal
153	5	make	cal
153	8	the	cal

159	26	to	aal
160	1	is	cal
160	3	of any;	aal
160	9	true	aal
160	13	Sentiment	cal
161	1	which	cal
161	2	to wit	cal
161	2–3	Disapprobation	cal
161	3	ought	cal
161	9	express	cal
161	10	wise	cal
161	15–16	having recourse to	cal
161	22	adorably	aal
161	24	said	cal
161	24–5	addressing himself to *Demea*	aal
161	33	who	cal
161	34	them	aal
162	1	much	cal
162	16	been	aal
162	18	in	cal
162	19	is	aal
163	1	the	aal
163	5	appear	cal
163	9	without hesitation	aal
163	13	proportionably	cal
163	19	analogical Reasoning	cal
163	20	when we	cal
163	24	If	cal
163	24	conclude	cal
164	6	so	cal
164	10	surely	cal
164	20	which	aal
164	24	on	aal
165	7	the	aal
165	8	*Cleanthes*	cal
165	9	that Argument	cal
165	11	set in its true Light.	cal
165	11–12	, in other respects,	cal
165	13	represented	cal
165	14	so to state the Matter to you	cal
165	14	will	cal
165	16	which	aal
165	18	the Universe	cal
165	18	to (2)	aal

165	20	which	aal
165	20	cou'd be esteemed	cal
165	22	wou'd be	cal
165	31	for	cal
166	1	to the rest	aal
166	7	that Principle	cal
166	8	Source or Spring	cal
166	15	(according to *Cleanthes*) *added in margin*	
166	20	inexplicable	aal
166	24	Means to Ends	cal
166	26	from the beginning	cal
167	8	the transferring	cal
167	10	in applying their *added in margin*	
167	10–11	to any particular Phænomenon. Every	cal
167	11	occasions	cal
167	22	hurry'd on	cal
167	26	to the Universe	cal
168	2	great	cal
168	7	allowing that we were	cal
168	9	*Origin* of the	aal
168	9	admitted	cal
168	12	which	aal
168	19	one	aal
168	26	, as we may well suppose,	aal
168	31	pardonable	cal
169	1	elsewhere	cal
169	2	appears	cal
169	20	Iron, Brass,	aal
169	21	minute	cal
169	25	Part	aal
169	25	the former	cal
169	26	Whole	cal
169	27	a certain Rule for	cal
169	32	after	cal
170	3	that	cal
170	3	lay	cal
170	14	are	cal
170	17	some	aal
170	23	it	aal
170	29	tho'	aal
171	13	revolve	cal
171	14	round	cal
171	15	primary	cal
171	15	round	cal

171	18	whether	cal
171	21	so much	cal
171	27	every	cal
172	4	carry'd	cal
172	5	to be	aal
172	14	these Bodies	cal
172	19	in which	cal
172	23	ever	cal
173	4	some sensible Appearances	cal
173	16	Suppose	cal
174	4	that	aal
174	17	every individual of	aal
174	21	brute	aal
174	23	are	cal
175	1	that	aal
175	9	asserting	cal
175	11	original	aal
176	4	*Livy* or *Tacitus*	cal
176	5	which	aal
176	12	here	aal
176	12	religious	aal
176	17	remote	aal
176	23	reject	cal
177	3	surely	aal
177	4	tho' abstruse	cal
177	15	in Writing	aal
177	17–18	to the	aal
178	4	religious	aal
179	6	become	cal
179	8	in (2)	cal
179	22–3	and so similar to a human Mind,	aal
180	1	preserving	cal
180	8	added	cal
180	13	wise	cal
180	20	ought to	cal
180	21	do not	cal
180	22	in the least	aal
181	4	can	aal
181	8	how	cal
181	8	you	aal
181	13	of	aal
181	14	other	aal
181	15	the	cal
181	17	shall	aal

181	19	cou'd	cal
181	20	wou'd	cal
181	26	he has	cal
182	7	Immutability and	aal
182	7	true	aal
182	14	ever (2)	aal
182	17	of his	aal
182	19	Judgement	cal
182	21	in which	aal
182	22	compleat	cal
182	23	which	aal
182	29	that is wholly	cal
183	1	immutable	cal
183	1	which	cal
183	9	be	cal
183	11	be	cal
183	11	Theologians	cal
183	12	so much celebrated, derived	aal
183	13	the	aal
183	17	Ground	cal
183	17	suppose	cal
183	18	to be	cal
183	20	the	cal
183	20	a	cal
183	20	which	aal
183	22	, I own,	aal
183	28	at least	aal
183	29	mental	aal
183	30	material World or	aal
184	4	the one Supposition	cal
184	6	Again	cal
184	8	neither can she	cal
184	12	of them	cal
184	19	of them	aal
184	24	World of Objects	cal
184	25	the World of Thought	cal
184	28	former,	cal
184	28	appear to Reason	cal
184	29	the latter	cal
185	3	of Food	aal
185	6	As	cal
185	10-11	the Cause of that Being,	cal
185	26	you (1)	cal
185	26	mundane System	cal

185	31	precise	aal
186	7	which	cal
186	8–9	, where the accurate Analysis of the Cause exceeds all human Comprehension	aal
186	10	which	cal
186	12	shou'd we	aal
186	16	It were,	cal
186	16	wise in us	aal
186	30	be assign'd by	cal
187	8	Even	aal
187	11	which	cal
187	28	perhaps	aal
188	3	satisfy'd me from the Beginning.	cal
188	6	a (2)	cal
188	6–7	, in its full force,	aal
188	7	indeed	aal
188	12–13	of itself,	aal
188	13	not a whit	cal
188	14	which	cal
188	19	please to	cal
189	1	doubt of	cal
189	2	reject	cal
189	6–7	of experimental Theism	aal
189	9	following	cal
189	22	greater must it have	cal
189	23	enlarg'd	cal
190	1	It is	cal
190	1–2	more unreasonable	cal
190	2	so	cal
190	2	a	aal
190	2–3	our Experience of	aal
190	3	Productions	cal
190	10	to	cal
190	18	Claim	cal
190	21	, upon your Suppositions,	aal
190	22	Attribute	cal
190	22	You will still insist, that, by	aal
191	1–2	give into the most arbitrary Hypothesis, and at the same time, weaken all Proofs	cal
191	3	, on your Theory, for	cal
191	4	for	cal
191	8	seeming	cal
191	10	according to	cal
191	13	to tell,	aal

191	14	contains	cal
191	16	, if the *Aneid* were read to him,	aal
191	17	to	aal
191	24	useful	aal
191	28	had been gradually improving?	aal
191	32	during infinite Ages	aal
193	3	that	aal
193	3–4	however, concealed from Sight,	aal
193	7	which	aal
193	9	Being	aal
193	10	vast	aal
193	10	necessary	cal
193	11	in	aal
193	13	*Cleanthes*;	aal
194	4	or conjecture,	aal
194	5	thing like	cal
194	5	Position	aal
194	8	Hypothesis	cal
194	11	lame Performance:	cal
194	24	, however,	cal
194	26–7	Indulgence of your	cal
195	1	which	cal
195	3	is	aal
195	6	supreme	cal
195	11	precarious and	aal
195	19	will	cal
196	3	in every Part	aal
196	11	chiefly	aal
196	21	are	aal
196	21	too,	aal
196	25	fell	cal
196	25	their	cal
197	1	, both of them,	aal
197	4	on	aal
197	4	which (2)	cal
197	7	an animal	cal
197	8–9	in supposing	cal
197	11	entirely	aal
197	11–12	since it is	cal
197	12	which	aal
197	16–17	as you call it,	aal
197	21–2	deliver any Opinion with regard to it	cal
197	22	Were	cal
197	22	examine	cal

197	24	in starting Objections and Difficulties to it	cal
197	28	also	aal
197	28	the most material:	aal
197	29	precise	cal
198	1	to (2)	aal
198	5	an	cal
198	6	I believe,	cal
198	8	Inference	cal
198	14-15	to have been in greater danger of entirely perishing	cal
198	17	now	aal
198	18	passed	cal
198	18	were it not	cal
198	23	for	cal
198	24	after	cal
198	25	When	cal
198	27	imagin'd	cal
198	28	later	cal
198	28	the true one	cal
198	28	vulgar	cal
199	2	that	cal
199	3	many	cal
199	5	passed	cal
199	6	transplanting so delicious	cal
199	9	Liberty	cal
199	11	*Greece*,	cal
199	13	since	cal
199	14	no	cal
199	17	arose	cal
199	19	all	aal
199	20	Sense	cal
199	21-2	or rather Infancy	cal
199	26	which	cal
200	1	may be trac'd	cal
200	2-3	that every part of this Globe has continu'd for many Ages entirely cover'd with Water.	aal
200	9	and Corruptions,	aal
200	9	ever had	aal
200	16	to the World;	cal
200	18	solves all Difficulties;	cal
200	18-19	, by being so general, is	cal
200	19-20	a Theory, that	cal
200	22	original,	aal
200	23	is very	cal
200	23	to	cal

200	24	of these	cal
201	5	for them	cal
201	5	ever	aal
201	8	which maintain'd, as we learn from *Hesiod*,	cal
202	9	heard,	cal
202	13–14	also resemble that of the other.	cal
202	14	very	aal
202	15	to wit (1)	cal
202	15	very	aal
202	15	to wit (2)	cal
202	17	*Cleanthes*	cal
202	23	universal	aal
203	1	therefore of the World,	cal
203	7	or this planetary System,	aal
203	10	fully	cal
203	15	shou'd	cal
203	21	Ressemblance	cal
203	24	ought they	cal
203	25	on which	aal
203	27–8	imperfect in itself, and so	cal
204	1	must	cal
204	6	does	cal
204	11	As much, at least,	cal
204	14–15	and that with as great Certainty as you	cal
204	16	*Generation, Reason*	aal
204	18–19	more than the other,	aal
204	21–2	the larger the	cal
204	22	are which we	cal
204	22	the better will they	cal
204	30	Fabric?	cal
204	32	Theory	cal
205	1	an egregious	aal
205	2–3	our own Minds	cal
205	3	this Principle	cal
205	3	that	cal
205	4	such a	cal
205	6	Vegetation;	cal
205	12	by (1)	cal
205	13	that	aal
205	14	according to	cal
205	14	in which	cal
205	17	Power	aal
205	20	which	aal
205	24–5	a Bird, on its Nest:	aal

205	26–7	Contrivance.	cal
205	28	proceeds	cal
205	30	, from its Nature,	aal
206	1	Thought,	cal
206	8	satisfying such Enquiries	cal
206	9	says he	aal
206	16	when	cal
206	18	great	aal
206	19	Principle	cal
206	21	and imperfect	aal
206	28	small	aal
206	29	a (1)	aal
207	6	and	cal
207	8	too,	aal
207	18	wholly	cal
207	18	(which is very possible)	aal
208	4	which	aal
208	4	raising	cal
208	11	while	cal
208	13	Whimsies,	cal
208	23	here	cal
208	24	that	aal
208	27	either Yours or	aal
208	27	mine	cal
209	3	that	cal
209	12	No-one, who	cal
209	13	will	aal
209	25	itself	aal
210	1	the (2)	aal
210	4	as	cal
210	5	, at present,	aal
210	9	Hypothesis	cal
210	16	that Order	cal
210	16–17	when once establish'd, supports itself,	cal
210	18	But	cal
210	19	in (1)	cal
210	19	a Constancy	cal
210	20	its Situation	cal
210	22	of each Form	aal
210	29	regular	aal
210	30	such	aal
210	32	feeble	aal
210	33	the rotten	cal
211	2	finite, tho'	cal

211	2	Revolutions	cal
211	3	and Organs	aal
211	5	(for we shall endeavour to vary the Expression)	aal
211	29	with	cal
211	32	, or rather be assur'd of it,	aal
212	5	in (2)	cal
212	8	so	aal
212	8	perishes	cal
212	11	well	aal
212	18	wou'd	cal
212	18	have	aal
212	19	expos'd	cal
212	20	Organs	cal
212	23	is fallen upon.	cal
212	26	necessary	cal
213	1	would	cal
213	1	have	aal
213	2	and useful	aal
213	3	Needle,	cal
213	3	would	cal
213	3	the	aal
213	3	have	aal
213	5	being	aal
213	6	of (2)	aal
213	7	which	cal
213	11	ever	aal
213	12	any	aal
213	12	erect	cal
213	14–15	our limited and imperfect Experience of the	cal
213	16	Advantage;	cal
213	18	Let us once more put it to Tryal.	aal
213	18	which	aal
213	22	which	aal
213	24	upon it	aal
213	25–6	the Equality of	aal
213	27	this	cal
213	31	all of us,	cal
214	3	we	cal
214	3	pronounce no-one to be	cal
214	5	All	cal
214	5	are	cal
214	8	Tenets	cal
214	11	For this plain Reason, that	cal
214	13	our	cal

214	13	Ressource.	cal
214	14	is	aal
214	17–18	on any Occasion,	aal
214	22	offering to us	cal
215	19	that	aal
215	23	which	cal
215	29	to be	aal
216	1–2	that the starting Objections	cal
216	2–3	to point out the Weakness of	cal
216	7	I shall	cal
216	7	is	cal
216	8	a	cal
216	8–9	or to prove it by any Arguments *a priori*.	aal
216	24	a	cal
216	30	pretended	aal
216	31	dare not affirm that we	cal
217	11	imagine	cal
217	14	assigned	cal
217	20	exists	cal
217	22	too,	aal
218	1	you	aal
218	11	any of	aal
218	13	is a	cal
218	15	either	aal
218	18	Numbers.	cal
220	1	oppress	cal
220	3	Ills	cal
220	7	every one	cal
220	10	is it necessary	cal
220	11	necessary	cal
220	12	, if possible,	aal
220	18	of	aal
220	18	immediate	aal
220	24	a	aal
220	25	the	aal
220	26	inspir'd	cal
220	31	who	cal
221	3	, so far as I can recollect,	aal
221	6–7	at least, the first, who made it essential to his philo-sophical System.	aal
221	16	amongst	cal
221	18	infirm	cal
221	22	in order	aal
222	3	still	aal

228	22	can	cal
229	6	often	cal
229	9	scarcely	cal
229	10	one	aal
229	18	is the Sole Cure of all Evil, but which,	aal
229	23	unawares	aal
229	25	fixing	cal
229	31	produc'd	cal
230	1	of	aal
230	2	your	aal
230	6	animal, or at least	aal
230	7	its	cal
230	15	and (1)	aal
230	16	all	aal
230	19	be contented to	aal
230	19	Retrenchment	cal
230	20	that (1)	aal
230	20	Pain or	aal
230	26	hopeful	cal
230	33	Grasp	cal
230	34	and of its Parts, particularly the latter,	aal
231	1	I believe	cal
231	2	then	aal
231	6	infinite (2)	aal
231	8	to (2)	aal
231	12	the Word,	aal
231	12	we meet	cal
231	24	mixture of	aal
231	28	be	aal
232	2	by	aal
232	7	reduce	cal
232	14	very	aal
232	15	however finite,	cal
232	16	it	aal
232	17	Attributes	cal
232	21	sublime and benevolent	cal
232	25	may be	cal
232	26–7	his Comprehension	cal
232	29	benevolent	cal
233	7	and to drop every	cal
233	11	were	cal
233	15	Ills	cal
233	18	in general,	aal
233	21	or most of	aal

240	5–6	, perhaps,	aal
240	18	not	aal
240	23	on any tolerable Reasons	aal
240	32	may	aal
240	33	can	cal
241	2	which we deduce	cal
241	18	which	cal
242	4	Source	cal
242	6	or to Drought above	cal
242	8	fram'd	cal
242	8	first	cal
242	14	by far	aal
242	17	no more	cal
242	18	Supreme Being	cal
242	19	resembles the human	cal
242	20	greater Cause	cal
242	20	from him	aal
242	25	which	cal
242	31	rest on	cal
243	5	Infidels;	cal
243	8	in	cal
243	8–9	Believe me, *Demea*; your Friend,	aal
243	16	, indeed,	aal
243	17	Principles	cal
243	19	the (2)	aal
244	3	Variation	cal
244	4	with that	aal
244	12	in	cal
244	14	*Philo*,	aal
244	18	when engag'd in an Argument;	aal
245	1	that	aal
245	11	its	cal
245	12	observ'd	cal
245	18	all the	cal
245	20	as	cal
245	26–7	which she propos'd;	cal
246	7	advance	cal
246	11	Species of	aal
246	25	which demonstrate	cal
246	28	every	cal
247	3–4	and no Understanding	cal
247	6	Principle	cal
247	12	Design in Nature,	cal
247	12	all	cal

255	17	to keep	cal
255	21–2	of this Spirit;	aal
255	23	greater	aal
255	23	Persons,	cal
255	25–6	Whence comes it then,	cal
255	26	in fact,	aal
255	27	, as far as possible,	aal
256	3–4	, to an uncertain Prospect of Tranquillity	cal
256	12	commonly	cal
256	13	Tenet	cal
256	14	the	cal
256	15	of that Principle,	aal
256	19	whether	cal
256	22	which	cal
256	23	even	aal
256	23	who	cal
256	25	with us	aal
257	2	*Punic* Faith	cal
257	2	antient	cal
257	3	as *Irish* Evidence has in modern;	cal
257	4	these vulgar Observations	cal
257	6	which	aal
257	17	in us	aal
257	21	which	aal
257	26	greater Part	cal
258	4	to	aal
258	5	, when afflicted,	aal
258	8–9	when they betake themselves to the Contemplation of them.	aal
258	10	all	cal
258	16	wou'd	cal
258	17	These	cal
258	20	Gloom	cal
258	20	which	cal
258	20	it	aal
258	25	Species	cal
258	29	upon	cal
259	3	which	cal
259	6	by exhausting the Spirits,	aal
259	8	State	aal
259	11	that	cal
259	14	the	cal
259	19	that	aal
259	21–2	one of	aal

260	3	most	cal
260	5	the	aal
260	15	*probably*	aal
260	16	not	cal
260	20	transfer'd,	cal
260	20–1	Appearance of	aal
260	21–2	If this really be the Case,	aal
260	28	of	cal
261	1	with regard to	cal
261	13	in	cal
261	23	to	aal

BIBLIOGRAPHICAL INDEX

The numbers in square brackets that follow each entry refer to the pages in this volume on which the allusion or citation may be found.

I. AUTHORS ALLUDED TO OR CITED BY HUME

(a) POST CLASSICAL AUTHORS

The editions cited are those consulted by the editor. Entries preceded by an asterisk have not been personally examined.

ARNAULD, Antoine, and NICOL, Pierre, *La Logique ou l'art de penser . . .*, 1662. [154, 155]

ARNOBIUS, *The Seven Books of Arnobius Against the Heathen*, trans. Hamilton Bryce and Hugh Campbell. In *The Ante-Nicene Fathers*, ed. Alexander Roberts and James Donaldson, vol. vi, Grand Rapids, Mich. 1957. [41, 48]

BACON, Sir Francis, *Essays*, London, 1706. [157]
—— 'Of Atheisme', in *Works*, ed. Spedding, Ellis, and Heath, vol. xii, Boston, Mass. 1861. [50, 157]

BAYLE, Pierre, *A General Dictionary, Historical and Critical*, vol. iii, London, 1735. [64]

*BOULAINVILLIERS, Count Henri de, *Abrégé chronologique de l'histoire de France*, 3 vols., Paris, 1733. [53]

*BRANDT, Geeraert, *La Vie de Michel de Ruiter*, Amsterdam, 1698. [69]

BRUMOY, Pierre, *Théâtre des Grecs*, vol. v, Paris, 1763. [40]

CHURCHILL, Charles, *Gotham*, London, 1764. [224]

CLARKE, Samuel, *A Discourse concerning the Being and Attributes of God*, London, 1732. [209, 217]

COPERNICUS, *De Revolutionibus Orbium Coelestrum*, Nuremberg, 1543. [153]

DRYDEN, John, 'Absalom and Achitophel', in *The Poems*, ed. James Kinsley, vol. i, Oxford, 1958. [71]
—— *Aureng-Zebe*, London, 1676. [226]

FONTENELLE, Bernard le Bovier de, *Histoire des Oracles*, Paris, 1687. [40]
—— *The History of Oracles and the Cheats of the Pagan Priests*, London, 1688. [Facsimile in Leonard M. Marsak, ed., *The Achievement of Bernard le Bovier de Fontenelle*, Johnson Reprint Corporation, New York and London, 1970.] [40]

GALEN, *De Foenum Formatione Libellus*. Galeni Operum, Basle, 1549. [245–6]

GALILEO, Galilei, *Dialogo ... sopra i due Massimi Sistemi del Mondo Tolemaico, e Copernicano*, Florence, 1632; trans. Thomas Salisbury, London, 1661. [171, 172]

HAKLUYT, Richard, *The Principal Navigations Voyages Traffiques and Discoveries of the English Nation*, vol. ii, New York, 1965. [A reprint of the Glasgow edition, 1903–5.] [88]

HOBBES, Thomas, *Leviathan* (*The English Works of Thomas Hobbes*, vol. iii), ed. William Molesworth, London, 1839. [94]

HUET, Peter Daniel, *Traité philosophique de la foiblesse de l'esprit humain* (1723); trans. Edward Combe, *A Philosophical Treatise concerning the Weakness of Human Understanding*, London, 1725. [156]

HYDE, Thomas, *Historia religionis veterum Persarum, earumque Magorum; Zoroastris vita, etc.*, Oxford, 1700. [55, 61]

KING, William, *De origine Mali*, Dublin, 1702; trans. Edmund Law, London, 1731. [221]

LECOMTE, Louis Daniel, *Nouveaux mémoires sur l'état présent de la Chine*, vol. ii, Amsterdam, 1698. [38]

—— *Memoires and Observations ... made in a late Journey through the Empire of China*, trans. from the Paris edn., London, 1697. [38]

LEIBNITZ, *Theodicée*, 1710. [221]

LOCKE, John, *An Essay concerning Human Understanding*, London, 1690. [156, 185]

MACHIAVELLI, Niccolò, *The Discourses*, trans. Leslie J. Walker, London, 1950. [63]

MACROBIUS, *The Saturnalia*, trans. Percival Vaughan Davies, New York, 1969. [59]

MALEBRANCHE, Nicolas, *De Recherche de verité. Ou l'on traite de la nature de l'esprit de l'homme*, Paris, 1678; trans. Richard Sault, 1694. [160]

MILTON, John, *Paradise Lost*, in *Poetical Works*, ed. Helen Darbishire, vol. i, Oxford, 1952. [28, 150, 193, 223]

NEWTON, Isaac, *Opticks*, London, 1704. [153]

Nouvelles de la République des Lettres, September, 1685. Amsterdam, 1685. [218]

PHILLIPS, Edward, 'The Life of Milton', in *Complete Poems and Major Prose*, ed. Merritt Y. Hughes, New York, 1957. [73]

*RAMSEY, Andrew Michael, *The Philosophical Principles of Natural and Revealed Religion, unfolded in a Geometrical Order*, vol. ii, Glasgow, 1749. [84–6]

REGNARD, Jean-François, 'Regnard's Journey to Lapland', in John Pinkerton, *A General Collection of the Best and Most Interesting Voyages and Travels in all Parts of the World*, vol. i, London, 1808. [39]

REID, Thomas, *Inquiry into the Human Mind, on the Principles of Common Sense*, Edinburgh, 1764. [158]

(*b*) GREEK AUTHORS

(All editions are Loeb Classical Library unless otherwise specified.)

ARISTOTLE, *Problems*, vol. ii, trans. W. S. Hett, rev. edn., 1957. [32]

ARRIAN, Flavius, *Anabasis of Alexander*, 2 vols., trans. E. Iliff Robson, 1929, 1933. [61, 63]

AURELIUS ANTONINUS, Marcus, *Communings with Himself*, trans. C. R. Haines, rev. edn., 1930. [77]

DIODORUS SICULUS, *The Library of History*, vols. i–ii, iv–vi, trans. C. H. Old-father, 1933–54; vol. vii, trans. Charles L. Sherman, 1952; vol. viii, trans. C. Bradford Welles, 1963; vol. x, trans. Russel M. Geer, 1954. [36, 39, 41, 43, 70, 88, 90]

DIOGENES LAERTIUS, *Lives of Eminent Philosophers*, vol. i, trans. R. D. Hicks, rev. edn., 1938. [48]

DIONYSIUS OF HALICARNASSUS, *Roman Antiquities*, vols. iii–v, trans. Earnest Cary, 1940, 1950, 1945. [35, 45]

EPICTETUS, 'Encheiridion', in *Discourses . . . Manual, and Fragments*, vol. ii, trans. W. A. Oldfather, 1928. [77]

EURIPIDES, 'Hecuba', in *Fabulae*, ed. Gilbert Murray, Oxford, 1966. [35]

—— *Iphigenia in Tauris*, trans. Gilbert West, London, 1766. [257]

HERODIAN, *History of the Empire from the Time of Marcus Aurelius*, vol. ii, trans. C. R. Whittaker, 1970. [48]

HERODOTUS, *History*, vols. i–iii, trans. A. D. Godley, 1926, 1938, 1922. [40, 42, 56, 60, 66, 87]

HESIOD, *Theogony* and *Works and Days*, trans. Hugh G. Evelyn-White, rev. edn., 1936. [32, 42, 44, 47, 54]

—— —— trans. Thomas Cooke, 1728 [201, 207]

—— *Theogonia, Opera et Dies, Scutum*, ed. Friedrich Solmsen, Oxford, 1970. [42]

HOMER, *Iliad*, 2 vols., trans. A. T. Murray, 1925. [40, 47, 53, 93]

LONGINUS, *On the Sublime*, in Aristotle, *The Poetics, etc.*, trans. W. Hamilton Fyfe, 1927. [40]

LUCIAN, 'Hermotimus', vol. vi, trans. K. Kilburn, 1959. [82]

—— 'Lover of Lies', vol. iii, trans. A. M. Harmon, 1921. [76]

—— 'Menippus', vol. iv, trans. A. M. Harmon, 1925. [84]

—— 'On Funerals', vol. iv, trans. A. M. Harmon, 1925. [42]

—— 'On Sacrifices', vol. iii, trans. A. M. Harmon, 1921. [39]

—— 'Zeus Catechized', vol. ii, trans. A. M. Harmon, 1915. [42]

PLATO, *Euthyphro, Laws, Phaedo, Republic.* [A handy edition with a variety of modern translations is the *Collected Dialogues*, ed. Hamilton and Cairns, New York, 1961.] [44, 77, 78, 80]

PLATO, *Timaeus*, in *Works*, vol. vii, trans. R. G. Bury, London, 1961. [207]

PLUTARCH, 'Pelopidas', *Lives*, vol. v, trans. Bernadotte Perrin, 1917. [47]

—— 'De Stoicorum repugnantiis', trans. Philemon Holland, London, 1657. [146]

—— 'Isis and Osiris', *Moralia*, vol. v, trans. Frank Cole Babbitt, 1936. [60]

—— 'Sayings of Kings and Commanders', *Moralia*, vol. iii, trans. Frank Cole Babbitt, 1931. [63]

—— 'Superstition', *Moralia*, vol. ii, trans. Frank Cole Babbitt, 1928. [83]

POLYBIUS, *The Histories*, trans. W. R. Paton, 1923. [256–7]

SEXTUS EMPIRICUS, 'Against the Physicists', *Works*, vol. iii, trans. R. G. Bury, rev. edn., 1953. [44, 80]

STRABO, *Geography*, vols. ii–iii, trans. Horace Leonard Jones, 1923–4. [37, 62, 236]

THUCYDIDES, *History of the Peloponnesian War*, vol. iii, trans. Charles Forster Smith, rev. edn., 1931. [63]

XENOPHON, *Anabasis*, vols. ii–iii, trans. Carleton L. Brownson, 1921–2. [78–9]

——, 'Constitution of the Lacedaemonians', *Scripta Minora*, trans. E. C. Marchant, 1925. [41]

—— *Memorabilia*, vol. iv, trans. E. C. Marchant, 1923. [60, 79, 82]

—— 'Ways and Means', *Scripta Minora*, trans. E. C. Marchant, 1925. [79]

(*c*) LATIN AUTHORS

(All editions are Loeb Classical Library unless otherwise specified.)

AUGUSTINE, *The City of God Against the Pagans*, vol. i, trans. George E. McCracken, 1957. [72]

CAESAR, Gaius Julius, *The Gallic War*, trans. H. J. Edwards, 1917. [40, 49, 236]

CICERO, Marcus Tullius, 'On Divination', *De Senectute, etc.*, trans. William Armistead Falconer, 1923. [73, 77, 94]

—— *Cato Major*, trans. John Logan, 1751. [226]

—— *De Natura Deorum*, trans. H. Rackham, 1933. [71, 80, 189, 196]

—— 'The Four Speeches against Lucius Sergius Catiline', *The Speeches*, trans. Louis E. Lord, 1937. [91]

—— 'In Defence of Cluentio', *The Speeches*, trans. H. Grose Hodge, 1927. [79]

—— *Letters to His Friends*, vol. iii, trans. W. Glynn Williams, 1954. [73]

—— *Tusculan Disputations*, trans. J. E. King, rev. edn., 1945. [71, 79]

CURTIUS RUFUS, Quintus, *History of Alexander*, vol. i, trans. John C. Rolfe, 1946. [41, 48]

EPICURUS, *The Extant Remains*, ed. and trans. C. Bailey, Oxford, 1926. [209]

HORATIUS FLACCUS, Quintus, *The Odes and Epodes*, trans. C. E. Bennett, rev. edn., 1927. [70]

JUVENALIS, Decimus Junius, *Satires*, trans. G. G. Ramsay, 1918. [79]

LIVIUS, Titus, *From the Founding of the City*, vols. i, iii, iv, trans. B. O. Foster, 1919, 1924, 1926. [77, 87]
LUCRETIUS CARUS, Titus, *De Rerum Natura*, trans. W. H. D. Rouse, rev. edn. 1928. [47, 79–80, 174, 189]

MANILIUS, *Astronomica* (*Collection des auteurs latins*, vol. ix), ed. M. Nisard, Paris, 1843. [39]

OVIDIUS NASO, Publius, *Metamorphoses*, 2 vols., trans. F. J. Miller, 1916, 1921. [39, 42, 86]

PETRONIUS, *Satyricon*, trans. Michael Heseltine, 1913. [72]
PLAUTUS, Titus Maccius, *Amphitryon*, vol. i, trans. Paul Nixon, 1916. [41]
PLINIUS CAECILIUS SECUNDUS, Gaius, *Letters and Panegyrics*, vol. i, trans. Betty Radice, 1969. [45]
PLINIUS SECUNDUS, Gaius, *Natural History*, vol. i, trans. H. Rackham, rev. edn., 1949; vol. viii, trans. W. H. S. Jones, 1963; vol. x, trans. D. E. Eichholz, 1962. [30, 32, 59, 73]

QUINTILIANUS, Marcus Fabius, *Institutio Oratoria*, vol. ii, trans. H. E. Butler, 1921. [76]

RUTILIUS NAMATIANUS, Claudius, 'A Voyage Home to Gaul', in *Minor Latin Poets*, trans. J. Wright Duff and Arnold M. Duff, rev. edn., 1935. [72]

SALLUSTIUS CRISPUS, Gaius, *The War with Catiline*, trans. J. C. Rolfe, rev. edn., 1931. [79, 91]
SENECA, Lucius Annaeus, *Ad Lucilium, Epistulae Morales*, vol. i, trans. Richard M. Gummere, 1917. [41, 79, 259]
SPARTIANUS, Aelius, 'Life of Hadrian', in *Scriptores Historiae Augustae*, vol. i, trans. David Magie, 1921. [72]
SUETONIUS TRANQUILLUS, Gaius, *Lives of the Caesars*, vol. i, trans. J. C. Rolfe, 1934. [42, 61, 62, 69, 70, 73]

TACITUS, Cornelius, 'Germania', in *Dialogues, etc.*, trans. Maurice Hutton, 1914. [49]
—— *The Histories* and *The Annals*, vols. i–ii, trans. Clifford H. Moore and John Jackson, 1937, 1931. [69–70, 76]

VARRO, Marcus Terentius, *On the Latin Language*, vol. I, trans. Roland G. Kent, rev. edn., 1951. [72]

VIRGILIUS MARO, Publius, *Georgics*, in *Works*, vol. i, trans. H. Rushton Fairclough, London, 1929. [199]

II. WORKS CITED BY THE EDITORS

ATTERBURY, Francis, *Sermons and Discourses on Several Subjects and Occasions*, London, 1735. [163]

AUGUSTINE, Saint, *De Duabus Animabus*, Cologne, 1616. [241]

BAKER, Henry, *Employment for the Microscope*, London, 1753. [190]
—— *The Microscope Made Easy*, London, 1743. [190]

BAYLE, Pierre, *Dictionary Historical and Critical*, trans. Pierre Des Maizeaux, London, 1734–8. [207, 224, 225, 227, 229, 241]
—— *Miscellaneous Reflections, Occasion'd by the Comet*, London, 1708. [203]

BEATTIE, James, *Dissertations Moral and Critical*, London, 1783. [174]

BEAUSROBE, Isaac de, *Histoire critique de Manichée et du Manicheisme*, Amsterdam, 1734–9. [241]

BENTLEY, Richard, *Sermons* in *A Defence of Natural and Revealed Religion: Being a Collection of the Sermons Preached at the Lecture founded by . . . Robert Boyle*, London, 1739. [175]

[BERKELEY, George], *Alciphron: or, The Minute Philosopher*, London, 1732. [147, 158, 173, 208]

BLACKLOCK, Thomas, *Paracelsis . . . in Two Dissertations*, Edinburgh, 1767. [260]

BLOK, P., *The Life of Admiral de Ruyter*, London, 1933. [69]

BURTON, John Hill, *Life and Correspondence of David Hume*, Edinburgh, 1846. [159]

BUTLER, Joseph, *The Analogy of Religion*, London, 1736. [200, 252]
—— *Fifteen Sermons Preached at the Rolls Chapel*, London, 1729. [188]

CAMPBELL, Dr. George, *The Philosophy of Rhetoric*, Edinburgh, 1776. [123]

CHAMBERS, E. K., *Elizabethan Stage*, Oxford, 1923. [84]

CHEYNE, George, *Philosophical Principles of Religion, Natural and Revealed*, London, 1725. [157, 162]

CHURCHILL, Charles, *Gotham*, 1764. [224]

CICERO, Marcus Tullins, *De Natura Deorum. Of the Nature of the Gods*, trans. R. Francklin, London, 1741. [160, 164, 170, 174–5, 178, 193, 196, 261]
—— *Epicurus's Morals*, trans. John Digby, London, 1712. [193]

CLARKE, Samuel, *A Collection of Papers . . . between . . . Mr. Leibnitz, and Dr. Clarke*, London, 1717. [221]
—— *A Discourse concerning the Being and Attributes of God*, London, 1732. [182, 190, 209, 215–16, 217, 246]

HUME, David, *Philosophical Essays concerning Human Understanding*, London, 1748. [105]

—— *A Treatise of Human Nature*, ed. Ernest C. Mossner, London, 1969. [149, 181–2]

—— *Two Essays*, [London], 1777. [118]

HURD, Richard, *Moral and Political Dialogues*, London, 1764; 3rd edn., London, 1765. [143, 144]

HURLBUTT, R. H., 'David Hume and Scientific Theism', *Journal of the History of Ideas*, xvii (1956), 486–96. [162, 177, 179]

—— *Hume, Newton, and the Design Argument*, Lincoln, Nebr., 1965. [177]

JORTIN, John, *Discourses concerning the Truth of the Christian Religion*, London, 1746. [144]

[KAMES, Henry Home, Lord], *Essays on the Principles of Morality and Natural Religion*, Edinburgh, 1751. [159, 163, 222, 234]

[——], *Sketches of the History of Man*, Edinburgh, 1774. [174]

KING, William, *An Essay on the Origin of Evil*, trans. Edmund Law, Cambridge, 1739. [221]

LOCKE, John, *The Reasonableness of Christianity*, London, 1695. [156]

LUCRETIUS CARUS, Titus, *De Rerum Natura. Six Books of Epicurean Philosophy*, *Done into English Verse* [by Thomas Creech], London, 1683. Also, trans. W. H. D. Rouse, London, 1959 (Loeb Classical Library). [174, 207, 209]

MACLAURIN, Colin, *An Account of Sir Isaac Newton's Philosophical Discoveries*, London, 1748. [177, 179, 261]

MALEBRANCHE, Nicholas, *Search after Truth. Or a Treatise of the Nature of the Humane Mind*, trans. Richard Sault, London, 1694. [160]

MANDEVILLE, Bernard, *The Fable of the Bees*, London, 1729 (ed. F. B. Kaye, Oxford, 1924). [95, 192]

MICHAUD, Joseph François and Louis Gabriel, *Biographie Universelle Ancienne et Modern*, Paris, 1843–65. [39].

MILNER, Joseph, *Gibbon's Account of Christianity considered: Together with some Strictures on Hume's Dialogues concerning Natural Religion*, London, 1781. [126]

MONTAIGNE, Michel de, *Apology for Raimond de Sebonde* in *Essays*, trans. Charles Cotton, London, 1743. [175]

MOSSNER, Ernest C., 'Hume's *Four Dissertations*: An Essay in Biography and Bibliography', *Modern Philology*, xlviii (1950), 37–57. [7–9]

—— *The Life of David Hume*, Oxford, 1970 (1st edn. Austin, Tex., 1954). [7]

[?NEWBERRY, John], '*Tom Telescope*', *The Newtonian System of Philosophy adapted to the Capacities of Young Gentlemen*, London, 1761. [171]

NEWTON, Isaac, *The Mathematical Principles of Natural Philosophy*, trans. Andrew Motte, London, 1729. [188]

PLATO, *Timaeus*, in *Works*, vol. vii, trans. R. G. Bury, London, 1961 (Loeb Classical Library). [196, 207]

PLOTINUS, *Enneads*, trans. Stephen MacKenna, London, 1962. [179]

[PRATT, Samuel Jackson], *Supplement to the Life of David Hume*, London, 1777. [112]

PRICE, J. V., *The Ironic Hume*, Austin, Texas, 1965. [95]

RAY, John, *Three Physico-Theological Discourses*, London, 1721. [200]

SCHEFFER, John, *History of Lapland*, Oxford, 1674; London, 1703. [39]

SERVIUS, Grammatici, *In Vergilii Bucolica et Georgica Commentarii*, recensuit Georgius Thilo, Hildesheim, 1961. [199]

SHAFTESBURY, Anthony Ashley Cooper, Third Earl of, *Characteristicks of Men, Manners, Opinions, Times*, London, 1711. [143, 205, 209, 261]

SIMPSON, Percy, *Proof-reading in the Sixteenth, Seventeenth, and Eighteenth Centuries*, Oxford, 1935. [133]

[SKELTON, Philip], *Ophiomaches: or, Deism Revealed*, London, 1749. [146]

SMITH, John, *The Printer's Grammar*, London, 1755. [138]

Spectator, The, ed. Donald F. Bond, Oxford, 1965. [158, 177]

STEWART, Dugald, *The Collected Works*, ed. Sir William Hamilton, Edinburgh, 1854–60. [106, 262–5]

SWIFT, Jonathan, *Irish Tracts 1720–1723*, ed. Herbert Davis, Oxford, 1963. [255]

—— 'On Poetry: A Rapsody', in *The Poems of Jonathan Swift*, ed. Harold Williams, Oxford, 1758. [222]

TERTULLIAN, *De Spectaculis*, trans. Gerald H. Randall, 1931. [84]

TINDAL, Matthew, *Christianity as Old as the Creation*, London, 1731. [143, 173]

TODD, William B., *Directory of Printers and Others in Allied Trades, London and Vicinity, 1800–1840*, London 1972. [127]

WOLLASTON, William, *The Religion of Nature Delineated*, London, 1726. [175]

INDEX OF NAMES